Chris Cooper

Essentials of
TOURISM

THIRD
EDITION

Los Angeles | London | New Delhi
Singapore | Washington DC | Melbourne

Los Angeles | London | New Delhi
Singapore | Washington DC | Melbourne

SAGE Publications Ltd
1 Oliver's Yard
55 City Road
London EC1Y 1SP

SAGE Publications Inc.
2455 Teller Road
Thousand Oaks, California 91320

SAGE Publications India Pvt Ltd
B 1/I 1 Mohan Cooperative Industrial Area
Mathura Road
New Delhi 110 044

SAGE Publications Asia-Pacific Pte Ltd
3 Church Street
#10–04 Samsung Hub
Singapore 049483

Editor: Matthew Waters
Editorial assistant: Jessica Moran
Production editor: Victoria Nicholas
Copyeditor: William Baginsky
Proofreader: Sharon Cawood
Marketing manager: Abigail Sparks
Cover design: Francis Kenney
Typeset by: C&M Digitals (P) Ltd, Chennai, India
Printed in the UK

Library of Congress Control Number: 2020931585

British Library Cataloguing in Publication data

A catalogue record for this book is available from
the British Library

ISBN 978-1-5264-9448-1
ISBN 978-1-5264-9447-4 (pbk)

BRIEF CONTENTS

CONTENTS

LIST OF FIGURES AND TABLES

FIGURES

TABLES

ABOUT THE AUTHOR

 **Chris Cooper** is Professor in the School of Events, Tourism and Hospitality Management, Leeds Beckett University in the UK. His PhD in Geography is from University College London. Chris has worked as a researcher and teacher in every region of the world and has extensive publishing experience. He gained experience in tour operation before returning to academic life. Chris works with international agencies including the United Nations World Tourism Organization (UNWTO). He held the Chair of the UNWTO's Education Council from 2005 to 2007 and was awarded the United Nations Ulysses Medal for contributions to tourism education and policy in 2009.

PREFACE

This third edition of *Essentials of Tourism* has moved to a new publisher – Sage, and I have been delighted with their enthusiasm for the book and in particular Matthew Water's support and insight as commissioning editor – the book is much better for his input. This edition sees a range of updates and new features, not least of which is a completely new set of cutting-edge, international case studies and two new sections in each chapter devoted to technology and employability. The literature and supporting materials have all been brought up to date and I hope that you find this edition even better than the first. As before though, *Essentials* aims to provide the reader with a text covering, literally, the 'essentials of tourism'. The book is structured into 14 chapters to allow tutors and students to complete the teaching and learning of the 'essentials' of tourism in a course over one 14-week semester. As such, the book does not assume any prior knowledge of tourism. The structure of the book was arrived at by analysing tourism curricula from leading schools around the world and then distilling those curricula into the 'essential' elements found at the core of every course. Naturally, different institutions and different parts of the world emphasise different aspects of tourism, but the 14 chapters in this book lie at the heart of tourism as it is taught internationally – it is therefore up to you, the reader, to contextualise this material within your own national systems of tourism.

The chapters fall naturally into five parts. Part 1 is designed to establish a framework for studying tourism, a way of thinking that has stood the test of time and, despite the fast-moving pace of change that tourism is experiencing, provides a stable analytical framework. Part 2 focuses on the destination, arguably the most important and exciting part of the tourism system. This part dissects the nature of the destination and examines the critical issues of the consequences of tourism for the destination and looks closely at just what is involved in sustainable tourism. Part 3 looks at the tourism sector, both public and private, and analyses the key issues concerning attractions and events, hospitality, intermediaries, transportation and the public sector in tourism. Clearly each of these sectors is distinct, but in fact they have much in common in terms of how they are managed and their economics. Only the public sector stands out as being separate here, simply because it is there to enable and guide tourism rather than to profit from it. Part 4 turns to the tourist in terms of demand and marketing, focusing in particular on the contemporary issues of marketing's 'service dominant logic' and how digital approaches have come to dominate contemporary marketing. Finally, the book ends with Part 5 examining tourism 'futures' – a term used because there are so many possible 'futures' and it is impossible to see which one 'future' will prevail.

To aid the use of the book, each chapter has three case studies illustrating contemporary practice in tourism and drawn from destinations and issues around the globe. These cases are international in focus and are designed to highlight important issues of the day. At the end of each chapter, a longer case study is provided to draw the chapter together. Each of these cases has discussion points and full sources. In addition, each chapter identifies a 'classic paper' – a paper that has acted as a milestone in the thinking of tourism and of the particular topic of the chapter. At the end of each chapter, there is an annotated list of key sources and a set of discussion questions.

Finally, throughout the book hyperlinks are provided to aid you in going rapidly to the original source of the material.

CASE MATRIX

Mini	Major	Case No.	Title	Destination
✓		1.1	De-colonising Tourism Research and the Curriculum	
✓		1.2	Types of Tourism: Characteristics of the Elements of the Ecotourism System	
	✓	1.1	Hypermobility – to Fly or Not to Fly?	
✓		2.1	The Itaipu Tourist Complex – Sustainable Technology as the Basis for a Destination Attraction	Paraguay
✓		2.2	Kronplatz, Italy, Cutting-Edge Destination Management	Italy
	✓	2.1	Astro-Destinations	Portugal
✓		3.1	Tourist Tax – the Case of Venice	Italy
✓		3.2	Contemporary Tourism Employment Issues	
	✓	3.1	Evaluating the Economic Effects of Events	
✓		4.1	Pallas-Yllästunturi National Park, Finland	Finland
✓		4.2	SEE Turtles, USA	USA
	✓	4.1	Climate Change Adaptation: The Events Sector	
✓		5.1	The TREE Alliance	Cambodia
✓		5.2	The Social Progress Index for Tourism Destinations	Dominican Republic
	✓	5.1	Sisterhood of Survivors Programme, Nepal	Nepal
✓		6.1	Education for Sustainability: The Eden Project, UK	UK
✓		6.2	Biosphere Expeditions	
	✓	6.1	The Roatan Marine Park, Honduras	Honduras
✓		7.1	The Masungi Georeserve, Philippines	Philippines
✓		7.2	Animals and Visitor Attractions	
	✓	7.1	Greening the Event Industry	

(Continued)

(Continued)

Mini	Major	Case No.	Title	Destination
✓		8.1	Lemon Tree Hotels, India	India
✓		8.2	The Accor Group – Research Leadership in Sustainability	
	✓	8.1	Airbnb – Redefining Hospitality	
✓		9.1	New Distribution Capability	
✓		9.2	CARMACAL – Carbon Calculator for Tours	
	✓	9.1	Intrepid Travel – a Benefit Corporation	
✓		10.1	Tren Ecuador	Ecuador
✓		10.2	Sustainable River Cruising	
	✓	10.1	Low Cost Carriers and the Environment: The Dilemma	
✓		11.1	Reinventing Government for Tourism: Banyuwangi, Indonesia	Indonesia
✓		11.2	Policy for Sustainable Tourism Development in Guanajuato State, Mexico	Mexico
	✓	11.1	The Heart of St. Kitts Foundation	St Kitts and Nevis
✓		12.1	Punta del Este, Uruguay – Overcoming Seasonality	Uruguay
✓		12.2	Climate Change and Tourism Demand: The Climate Index for Tourism	
	✓	12.1	User Generated Reviews – TripAdvisor.com	
✓		13.1	De-marketing the Faroe Islands	Faroe Islands
✓		13.2	Should Destinations be Marketed?	
	✓	13.1	Digital Marketing Strategy: Etihad Airways	
✓		14.1	Food Futures	
✓		14.2	New Realities	
	✓	14.1	Artificial Intelligence, Robotics and Automation Technologies	

ONLINE RESOURCES

Essentials of Tourism, third edition, is supported by online resources. Visit https://study.sagepub.com/cooper3e to take advantage of the teaching and learning resources for students and lecturers.

FOR STUDENTS

- **SAGE Video**, including videos of author, Chris Cooper, discussing seaside tourism and practitioner, Sean Taylor, discussing adventure tourism.
- A **multiple-choice questions testbank** with ten questions per chapter to test student understanding and aid assessment preparation.

FOR LECTURERS

- **PowerPoint slides** featuring figures, tables, photos and key topics from the textbook that can be downloaded and customised to suit teaching needs.
- **Flipped classroom activities** for both groups and individuals, designed to enhance student learning both online and in the classroom.

PART 1
TOURISM ESSENTIALS: AN INTRODUCTION

Tourism is both a victim and a vector of many contemporary trends in the world – climate change, for example, will impact severely upon destinations, but it can be argued that tourism is also a partial cause of climate change. In a complex world of constant and unexpected change, it is important to take a disciplined and analytical approach to the teaching and learning of tourism. This is particularly the case when tourism is the focus of so much media attention – newspaper travel supplements, TV programmes and an explosion of social media coverage and travel literature. Tourism, too, is a controversial activity, not just in terms of climate change – tourism is high-carbon activity – but also there are other consequences of tourism for, say, indigenous peoples. Again, it is important to provide a balanced view, taking into account the evidence and the burgeoning literature. It is important, too, to recognise that, as tourism matures as a subject area, there are new approaches to studying and analysing tourism to complement the more traditional ways of thinking. Examples here include the *mobilities paradigm* and the *critical turn in tourism studies,* based upon taking perspectives of cultural studies, feminism, ethics, postmodernism, power/politics and world-making and applying them to tourism (Ateljevic et al., 2018). This adds up to tourism as an exciting subject to study – after all, most of us have experienced tourism and can relate the material in this book to our own experiences.

This first chapter sets out to provide a framework for the book and a way of thinking about tourism. The chapter begins with a historical perspective on tourism before introducing the concept of a tourism system. It goes on to outline the role of a tourism system in offering a way of thinking about tourism and in providing a framework of knowledge for those of you studying the subject. This framework is particularly important in the twenty-first century when the world is increasingly complex and experiencing rapid and unexpected change caused by both human and natural agents. In addition, tourism has now become a major economic sector in its own right and this chapter demonstrates the scale and significance of tourism. At the same time, the chapter identifies some of the issues that are inherent both in the subject area and in the study of tourism. In particular, it emphasises the variety and scope of tourism as an activity and highlights the fact that all elements of the tourism system are interlinked, despite the fact that they have to be artificially isolated for teaching and learning purposes. Finally, the chapter considers the difficulties involved in attempting to define tourism and provides some ideas as to how definitions are evolving.

1

TOURISM ESSENTIALS

LEARNING OUTCOMES

This chapter focuses on the concepts, history, terminology and definitions that underpin tourism. It also provides a framework for the study of tourism to guide you through this book. The chapter is designed to provide you with:

- an awareness of the historical background to tourism;
- an understanding of the nature of the tourism system;
- an awareness of the issues associated with the academic and practical study of tourism;
- an appreciation of the vexed terminology associated with tourism; and
- a knowledge of basic supply-side and demand-side definitions of tourism.

INTRODUCTION

In a world of change, one constant since 1950 has been the sustained growth and resilience of tourism both as an activity and an economic sector. This has been demonstrated despite the 'shocks' of '9/11', other terrorist attacks and natural disasters. Despite a number of more recent crises, it was the events of '9/11' that triggered changes in both consumer behaviour and the tourism sector itself, changes which impacted on travel patterns and operations around the world. Yet, even with these challenges, the World Travel and Tourism Council (WTTC; www.wttc.org) demonstrate the tremendous scale of the world's tourism sector:

- The travel and tourism industry's percentage of world gross domestic product is 10.4 per cent.
- The world travel and tourism industry supports 319 million jobs (1 in 10 of world jobs).
- By 2018 there were 1.4 billion international tourism trips and well over 6 billion domestic trips.

It is clear that tourism is an activity of global importance and significance and a major force in the economy of the world. It is also a sector of contrasts. It has the capacity to impact negatively upon host environments and cultures – the raw materials of many tourism products – but it can also promote peace, help alleviate poverty and spearhead both economic and social development.

As the significance and diversity of tourism as an activity have been realised, increased prominence has been given to tourism in United Nations summits such as the World Summit on Sustainable Development in Johannesburg in 2003, when tourism featured for the first time. International mass tourism is at best only 50 years old, and the 'youth' of tourism as an activity – combined with the pace of growth in demand – has given tourism a Cinderella-like existence; it is important, but it is not taken seriously. This has created three issues for the sector:

1. As well as demonstrating sustained growth, tourism has been remarkable in its resilience to adverse economic and political conditions. Natural and man-made disasters clearly demonstrate the sector's ability to regroup and place emphasis on a new vocabulary, including words like 'safety', 'security', 'risk management', 'crisis' and 'recovery'. Inevitably, though, growth is slowing as the market matures and, as the nature of the tourist and their demands change, the sector will need to be creative in supplying products to satisfy the 'new tourist'.

2. Technology increasingly pervades the tourism sector: from the use of the Internet to book travel and seek information about destinations, through to the use of mobile technology to revolutionise the way that tourism information can be delivered direct to the user *in situ* at the destination, to the innovative role that the Internet of Things and Big Data play in managing and curating the visit to destinations. Tourism is ideally placed to take advantage of developments in information technology. But change has come at the price of restructuring the distribution channel in tourism and in changing the nature of jobs in the sector as artificial intelligence (AI) and robotics arrive on the wave of the fourth industrial revolution.

3. International organisations support tourism for its contribution to world peace, its ability to deliver on the UN's Sustainable Development Goals – in particular poverty alleviation, the benefits of the intermingling of peoples and cultures, the economic advantages that can ensue, and the fact that tourism is a relatively 'clean' industry. But an important issue is the stubbornly negative image of tourism as a despoiler of destinations, a harbinger of climate change, and even the employment and monetary gains of tourism are seen to be illusory in many destinations. The International Labour Organization (ILO), for example, views tourism jobs as of low quality, arguing that the sector should deliver 'decent work', not just create jobs of low quality. A critical issue, therefore, for all involved in the successful future of tourism, will be to demonstrate that the tourism sector is responsible and worthy of acceptance as a global activity. The WTTC has been an influential lobbyist in this regard (see www.wttc.org). As the representative body of the major companies in the tourism sector, it has led an active campaign to promote the need for the industry to take responsibility for its actions and for close public and private sector coalitions. Nonetheless, there is a backlash against the fact that tourism is a 'high carbon activity', reflected in the campaign against flying, as explained in the major case study at the end of this chapter.

All of these points connect to mean that the tourism sector must take responsibility for the consequences of tourism as an activity, particularly as a high-carbon activity. This will involve engaging with the big issues of this century – ensuring that tourism wholeheartedly embraces the green economy and reduces its carbon footprint to help alleviate climate change; that tourism does not exacerbate the global issues of food and water security; and that tourism makes a real contribution to poverty alleviation. And, of course, despite the relative youth of international mass tourism, other types of tourism have, in fact, a very long history, dating back thousands of years. In the following section, we turn to the historical development of tourism.

FOCUS ON TECHNOLOGY

Landmarks of Information Technology and Tourism

Information technology has transformed tourism, not only how business is done and organised but also how the tourist searches for and purchases products and enjoys the experience. Of course, the relationship between technology and tourism has evolved over the years as the physical is replaced by the virtual and the analogue by the digital. These are developments that Buhalis (2019) has charted:

- In the 1980s, computing power and rapid communications supported developments such as hotel and airline distribution systems, travel agency systems and the larger global distribution systems. These transformed the travel trade's approach to ticketing, yield management, customer service, productivity and reservations.

- But it was the Internet in the 1990s that saw the real revolution in how tourism business was done. The Internet levelled the playing field allowing a teenager in their bedroom to have the same marketing reach as a global corporation. It allowed e-intermediaries to decimate old-fashioned, bricks-and-mortar tour operators and agents. It facilitated the development of search engines, online tourism communities, blogs and social media, so transforming the relationship between the consumer and the sector. It also saw the rise of online review sites such as TripAdvisor as 'user-generated content sites' and saw the phrase 'e-word of mouth' enter the tourism vocabulary.

- In the future, the relationship will change again as the tangible meets the virtual in 'phygital' relationships, big data allows for personalised experiences, and new virtual destinations, peopled by androids and robots, will deliver curated and memorable experiences.

Source: Buhalis, D. (2019) 'Technology in tourism – from information communication technologies to eTourism and smart tourism towards ambient intelligence tourism: a perspective article', *Tourism Review*, 75 (1): 267–72.

THE HISTORY OF TOURISM

Early tourism

Most sources point to the Sumerians' development of trade around 4000 BCE as the birth of travel (Walton, 2015). Trade remained the major motivation for travel with the development of vast trading networks during the fifteenth and sixteenth centuries – the Silk Roads being a prime example. Travel was difficult and dangerous, however, and only conducted when necessary. As well as trade, military and administrative purposes were also motivations for early tourism, although religious festivals and pilgrimages were evident too. Travel for pilgrimage is evident in many Asian countries from an early period when people journeyed to the mountains and rivers to visit ancestral gods and spirits (Sofield and Li, 1998). Indeed, from the time of the ancient Egyptians, pilgrimages and festivals have taken travellers across borders but tourism, as travel for pleasure, is evident in Egypt from 1500 BCE onward (Casson, 1994). Travel at this time, however, was still disjointed and a difficult undertaking on treks over long distances.

The building of roads during the Roman Empire facilitated a new, faster medium for travel. As a result, leisure travel across Europe gained popularity in Roman times. Augustan Rome (44 BCE – 69 CE) saw hotels, museums, guidebooks, souvenir shops and seaside resorts (Lomine, 2005). The Bay of Naples saw the emergence of villas as second homes for wealthy Romans (Towner and Wall, 1991). However, after the collapse of the Roman Empire the roads were not maintained and travel once again became difficult and dangerous. Despite this, pilgrimages continued across Europe during the medieval period with travellers crossing regions to visit religious sites. Consequently, as the main sources of reception along the road, churches and monasteries were early sources of hospitality.

The Grand Tour

From the late fifteenth century, the sons of the upper classes were sent to tour abroad as a means of completing their education. The Grand Tour, as it became known, was seen as part of the process of induction into society, as 'tourists' expanded their knowledge and experience. Over the course of the seventeenth and eighteenth centuries, thousands of Britons, Germans, French and Russians travelled around the continent, principally to France, Italy, Switzerland and Germany. The term 'tourist' was first coined in the late eighteenth century to describe these travellers. The eighteenth and nineteenth centuries saw travel more through the lens of scientific exploration and expedition, transforming the approach to natural history, and scientists travelled across the world. At this time, travel was still very much a privilege of the upper classes, but this soon changed.

The nineteenth century

Cooper (2011) states that the impact of the Industrial Revolution on technology and work transformed tourism. The revolution in transportation technology opened up leisure travel to greater numbers of people and the emergence of a tourism industry made the process of travelling much more organised. The railway, in Britain and later in Europe and North America, allowed greater access to a destination at greater speed. Thomas Cook's organised trip from Leicester to Loughborough in 1841 saw the start of mass rail travel for pleasure trips. And in North America, roads and then railways were constructed to facilitate travel across the country as the population spread west over the course of the nineteenth century. Sailing ships were replaced by steamships and allowed greater access to the world, not only for trade and scientific exploration but also for leisure. Other developments of the industrial age, such as the opening of the Suez Canal in 1869, also facilitated this movement abroad.

The twentieth and twenty-first centuries

The relative peace in Europe in the late nineteenth century meant that these trends in tourism continued, and a growth in travel occurred up until the First World War. In the years after the war, the car emerged as the new technology to dominate tourism. The first half of the twentieth century saw the car emerge as the main form of transport and the construction of highways and motels, particularly in North America and Australia, facilitated this desire for travel. The popularity of the car for leisure travel began in the United States and moved to Europe by the 1930s, but the car remained much more dominant in the United States. The majority of car travel was domestic, challenging the dominance of the train, with day trips to pleasure grounds and theme parks increasingly popular during this interwar period (Pussard, 2005). The mid-twentieth century saw a dramatic shift away from surface transport for longer trips with the emergence of passenger air travel.

The aeroplane transformed the way people travelled and opened up new regions, cultures and populations to tourism. Initially used for commercial purposes, aeroplanes began taking passengers in the 1920s. Air travel for tourism took off, literally, after the Second World War. The development of the jet engine, which increased the speed and range of aircraft, made international travel more accessible and, with greater affluence on both sides of the Atlantic from the 1950s onward, the tourism industry responded to demand for overseas travel by introducing cheap package holidays. This heralded the industrialisation of the industry and the onset of mass tourism in the second half of the century and into the new Millennium, and the types of tourism that we are familiar with today. The tourism industry developed across the world over the second half of the twentieth century and into the twenty-first. Technological developments in transport opened up new destinations and made travel easier and safer. The 1990s saw the development of budget airlines transforming the way people took holidays, increasing the popularity of short city breaks and further opening up new destinations across the world. It is not just the activity of tourism that has gained attention, but also in the last 50 years tourism as a subject in education has emerged. This is covered in the next section.

THE SUBJECT OF TOURISM

In historical terms then, tourism activity is a relatively new development and one which has only recently been considered worthy of serious business endeavour or academic study (Fidgeon, 2010). However, the tourism sector is of sufficient economic importance and its impact upon economies, environments and societies is significant enough for the subject of tourism to deserve serious academic consideration. There is no doubt therefore that tourism is a subject area or domain of study, but that at the moment it lacks the level of theoretical underpinning that would allow it to become a discipline. Nevertheless, the popularity of tourism as a subject, and the recognition of its importance by governments, has accelerated the study of tourism.

Tourism as a subject is showing signs of maturity with its growing academic community, increasing numbers of journals and textbooks – which are becoming specialised rather than all-embracing – and its measure of professional societies, both internationally and within individual countries. There is a greater confidence in the approaches used to research tourism as the positivist and scientific approaches are augmented with qualitative and more experimental methods. All of these indicators point to the increasing professionalism of the tourism sector (see Airey, 2018).

CLASSIC PAPER

Tribe, J. (1997) 'The indiscipline of tourism', *Annals of Tourism Research*, 24 (3): 638–57

John Tribe's classic paper provides valuable insights into the nature of tourism as a subject and how tourism knowledge is created. The article examines a range of issues, including whether tourism is a discipline or a science, the type of knowledge that exists in tourism and the implications of the very name 'tourism' as unlike, say, physics; it also represents a common activity. The paper begins by stating that tourism is 'conscious of its youthfulness and thus potential lack of intellectual credibility' (p. 638) and goes on to explain that epistemology encourages a systematic review of tourism knowledge and also helps to map the boundaries of the subject.

Tribe says that tourism can be thought of in three ways: (i) as an activity engaged in by people; (ii) as an area of academic interest; and, finally, (iii) as an area of education and training. These multiple perspectives lead to difficulties in defining tourism, as noted in this chapter. Definitions of the subject increasingly draw on business and management viewpoints whilst others come from psychology or behavioural dimensions. Tribe states the following as a definition of tourism: 'The sum of phenomena and relationships arising from the interaction in generating and host regions, of tourists, business suppliers, governments, communities and environments' (p. 641).

The article goes on to explain that tourism fails the test of being a discipline due to its lack of theory, as well as not having a coherent knowledge framework or a strong network of academic concepts. Similarly, it fails the test of a 'science' partly because it, rightly, does not confine its research to the scientific method. Tourism can, however, be thought of as a 'field of study' by concentrating on particular phenomena and bringing various disciplines and subject perspectives to bear upon those phenomena.

Tribe's model of the types of knowledge that make up the field of tourism is one of the important contributions of the paper. He thinks of tourism knowledge as:

TF1 – knowledge focused around tourism business studies; and

TF2 – knowledge focused around environmental impacts, tourism perceptions, carrying capacity and social impacts.

Both of these combine to create tourism knowledge itself (TF). He goes on to outline two main ways of generating tourism knowledge:

Mode 1 – primarily academic research originating in higher education; and

Mode 2 – applied knowledge originating from government industry and other non-academic organisations.

(Continued)

At the time of working (the late 1990s), he felt that mode 2 was economically increasingly important and helped to promote the TF1 part of tourism knowledge, which he felt was becoming dominant.

The paper concludes with a number of observations, notably that tourism is a rather messy subject area, not characterised by a discipline, but rather the 'indiscipline' of the title. Tribe feels that tourism should not be concerned with whether it is a discipline or not but instead should celebrate its diversity.

Nonetheless, the relative youth of tourism as an area of study creates a range of issues not only for the sector in general but also for everyone involved in teaching, researching and studying the subject:

- The subject area itself remains bedevilled by conceptual weakness and fuzziness. This leaves many questions that would be taken as common ground in other subjects (such as navigating the maze of terminology related to the type of tourism which is less destructive – green, alternative, responsible, sustainable, eco...). This results in a basic lack of rigour and focus, leaving tourism as a subject area open to criticism by others. Franklin and Crang, for example, are unrelenting: 'The rapid growth of tourism has led researchers to simply record and document tourism in a series of case studies, examples and industry-sponsored projects' (2001, p. 6). This highlights the apparent conflict between 'academic' and 'applied' approaches – which is also an unresolved issue.

- The subject encompasses a number of diverse industrial sectors and academic subjects, raising the question for those studying tourism as to whether or not tourism is, in fact, too diverse and chaotic to merit separate consideration as a subject or an economic sector. According to Gilbert (1990), what makes tourism difficult to define is the very broad nature of both the concept and the need for so many service inputs. Tourism also envelops other sectors and industries and therefore has no clear boundary, due to the expansive spread of activities it covers (Gilbert, 1990, p. 7). In reality, the tourism industry consists of a mass of organisations operating in different sectors, each of which supplies those activities which are termed tourism. This book argues, of course, that it should warrant a subject and sector in its own right, but that there is a need for a disciplined approach to help alleviate potential sources of confusion for students. It is therefore important in this respect to provide a framework within which to locate these subject approaches and industries, something that this book does.

- As if these problems were not sufficient, tourism also suffers from a particularly weak set of data sources – in terms of both comparability and quality – although the UN World Tourism Organization (UNWTO) (www.unwto.org) has made significant progress in this regard.

- Traditional approaches have tended to operationalise and reduce tourism to a set of activities or economic transactions, while more recent authors have been critical of this 'reductionism', stressing instead postmodern frameworks which analyse the significance and meaning of tourism to individuals and therefore provide more explanation of the activity of tourism itself.

- Finally, tourism does suffer from an image problem in academic circles. Nonetheless, many are attracted to it as an exciting, vibrant subject and an applied area of economic activity – which this book believes that it is. But to be successful, tourism demands very high standards of professionalism, knowledge and application from everyone involved. This is sometimes felt to be in contrast to the image of jet-setting, palm-fringed beaches and a leisure activity.

MINI CASE STUDY 1.1

De-colonising Tourism Research and the Curriculum

There have been a number of instances recently where academics and students have called for the removal of statues, sponsorship or readings from individuals who demonstrated a poor historical awareness of the contexts of their work. More specifically, arguments dating back to the 'critical turn in tourism studies' suggest that much of tourism knowledge has been produced in the developed world, by white, male academics (Ateljevic et al., 2010). This is part of a wider movement to 'de-colonise the curriculum'. In a blog from the London School of African and Oriental Studies, three interpretations of this de-colonisation movement were put forward:

- First, the movement suggests that shared assumptions about the world and our understanding of it, and what is worth researching, were informed by a 'racial and civilisation hierarchy' which omits other worldviews. This does not imply the wholesale removal of Western knowledge in the curriculum, but rather a decentring of it.
- Second, the movement questions the researcher's 'location and identity' – whether, for example, they write purely from the viewpoint of Western developed societies or take a male 'gaze' of research.
- Third, the movement encourages a diverse student population and approach in terms of teaching and learning, and ensures that racial minorities are not disadvantaged.

For tourism scholarship, Chambers and Buzinde (2015) are clear: 'We present the central argument of our discussion which is that despite the mentioned advances in tourism research and scholarship our knowledge about tourism is still predominantly "colonial"' (p. 4). So how has this 'skewed' view of the world come about? Surely tourism is an international activity and scholarship must be informed by, be aware of, and learn from all regions and cultures in the world. Indeed, many scholars would argue, rather smugly, that this is the case. However, the argument here is that tourism reflects a post-colonial stance rather than one of de-colonisation. A post-colonial stance encompasses an examination of tourism in the South and the relationship between Western societies and other cultures (Chambers and Buzinde, 2015).

Additional reasons for the 'colonial' stance focus on language, namely the dominance of English as the academic global language. This marginalises research in other languages and the impact that it has. It is also partly due to the fact that many tourism scholars have come from parent disciplines such as geography or economics where the worldview has been typically Eurocentric, dismissive of knowledge from other cultures. This includes indigenous knowledge, such as how indigenous cultures view the environment and its exploitation by tourism.

(Continued)

There are now increasing examples of a de-colonising approach in tourism. For example, Aquino (2019) closely examined Filipino academics' tourism and hospitality research knowledge creation in the Philippines. He found that it was dominated by positivist thinking and methodology, indicating that their work was strongly influenced by the legacies of the colonies and neocolonial contexts. He suggests this can be combatted using an indigenous approach to knowledge production based upon Sikolohiyang Pilipino (Filipino psychology), a native epistemological perspective.

Discussion Questions

1. Take a tourism course in your university – does the reading list reflect colonial thinking?
2. Do an Internet search for indigenous cultures – what can they teach tourism scholars?
3. In class, debate whether tourism should fully embrace the de-colonisation philosophy.

Sources: Aquino, R.S. (2019) 'Towards decolonising tourism and hospitality research in the Philippines', *Tourism Management Perspectives*, 31: 72–84; Ateljevic, I., Morgan, N. and Pritchard, A. (2010) *Critical Turn in Tourism Studies: Innovative Research Methodologies*. London: Routledge; Chambers, D. and Buzinde, C. (2015) 'Tourism and decolonisation: locating research and self', *Annals of Tourism Research*, 51: 1–16; www. soas.ac.uk/blogs/study/decolonising-curriculum-whats-the-fuss

But there is light at the end of this tunnel. To quote Coles et al. (2006), tourism suffers from the difficulties of location 'in a sea of competing academic territoriality and competing constituencies' (p. 294). They suggest that the approach to tourism should be more flexible and fluid, recognising the inputs and value of differing subjects and disciplines to explanation in tourism. This is termed a 'post-disciplinary' approach, and it differs from the earlier ideas of multi- or interdisciplinary approaches to tourism by being a flexible and creative approach that breaks through the parochial boundaries of disciplines (Coles et al., 2006). It is against this background that an innovative movement has developed known as the 'tourism education futures initiative' (TEFI). TEFI argues that tourism education is stuck in the twentieth century, with a tired curriculum that is not fit for the twenty-first century tourism environment. Tackling this challenge head on, TEFI sets out to create a new and contemporary approach to tourism education, rethinking curricula, values and approaches (www.tourismeducationfutures.org).

FOCUS ON EMPLOYABILITY

Teaching Tourism as a Career

It is interesting that in the menus and lists of jobs that encompass tourism, few include the key role of tourism educators. Yet these jobs are relatively secure, well paid and allow for mobility as well as part-time and sessional modes. Of course, there are different levels of tourism educator:

- At the highest level is education in universities and institutions of higher education. These jobs are highly sought after and often demand a second subject area as well as tourism. This may be a business discipline such as marketing, or another field such as economics. This is because increasingly tourism is taught in business schools rather than in stand-alone departments of tourism. Being an educator at this level normally demands a PhD and some publications, as well as a teaching qualification.

- Teaching tourism at further education (FE) or college level has lower barriers to entry. Here, teachers are expected to be in the classroom for more hours than at university level (where research is also expected). For FE, at least an honours degree is needed as well as a teaching qualification and sometimes industry experience. Often, the courses have a more vocational flavour than in universities.

Educator jobs include:

- Planning and delivering teaching programmes;
- Designing and updating courses;
- Assessing students and marking their work;
- Monitoring students' progress;
- Administration;
- Student recruitment, including interviewing and open days;
- Being a personal tutor; and
- Supervising essays, dissertations and practical work.

A TOURISM SYSTEM

In response to the issues identified above, it is important at the outset to provide an organising framework for the study of tourism. There are many ways to do this. Individual disciplines, for example, view the activity of tourism as an application of their own ideas and concepts, and an approach from, say, geography or economics could be adopted. An alternative is to take a post-disciplinary approach as noted above. Figure 1.1 shows one such attempt to integrate a variety of subjects and disciplines and to focus upon tourism. It explains the richness and diversity of the subject of tourism.

However, in a book of this nature it is impossible to cover the complete range of approaches to tourism. Instead, as an organising framework, the book adopts the model suggested by Leiper in 1979 and updated in 1990 (Figure 1.2). As Figure 1.2 shows, Leiper's model neatly takes into account many of the issues identified above by considering the activity of tourists, allowing industry sectors to be located and incorporating the geographical element which is inherent to all travel. Finally, it places tourism in the context of a range of external environments such as society, politics and economies. There are three basic elements of Leiper's model:

1. Tourists;

2. Geographical elements; and

3. The tourism sector.

Tourists

The tourist is the actor in this system. Tourism, after all, is a very human experience, enjoyed, anticipated and remembered by many as some of the most important times of their lives. Definitions and classifications of tourists are dealt with later in this chapter.

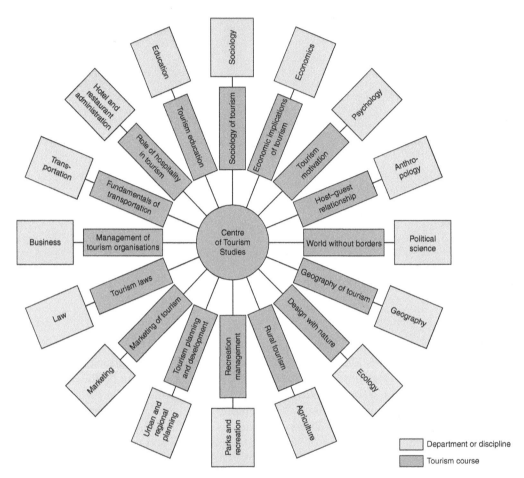

FIGURE 1.1   A study of tourism and choice of discipline and approach

Source: Jafari and Ritchie, 1981; McIntosh and Goeldner, 1990

Geographical elements

Leiper outlines three geographical elements in his model as:

1.   The traveller-generating region;

2.   The tourist destination region; and

3.   The transit route region.

The traveller-generating region represents the generating market for tourism and, in a sense, provides the 'push' to stimulate and motivate travel. It is from here that the tourist searches for information, makes the booking and departs.

In many respects, the tourist destination region represents the 'sharp end' of tourism. At the destination, the full consequences of tourism are felt, and planning and management strategies are implemented. The destination, too, is the raison d'être for tourism, with a range of special places distinguished from the everyday by their cultural, historic or natural significance (Rojek and Urry, 1997). The 'pull' to visit destinations energises the whole tourism system and creates demand for travel in the generating region. It is therefore at the destination where the innovations in tourism take place – new products are developed and 'experiences' delivered, making the destination the place 'where the most noticeable and dramatic consequences of the system occur' (Leiper, 1990: 23). The tourist destination is analysed in Chapter 2.

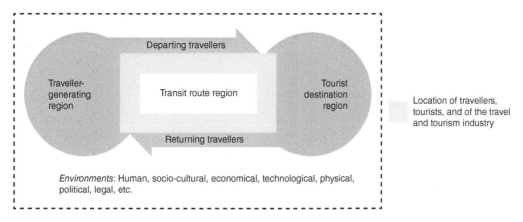

FIGURE 1.2   A basic tourism system

Source: Leiper, 1990

The transit route region does not simply represent the short period of travel to reach the destination, but also includes the intermediate places that may be visited en route: 'There is always an interval in a trip when the traveller feels they have left their home region but have not yet arrived...[where] they choose to visit' (Leiper, 1990: 22). Transport for tourism is analysed in Chapter 10.

The tourism sector

The third geographical element of Leiper's model is the tourism sector, which can be thought of as the range of businesses and organisations involved in delivering the tourism product. The model allows the location of the various industrial sectors to be identified. For example, travel agents and tour operators are mostly found in the traveller-generating region; attractions and the hospitality industry are found in the destination region; and the transport industry is largely represented in the transit route region. The tourism sector is analysed in Part 3 of the book.

Each of the elements of Leiper's tourism system interacts, not only to deliver the tourism product, but also in terms of transactions and impacts and, of course, the differing contexts within which tourism occurs (Figure 1.3). The fact that tourism is also a sector of contrasts is illustrated by examining two major elements of Leiper's model. Demand for tourism in the generating region is inherently volatile, seasonal and irrational. Yet this demand is satisfied by a destination region where supply is fragmented, inflexible and dominated by fixed investment costs – surely a possible recipe for the financial instability of tourism.

The major advantages of Leiper's model are its general applicability and simplicity, which provide a useful 'way of thinking' about tourism. Indeed, each of the alternative models that could be considered tend to reveal Leiper's basic elements at their core when they are dissected.

There are also other advantages of this approach:

- It has the ability to incorporate interdisciplinary approaches to tourism because it is not rooted in any particular subject or discipline, but instead provides a framework within which disciplinary approaches can be located.

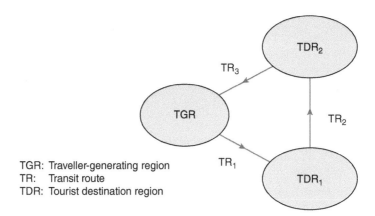

FIGURE 1.3   Geographical elements in a tourism system with two destinations

Source: Leiper, 1990

- It is possible to use the model at any scale or level of generalisation – from a local resort to the international industry.
- The model demonstrates a highly important principle of tourism studies: that all the elements of tourism are related and interact; that, in essence, tourism represents a system of customers and suppliers who demand and supply tourism products and services. Inevitably in any textbook or course, Leiper's elements of tourism have to be separated and examined individually, but in reality all are linked and the realisation of their interrelationships provides a true understanding of tourism.
- Finally, the model is infinitely flexible and allows for the incorporation of different types of tourism, while at the same time demonstrating their common elements. This shows that the various types of tourism – such as dark tourism or rural tourism – are simply different blends of the characteristics of Leiper's elements; they are not different tourism systems in themselves. So, for example, ecotourism can be analysed using the

model shown in the mini case study below. Here, it is clear that ecotourism does not require a completely new approach, but simply an analysis of each of the particular characteristics of the elements of the ecotourism system.

MINI CASE STUDY 1.2

Types of Tourism: Characteristics of the Elements of the Ecotourism System

Leiper's tourism system can be used to understand how different 'types of tourism' are distinct from each other in terms of the features of the market, the destination and the transit zone.

A hut made of bamboo and straw on an ecotourism resort

Source: © Love Sea Travel/Shutterstock.com

The distinctive characteristics of each of the elements of the system that make up ecotourism are as follows:

Generating Region

Demand for ecotourism:

- Is purposeful;
- Is poorly documented;
- Desires first-hand experience/contact with nature/culture;
- Has the motive to study, admire and/or enjoy nature/culture;
- Is tempered by the need to consume tourism responsibly and offset carbon emissions;
- Can be segmented in many ways including by level of commitment, level of physical effort, motives; and
- Comes from those who are more likely to be well educated, have a higher income and are slightly older than the average tourist.

Destination Region

Destinations for ecotourism:

- Are relatively natural areas which are undisturbed and/or uncontaminated;
- Have attractions of scenery, flora, fauna and/or indigenous culture;
- Allow ecotourism to deliver economic and conservation benefits to the local people, including employment;

(Continued)

- Develop ecotourism with a view to conserving/enhancing/maintaining the natural/cultural system;
- Apply integrated planning and management techniques;
- Apply environmental impact and auditing procedures to all elements of the tourism destination (such as accommodation – a major emitter of carbon – and other facilities);
- Attempt to be carbon neutral; and
- Encourage local ownership of facilities.

Transit Zone

Transport for ecotourism:

- Should monitor emissions and environmental impacts;
- Should be of low impact to the environment in terms of noise, carbon emissions, congestion, fuel consumption and waste;
- Should promote the conservation ethic;
- Should be used as a management tool;
- Should encourage the use of public transport;
- Should encourage the use of locally owned transport companies; but reaching a long haul eco-tourism destination may consume large amounts of aircraft fuel and be more damaging to the environment than the tourist realises, and thus defeat the purpose of the trip itself.

Discussion Questions

1. Do the principles of ecotourism apply equally to each of the elements of the ecotourism system?
2. Should ecotourists be true to their beliefs and not fly?
3. There is a view that ecotourism is used by developers as a 'soft' medium to access valued natural resources to 'pave the way' for more aggressive tourism development – do you agree with this view?

DEFINITIONS OF TOURISM

Leiper's model shows that tourism may be thought of as a whole range of individuals, businesses, organisations and places which combine in some way to deliver a travel experience. Tourism is a multidimensional, multifaceted activity, which touches many lives and many different economic activities. Not surprisingly, tourism has therefore proved difficult to define – while the word 'tourist' first appeared in the English language in the early 1800s, more than two centuries later definitions remain problematic. In some senses, this is a reflection of the complexity and diversity of tourism, but it is also indicative of its youth as a field of study. As a result, it is difficult to find an underpinning coherence of approach in defining tourism, aside from the need to characterise the 'otherness' of tourism from similar activities such as migration. Yet even this approach is under criticism as both geographers and sociologists increasingly believe that tourism is but one form of 'mobility' and should not be separated out. In other words, definitions of tourism have been created to cater for particular needs and situations.

Despite these difficulties, it is vital to attempt definitions of tourism, not only to provide a sense of credibility and ownership for those involved, to justify investment in tourism and tourism education, but also for the practical considerations of both measurement and legislation. Definitions of tourism can be thought of as either:

- Demand-side definitions; or
- Supply-side definitions.

Tourism definitions are unusual in that, until the 1990s, they were being driven more by demand-side than supply-side considerations. Some writers find this surprising: 'Defining tourism in terms of the motivations or other characteristics of travellers would be like trying to define the healthcare professions by describing a sick person' (Smith, 1989: 33). The UNWTO provides the stimulus for developing the measurement of tourism from both a demand- and supply-side perspective for 'furthering knowledge of the sector, monitoring progress, evaluating impact, promoting results-focused management, and highlighting strategic issues for policy objectives' (www.unwto.org). The benchmark was reached with the publication of international recommendations for tourism statistics in 2008. The 1990s saw major landmarks towards this benchmark:

1. **Demand-side definitions.** The UNWTO's 1991 International Conference on Travel and Tourism Statistics was called to tidy up definitions, terminology and measurement issues. The recommendations of this conference were adopted by the United Nations Statistical Commission (UNSTAT) and published as *Recommendations on Tourism Statistics* (WTO and UNSTAT, 1994). The conference and the subsequent publications represent the official 'technical' definitions of tourism.

2. **Supply-side definitions.** In March 2000, the United Nations Statistical Commission approved the adoption of tourism satellite accounts as the method of measuring the economic sector of tourism.

Demand-side definitions of tourism

Demand-side definitions have evolved firstly by attempting to encapsulate the idea of tourism into 'conceptual' or 'heuristic' definitions, and secondly through the development of 'technical' definitions for measurement and legal purposes.

From a conceptual point of view, tourism can be thought of as: 'The activities of persons travelling to and staying in places outside their usual environment for not more than one consecutive year for leisure, business and other purposes' (WTO and UNSTAT, 1994). While this is not a strict technical definition, it does convey the essential nature of tourism, that is:

- Tourism arises out of a movement of people to, and their stay in, various places, or destinations.
- There are two elements in tourism – the journey to the destination and the stay (including activities) at the destination.
- The journey and stay take place outside the usual environment or normal place of residence and work so that tourism gives rise to activities that are distinct from the resident and working populations of the places through which they travel and stay.

- The movement to destinations is temporary and short term in character – the intention is to return within a few days, weeks or months.

- Destinations are visited for purposes other than taking up permanent residence or employment in the places visited.

However, these 'conceptual' approaches are vague and do not allow precision for measurement or legislative purposes. As a result, 'technical' definitions were developed by the UNWTO in an attempt to isolate tourism trips from other forms of travel for statistical purposes (Figure 1.4). These 'technical' definitions demand that an activity has to pass certain 'tests' before it counts as tourism. Such tests include the following (overleaf):

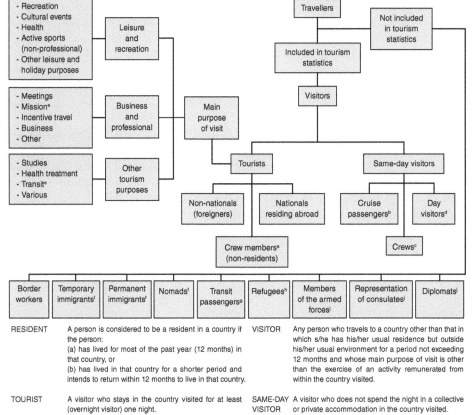

RESIDENT A person is considered to be a resident in a country if the person:
(a) has lived for most of the past year (12 months) in that country, or
(b) has lived in that country for a shorter period and intends to return within 12 months to live in that country.

VISITOR Any person who travels to a country other than that in which s/he has his/her usual residence but outside his/her usual environment for a period not exceeding 12 months and whose main purpose of visit is other than the exercise of an activity remunerated from within the country visited.

TOURIST A visitor who stays in the country visited for at least (overnight visitor) one night.

SAME-DAY VISITOR A visitor who does not spend the night in a collective or private accommodation in the country visited.

Notes:
[a] Foreign air or ship crews docked or in lay over and who use the accommodation establishments of the country visited.
[b] Persons who arrive in a country aboard cruise ships (as defined by the International Maritime Organization, 1965) and who spend the night aboard ship even when disembarking for one or more day visits.
[c] Crews who are not residents of the country visited and who stay in the country for the day.
[d] Visitors who arrive and leave the same day for leisure and recreation, business and professional or other tourism purposes, including transit day visitors en route to or from their destination countries.
[e] Overnight visitors en route from their destination countries.
[f] As defined by the United Nations in the *Recommendations on Statistics of International Migration,* 1980.
[g] Who do not leave the transit area of the airport or the port, including transfer between airports or ports.
[h] As defined by the United Nations High Commissioner for Refugees, 1967.
[i] When they travel from their country of origin to the duty station and vice versa (including household servants and dependants and dependants accompanying or joining them).

FIGURE 1.4   Classification of international visitors

Source: WTO, 2000

- Minimum length of stay – one night (visitors who do not stay overnight are termed same-day visitors or excursionists – and are notoriously difficult to measure).

- Maximum length of stay – one year, which is easy to control through immigration and also, as a consequence of being in a destination for more than one year, the behaviour of a 'visitor' may change to reflect that of locals.

- Strict 'purpose of visit' categories, including leisure, business and common interest.

- A distance consideration is sometimes included on the grounds of delineating the term 'usual environment' – the UNWTO recommendation is 160 kilometres.

Supply-side definitions of tourism

The very nature of tourism as a fragmented, diverse product, spread over many industries and comprising both intangible and tangible elements, means that it is a difficult sector to define. As with demand-side definitions, there are two basic approaches to defining the supply-side of the tourism sector – the conceptual, or descriptive, and the technical. From a conceptual point of view, Leiper suggests: 'The tourist industry consists of all those firms, organisations and facilities which are intended to serve the specific needs and wants of tourists' (1979: 400).

A major problem concerning 'technical' supply-side definitions is the fact that there is a spectrum of tourism businesses and organisations, ranging from those which are wholly serving tourists to those who also serve local residents and other markets. The tourism satellite account (TSA) is the agreed approach to defining the tourism sector as it measures the goods and services purchased by visitors to estimate the size of the tourism economic sector (WTO, 2001) (see also Table 1.1). The TSA:

- Provides information on the economic impact of tourism, including contribution to gross domestic product, investment, tax revenues, tourism consumption and the impact on a nation's balance of payments;

- Provides information on tourism employment and its characteristics; and importantly

- Allows tourism to be compared with other economic sectors.

TABLE 1.1   UNWTO supply-side definition of tourism (International Standard Industrial Classification, ISIC)

ISIC divisions	Business activity[a]	Example
Construction	T	Hotels, recreational facilities, transport facilities, resort residence
Wholesale and retail	P	Motor vehicles sales, sales of motor vehicle fuels, retail food sales, retail sales of textiles
	T	Retail sales of travel accessories, souvenir sales, etc.
Hotels and restaurants	P	Fast food restaurants, food
	T	Hotels, camping sites
Transport, storage and communications	P	Transport via railways, chauffeured vehicles, inland water transport

(Continued)

TABLE 1.1   (Continued)

ISIC divisions	Business activity[a]	Example
	T	Inter-urban rail, airlines, special rail tour service, long-distance bus services, cruise ships
Financial intermediation	P	Exchange of currencies, life insurance, credit cards
	T	Travel insurance
Real estate, renting and business activities	P	Buying or selling of leased property, letting or owning of leased property
	T	Rental of ski equipment, letting of owned tourism property
Public administration	P	Translation services, customs administration, fishing regulation, foreign affairs, border guards
	T	Tourism administration, information bureaux, visa issuance, regulation of private transport
Education	P	Adult education, driving schools, flying schools, boating instruction
	T	Hotel schools, tourism education programmes, recreation and park service schools, tourist instruction
Other community	P	Swimming, scuba instruction, flying instruction, boating instruction, motion picture entertainment
	T	Visitor bureaux, travel clubs, travel unions
Extra-territorial organisations	P	OECD, World Bank, IMF, ASEAN
	T	International tourism bodies

[a]P = part involvement with tourism; T = totally dedicated to tourism

Source: WTO and UNSTAT, 1994

It is clear from this section that the tourism sector has been late in recognising the importance of supply-side definitions. However, the benefits of doing so are clear. The TSA allows tourism to be compared with other economic sectors, delivers important data for planning and policy, as well as providing an important conceptual framework for studying and researching tourism.

TOURISM SUPPLY AS A COMPLEX SYSTEM

Another approach to conceptualising the supply side of tourism is the 'systems approach'. Researchers increasingly view the supply-side structure of tourism as a complex system. Here the components of the system are autonomous agents (such as businesses or community groups) who interact, but who pursue their own objectives – hence the difficulties faced by any organisation in trying to manage the tourism sector or a destination. This is because the challenges of managing the tourism system are twofold (Fennell and Cooper, 2020):

1.   The agents in the system do not act with the overall goals of the system in mind – for example, small businesses may not engage with sustainability initiatives; and

2. There is no way to know how stable these systems are and, if they are subject to change, how they will respond – climate change is a good example here.

Hall et al. (2017) define a system as: 'A group of elements organised such that each element is, in some way, either directly or indirectly interdependent with every other element' (Hall et al., 2017: 16).

There are four characteristics of tourism systems (Fennell and Cooper, 2020):

1. Tourism represents an open system as it interacts with elements and influences external to tourism.

2. The system is made up of a series of subsystems – for example, the distribution networks of accommodation or the public sector marketing system.

3. The causes behind some of the system linkages are understood, but many are not as, for example, with the complex relationship between the environment and tourism at the destination.

4. Tourism systems are subject to 'feedback'. Here Hall et al. (2017) provide the example of an ecotourism destination where its very success leads to further tourists visiting and the loss of the original purpose of ecotourism.

The nature of tourism as a complex system means it has to be conceptualised and understood as a whole; it is impossible to break it down into constituent parts without losing the integrity of the system. This is why when tourism is being taught, educators have to break it down for ease of communication, but the use of case studies allows for the whole system to be understood.

SPATIAL INTERACTION BETWEEN THE COMPONENTS OF THE TOURISM SYSTEM: TOURIST FLOWS

The consideration of tourist flows between the generating region and the destination is fundamental to the study of tourism and critical for managing the environmental and social impacts of tourism, securing the commercial viability of the tourism industry and for planning new developments. There are regular patterns of tourist flows as they do not occur randomly but follow certain rules, influenced by a variety of 'push' and 'pull' factors:

- **Push factors** are mainly concerned with the stage of economic development in the generating area and will include such factors as levels of affluence, mobility and holiday entitlement. An advanced stage of economic development will give the population the means to engage in tourism whilst an unfavourable climate will also provide a strong impetus to travel.

- **Pull factors** include accessibility, and the attractions and amenities of the destination area. The relative cost of the visit is also important, as is the effectiveness of marketing and promotion by the destination.

Tourist flows are complex and are influenced by a wide variety of interrelated variables. A number of attempts have been made to explain the factors that affect tourist flows and to provide rules governing the magnitude of flows between regions. An early attempt by Williams and Zelinsky (1970) selected 14 countries that had relatively stable tourist flows over several years and which accounted for the bulk of the world's tourist traffic. They identified the following factors:

- Distances between countries (the greater the distance, the smaller the volume of flow);
- International connectivity (shared business or cultural ties between countries); and
- The general attractiveness of one country for another.

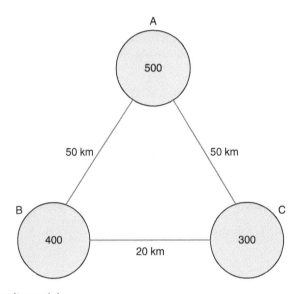

FIGURE 1.5   The gravity model

Source: Boniface and Cooper, 2009

The 'gravity model' is another way of explaining tourist flows (see Figure 1.5). Push and pull factors generate flows, and the larger the mass (population) of country 'A' or country 'B', the greater the flow between them. The other contributing factor, known as the friction of distance, refers to the cost in time and money of longer journeys, and this acts to restrain flows between the country of origin and more distant destinations.

INTERRELATIONSHIPS AND CLASSIFICATIONS

Not only are the elements of the tourism system all interlinked, but tourism also has close relationships with other activities and concepts. It is therefore a mistake to consider tourism in isolation from these other, related activities. For example, most tourism throughout the world is a leisure activity and as such it is important to locate tourism in the spectrum of leisure activities (Figure 1.6), so 'leisure' could be taken as an example of one activity to which tourism is related.

Although the translation from the Latin word for leisure literally means 'to be free', defining leisure is, if anything, more problematic than defining tourism. In essence, leisure can be thought of as a combined measure of time and attitude of mind to create periods of time when other obligations are at a minimum. Recreation can be thought of as the pursuits engaged in during leisure time, and an activity spectrum can be identified with, at one end of the scale, recreation around the home, through to tourism, at the other end, where an overnight stay is involved.

Although same-day visits or excursions are a common recreational activity, for tourism to occur leisure time has to be blocked together to allow a stay away from home. Traditionally, these blocks of leisure time were taken as paid holiday entitlement, though innovations such as flexitime and three-day weekends have also facilitated tourism.

Tourists

While all-embracing definitions of tourism and the tourist are desirable, in practice tourists represent a heterogeneous, not a homogeneous, group with different personalities, demographics and experiences. Tourists can be classified in four basic ways which relate to the nature of their trip:

1. A basic distinction can be made between domestic and international tourists, although this distinction is blurring in many parts of the world (for example, in the European Union). Domestic tourism refers to travel by residents within their country of residence. There are rarely currency, language or visa implications, and domestic tourism is more difficult to measure than international tourism. As a consequence, domestic tourism has received little attention. In contrast, international tourism involves travel outside the country of residence and there may well be currency, language and visa implications.

2. The type of travel arrangements purchased, such as:
   o An inclusive tour where two or more components of the trip are purchased together and one price is paid;
   o Independent travel arrangements where the traveller purchases the various elements of the trip separately; and
   o Tailor-made travel, which is a combination of the two and increasingly common due to the use of the Internet to purchase travel.

3. Distance travelled, which is used to make the distinction between long haul tourism (generally taken to mean travel over a distance of at least 3000 kilometres), and short-haul or medium-haul tourism (involving shorter journeys). This is important in terms of marketing and aircraft operations (and has implications for carbon emissions). Because of their geographical location, Australians and North Americans are more likely to be long haul tourists than their counterparts in Europe.

4. Tourists can also be classified by 'purpose of visit category'. Conventionally, three categories are used:
   o Leisure and recreation – including holiday, sports and cultural tourism and visiting friends and relatives (VFR);

    o   Other tourism purposes – including study and health tourism; and

    o   Business and professional – including meetings, conferences, missions, incentive and business tourism.

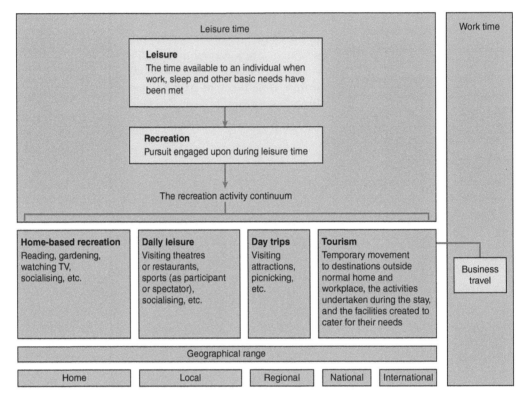

FIGURE 1.6 **Leisure, recreation and tourism**

Source: Boniface and Cooper, 2009

Not only are these categories used for statistical purposes, they are also useful for the marketing of tourism. Consider, for example, Figure 1.7 which demonstrates the flexibility of travel for each of the categories from the point of view of airline fare pricing and validity.

    There are many other ways to classify tourists. These range from simple demographic and trip classifications, through to their lifestyles and personalities, to their perception of risk and familiarity and postmodern interpretations of consumers and commodities. However, one approach with increasing relevance to contemporary tourism is to classify tourists according to their level and type of interaction with the destination.

    Classifications of tourists that adopt this approach commonly place mass tourism at one extreme and some type of alternative, small-scale tourism at the other with a variety of classes in between. It is then argued that mass tourism has a major impact upon the destination because of the sheer scale of the industry and the nature of the consumer. On the other hand, small-scale, alternative types of tourism are said to have a much-reduced impact upon the destination, not only because of the type of consumer involved but also because they will shun the travel trade and stay in local pensions or with families. It is argued, then, that the impact of this type of tourism is less disruptive than for mass tourism.

However, some commentators have oversimplified the complex relationship between the consumption and development of tourism resources. This is particularly true of the so-called 'alternative' tourism movement, which is lauded by some as a solution to the ills of mass tourism. Indeed, the tenor of much of the writing about alternative tourism is that any alternative tourism scheme is good whilst all mass tourism is bad. There is, of course, a case for alternative tourism, but only as another type of tourism in the spectrum. It can never be an alternative to mass tourism, nor can it solve all the problems of tourism (Archer et al., 2004). Indeed, 'enlightened mass tourism' may now be the way forward, combining large volumes of tourists with sympathy for, and understanding of, the destination.

These issues, and the fallacy of lauding 'alternative' tourism as a literal alternative to mass tourism, come into clear focus when examined against the frameworks of analysis developed in this book. For example, only by matching appropriate types of visitor to particular types of destination will truly sustainable tourism development be achieved. This leads to consideration of the fact that the configuration of the components of Leiper's tourism system combine to create a wide variety of different types of tourism. These types of tourism are created by an interaction with the type of destination and the market. Here, the nature of the destination influences the other components of the tourism system, namely the market with its particular motivations to travel, and the means of transport used. Thus, we can distinguish many types of tourism, including heritage, cultural, urban, rural, eco- and nature-based tourism.

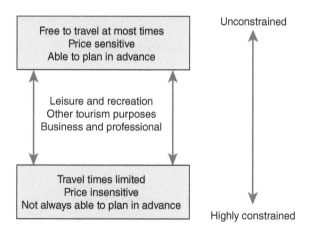

FIGURE 1.7   Airline pricing and purpose of visit categories

THE TOURIST EXPERIENCE

All of the types of tourism noted above are effectively 'experiences'. In analysing and defining tourism, it is easy to forget the tourist as an individual and the extent to which travel and recreation satisfy the need for self-fulfilment through experiences. Tourism is very much a part of the 'experience economy' and the design, staging, marketing and evaluation of the experience has become an important part of tourism product design (Pine and Gilmore, 1999). Every tourism trip can be thought of as an experience with a series of stages:

1. The **anticipation phase** takes place before the trip and involves perceptions and expectations of the destinations as the tourist embarks on making their travel decision.

2. In the **realisation phase** the destination experience is the goal of the trip and is combined with both the outward and return journeys as part of the total experience (Figure 1.8). It is here that the tourist can instantly communicate their impressions of the experience to the world, for instance through blogs or twitter (www.twitter.com).

3. In the **recollection phase** after the trip, the extent to which the quality of these experiences met expectations will influence future travel decisions.

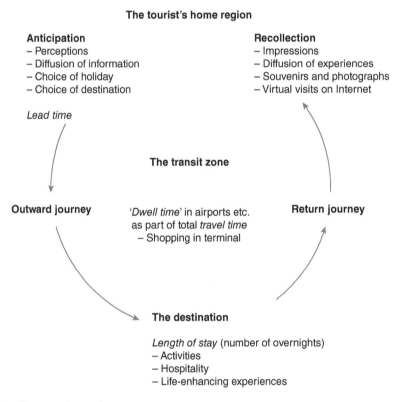

FIGURE 1.8   The travel experience

Source: Boniface and Cooper, 2009

SUMMARY

Although tourism has long historical roots, mass international tourism is a relatively recent activity. As a result, while it has experienced unprecedented growth rates in the past five decades, the study of tourism inevitably lacks the maturity of other subject areas and disciplines. This lack of maturity is manifested in many ways, not least the lack of agreement as to what actually constitutes tourism activity on both the demand and supply sides. Nevertheless, the economic importance of tourism has guaranteed increased governmental and international attention. Accompanying this has not only been a growing recognition of the significance and importance of tourism and the need to be able to define and measure all aspects of it, but also a need for the sustainable development and management of tourism. Of course, recent natural and man-made events have checked the inexorable growth of tourism, particularly awareness of climate change, but overall the sector has demonstrated its resilience to such setbacks.

This introduction provides the basic underpinning framework for the remainder of this book, offering contemporary views on important tourism-related definitions, acquainting the reader with the fundamentals of the history of tourism, the dynamics of the tourism system and how they conspire to create different types of tourism. In a rapidly changing world, it is important to have enduring organising frameworks within which to locate changing practices, world events and their implications for tourism and future trends, which will impact on how tourism operates.

DISCUSSION QUESTIONS

1. Draft a justification for the introduction of a new tourism programme at your educational institution.

2. It has been suggested that tourism is a fragmented sector in search of an industry. Discuss this assertion.

3. Design a PowerPoint presentation outlining the role of transport in the history of tourism since 1840.

4. In groups, design a table describing as many forms of mobility as you can think of – for example, commuting, migration, day trips. In a second column, identify with reasons those that can be thought of as tourism and those that cannot.

5. Discuss the view that responsible or alternative tourism can never be a replacement for mass tourism.

ANNOTATED FURTHER READING

Airey, D. (2018) 'Tourism education and scholarship', in C. Cooper, S. Volo, W.C. Gartner and N. Scott (eds), *The Sage Handbook of Tourism Management: Applications of Theories and Concepts to Tourism*. London: Sage. pp. 49–60.

Insightful overview of tourism education.

Fennell, D.A. and Cooper, C. (2020) *Sustainable Tourism: Principles, Contexts and Practices*. Bristol: Channel View.

Contemporary and thorough text covering all aspects of tourism and sustainability.

Jafari, J. and Xiao, H. (2016) *Encyclopedia of Tourism*. Cham: Springer.

Complete reference book of tourism with definitions and brief reviews of every topic.

www.unwto.org

An all-embracing website providing the official United Nations' view on tourism issues such as pro-poor tourism and providing definitions, definitive statistics and approaches to tourism.

Zuelow, E.G.E. (2015) *A History of Modern Tourism*. London: Palgrave.

A state-of-the-art review of tourism history, specialising in the more recent history of tourism.

REFERENCES CITED

Airey, D. (2018) 'Tourism education and scholarship', in C. Cooper, S. Volo, W.C. Gartner and N. Scott (eds), *The Sage Handbook of Tourism Management: Applications of Theories and Concepts to Tourism*. London: Sage. pp. 49–60.

Archer, B.H., Cooper, C.P. and Ruhanen, L (2004) 'The positive and negative aspects of tourism', in W.F. Theobold (ed.), *Global Tourism*. Oxford: Elsevier Butterworth-Heinemann. pp. 79–102.

Ateljevic, I., Pritchard, A., Morgan, N., Cuasevic, S. and Minnaert, L. (2018) 'Critical turns in tourism studies', in C. Cooper, S. Volo, W.C. Gartner and N. Scott (eds), *The Sage Handbook of Tourism Management: Applications of Theories and Concepts to Tourism*. London: Sage. pp. 12–21.

Boniface, B. and Cooper, C. (2009) *Worldwide Destinations: The Geography of Travel and Tourism*. London: Heinemann.

Casson, L. (1994) *Travel in the Ancient World*. Baltimore, OH: JHU Press.

Coles, T., Hall, C.M. and Duval, D.T. (2006) 'Tourism and post-disciplinary enquiry', *Current Issues in Tourism*, 9 (4–5): 293–319.

Cooper, R. (2011) 'Tourism', in *The Berkshire Encyclopedia of World History*. Great Barrington, MA: Berkshire Publishing. pp. 2519–24.

Fennell, D.A. and Cooper, C. (2020) *Sustainable Tourism: Principles, Contexts and Practices*. Bristol: Channel View.

Fidgeon, P.R. (2010) 'Tourism education and curriculum design: a time for consolidation and review?', *Tourism Management*, 31: 699–723.

Franklin, A. and Crang, M. (2001) 'The trouble with tourism and travel theory', *Tourism Studies*, 1 (1): 5–22.

Gilbert, D. (1990) 'Conceptual issues in the meaning of tourism', in C. Cooper (ed.), *Progress in Tourism, Recreation and Hospitality Management*. London: Belhaven Press. pp. 4–27.

Hall, C.M., Prayag, G. and Amore, A. (2017) *Tourism and Resilience: Individual, Organisational and Destination Perspectives*. Bristol: Channel View.

International Maritime Organization (1965) *Convention on Facilitation of International Maritime Traffic*. London: IMO.

Jafari, J. and Ritchie, J.R.B. (1981) 'Towards a framework for tourism education', *Annals of Tourism Research*, 8 (1): 13–34.

Leiper, N. (1979) 'The framework of tourism', *Annals of Tourism Research*, 6 (4): 390–407.

Leiper, N. (1990) *Tourism Systems*. Auckland: Massey University Department of Management Systems, Occasional Paper 2.

Lomine, L. (2005) 'Tourism in Augustan Society (44BC to AD69)', in J.K. Walton (ed.), *Histories of Tourism: Representation, Identity and Conflict*. Clevedon: Channel View. pp. 69–87.

McIntosh, R.W. and Goeldner, C.R. (1990) *Tourism: Principles, Practices, Philosophies*. New York: Wiley.

Pine, J. and Gilmore, J. (1999) *The Experience Economy*. Cambridge, MA: University of Harvard Press.

Pussard, H. (2005) 'The development of domestic tourism at pleasure grounds in inter-war England', in J.K. Walton (ed.), *Histories of Tourism: Representation, Identity and Conflict*. Clevedon: Channel View. pp. 195–210.

Rojek, C. and Urry, J. (1997) *Touring Cultures: Transformations of Travel Theory*. London: Routledge.

Smith, S.L.J. (1989) *Tourism Analysis: A Handbook*. Harlow: Longman.

Sofield, T. and Li, S. (1998) 'Tourism development and cultural policies in China', *Annals of Tourism Research*, 25 (2): 362–92.

Towner, J. and Wall, G. (1991) 'History and tourism', *Annals of Tourism Research*, 18 (1): 71–84.

Walton, J. (2015) 'Tourism and history', in C. Cooper (ed.), *Contemporary Tourism Reviews*. Oxford: Goodfellow Publishers. pp. 41–66.

Williams, A. and Zelinsky, W. (1970) 'On some patterns of international tourism flows', *Economic Geography*, 46 (4): 549–67.

WTO (2000) *Data Collection and Analysis for Tourism Management, Marketing and Planning*. Madrid: World Trade Organization.

WTO (2001) *Basic Concepts of the Tourism Satellite Account (TSA)*. Madrid: World Trade Organization.

WTO and UNSTAT (1994) *Recommendations on Tourism Statistics*. Madrid: World Trade Organization and New York: United Nations.

MAJOR CASE STUDY 1.1

Hypermobility – to Fly or Not to Fly?

An aeroplane flying at cruise altitude with contrails

Source: ©Milan Rademakers/Shutterstock.com

Introduction

As the awareness of climate change grows amongst the public, attention has turned to the carbon emissions from aircraft. Of course, air travel has brought huge benefits to society, not just in terms of tourism, but also for trade, commerce and society more broadly. However, it is now recognised that flying is bad for the environment and, as a consequence, there has been considerable media attention directed to whether we should still fly or seek alternative forms of transport, and indeed the activity of tourism itself – 'to fly or not to fly' has therefore become an important public debate. Butt and Shaw (2012), for example, found that whilst there is still a majority of people who support freedom to fly, there is an increasing number who feel that flying, particularly by frequent fliers, should be curtailed or even taxed.

The Backlash

However, this will involve a major social movement against flying which will then inspire a new way of

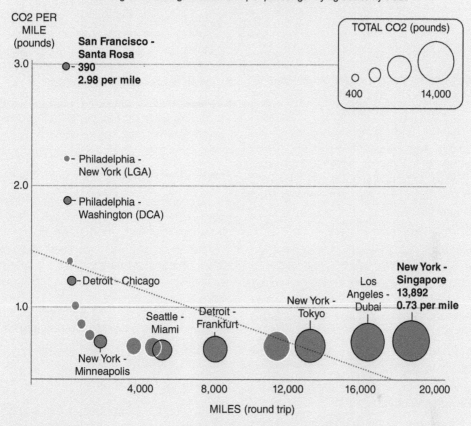

**Shorter flights are less efficient,
but longer flights have a larger carbon footprint**
Pounds of greenhouse gas emissions per passenger flying economy class

FIGURE 1.9   Shorter flights are less efficient, but longer flights have a larger footprint

Source: Green Car Congress

thinking and in turn will influence policy and practice. This will mean that air travel becomes no longer glamorous such that Facebook or Instagram posts from exotic destinations will cease to impress. There are already signs that this movement is gaining traction. In Sweden, for example, 'the Greta Thunberg effect' means that Swedes now have words for the 'shame' of flying – 'flygskam', as well as 'flygfritt' (flight free), and 'vi stannar på marken' (we stay on the ground).

Resistance is already evident in the business community too. A large number of frequent fliers do so on business, with fares paid by their organisation. Business travel is commonly seen as a benefit of the job, a perk that is enjoyed by senior executives enjoying a glamorous life in business class. Of course, this does not help the case of those who argue that flying should be curtailed. Indeed, Cohen and Gössling (2015) argue that this 'hypermobility' can have negative medical and psychological effects on the individuals concerned, including disruption of circadian rhythms, traveller exhaustion, radiation exposure, loneliness and isolation. Realisation of these impacts of flying has prompted leading

(Continued)

companies to develop policies to safeguard against frequent flying and its adverse effects.

To Fly?

If we have to fly, how can emissions be minimised?

- Emissions depend upon where passengers sit, lowest for economy and highest for first class, simply because there is more space for each seat.
- Short haul flights use more fuel on take-off and landing than long haul because on long haul, a greater part of the journey is high altitude cruising. However, long haul produces contrails and at high altitude carbon has a more harmful effect (see Figure 1.9).
- Newer aircraft are more efficient.
- 'Thicker' routes are more efficient as they carry more passengers per aircraft – hence some argue that budget airlines are better than scheduled carriers in terms of emissions. However, their rapid growth means that, in absolute terms, emissions are higher.
- Flying less but staying longer reduces emissions per trip.
- Fly during the day – at night contrails have a greater warming effect.
- Fly in the summer as the warmer temperatures reduce the contrails.

Or Not to Fly?

Switching transport modes from air to surface transport can be beneficial but it depends upon factors such as the age of the motive power, the number of passengers carried, speed, length of the trip and the type of power/fuel used.

- Train – normally a much better option, but diesel trains are larger emitters than electric ones. It also depends upon the source of electricity.
- Road – for cars, emissions depend on how many people are in the car but generally all forms of fuel (electric, hybrid, petrol or diesel) are better than flying, depending upon the length of the journey. Coaches and buses generally come out well, depending upon their age.
- Sea – this option is not as good as might first seem. Cruising has significant emissions and other environmental impacts.

Destination Impacts

If flying becomes too toxic, then long haul destinations – many in the developing world – will suffer. Similarly, air transport delivers food and supplies to remoter destinations in, say, Australia, and if flying stops then the economies of many long haul destinations will be hit – they are often reliant on tourism as the only viable economic option, and tourism is an important export earner and driver of development. So, climate adaptation must take this into account by creating other options for sustainable livelihoods.

Discussion Questions

1. To fly or not to fly – debate this in class.
2. Map out a future scenario for yourself if flying ceases to be a transport option.
3. How true is the assertion that technology will always come up with a solution to global problems such as the flying dilemma?

Sources: Butt, A. and Shaw, A. (2012) 'Pay more, fly less? Changing attitudes to air travel', in A. Park, J. Curtice, K. Thomson, M. Phillips and E. Curry (eds), *British Social Attitudes: The 25th Report*. London: Sage. pp. 129–54; Cohen, S.A. and Gössling, S. (2015) 'A darker side of hypermobility', *Environment and Planning A: Economy and Space*, 47, 1661–79; www.greencarcongress.com

PART 2
DESTINATION ESSENTIALS

This part focuses upon the tourism destination as a fundamental unit of analysis for tourism. Not only do destinations, their images and their digital traces attract tourists, motivate the visit and therefore energise the tourism system, but they are also at the sharp end of tourism, at the same time suffering and benefiting from visitation. The richness and variety of destinations is a key driver of the success of tourism and they demonstrate a complex pattern across the world where tourism is attracted to the unique, the exotic and the vulnerable. At the same time, tourism destinations are forever expanding as the pleasure periphery reaches ever more distant and remote locations, including the Polar Regions, and ever more controversial places through 'dark tourism'. They are also increasingly represented through tourists leaving digital traces of their visits, recommendations through e-word of mouth, and memories via online posts as Facebook becomes the new 'postcard'.

The destination is where the consequences of tourism occur – whether they are positive or negative, and it is therefore the focus for planning and management of tourism, all wrapped into a framework of sustainability. We can think of the destination as a loosely formed network of organisations that deliver the tourist experience. Destinations have many common features, but a key distinction is between the 'attractions', which draw the visit, and the 'support facilities', which, although essential for tourism, support rather than draw the visit. Sustainability is a key consideration for destinations and this part of the book shows how it is delivered through an understanding of carrying capacity and the techniques of destination management and strategic planning. The sustainable destination is a competitive one and the first chapter shows the features of a competitive destination and the idea of destination evolution through the notion of a tourist area life cycle.

There is no doubt that sustainability has become the organising concept for destinations. It is a deceptively simple concept and one with a long pedigree. Sustainability has grown in response to the view that tourism can be very damaging for destinations unless it is effectively planned and managed. This part of the book considers the important economic, environmental, social and cultural consequences of tourism at the destination. Of course, tourism brings many benefits but it can also destroy the very resources that attract tourists. Gauging the consequences of tourism is difficult. There is often no baseline against which to measure the changes wrought by tourism, and often tourism is a scapegoat for changes that may have occurred anyway, or were caused by other factors. Destinations are also concerned with complex environmental and social systems where the relationships between the various consequences of tourism are only just beginning to be understood. There is no doubt that with concerns for climate change we will move to quadruple bottom-line sustainability – environment, the economy and the community with the fourth element being carbon. Indeed, this book stresses throughout the vital need for tourism to embrace the low-carbon economy and, wherever possible, contribute to reducing climate change.

2

THE DESTINATION

LEARNING OUTCOMES

This chapter considers the destination as a crucial element of the tourism system, outlining the key components of the destination, what makes a destination sustainable and competitive, and showing how destinations evolve. The chapter is designed to provide you with:

- an understanding of the destination as the focal point of tourism activity;
- an awareness of the individual features and components of the tourism composite and the contribution of each to the destination product;
- an appreciation of the role of destination management and strategic planning in destination sustainability;
- an understanding of destination competitiveness; and
- an awareness of the tourism area life cycle.

INTRODUCTION

Globally, the richness and variety of destinations continue to contribute to the success of the tourism sector. The supply of tourism demonstrates a complex pattern across the world because it is located in diverse environments and in differing economic and social contexts. The supply of tourism is also continually expanding as the pleasure periphery reaches ever more distant and remote locations. This chapter focuses on the tourism destination, which can be thought of as a loosely bounded network of organisations that deliver the tourism experience. The destination represents the third element of Leiper's tourism system (see Chapter 1), but in many respects the most important one because destinations, their images and their digital traces attract tourists, motivate the visit and therefore energise the whole tourism system. The destination brings together all aspects of tourism – demand, transportation, supply and marketing – in a useful framework, and the chapter identifies these key elements and their contribution to the destination 'amalgam'. The chapter shows how the concept of carrying capacity contributes to the sustainable planning and management of the destination and identifies the elements that contribute to destination competitiveness. Finally, the chapter shows how destinations evolve using the framework of the tourism area life cycle.

DEFINING THE DESTINATION

Despite the fact that the destination can be considered alongside the tourist as the basic unit of analysis in tourism, defining destinations has generated controversy, with some arguing for a geographical definition, whilst others see it as a flexible space, an idea or a concept that cannot be confined within hard geographical or political boundaries (Fyall and

Garrod, 2018). Effectively, the destination is a focal point for the generation and delivery of tourism products and experiences and the implementation of management planning and policy. It provides the facilities and services to meet the needs of the tourist. Destinations are also both tangible as physical spaces, and intangible as they generate images, expectations, digital traces and memories. In an attempt to generate some clarity to the debate, the UNWTO held a think tank in 2002 to establish a definition, although this proved more difficult than they expected. The following definition resulted from the meeting:

> A tourism destination is a physical space in which tourists spend at least one overnight. It includes tourism products such as support services and attractions and tourist resources within one day's return travel time. It has physical and administrative boundaries defining its management, images and perceptions defining its market competitiveness. Destinations incorporate various stakeholders often including a host community, and can nest and network to form larger destinations. Destinations can be on any scale, from a whole country, a region, or an island, to a village, town or city, or a self-contained centre. (UNWTO Destination Think Tank, Madrid, December 2002)

This definition is more of an all-encompassing list of destination attributes and already seems rather dated. Contemporary thinking now views destinations as loosely bounded networks of organisations that deliver the tourism experience. This immediately recognises the importance of stakeholders and their governance, relationships and the fact that destinations can nest within each other – Orlando within Florida, for example.

COMMON FEATURES OF TOURIST DESTINATIONS

While destinations are very varied, there are four common features of most destinations:

1. Amalgams;
2. Cultural appraisals;
3. Inseparability: that is, tourism is produced where it is consumed; and
4. Multiple use of destinations.

Amalgams

Most destinations comprise a core of the following components – the four 'A's:

1. **Attractions** act to pull the visitor to the destination. They include both natural and man-made attractions as well as events.
2. **Amenities** include accommodation, food and beverage outlets, entertainment, retailing and other services.
3. **Access** includes both local transport around the destination and access to and from the destination (air, road and sea), through transport terminals.
4. **Ancillary services** come in the form of local organisations.

Of course, each of these components has to be in place before tourism can occur – accommodation alone, for example, will rarely suffice (except perhaps in the case of iconic luxury hotels such as the Raffles Hotel in Singapore: www.raffles.com). The mix of facilities and services at a destination is therefore known as an amalgam – the complete mix has to be present for it to work and the total tourism experience to be delivered.

This amalgamation of the components of a destination comes together in many different ways, and in many different cultural, economic and environmental contexts to create the range of destinations available. The very fact that the destination is an amalgam has a number of implications. In particular, it is important that the quality of each component of the destination and the delivery of the tourism service by these components is reasonably uniform: a poor restaurant can detract from an otherwise satisfactory experience. This *complementarity* of destination components is difficult to control by destination managers given the fragmented nature of enterprises in tourism. Integration of enterprises by larger organisations (tour operators owning hotels and transport carriers) is one means of such control, but for public-sector tourist boards the problem is a critical one.

Cultural appraisals

Visitors have to consider a destination to be attractive and worth the investment of time and money to visit. Because of this, destinations can be thought of as cultural appraisals. For example, in the nineteenth century the perception of mountains changed from fearsome places to attractive landscapes, which then became popular tourist destinations. An example of this idea is the desire of tourists to visit hostile environments such as Antarctica, or places associated with death, war or crime as in dark tourism. As tastes and fashion change, so they are reflected in the destinations that tourists patronise. This means that, while new opportunities are always available, there is also a constant threat to established destinations, which may go out of fashion. It is, therefore, vital to maintain the difference between the destination and the tourist's home environment through good design and management, and to avoid the development of uniform tourism landscapes. In the twenty-first century, there are two further considerations which tourists take into account when judging whether to visit:

1. The first is their safety and security at the destination and whether they can trust that they will be safe and secure at the destination, given recent events where tourists have been targets of terrorism or victims of natural disasters. Here, Liu et al. (2019) state that a tourist's trust in a destination depends upon the many destination stakeholders, including authorities, tourists, residents, employees and the destination management agency itself.

2. Sustainability and whether the destination is judged to be well managed in terms of the environment and the host community.

Inseparability

Tourism is consumed where it is produced as visitors have to be physically present at a destination to experience tourism. Because tourism, by its very nature, is attracted to the unique and the fragile parts of the world, destinations are vulnerable to tourist pressure and may suffer alteration. This is exacerbated by the fact that visitor pressure is often concentrated seasonally in time and at specific popular locations.

Like all services, the destination is perishable in the sense that if it is not used it is lost – the availability of beds or attraction tickets cannot be stored in the off-season for sale in the peak. Seasonality is a major problem for many destinations, prejudicing profitability and rendering them inefficient in terms of the use of their assets. This is because most elements of a destination have a high ratio of fixed to variable costs and, therefore, for a highly seasonal destination, the peak (of, say, two or four months) has to make the majority contribution to fixed costs, which are chargeable for 12 months of the year. For example, for many tourist destinations anything up to 80 per cent of total costs are in physical plant, and construction involves long lead times.

Multiple use

Destinations serve residents and workers throughout the year, but at some times of the year they are also used by day visitors or tourists, away from their normal place of residence and work. This multiple use of destinations means that it is possible to classify enterprises according to whether they depend only upon tourism, only upon residents, or a mix of the two. In fact, only purpose-built destinations (such as theme parks) exist purely to serve the tourist. Most destinations have to share tourism with other uses; indeed, tourists are often the most recent and least respected users. For example, tourism in rural areas is shared with nature conservation, agriculture and forestry. Tourism may therefore become a source of conflict in shared destinations, with open antagonism displayed between tourists and other users. Solutions to this problem involve the careful integration of tourism activities in a variety of ways:

- Phasing tourism uses in time;
- Zoning tourism uses in space;
- Management schemes to reduce tension and conflict by intervening in problem situations;
- Involving all stakeholders and understanding their differing needs;
- Community-driven tourism planning to ensure that tourism develops in harmony with community wishes;
- Publicity campaigns to inform local residents of the benefits of tourism; and
- Information campaigns and codes of conduct targeted at the tourist.

Components of the destination amalgam

Before introducing the components of a destination and demonstrating their place in the destination amalgam, it is important to make the major distinction between attractions and support services. *Attractions* generate the visit to a destination, while *support services* and facilities are also essential for tourism at the destination, but would not exist without attractions. A particular focus of these components is the resort, which we can define as 'a place that attracts large numbers of tourists and that tourism endows with special characteristics, so that revenue produced by tourism plays an important role in its existence'.

Attractions and events

It is the attractions of a destination – whether they be artificial features, natural features or events – that provide the initial motivation to visit. Traditionally, attractions have been a neglected sector of the tourist industry, owing to their variety and fragmented ownership pattern. However, the sector is now demonstrating maturity with increased professionalism in the management of attractions and events. This includes a closer match between the market and supply through:

- The adoption of marketing philosophy;
- Better training for attractions and event personnel;
- Greater involvement of technology in the development of new types of attraction and in both co-creating and 'curating' the experience; and
- Renewed focus upon and professional management of mega events.

Alongside this more enlightened management approach, the attraction and events sector is forming professional bodies and seeking representation in wider tourist industry circles. Attractions and events are dealt with in detail in Chapter 7. Mini Case Study 2.1 outlines a destination which has the generation of sustainable energy and a technology park as the basis for its attraction.

MINI CASE STUDY 2.1

The Itaipu Tourist Complex – Sustainable Technology as the Basis for a Destination Attraction

Introduction

The Itaipu Tourist Complex lies on the border between Brazil, Argentina and Paraguay. It is part of a rich, biodiverse ecosystem threatened by human activity. The complex is located between two national parks – Iguazu Falls and Ilha Grande. The location of the complex therefore helps to attract visitors, and tourism is used to stimulate the development of the border region.

However, the real reasons for using Itaipu as a case study are twofold. Firstly, its attraction is based upon a technology park and huge dam that create renewable energy; and secondly, it has developed a sustainable approach to destination territory development.

The Itaipu Technological Park (ITP)

The ITP is based upon the dam and reservoir system that generates renewable energy. It stretches over an area of 50,000 square meters and is home to 2000 employees, trainees, partners, entrepreneurs, researchers, teachers and students. The park hosts research and research support agencies, a business development centre and a university campus. It is the world's leading generator of clean and renewable energy, alone supplying 15 per cent of Brazil's and 75 per cent of Paraguay's energy.

Tourism was involved in the dam project from the start with visitors coming to see the construction, but the tourism side of the park was not professionally run. So, in 2006, the Itaipu Technological Park

Foundation (ITPF) was created to run the ITP and manage the visitors. The Foundation developed a new mission: 'To generate electricity with quality, social and environmental responsibility, propelling the economic, touristic, technological and sustainable development, in Brazil and Paraguay', and a new strategic purpose to: 'Effectively avail the touristic and technological potential of Itaipu and its region, seeking the income-generation and opportunities for the community, becoming a hub of knowledge and integration in South America'.

Sustainability

The Itaipu Sustainability Policy was approved by both Brazil and Paraguay in 2014 and covers all activity in the destination and the park. Its purpose is:

> to establish sustainability principles and values which must be taken into account when carrying out daily activities that are inherent to the Company and actions that are meant to foster sustainable development both in Paraguay and Brazil for the common good and a better future.

The sustainability principles and values are classified into four balanced dimensions:

1. **Corporate dimension**, managing people, resources and business processes in a rational, balanced and efficient way, operating sustainable purchasing and developing local suppliers.
2. **Environment dimension**, using and encouraging the use of, and generating energy from, clean and renewable sources. Working in partnership with social actors in favour of sustainability and conserving and preserving the environment and respecting biodiversity.
3. **Socioeconomic development dimension**, actively acting in sustainable human development.
4. **Cultural dimension**, fostering and reinforcing sustainability culture as an example for the world and valuing sustainable actions.

Discussion Questions

1. The ITP is a serious contributor to clean energy production. What do you think is the core attraction of the park?
2. Debate the most effective model for managing a destination like the ITP – government, private enterprise or a different model?
3. Do you think that part of the success of the park is its proximity to Iguazu Falls?

Source: www.itaipu.gov.py

Amenities

A tourist at a destination requires a range of amenities, support facilities and services. This sector can be characterised as having a low level of concentration of ownership as these enterprises are often operated by small to medium-sized enterprises (SMEs). On the one hand, this is an advantage because it means that tourist expenditure flows quickly into the local economy. On the other hand, however, SMEs are both fragmented and lack a coherent lobby. Often, too, they lack investment capability and the management/marketing expertise demanded by an increasingly discerning tourism marketplace.

The provision of amenities demonstrates the multisectoral nature of tourism supply and the interdependence of the various sectors. For example, the supply of many facilities and services at a resort depends upon the number of bed spaces available; that is, the number of tourists who will visit. For example, provision of around 1000 beds will support up to six basic retail outlets, while 4000 beds will support specialist outlets such as hairdressers. Similar ratios can be calculated for restaurants, car parking or entertainment.

ACCOMMODATION, FOOD AND BEVERAGE

The accommodation/food and beverage sector of the destination not only provides physical shelter and sustenance, but also creates the general feeling of welcome and a lasting impression of the local cuisine and produce. Traditionally dominated by SMEs, the accommodation sector usually offers a mix of type of establishment, and it is important for destinations to adapt and change this mix to meet market aspirations. In some resorts, for example, there is a movement towards flexible forms of accommodation, such as apartments and time-share, and away from more traditional serviced establishments (hotels or self-catering apartments). Finally, there is the private informal sector (including second homes and caravans), which is a large though neglected part of the accommodation industry, and the hugely disruptive innovation of Airbnb (dealt with in detail in Chapter 8).

RETAILING AND OTHER SERVICES

There is an increasing range of facilities and services available to a tourist as the size of destination increases. These include retailing, security services and other functions, such as hairdressing, banks, exchange bureaux and insurance. These services tend to locate close to the main attractions of a destination, often creating an identifiable 'recreational business district'.

ACCESS

Clearly, the development and maintenance of efficient transport links to the generating markets are essential for the success of destinations. Indeed, there are examples of destinations where transport has made, or broken, the tourist industry. Small islands, for example, are dependent upon their carriers to provide market access, while destinations such as Spain and Mexico are ideally situated to take advantage of international tourism from Europe and North America respectively. In international terms, developing countries have particular problems attracting a share of the market because they are generally distant from the generating markets and, as society begins to question long haul flights, they will be a victim of climate change.

Catchment areas will also vary according to the drawing power of the destination. Tightly drawn geographical catchments will characterise smaller resorts without a major distinguishing attraction. However, major destinations, such as the theme parks of Orlando, can draw upon an international catchment.

Both physical and market access to the destination are important, as is the provision of services such as car rental and local transport, in order to service excursion circuits and provide transfers to accommodation at the destination. An increasingly creative approach to transportation at the destination adds to the quality of the tourist experience, and there are many examples of innovative transport provision in this respect, including:

- Scenic drives;
- Park and ride schemes;
- Shuttle buses for walkers;
- Cycle ways; and
- Innovative vehicles such as Aquaducks or CityCats.

ANCILLARY SERVICES

Most major destinations provide ancillary services to both the consumer and the industry through a destination management organisation (DMO) (Pike and Page, 2014). These services include marketing, development and coordination activities. The DMO may be in the public sector, may be a public–private sector cooperative or, in some cases, may exist totally within the private sector. Such organisations are often linked to regional and national tourist boards and provide the framework within which tourism operates at the destination. A particular issue for DMOs is to prove their effectiveness in terms of marketing and competitiveness, as noted by Morgan et al. (2012).

The main services normally provided by the DMO are as follows:

- Promotion of the destination;
- Coordination and control of development;
- Provision of an information/reservation service to the trade and the public;
- Oversight of human resources and training (such as for local guides);
- Advice to and coordination of local businesses;
- Provision of facilities such as catering or sports; and
- Provision of destination leadership and partnership building.

INFRASTRUCTURE AND SUPERSTRUCTURE

Infrastructure and superstructure are alternative ways of looking at the components of a destination. Infrastructure represents all the forms of construction above or below ground needed by an inhabited area, with extensive communication with the outside world as a basis for tourism activity in the area. Adequate infrastructure is essential for destinations and is mainly in the form of:

- Transportation (road, railway, airport, car parks);

- Utilities (electricity, water, communications); and
- Other services (healthcare and security).

Infrastructure is normally shared by residents and visitors alike. There are examples where lack of adequate infrastructure has prevented the growth of tourism (such as restricted water supplies on the Kenyan Mombassa coast). Infrastructure does not normally generate income and is treated as a public investment in most tourist developments. Seasonality is a major problem for infrastructure development and most construction is planned to meet a percentage of peak load rather than peak.

Whereas infrastructure tends to be provided by the public sector, *superstructure* is normally a private sector activity, as it is the profit-generating element of the destination. It includes accommodation, built attractions and retailing and other services. In many countries, the public sector is active in providing financial incentives (grants, loans, tax holidays) for private sector tourism investment. Although the norm is for the public sector to provide infrastructure as a prerequisite for private sector development of the superstructure, in many cases combinations of public and private sector finance are used to develop destinations.

TYPES OF TOURISM

The particular combination and features of the destination amalgam characterise various 'types of tourism' such as heritage tourism, pink tourism or astro-tourism, which is examined in Major Case Study 2.1. For example, destinations delivering the type of tourism known as 'dark tourism' or 'thanatourism' are characterised by sites of death, disaster or where something dark has occurred. These may be battlefields, sites of assassination, or sites such as concentration camps. Of course, these could hardly be called attractions and their interpretation and display for the dark tourists demand sensitivity, as Light (2017) questions in his paper on the conflict between dark and heritage tourism. Another type of tourism, adventure tourism, also demands particular configurations of destination components. Here, the destination is often surveyed to create an adventure tourism 'template' where particular sites and resources can be identified for activities such as mountain biking, bungee jumping, white water rafting or mountaineering. Adventure tourism is a rapidly growing type of tourism as tourists seek out the unusual and the dangerous at the destination; this growth has been facilitated by innovations in technology such as GPS on mobile phones and social networking. For all the many 'types of tourism', it is the combination of these destination components with the particular wants and needs of the market that define each 'type'.

DESTINATION STAKEHOLDERS

A final way of viewing the components of destinations is by looking at the fact that tourism destinations comprise a mosaic of different actors that can be termed stakeholders. A truly sustainable destination will recognise that it must satisfy all of its stakeholders in the long term. This can be achieved by a strategic planning approach which balances a marketing orientation focused on tourists, with a planning orientation focused on the needs of local people. It must also be remembered that the tourist experience is made up of a series of small *encounters* with many stakeholders and that these encounters strongly influence the success or otherwise of the visit. In every destination there are several stakeholders, which have a wide range of both compatible and conflicting interests:

- **The host community** is the most important stakeholder as these people live and work at the destination and provide local resources to visitors. It is therefore important to involve the local community in decision-making, and to ensure that tourism does not bring unacceptable impacts upon the local people and their homes.

- **Tourists** are looking for a satisfying experience, through properly segmented and developed products. They seek a high quality of service and a well-managed and organised destination.

- **The tourism industry** is, to a large extent, responsible for the existing development of tourism and the delivery of the tourism product. It seeks an adequate return on investment. The industry can be thought of as polarising between global and niche players. The global players tend to be multinational and well resourced with capital, expertise and power. Often, they have limited interest in and commitment to destinations. Niche players are traditionally small, family-based enterprises lacking capital, expertise, qualified human resources and influence at the destination.

- **The public sector** sees tourism as a means to increase incomes, stimulate regional development and generate employment. The public sector is an important stakeholder, often taking a destination leadership, stewardship or governance role.

- **Other stakeholders** include pressure groups, chambers of commerce and power brokers within the local, regional or national community.

Mini Case Study 2.2 shows how the many stakeholders involved in delivering an Italian Alpine destination product are managed through a smart 'umbrella' management arrangement.

MINI CASE STUDY 2.2

Kronplatz, Italy, Cutting-Edge Destination Management

Introduction

The Italian ski resort of Kronplatz is one of the major winter sports resorts in the Southern Tyrol, accounting for over 85 per cent of the bed-nights in the region. It has about 150 days of skiing annually and at peak times there are more than 10,000 skiers on the mountain. Kronplatz is a triangular mountain with 116 kilometres of slopes and 36 state-of-the-art ski lifts.

Kronplatz, Italy

Source: 'Kronplatz' by SimSullen is licensed under CC BY-SA 2.0

(Continued)

The mountain's morphology allows for a number of ski trails and chairlifts to the summit, starting from geographically scattered points in the lower valleys. This allows skiers to ascend by one route and then ski down another. The chairlift access points in the valleys are linked by public transport to facilitate flexibility.

Destination Investment and Management

What marks Kronplatz out as worthy of a case study is, firstly, the level of investment that has been put into the destination, and secondly, the cutting-edge way that the various components of the destination amalgam are managed. Ski resorts are complex with, like all destinations, many different suppliers coming together to deliver the product. By managing the mountain holistically, investment is encouraged and the visitor experience is enhanced.

Investment

Kronplatz is investing in the destination in three key areas:

1. There has been significant investment in the ski lifts – almost 40 lifts operate with state-of-the-art comfort and facilities, including wifi.
2. Like all Alpine resorts, Kronplatz is subject to climate change with forecasts that there will be no snow above 12,000 metres by 2024. In response, the destination has invested in a state-of-the-art system of snow making with the use of quiet snow guns/lances. The system is fully automated and includes water management, energy limitation and wind tracking.
3. Kronplatz is also investing in diversifying away from winter sports and a dependence upon snow. Investments include museums (such as the Messner Mountaineering Museum (www. messner-mountain-museum.it) and the Mountain Photography House on the summit), hiking and biking trails, gastronomy and new forms of accommodation including lodges and chalets on the slopes.

This diversification will also help to even out the seasonality of the region, which is an issue for the labour force.

Management

Over ten companies operate the ski lifts and many more are involved in ski schools, hospitality, après ski and transport. The Kronplatz mountain has an overall management company – Consorzio Skirama Plan de Corones. The company acts as an umbrella management company for the destination, collecting and disbursing revenues to the individual companies. This is a very 'smart' management approach for two reasons:

1. It creates a seamless experience for the visitor – they do not need separate tickets for each lift, bus ride or even for cafes and bars – it is all handled by the one company through the use of smart card ski passes. These cards can also be used in competing resorts in a spirit of regional 'co-opetition'; and
2. It removes the notion of competition between enterprises and encourages cooperative investment in the destination.

Discussion Questions

1. Visit the Kronplatz website. How evident is it that the mountain is managed as a complete destination?
2. Are snow-making machines simply a 'King Canute style' denial of climate change?
3. What other ways can winter sports destinations such as Kronplatz diversify away from a dependence upon snow?

Source: www.kronplatz.com/en

THE SUSTAINABLE DESTINATION

Clearly, the components of the tourist destination can be effective only if careful planning and management deliver a sustainable tourism product, and in so doing ensure that one or more of the components does not surge ahead of the others (see Kurniawan et al., 2019, for a case study of Indonesia). The concept of sustainable tourism is explored in detail in Chapter 6. It is clear that the concept of sustainability demands a long-term view of tourism and ensures that consumption of tourism does not exceed the ability of a host destination to provide for future tourists. In other words, it represents a trade-off between present and future needs. In the past, sustainability has been a low priority compared with the short-term drive for profitability and growth, but as pressure has grown for a more responsible tourism industry, it is difficult to see how such short-term views on consumption can continue. To understand how to deliver sustainable tourism destinations, we need to consider three key concepts:

1. Carrying capacity;
2. Destination management; and
3. Strategic planning.

Carrying capacity

Central to the concept of sustainability is the idea of carrying capacity. Carrying capacity of a destination is a deceptively simple idea – quite simply, it refers to its ability to absorb tourism use without deteriorating. In other words, capacity intervenes in the relationship between the tourist and the destination. As Table 2.1 shows, carrying capacity comes in a variety of forms. Mathieson and Wall (1982) define carrying capacity as: 'The maximum number of people who can use a site without an unacceptable alteration in the physical environment and without an unacceptable decline in the quality of experience gained by visitors' (p. 21).

The main problem with carrying capacity is that the concept is easy to grasp but very difficult to put into practice because it is a management decision. Managers of the tourist destination, as well as the tourists themselves, decide what is unacceptable and when the quality of experience has declined. For example, Jacobsen et al. (2019) discovered that cruise tourists are more crowd tolerant than independent tourists. The idea of a deteriorating destination has become known as 'overtourism' but it is simply a recognition that the destination is 'over capacity'. Indeed, any destination can be managed to a high or low capacity, a level that is determined as much by management as by the innate characteristics of the resource and its culture.

Destination management

Destination management is about 'place making' to deliver a high-quality experience to the visitor and to manage the consequences of visitation at the destination (see Fyall and Garrod, 2018). It provides the tools to produce sustainable and competitive tourism at a destination, going one step beyond destination marketing to take a more holistic and integrative approach to managing the 'whole destination'. Destination management tends to be led by the relevant DMO through the medium of policy, planning legislation and partnership building with destination stakeholders. It also reflects contemporary thinking that the local destination is the most meaningful building block for marketing, development and engagement with stakeholders.

TABLE 2.1   Types of carrying capacity

Physical Carrying Capacity

This relates to the amount of suitable land available for facilities and also includes the finite capacity of the facilities (such as car parking spaces, covers in restaurants or bedspaces in accommodation). It is the most straightforward of all capacity measures and can be used for planning and management control (by, say, limiting car parking spaces at sensitive sites).

Psychological Carrying Capacity

The psychological capacity of a site is exceeded when a visitor's experience is significantly impaired. Of course, some people are crowd tolerant and enjoy busy places, whilst others shun them. Psychological capacity is therefore a very individual concept and difficult to influence by management and planning, although landscaping can be used to reduce the impression of crowding.

Biological Carrying Capacity

The biological capacity of a site is exceeded when environmental damage or disturbance is unacceptable. This can relate to both flora and fauna, for example, at picnic sites, along paths or in dune-ecosystems. More research has examined the capacity thresholds of vegetation than has looked at the tolerance of animals or birds to tourism (at, say, whale-watching locations). It is also important to consider the total ecosystem rather than individual elements.

Social Carrying Capacity

The concept of social carrying capacity is derived from ideas of community-based tourism planning and sustainability. It attempts to define levels of development, which are acceptable to host community residents and businesses and may use techniques that attempt to gauge residents' threshold *limits to acceptable change* (LAC).

The UNWTO (2007) defines destination management as:

> The coordinated management of all of the elements that make up a destination. Destination management takes a strategic approach to link up these sometimes very separate entities for the better management of the destination. Joined-up management can help to avoid duplication of effort with regards to promotion, visitor services, training, business support and identify any management gaps that are not being addressed. (p. 4)

As shown in Figure 2.1, destination management combines the practices and principles of:

- Development planning;
- Marketing; and
- Management.

The key to effective destination management is to encourage cooperation and collaboration to strengthen partnerships between all stakeholders at the destination. This delivers a shared vision and an integrated, holistic approach to managing the destination. The benefits of destination management are as follows:

- It ensures that the destination is competitive.
- It ensures that the destination is sustainable.
- It ensures that tourism delivers economic benefits to the host community.
- It ensures the delivery of quality experiences to the visitor.
- It delivers an overarching destination vision.
- It promotes continuous destination improvement.

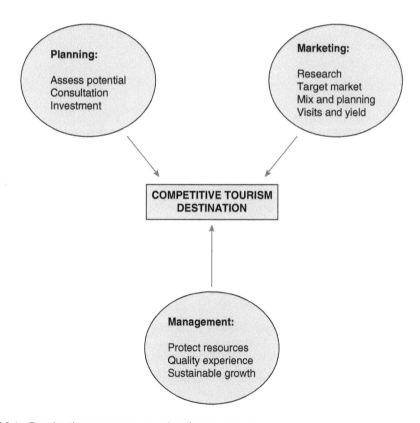

FIGURE 2.1   Destination management planning concepts

TABLE 2.2   Strategic planning – from the traditional approach to experience strategies

Traditional Strategic Planning

In the early years of destination strategies, managers tended to adopt a traditional and rather rigid sequential approach. This consisted of a series of stages, typically:

- situation analysis/environmental scanning;
- objectives and goals;
- strategy formulation;
- marketing, positioning and mix; and
- implementation and monitoring.

By the late 1990s, this approach had become less relevant to the changing operating environment of destinations in a world of continuous and unexpected change.

The Visioning Approach

In the late 1990s, a number of destinations began to adopt a 'visioning' approach to strategy. Here visions are crafted that present a practical and achievable picture of where the destination sees itself in the future.

Visioning is a dynamic, engaging and bottom-up approach, allowing the destination to be flexible and responsive to changing circumstances. It is focused upon bringing together stakeholders in a collaborative and participative goal-setting approach to generate a 'shared vision'. Visions are inspiring, imaginative and reflect the shared aspirations of the destination.

Experience Strategies

In the new millennium, a small number of forward-looking destinations have developed experience strategies in recognition of tourism as an experience. This approach accepts that visitors are accustomed to high-quality entertainment experiences and so, to be competitive, destinations must engineer memorable, personal and transforming experiences to match the expectations of the visitor.

This approach recognises that meaningful experiences cannot be guaranteed, but they can be managed. Tourism Tasmania's Experience Strategy is a leading example here.

The focus on technology box examines how technology is playing an increasing role in destination management.

FOCUS ON TECHNOLOGY

Smartphone Itinerary Apps

Destination management is increasingly reliant upon technology. The development of apps for smartphones is an example of how visitors can explore the way that a destination has been transformed. These apps act as an effective visitor management tool by influencing itineraries to protect vulnerable resources and encourage visitors to go to 'hardened' parts of the destination, as well as to restaurants and hotels. Many apps are now available – some are destination specific, whilst others are comprehensive. Leading apps include:

- **Visit a City** – a standard trip-planning app;
- **Google Trips** – a comprehensive app allowing the user to plan themed itineraries and customise day plans;
- **TripAdvisor** – acts as a social media centre allowing visitors to crowd source attractions and itineraries, follow other travellers and share ideas and reviews, acting as a 'social network for travel planning';

- Gogobot – provides itineraries and recommendations on hospitality;
- Triposo – focuses on the destination's history and culture, as well as the usual recommendations for restaurants and hotels;
- Tripomatic – a comprehensive city guide with long lists of attractions and activities;
- Foursquare – uses recommendations from local residents in terms of tips and reviews;
- Sidewalk – similar to Foursquare, sharing local culture, history and food information, using self-guided walks created by a local expert.

For the future, these apps and their smartphones will interact with embedded devices in the destination itself, using the Internet of Things – effectively the destination will become a computer interface, interacting with the visitor to help them curate the visit and with destination managers to influence visitor behaviour.

Strategic planning

There is a real synergy between sustainability and the long-term perspective. It is no longer acceptable for the industry to exploit destinations and then move on, as has happened, for example, in some coastal areas of Spain. This changing perspective away from the short term has led to a realisation of the importance of taking a strategic approach to both markets and destination management. It is possible to devise appropriate strategies for destinations at each stage of their development such that the destination formula is constantly reviewed and adjusted in order to achieve sustainable tourism at each stage. This long-term perspective provides control and responsibility to prevent the destination exceeding capacity and the inevitable decline in visitation that follows. In other words, what is involved is the crafting of a strategic vision for a destination which allows the destination to take control of its own future in a turbulent world. Over the years, the approach to strategic planning has evolved, as shown in Table 2.2.

The defining characteristics of the strategic planning approach are:

- The adoption of a long-term perspective;
- The development of a holistic and integrated plan which controls the process of change through the formation of goals;
- A formalised decision process focused on the deployment of resources, which commits the destination to a future course of action; and
- The political process at the destination is critical to success.

The benefits of the strategic approach to the destination are clear:

- It provides a common sense of ownership and direction for the myriad stakeholders, while at the same time sharpening the guiding objectives of the destination.
- The coherence provided by the approach provides a framework for joint initiatives between the commercial and public sectors, demands the clear identification of roles and responsibilities, and provides a sense of ownership for all.

- Finally, the approach delivers a range of performance indicators against which the destination's performance can be judged.

However, the introduction of a longer-term strategic planning perspective by destinations is problematic. Simply, the adoption of strategic planning at the destination is not as straight-forward as in a commercial organisation where responsibilities and reporting lines are well defined. As this chapter has shown, destinations comprise a constantly shifting mosaic of stakeholders and value systems. Each of these groups has a different view of the role and future of tourism at the destination and therefore the adoption of strategies becomes a political process of conflict resolution and consensus, all set within a local legislative context and where power brokers have a disproportionate influence. The power of this political process should not be underestimated. Politics influences those who are responsible for the planning process, and lack of political support commonly leads to the failure, or non-implementation, of plans. In addition, the tourist sector at destinations is characterised by fragmentation and a dominance of small businesses, which often trade seasonally. This has led to a lack of management expertise at destinations, a divergence of aims between the commercial and public sectors and a short-term planning horizon which in part is driven by public sector, 12-monthly budgeting cycles, but also by the tactical operating horizon of small businesses. At the same time, the stage of the destination in the life cycle influences the acceptability of a destination-wide marketing exercise. In the early stages of the life cycle, for example, success often obscures the long-term view, while in the later stages, particularly when a destination is in decline, opposition to long-term planning exercises may be rationalised on the basis of cost.

Finally, the performance indicators adopted in such exercises can be controversial since tourist volume is the traditional, and politically acceptable, measure of success in many destinations. Yet, from the point of view of sustainability, more appropriate measures are likely to be the less tangible ones of environmental and social impacts. Of course, to be competitive a destination must be sustainable – it is all too easy to go for growth and, at the same time, destroy the very resource that the tourist wants. Destination competitiveness is covered in the next section.

THE COMPETITIVE DESTINATION

An imperative for all destinations is to be competitive in order to deliver benefits to all stakeholders. In the bigger picture, it is in fact destinations that compete with each other rather than the individual businesses within the destination. Being competitive demands that destinations (Fyall, 2019):

- Thoroughly understand changes in the external environment;
- Are aware of shifting consumer preferences and expectations;
- Understand their positioning against competitors' offerings in terms of both image and reputation; and
- Constantly innovate in terms of their product offering and their marketing.

In other words, destinations must research their own characteristics, product offering and markets as well as those of their competitors (see Croes and Semrad, 2018). Ritchie and Crouch have published widely on the issue with a comprehensive framework for analysing destination competitiveness (Figure 2.2), and the classic paper in this chapter is based on their work.

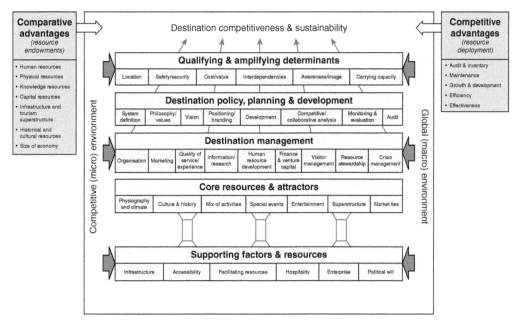

FIGURE 2.2   Conceptual model of destination competitiveness

Source: Ritchie and Crouch, 2003

The paper is a classic for two reasons:

1. It systematically maps out a model for destination competitiveness based upon a considerable amount of research, as well as discussion and refinement through debates and focus groups with students and destination managers. For example, the 2000 version of the model introduces tourism policy as an important influence upon competitiveness. Here, Ritchie and Crouch see policy as comprising three parts – the structure of the policy in terms of umbrella guidelines, the content of the policy, and policy process in terms of how the policy is delivered.

2. It provides a useful framework for defining the tourism destination. Ritchie and Crouch emphasise the importance of coming up with an agreed definition of the destination – not simply from an academic point of view, but also from the practical point of view of destination managers who need to share their understanding of the destination with their stakeholders. Their model of a destination has four key features:

    a. It distinguishes between the *physical resources* of a destination – such as beaches, and the *processes and activities* that occur around them to create tourism;

    b. It distinguishes between *natural resources* (climate, for example) and *human elements* such as buildings, technology and culture;

    c. It identifies and defines the *actors* who create the destination; and

    d. It defines *destination governance* 'vertically' by tier of government and 'horizontally' by partnerships.

The paper goes on to identify the following key components of destination competitiveness:

*   **Core resources and attractions** – these are the main attractions that draw tourists to a destination.

*   **Supporting factors and resources** – these are the facilitating resources that sustain and support the visit, although they are not the main reason for visiting; they include access, accommodation, food and beverage.

*   **Qualifying and amplifying determinants or situational conditioners** – these determinants limit or nurture the ability of the destination to compete. They include factors such as the size and scale of the destination and levels of security. Of course, these may be outside the control of the destination itself – for example, the unrest in the Middle East renders many otherwise highly desirable destinations almost as no-go areas.

*   **Destination policy, planning and development** – this approach is effective and coordinates a 'whole of destination' policy and planning which influences the competitiveness of a destination. In contrast, a badly planned and managed destination will always find it difficult to be competitive.

*   **Destination management** – as already shown, effective destination management delivers the visitor experience on the ground and ensures

quality management and coordination of the destination products. Again, this can make or break a destination.

- **Comparative versus competitive advantage** – in their model, Ritchie and Crouch make the distinction between the *comparative advantage* of a destination, which comes from its endowed resources of, say, natural beauty or cultural heritage, and *competitive advantage*, which is linked to how effectively the comparative resources are employed. This will very much depend upon the local DMO.

- **Global (macro) versus competitive (micro) environment** – here the model recognises that all destinations exist within a global environment and will be subject to forces outside their control. Examples are demographics or global economic cycles. Equally, there are micro-level influences upon the destination which come from the tourism system itself, including, say, changes in distribution methods of the product, or changes in transport provision to the destination. Both sets of factors influence destination competitiveness.

This paper deserves to be read because of its wide-ranging nature, its clarity of thinking about the destination and its contribution to our understanding of the structure and functioning of tourism destinations.

FOCUS ON EMPLOYABILITY

Job Functions in Sustainable Competitive Destinations

Careers and job functions in destination management are changing to reflect the shift to sustainable destinations – from green engineering to local guides – which in turn delivers a competitive destination. The new batch of jobs focuses around:

- Sustainable construction, engineering and consultancy, including environmental auditing, feasibility studies and supervision of design. This will also include tourism development specialists, sustainable tourism business development managers and human resources advisors, all focused on delivering sustainable construction.

- Accommodation managers and staff who can offer advice on sustainable practices and environmental education to guests. This will also include sustainable tourism managers, eco-lodge managers and sustainable consumption and conservation managers, reflecting a shift in thinking at the destination.

- Environmental management including national park managers, wildlife reserve rangers, nature tourism park managers, conservation project managers, naturalists, and conservation scientists.

- Marketing roles moving away from traditional approaches and increasingly focusing on environmental concerns and ethical behaviour as well as working in social media to promote sustainability. They include guidebook writers and responsible tourism marketing managers.

(Continued)

- The public sector, from local authorities to NGOs such as the UNWTO, having roles focusing on destination sustainability.
- Roles in sustainable destination certification and monitoring at the destination.
- Finally, guides playing a key role in sustainability, though the profession is much under-rated. They act as an intermediary between the visitor and the destination and so can influence behaviour and leave a lasting impression on the visitor. Many countries have compulsory guide training programmes.

THE EVOLVING DESTINATION

There is no doubt that the evolution of tourism has been closely linked to the evolution of destinations and, in particular, resorts. As markets also develop and change, resorts have had to respond in terms of their tourist facilities and services, for example through adaptation to climate change. A more formalised representation of this idea is expressed by Butler's (1980) tourist area life cycle (TALC) (see Figure 2.3). This states that destinations go through a cycle of evolution similar to the life cycle of a product (where sales grow as the product evolves through the stages of launch, development, maturity and decline). Simply, numbers of visitors replace sales of a product (Table 2.3). Obviously, the shape of the TALC curve will vary, but for each destination it will be dependent upon factors such as:

- The rate of development;
- Access;
- Government policy;
- Market trends; and
- Competing destinations.

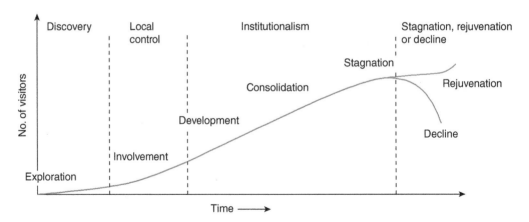

FIGURE 2.3   The tourist area life cycle

Source: Butler, 1980; Boniface and Cooper, 2009

TABLE 2.3 The tourist area life cycle

Exploration Stage

Here the resort is visited by a small volume of explorer-type tourists who tend to shun institutionalised travel. The natural attractions, scale and culture of the resort are the main draw, but volumes are constrained by lack of access and facilities. At this stage, the attraction of the resort is that it remains as yet unchanged by tourism and contact with local people will be high. Parts of Latin America and the Canadian Arctic are examples here.

Involvement Stage

At the involvement stage, local communities have to decide whether they wish to encourage tourism and, if so, the type and scale of tourism they prefer. Local initiatives will begin to provide for visitors and advertise the resort, which may lead to an increased and regular volume of visitors. A tourist season and market area emerge and pressures may be placed on the public sector to provide infrastructure and institute control. At this point, it is important to establish appropriate organisation and decision-making processes for tourism. Here, involvement of the local community should ensure that locally determined capacity limits are adhered to and that sustainable principles are introduced. The smaller, less-developed Pacific and Caribbean islands are examples here, as are countries such as Yemen.

Development Stage

By the development stage, large numbers of visitors are attracted, at peak period perhaps equalling or exceeding the number of local inhabitants. By this stage, the organisation of tourism may change as control passes out of local hands and companies from outside the area move in to provide products and facilities. These enterprises may have differing aims and timescales from those of the local community in terms of sustainable development. It is therefore at this stage that problems can occur if local decision-making structures are weak. Control in the public sector can also be affected as regional and national planning may become necessary, in part to ameliorate problems but also to market to the international tourist-generating areas as visitors become more dependent upon travel arrangements booked through the trade. This is a critical stage as these facilities, and the changing nature of tourism, can alter the very nature of the resort, and quality may decline through problems of overuse and deterioration of facilities. Parts of Mexico and the north African coast exemplify this stage.

Consolidation Stage

In the later stages of the cycle, the rate of increase of visitors declines, though total numbers are still increasing and exceed permanent residents. The resort is now a fully fledged part of the tourism industry with an identifiable recreational business district (RBD). Many Caribbean and Mediterranean destinations are examples here.

Stagnation Stage

At stagnation, peak tourist volumes have been reached and the destination is no longer fashionable, relying upon repeat visits from more conservative travellers. Business use of the resort's extensive facilities is also sought, but generally major promotional and development efforts are needed to maintain the number of visits. Resorts in this stage often have environmental, social and economic problems and find that competition for visits is fierce and coming from a number of well-entrenched, mature resorts. A number of Spanish resorts (such as on the Costa Brava) exemplify this stage.

Decline Stage

Visitors are now being lost to newer resorts and a small geographical catchment for day trips and weekend visits is common. However, resorts should not await decline as inevitable but should look to revitalise visits by seeking new markets, repositioning the resort or finding new uses for facilities.

Rejuvenation Stage

Destination managers may decide to rejuvenate or relaunch the destination by looking at new markets or developing the product. Introduction of new types of facility such as casinos is a common response. Here a destination should seek to protect its traditional markets, whilst also seeking new markets and products such as business, conference or special interest tourism. This helps to stabilise visitation, may combat seasonality and reduces dependence on declining market segments.

Rejuvenation strategies are difficult to implement as managers are dealing with the built fabric of tourist destinations rather than with a consumer product. Indeed, it is at this stage that the analogy of a product life cycle and the destination cycle breaks down, simply because tourism is so closely woven into the very way of life of resorts and supports jobs, services and carriers. The classic examples of this stage are Atlantic City, USA; Scheveningen, the Netherlands; and a number of Spanish destinations (Benidorm and Majorcan resorts) and Welsh destinations (Rhyl and Llandudno).

Each of these factors can delay or accelerate progress through the various stages. Indeed, destination strategy can arrest development at any stage in the cycle, and only tourist developments promising considerable financial returns will mature to experience all stages of the cycle. In turn, the length of each stage, and of the cycle itself, is variable. At one extreme, instant resorts such as Cancun (Mexico) (www.visitmexico.com/en/main-destinations/quintana-roo/cancun) move almost immediately to growth; at the other extreme, well-established resorts such as Scarborough (England) (www.scarborough.co.uk) have taken three centuries to move from exploration to rejuvenation.

One particular benefit of the tourist area life cycle is as a framework for understanding how destinations and their markets evolve (see Butler, 2015). The shape of the curve varies depending upon supply-side factors such as:

- Investment;
- Capacity constraints;
- Tourist impacts; and
- Planning responses.

Indeed, it could be argued that an understanding of the cycle aids the development of community-based and sustainable tourism strategies at the involvement stage. To implement such approaches in later stages may be inappropriate and certainly are more difficult. In other words, tourist destinations are dynamic, with changing provision of facilities and access matched by an evolving market in both quantitative and qualitative terms, as successive waves of different numbers and types of tourists with distinctive preferences, motivations and desires populate the resort at each stage of the life cycle.

The TALC is best utilised as a conceptual framework, although other writers have suggested that it can be used to guide strategic planning at destinations, or as a forecasting tool. There are, however, significant problems with these approaches:

- The difficulty of identifying stages and turning points;
- The difficulty of obtaining long runs of visitor arrivals data from which to assemble the curve;
- The danger of planners responding to (possibly false) warning signs, which can be influenced anyway by management intervention;
- The danger of a tailor-made strategy for each stage;
- The level of aggregation is open to many interpretations. After all, there will be a life cycle for nested destinations – a hotel, a resort and a region – as well as differing curves for each market segment.

The TALC has many critics, in part drawn by its very simplicity and apparent deterministic approach. Some argue that, far from being an independent guide for decisions, the TALC is determined by the strategic decisions of management and is heavily dependent on external influences. However, as a framework within which to view and understand the development of destinations, albeit with hindsight, and as a way of thinking about the interrelationship of destination and market evolution, it provides many useful insights.

SUMMARY

This chapter has focused upon the tourism destination as a fundamental unit of analysis for tourism. The chapter has demonstrated the various approaches to defining and thinking about the destination and recommends viewing destinations as networks of organisations that deliver the tourist experience. The chapter went on to identify the common features of destinations, including events, and the fact that they are amalgams, and showed how this has implications for destination management as well as understanding the different types of tourism. The chapter showed that sustainability has become the organising concept for destinations and that this is delivered through an understanding of the carrying capacity and the techniques of destination management and strategic planning. Sustainability delivers a competitive destination and the chapter showed the various influences on destination competitiveness. Finally, the chapter introduced the idea of destination evolution through the notion of a tourist area life cycle.

DISCUSSION QUESTIONS

1. In class, discuss the various approaches to defining the destination. Decide your preferred approach and justify it.

2. Taking a destination of your choice, identify the key components of the destination and consider the implications of the 'amalgam' concept.

3. There are a number of types of carrying capacity – discuss which should be the ultimate limiting factor for tourism at a destination with which you are familiar.

4. Using the Internet, identify a destination strategy and write a critique of its approach.

5. Taking a destination which you know well, research the history of demand and plot visitor numbers against time on a graph – can you identify any of the TALC stages on the graph?

ANNOTATED FURTHER READING

Butler, R.W. (2015) 'Tourism area life cycle', in C. Cooper (ed.), *Contemporary Tourism Reviews, Volume 1*. Oxford: Goodfellow. pp. 183–226.

Authoritative and up-to-date review of the life cycle.

Croes, R. and Semrad, K. (2018) 'Destination competitiveness', in C. Cooper, S. Volo, W.C. Gartner and N. Scott (eds), *The Sage Handbook of Tourism Management: Applications of Theories and Concepts to Tourism*. London: Sage. pp. 77–90.

Excellent and thorough review of destination competitiveness.

Crouch, G. and Ritchie, J.R.B. (2012) *Competitiveness and Tourism*. Cheltenham: Edward Elgar.

The full version of their competitiveness model in a comprehensive volume.

Fyall, A. (2019) 'Tourism destination re-positioning and strategies', in E. Fayos-Sola and C. Cooper (eds), *The Future of Tourism: Innovation and Sustainability*. Cham: Springer. pp. 271–84.

Thoughtful review of destination strategy

Page, S. and Connell, J. (2014) *The Routledge Handbook of Events*. London: Routledge.

Excellent and comprehensive coverage of all aspects of events and destinations.

REFERENCES CITED

Boniface, B. and Cooper, C. (2009) *Worldwide Destinations: The Geography of Travel and Tourism*. London: Heinemann.

Butler, R.W. (1980) 'The concept of a tourist area cycle of evolution', *Canadian Geographer*, 24: 5–12.

Butler, R.W. (2015) 'Tourism area life cycle', in C. Cooper (ed.), *Contemporary Tourism Reviews, Volume 1*. Oxford: Goodfellow. pp. 183–226.

Croes, R. and Semrad, K. (2018) 'Destination competitiveness', in C. Cooper, S. Volo, W.C. Gartner and N. Scott (eds), *The Sage Handbook of Tourism Management: Applications of Theories and Concepts to Tourism*. London: Sage. pp. 77–90.

Fyall, A. (2019) 'Tourism destination re-positioning and strategies', in E. Fayos-Sola and C. Cooper (eds), *The Future of Tourism: Innovation and Sustainability*. Cham: Springer. pp. 271–84.

Fyall, A. and Garrod, B. (2018) 'Destination management', in C. Cooper, S. Volo, W.C. Gartner and N. Scott (eds), *The Sage Handbook of Tourism Management: Applications of Theories and Concepts to Tourism*. London: Sage. pp. 91–110.

Jacobsen, S., Iversen, N. and Hem, L. (2019) 'Hotspot crowding and over-tourism: antecedents of destination attractiveness', *Annals of Tourism Research*, 76: 53–66.

Kurniawan, F., Adrianto, L., Bengen, D. and BudiPrasetyo, L. (2019) 'The social-ecological status of small islands: an evaluation of island tourism destination management in Indonesia', *Tourism Management Perspectives*, 31: 136–44.

Light, D. (2017) 'Progress in dark tourism and thanatourism research: an uneasy relationship with heritage tourism', *Tourism Management*, 61: 275–301.

Liu, J., Wang, C., Fang, S. and Zhang, T. (2019) 'Scale development for tourist trust toward a tourism destination', *Tourism Management Perspectives*, 31: 383–97.

Mathieson, A. and Wall, G. (1982) *Tourism: Economic, Physical and Social Impacts*. Harlow: Longman.

Morgan, N., Hastings, E. and Pritchard, A. (2012) 'Developing a new DMO marketing evaluation framework: the case of Visit Wales', *Journal of Vacation Marketing*, 18 (1): 73–89.

Pike, S. and Page, S. (2014) 'Destination marketing organizations and destination marketing: a narrative analysis of the literature', *Tourism Management*, 41: 202–27.

Ritchie, J.R.B. and Crouch, I. (2003) *The Competitive Destination: A Sustainable Tourism Perspective*. Wallingford: CABI.

UNWTO (2007) *A Practical Guide to Destination Management*. Madrid: UNWTO.

MAJOR CASE STUDY 2.1

Astro-Destinations

Astro-Tourism at Great Alqueva Lake Dark Sky Reserve, Portugal

Source: 'Alqueva lake, Portugal. Single shot image' by Kees Scherer is licensed under CC0 1.0

Introduction

As tourists search for authentic, well-managed experiences, new forms of tourism are emerging to satisfy this demand. In this case study, a new type of special interest tourism – astro-tourism – is examined in terms of the implications for destinations.

Astro-tourism is for tourists who are interested in aspects of astronomy and it can be thought of as: 'tourism using the natural resources of unpolluted night skies and appropriate scientific knowledge for astronomical, cultural or environmental activities' (Cooper et al., 2019: 112).

This form of tourism demands particular weather conditions, as well as dedicated infrastructure on the ground. In terms of the weather, astro-tourism needs clear, pollution-free skies at night combined with geographical locations that offer a good configuration for viewing the night sky. It is sensitive to

(Continued)

atmospheric conditions and light pollution. In terms of destination resources, successful astro-tourism destinations are not only based upon observatories and viewing equipment, but they also benefit from a heritage in astronomy by, say, indigenous populations as well as astro-related features from the past (such as Stonehenge in the UK). Examples of observatories that attract tourists include the Dish at Parkes in New South Wales, Australia; the Greenwich Observatory in London, UK; and the Lowell Observatories in the USA. Successful astro-tourism destinations include Western Australia and Hawaii, whilst Cyprus is working to develop open-air astro-parks featuring innovative use of augmented and virtual reality – they plan to accredit up to six 'Dark Sky Reserves'. The advantage of astro-tourism for the destination is the opportunities that it creates for cooperation between scientists, the tourism sector and local communities – even Airbnb now includes astro-tourism properties.

There are two bodies that accredit astro-tourism destinations:

- The conditions for astro-tourism are defended by the Starlight Foundation and their declaration: 'in defence of the night sky and the right to starlight' (https://fundacionstarlight.org). A starlight tourist destination must not only prove the quality of its air, and the means to ensure its protection but it must also have appropriate tourism infrastructure including accommodation, food and beverage, equipment for observation available to visitors, and trained staff and interpreters. The foundation has established the Starlight Tourist Certification System.
- The other organisation which designates areas for astro-tourism is the International Dark Sky Association (www.darksky.org). It designates dark sky reserves which are public or private land with 'an exceptional or distinguished quality of starry nights and nocturnal environment that is specifically protected for its scientific, natural, educational, cultural, heritage and/or public enjoyment' (www.darksky.org).

Dark sky reserves have a core area which meets the minimum criteria for dark sky quality and natural darkness, and a peripheral area that supports dark sky preservation in the core. Reserves are often formed through a partnership of multiple agencies, as in the Portuguese example below. The association supports astro-tourism and has a particularly useful set of lighting plans and guidelines to reduce light pollution.

Astro-Tourism in Alqueva, Portugal

The Portuguese region of Alqueva has been recognised as an exceptional place for stargazing and, in response, the municipalities around the Great Alqueva Lake joined together to preserve this special feature and reduce public lighting at night. The destination is a protected area and certified as both a 'Dark Sky Reserve' and a 'Starlight Tourism Destination'. It extends over about 3000 square kilometres. This state-of-the-art astro-tourism destination has been developed not only with all the necessary viewing equipment and weather conditions, but also a range of added-value destination features. The HQ and observatory are in a historical building and old school.

The core astro-tourism product

Alqueva has an astro-photography exhibition for visitors and a mini museum as well as an official dark sky observatory equipped with cutting-edge telescopes for solar and astronomical observations. These allow the visitor to view the planets and craters on the moon, as well as the opportunity to view remoter nebulae, galaxies and swarms of stars. Stargazing sessions can be booked depending on the phases of the moon and the time of year. In addition, solar observations can be booked using safe telescopes. These sessions are mixed with outdoor observations with binoculars and the naked eye.

Added value sessions

In addition to the core astro-tourism destination product, Alqueveda has developed a number of added value sessions. These include:

- Night-time canoe tours where visitors can walk around the Great Alqueva Lake and see the dark night sky. They can also go on canoe trails and swim in the lake;

- Boat tours on the Great Alqueva Lake on the Westlander – a sailboat built in 1913 in the Netherlands – with hospitality as well as functions such as weddings and birthday parties;

- Other local guided tours, including the archaeological Circuit of Évora, a tour of medieval Monsaraz and winery, a visit to the embroiderers of Arraiolos, a tour of the castles of Raia and the Jewish settlements of the North Alentejo including a World Heritage candidate village;

- Blind wine tasting at night;

- Night-time astro-tourism parties;

- Astronaut visits; and

- Astro-photography workshops.

Discussion Questions

1. The Alqueva dark sky reserve has cleverly mixed core and add-on products to develop the destination. Is there anything missing from the destination formula?

2. Do you think that astro-tourism is an early form of space exploration, or is it a destination product in its own right?

3. Draft a marketing plan for a new dark sky destination in Cyprus.

Sources: www.darksky.org; https://darkskyalqueva.com; https://fundacionstarlight.org; Cooper, C., Fayos Sola, E., Jafari, J., Lisboa, C., Marin, C., Perdomo, Y. and Urosevic, Z. (2019) 'Case studies in technological innovation', in E. Fayos Sola and C. Cooper (eds), *The Future of Tourism: Innovation and Sustainability*. Cham: Springer. pp. 111–27.

3

THE ECONOMIC CONSEQUENCES OF TOURISM

LEARNING OUTCOMES

This chapter considers the economics of tourism, taking into account the unique characteristics of the sector and both the positive and negative consequences of tourism for a destination. The chapter is designed to provide you with:

- an understanding of the unique characteristics of the tourism sector;

- an awareness of the importance of the economic evaluation of tourism and events;

- an appreciation of the tourism multiplier concept and its development;

- an understanding of the ways that tourism can bring economic benefits to a destination; and

- an awareness of the economic costs of tourism to a destination.

INTRODUCTION

Tourism is often described as one of the world's largest industries. It employs millions of people, has a turnover in billions of dollars and encourages millions of people to travel, as shown in Chapter 1. In other words, it is a substantial economic sector and economists bring a level of discipline to its analysis. There is no doubt that economics has made a fundamental contribution to the study and understanding of tourism, evidenced by the establishment in 1995 of the journal *Tourism Economics*. Economic analysis based upon tourism statistics is vital for decisions in the tourism sector, whether for investment, marketing or planning (Dwyer et al., 2015); after all, there is little point in embarking on the expensive process of collecting statistics and economic modelling if it does not inform policy. Sometimes though, economists have been accused of developing a bewildering array of technical terms, models and approaches – indeed, there is no simple recipe for assessing the economic contribution of tourism, and economists themselves often disagree about techniques. For example, there is a debate about how to assess the economic contribution of events to a destination, as shown in Major Case Study 3.1. Nonetheless, it is important for the language of economists to be clear, transparent and so able to inform policy. An example here is the classic paper for this chapter by Sinclair et al. (2003), which shows how economists can make a clear and unambiguous contribution to understanding tourism.

THE SUPPLY SIDE OF TOURISM: DEFINITIONS AND CHARACTERISTICS

Economists remain in dispute as to whether tourism is really an industry and, if so, how to define and measure it (Hara et al., 2018). In part, these problems arise because many industries are involved in delivering the tourism product as a service or 'experience' and tourism has distinctive characteristics that have to be taken into account. As a result, Sinclair et al. (2003) state that research on tourism supply has focused on individual sectors rather than the structure of the sector as a whole. Leiper (1990) is clear in his view that tourism is in fact only partially an industry as governments, communities and others are involved in delivering the tourism product. Tourism is therefore an industry that challenges conventional economic paradigms. Yet it is important to understand how its complex system functions if tourism is to be managed effectively. Debbage and Ioannides (1998) speak of the commodification of tourism that has created such a machinery of production:

> Although changes in consumer demand and the evolution of increasingly more sophisticated consumer preferences can play substantive roles in shaping the tourism product, it is the actual 'machinery of production' that helps to manipulate and facilitate origin-destination tourist flows across the world. (p. 287)

The authors go further by saying that tourism economists have tended to neglect the supply side of tourism. This is despite the fact that tourism is an increasingly important focus of policy intervention and of development in many countries, as economic strategies focus on the revenue and employment-generating potential of tourism. There is no doubt that the dilemma of analysing the supply side of tourism from an economic point of view has arisen because of the unique characteristics of tourism, including:

- The sector is an invisible export as there is no tangible product to show in a balance of payments account.
- It comprises both tangible and non-tangible elements.
- It is produced where it is consumed. In other words, it is one of the few industries where the consumer has to physically visit the site of production in order to consume it. As a result, the producer does not bear any transport costs as they are borne by the tourist.
- Tourism is not a single product but a diverse range of products and services that interact. This means that although the sector is fragmented, for the product to be delivered there has to be collaboration at the destination across the various enterprises that deliver aspects of the product – such as accommodation, transport and attractions. As a result, unless there is considerable integration of these aspects within a destination there is scope for substantial leakage of income away from the destination.
- Tourism is also a fragmented sector in that it comprises many different types of provider and has no single voice to represent it – indeed, Leiper (1990) terms it a set of businesses in search of an industry.
- The tourism industry is highly diverse – from size of establishment (SMEs to corporations); through business type (IT to service provision); sector (air transport to accommodation); organisation (public and private sector); to process. It is therefore more a collection of industries than a single industry.
- The sector is characterised by very unstable demand, which makes it a risky investment prospect from a financier's point of view.
- Tourism is a traditional industry that is slow to innovate and accept change, yet it is also one that promotes travel and thus contributes to climate change through carbon emissions. As a result, there is a constant need to innovate and adapt to new technologies.

Measuring the size and scope of the contemporary tourism industry has traditionally been a major challenge, in terms of developing a coherent and shared view of just what comprises the supply side of tourism, and how to measure it. Here, development and implementation of the Tourism Satellite Account (TSA) methodology have proved to be a major breakthrough in supply-side measurement and for the credibility of the tourism sector. The TSA is based upon the framework of the System of National Accounts (SNA) and allows the tourism component of the economy to be identified as explained below.

A satellite account is a term developed by the United Nations to measure the size of economic sectors that are not defined as industries in national accounts. By the conventional definitions used by economists for an industry, tourism would not qualify – there is not a single production process, the product is fragmented and varied, and there is no geographical catchment for the market. The concept of the satellite account is based upon the fact that the tourist (the demand side) receives a single product in the form of the visit, and all the consumption associated with that visit. Effectively then, the TSA is a subset of a nation's accounts that involves expenditures by individuals defined as tourists by the UNWTO.

The TSA allows tourism to be compared for the first time with other industries, as well as allowing economists to compare tourism sectors between different countries. The TSA measures:

- Tourism's contribution to GDP;
- Tourism's ranking compared to other economic sectors;
- The number of jobs created by tourism;
- The amount of tourism investment tax revenues generated by tourism industries;
- Tourism consumption;
- Tourism's impact on a nation's balance of payments; and
- The characteristics of tourism human resources.

Using the tourism satellite account

The potential uses of the TSA are really significant. They encourage planners and economists to increase and improve knowledge of the relative importance of tourism in a country or region. As a result, it is also an important instrument for politicians wishing to advocate support for the sector and provides support for designing more efficient policies relating to tourism and its employment aspects. The data from the TSA can be used to create awareness among tourism stakeholders of the economic importance of tourism and its contribution to the wider economy. Following the 2016 meeting of the UN's Statistics Division, current and future work on the TSA is focusing on the regional level, human resources, culture, transport and the environment, specifically through carbon emissions (see Dwyer, 2018; Hara et al., 2018; Jones, 2013).

THE DEMAND SIDE OF TOURISM: MEASUREMENT ISSUES

Whilst measuring the complex phenomenon that is tourism is difficult, it is important for two key reasons:

1. Estimates of the number of tourists to a destination drive the economic models that assess the role of tourism in an economy.

2. Governments are keen to monitor and attach measures to the movement of people within, into and out of their countries. Measures of incoming tourism are particularly important because of the economic benefits.

Most statistics of tourism demand represent the best estimates available rather than an absolute value. They have the following broad benefits:

- They often provide valuable trend data, where information is produced over a number of time periods.
- Information about the origins of visitors, their trip and attitudes can be used in marketing or planning.
- They enable the effects of decisions or changes to be monitored.
- They provide a means of making forecasts.
- They allow economists to measure the contribution of tourism to the overall economy.
- They assist in providing a platform of data to inform policy.
- Commercial organisations use tourism statistics for marketing purposes.

In addition to the above, local and regional tourism organisations and individual businesses make use of domestic tourism statistics as an aid to decision-making.

The measurement of demand normally includes statistics of volume, value and visitor profiles. In addition, during the collection of such data from visitors, questions are also often asked that relate to visitor opinions and attitudes.

Measures of demand

Volume statistics

The total number of international tourist arrivals, the total number of international tourist departures and domestic tourism are the three key measures of demand. These measures are actually of trips and not counts of individuals. A serious weakness in using tourism arrivals, as far as most tourism suppliers are concerned, is that the length of stay is not taken into account. The length of stay is important for accommodation establishments. A better measure of volume for many purposes is therefore total tourist nights. This also acts as a measure of likely impact on a tourist destination.

Value (expenditure) statistics

Total visitor expenditure is a simple measure of the economic value of visitors to a destination. It normally includes spending within the destination and excludes fare payments made to international passenger carriers for travel into and out of that country.

Visitor profile statistics

Profile statistics are made up of statistics relating to the visitor and include trip characteristics and demographics.

Measurement methods

Tourism statistics are normally estimates rather than exact values. This is mainly because monitoring and measuring what are at times complex movements of people is not easy and is a process subject to error.

Volume statistics are often obtained using counting procedures at entry and exit points to a country or (for inbound tourism) sometimes through the use of registration forms at accommodation establishments. Nevertheless, there are many countries that do make counts and collect information at frontiers for tourism-related purposes. Clearly, islands have an advantage in this respect, since there are likely to be fewer entry/exit points. A major problem with using counts made by accommodation establishments alone is that they give only partial coverage as they omit those staying with friends or relatives or using sites such as Airbnb.

Expenditure statistics are notoriously difficult to collect. They can be derived using foreign currency estimates from banks, or from suppliers of tourism services and facilities such as hotels or attractions. These methods are cumbersome and normally not satisfactory as they require the cooperation of these organisations and often are only provided as estimates. Increasingly, therefore, information is collected directly from the tourists themselves, through sample surveys of foreign tourists as they leave the country, and from nationals as they return from a foreign trip, either on entry to the country or through household surveys.

Household surveys are used to measure domestic and outbound tourism. A structured sample of households is constructed and interviewers are employed to collect information using a questionnaire. Questions normally relate to past behaviour, covering trips already made, although studies of intentions are sometimes undertaken.

En route surveys are surveys of travellers during the course of their journey. Strategic points are selected on key surface transport routes to stop or approach people, who are then either interviewed or given a questionnaire or other documentation to complete in their own time for return by post. A major problem with this type of work is that the representativeness of the sample can be in doubt because of incomplete knowledge of traffic movement within a country.

Surveys are often conducted at popular tourist destinations or in areas where there are high levels of tourist activity. They typically lead to estimates of the volume and value of tourism to the destination, and to profiles of visitors and their visits. Questions are also asked to elicit opinions about the destination and associated attitudes.

Surveys of suppliers of tourism services are sometimes undertaken in order to gain information on topics such as occupancy rates or visitor numbers.

FOCUS ON TECHNOLOGY

Using Social Media and Big Data as a Research Tool

Tourists leave digital traces of their activity and these can be measured using online sources to capture their behaviour and opinions. Technology therefore allows the move away from traditional market research towards harvesting data readily available on social media sites such as Twitter and Facebook in a process of 'datafication' (Volo, 2018). Social media provide a rich source of data for tourism research as they are prolific, accessible and highly visible. No longer does the researcher have to question the consumer in the high street or in their home; instead, the tourist is constantly posting their thoughts and opinions online and, whilst the social media companies own the data, they can be accessed through research companies as well as through some sites (such as Facebook) that provide free monitoring tools.

Traditional market research can be costly and time-intensive; as a result, many organisations have begun to turn to social media as a cost-effective and in-depth tool for gaining real-time insights into their customers, market, brand appearance and other important market research aspects, assisted by social media aggregation tools such as Hootsuite (https://hootsuite.com).

Using tourism statistics

There are a number of points to bear in mind when using tourism statistics:

- For measurements which result from sample surveys, in general the smaller the sample size, the greater the probable error.

- Even though the sample size for data relating to a region or country may give rise to acceptable levels of error, an analysis of a subset of the data, pertaining to a smaller area or region, may not be feasible owing to the much-reduced sample size.

- Sample size is not everything. The true random sampling of tourists who are, by their very nature, on the move is not normally possible. A sample has to be formally and carefully constructed.

- Where methodology in collecting data changes (even when it is for the better), it is dangerous to compare results.

- There are serious problems involved in attempting either to compare or to combine figures collected by different countries or organisations.

THE ECONOMIC CONSEQUENCES OF TOURISM

Introduction

As an activity of global significance, tourism has economic consequences for enterprises, communities, destinations, regions and countries. Quite simply, the economic significance of tourism is the fact that tourists earn money in their place of residence but spend it at the destination (see Comerio and Strozzi (2019) for a comprehensive review of the economic consequences of tourism). Economic impact analysis tracks and aggregates these monetary payments as they move through the destination's economy (Dwyer et al., 2020). As a result, tourism generates significant revenues, estimated at US$1.7 trillion in 2018, from international tourism and transport, and generates significant numbers of jobs globally, estimated by the World Travel and Tourism Council at 319 million jobs in 2018 (www.wttc.org). One of the key areas of research has been the way that the money and jobs generated by tourism circulate around the destination economy and 'multiply' to create further income and jobs (Dwyer et al., 2015). We deal with this aspect of the economics of tourism later in this chapter.

An important development is the conceptualisation of the tourism-related sector of the economy as the 'visitor economy', encompassing not only the economic significance of tourism, but also allowing the analysis of the supply chain and policy-related decisions which may impact upon the sector (Deloitte, 2008). Mini Case Study 3.1 examines the potential impact of a tourist tax on an iconic destination.

MINI CASE STUDY 3.1
Tourist Tax – the Case of Venice

The Issue

The Italian city of Venice is an iconic destination, but a highly fragile one. Tourism has become a major issue for the city, exacerbated by the rise in the number of cruise ships and excursionists (day visitors), the growth of Airbnb and the impact of low-cost airlines. This has resulted in a very different scale of tourism in the twenty-first century and has prompted discussions as to how sustainable these trends are for the city.

Venice, Italy

Source: 'IMG_20160530_210442' by Tim Pearce, Los Gatos is licensed under CC BY 2.0

In the twenty-first century, the number of tourist arrivals to Venice has quadrupled with excursionists estimated to be approaching 24 million per year, with an additional six million staying visitors (UNWTO, 2019); yet estimates suggest that the maximum carrying capacity of the city is 18 million visitors at the most. As a result, Venice is much studied and reported on, but has yet to find a solution to balancing the needs of its fragile ecosystem, the 50,000 local residents and 30 million tourists. One solution, implemented in 2019, is the controversial introduction of a tax on excursionists – there is already a bed tax in the city which earns around 30 million euros for Venice.

The Tax

The tax is being levied in order to pay for many of the services in the city such as rubbish removal and maintenance of the fabric of the city itself, including the bridges, canal banks and the cultural heritage. These costs are estimated at 41 million euros per annum. The tax is variable by season with a three-euro tax in low season, rising to 10 euros in the high season by 2022. In addition, there are early plans to ration visits to the city through a pre-booking system. The tax will be collected by transport operators who bring tourists into the city and will be built into the ticket price of cruises and air carriers.

The question is whether the tax will act to dissuade tourists from visiting; indeed, many are speaking of Venice 'exiting' the tourism industry through a form of 'trexit'. But the small amount of the tax is unlikely to trigger this. What is needed is a holistic approach to managing the city – the jury is out as to whether this controversial tax will help.

Discussion Questions

1. In class, debate the pros and cons of the tax for the city.
2. Do you think that the tax will dissuade visitors from coming to Venice?
3. What would be the impact of 'trexit' on the economy of Venice?

Sources: City of Venice (2018), www.comune.venezia.it; Hugues, S., Sheeran, P. and Pilato, M. (2018) 'Over-tourism and the fall of Venice as a destination', *Journal of Destination Marketing & Management*, 9: 374–6; UNWTO (2019) *Overtourism? Understanding and Managing Urban Tourism Growth beyond Perceptions, Volume 2: Case Studies*. Madrid: UNWTO; van der Borg, J. (2017) 'Sustainable tourism in Venice: what lessons for other fragile cities on water?', in R. Caroli and S. Soriani (eds), *Fragile and Resilient Cities on Water: Perspectives from Venice and Tokyo*. Cambridge: Cambridge Scholars Publishing.

In the past, research focusing upon the economic consequences of tourism was more commonly done at the national scale rather than the regional or the local. As Wall and Mathieson (2006) state, there are a variety of reasons for this:

- The economic consequences of tourism are more readily measurable than, say, environmental or social impacts. As a result, data are available, and these are more commonly collected at the national level.

- The methodologies for assessing the economic consequences of tourism are well established. Indeed, contemporary econometric models and, in particular, 'computable general equilibrium (CGE) models', allow us to estimate the impact of policy changes or changes in demand upon the economic value of tourism by modelling the whole economy within which tourism lies (Dwyer, 2018).

- Research funding agencies and tourist boards believe that the results of investigations into the economic value of tourism will deliver positive results that can be used for political purposes, whilst studies focusing on the environment or host communities will tend to be more negative. It is interesting to note, however, that the contemporary approach of the CGE model does not always place tourism in a positive economic light.

Wall and Mathieson (2006) observe that the consequences of tourism for a destination will depend upon:

1. The type of tourism generated to the destination. For example, international tourists tend to spend more than domestic tourists, and sectors such as business or conference tourism spend more than leisure tourists. The consequences will also differ according to the length of stay of the visitor and the generating regions of the tourists.

2. The ability of the national economy to leverage from the economic consequences of tourism in terms of the capacity to invest in tourism, and whether the level of tourism development is sufficient to allow economies of scale for suppliers.

3. The organisation of capital at the destination in terms of how much foreign investment is present and the capacity of the domestic economy to generate capital to support tourism. In many destinations, the hotel sector is a popular form of investment for foreigners.

4. The greater the level of foreign capital, the greater the 'leakage' of profits on the investment back to the foreign company. This is a common issue for destinations dependent upon international tour operators for their market and developments – Cyprus is a good example here.

5. Attributes of the destination in terms of the structure of the market, the degree of dependence upon intermediaries, and the degree of seasonality.

6. The setting of the destination in terms of being in a developing or developed economy, the political structures and its geographical location, and whether it is peripheral or more central in a region.

The concept of the tourism multiplier

Tourism economists have focused much of their research upon the fact that tourist expenditure at the destination increases the income of the destination by an amount greater than that which was originally spent. In other words, expenditure 'multiplies' as it circulates around the destination. This is known as the 'multiplier effect'. The actual multiplier is the numerical coefficient indicating how much destination income will increase due to the initial injection of tourist spending – the higher the multiplier, the greater the amount of additional income generated. In other words, an income multiplier of 1.5 means that for every $10 spent at the destination by the tourist, $15 will be generated as the tourist initially pays for accommodation, and the hoteliers themselves purchase food and other services and their suppliers pay out, say, wages or rent to stay in business. This is an example of the 'dynamic' nature of destination economies and shows that the initial spending by the visitor is only the first stage of the economic consequences of tourism for a destination (Figure 3.1).

The tourism *income multiplier* is the most commonly used coefficient, but it is also possible to calculate tourism *employment multipliers* and *government revenue multipliers*. Multipliers give different values according to the type of consequence desired:

- **Direct effects** – the actual expenditure or jobs generated by spending on tourism commodities.
- **Indirect effects** – the secondary effect of tourist spending as money is paid to traders and other suppliers by the primary recipients of the revenue. In other words, hotels pay the laundry companies to clean the bed linen and, in turn, they generate jobs.
- **Induced effects** – created by the contribution of tourist spending as it feeds into the general health of the economy in terms of income, jobs and government revenue.

Tourism multipliers have generated a large and sometimes controversial literature, in part because the calculation of the multiplier coefficient is so important for supporters of tourism at a destination. The methodology for multipliers is also complex, with three main approaches – the input–output model, the social accounting matrix and the computable general equilibrium model (Baggio, 2019). The size of the multiplier depends on three key factors:

1. **The economic self-sufficiency of the destination.** The more self-sufficient a destination, the higher will be the multiplier as the linkages between the different sectors of the economy will be closer. This means that the indirect and induced effects will be greater and there will be less 'leakage' of income and jobs out of the destination. Leakages occur when spending or jobs are lost to other sectors, or income is taken out of the economy by placing it into savings. Of course, self-sufficiency is closely linked

to scale – a small destination will be less self-sufficient than a larger one and so the size of the multiplier tends to increase with scale (Figure 3.1).

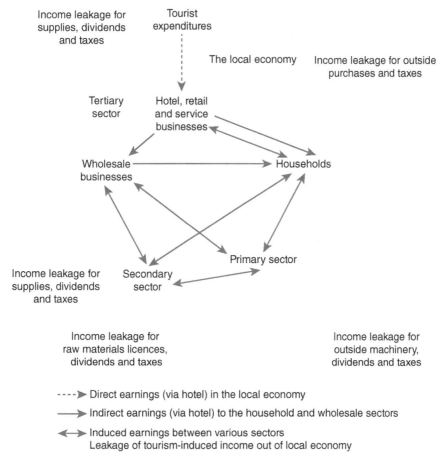

FIGURE 3.1   The economic impact of tourism in a locality and leakage effect

Source: Page and Connell, 2009

2. **The econometric technique used.** Tourism economists use different multiplier techniques, and as computing power has increased, these 'econometric techniques' have become increasingly complex. The current debate is between 'input–output models' and the more contemporary 'CGE models' (Dwyer et al., 2020). The development of Tourism Satellite Accounts has been possible due to the CGE models and gradually they are being used as best practice.

3. **The sources of data for the multiplier.** One point that is often overlooked is that all of these techniques are only as good as the data that they use. For multipliers, data at the national level are reasonably reliable, but for multipliers for ever smaller geographical areas – regions and individual destinations, for example – the data become less reliable and often have to be collected by the research team. For example, as shown above, most demand statistics – the fuel of multipliers – are estimates only.

This all adds up to the fact that these multipliers are prone to error (see Gunter et al., 2019) and it must be recognised that multipliers are, in reality, only a tool to allow policy makers and politicians to assess the economic value of tourism to a destination. The next section of this chapter considers the economic benefits and the economic costs of tourism to a destination. It is important to understand these consequences, as any defence of tourism as an activity tends to use positive economic arguments, whilst minimising the economic costs.

CLASSIC PAPER

Sinclair, M.T., Blake, A. and Sugiyarto, G. (2003) 'The economics of tourism', in C. Cooper (ed.), *Classic Reviews in Tourism*. Clevedon: Channel View. pp. 22–54

Thea Sinclair and her colleagues have written a 'classic' review paper covering all the main elements of the economics of tourism. The paper is a 'classic' because not only is it complete and thorough in its coverage, but it is also written by specialist tourism economists who are technically highly accomplished yet write in a very accessible style. As with all review papers, one of its strengths is its provision of an extensive reference list. This list reads like a road map of the development of tourism economics, with names including Brian Archer, Larry Dwyer, John Fletcher, Haiyan Song, Stephen Wanhill and Stephen Witt.

The paper is organised into five sections:

1. **Introduction.** The introduction is authoritative and clear. It begins with a definition: 'The economics of tourism is concerned with the allocation of scarce resources to satisfy consumers' demand for tourism and with the impact of tourism at the macroeconomic and microeconomic levels' (p. 22). The introduction stresses that literature on tourism supply has tended to focus on certain sectors such as transport and accommodation, but the authors rightly point out that demand for tourism has much more coverage.

2. **The demand for tourism.** The authors state that demand analysis is 'useful for increasing our understanding of the relative importance of different economic determinants of demand for forecasting and for related policy formation' (p. 23). In this section of the paper, they analyse the various approaches taken by economists to tourism demand based upon the technical approaches offered by different models.

3. **The supply of tourism.** Supply-side issues have long been neglected, mainly due to the complexities of tourism and also the lack of data. However, the development of Tourism Satellite Accounts is redressing this imbalance.

4. **The wider impacts of tourism.** Tourism has wide economic impacts at both the macro and the micro levels, but the strength of this paper is that it considers the relationship between economic impacts and others, such as environmental considerations.

5. **Conclusions.** The authors conclude that demand studies have dominated the study of tourism economics and that there is a need for more

policy-related work. They observe that whilst the demand work is analytical, the work required on the supply of tourism is more descriptive. Work on tourism impacts has changed in focus as different techniques have been used, but work linking economic impacts with others, such as the environment, is less common.

This is a thorough, technically adept and wide-ranging paper written in an accessible, authoritative style – a deserved classic.

THE ECONOMIC BENEFITS OF TOURISM

The economic benefits of tourism to a destination can be summarised as three areas – income, employment and regional development.

Income

One of the most significant economic consequences of tourism is the spending generated by tourists at the destination. This 'multiplies' through the destination to generate additional income and contribute to the gross domestic product of regions and countries. The World Travel and Tourism Council estimates that tourism contributes on average 10.4 per cent to the gross domestic product of countries worldwide (www.wttc.org).

At the national scale, income from spending by international tourists counts as an invisible 'export' as it is income that was earned overseas in country A and then spent on products at the destinations of country B. This means the income counts as part of the balance of payments of a country on the travel account. The balance of payments is a country's financial account. Tourism earnings are an 'invisible' export because no tangible goods are involved. This earned income is set against income spent by residents of that country when they travel abroad. This income spent abroad counts as an 'invisible import' for country A. For countries that have a highly successful inbound tourism industry – such as Spain – this means that the travel account is in credit, whilst for countries such as the UK or Germany, which are major generators of international tourism, the travel accounts are in debit. For the major destinations of the world, the scale of their export income is highly significant for the travel account. In contrast, for the major generators of tourism or importers their impact on the travel account is much less significant. Countries with significant international tourism spending and receipts are shown in Table 3.1.

TABLE 3.1   The ten leading generators and destinations for international tourism 2018

The leading generators of international tourism (based upon spend)	The leading destinations for international tourism (based upon volume)
China	France
USA	Spain
Germany	USA
UK	China
France	Italy

(Continued)

TABLE 3.1   (Continued)

The leading generators of international tourism (based upon spend)	The leading destinations for international tourism (based upon volume)
Australia	Turkey
Russian Federation	Mexico
Canada	Germany
Korea (ROK)	Thailand
Italy	UK

Source: based on data from UNWTO

The travel account of the balance of payments is based upon direct spending by international tourists. The categories of spending are normally:

- expenditure on tourism commodities such as accommodation, food and beverage, and retail;
- tourist expenditure on capital goods, such as antiques;
- imports and exports of goods for tourism, such as wine or equipment;
- payments to carriers for fares;
- money transfers, often by expatriates;
- interest, profits and dividends; and
- foreign capital investment (often in accommodation).

In the future, tourism will be increasingly important in the developing world and many countries are now using tourism as a development option to stimulate their economies. Whilst in the past this was more the case for countries that did not have other forms of income, tourism is increasingly used as a way to diversify economies, as in the oil-rich countries of the Middle East.

Of course, the economic benefits will reduce if the country imports many of the goods and services needed to support the tourism sector. For example, in the early years of the development of tourism in many Asian and African countries, expatriate managers and senior staff dominated the hotel sector and governments were prompted to develop strategies to reduce the level of expatriate labour in favour of locally trained managers. In part, this influx of expatriate labour was caused by a second problem for the countries themselves: a dominance of foreign investment and ownership in the hotel sector.

Finally, tourism spending acts to stimulate investment in the sector and also contributes to government tax revenues, most commonly through indirect taxation of spending but in some countries through a tourism tax on arrivals, departures or beds.

Employment

Tourism is favoured as an economic sector due to its ability to generate and sustain significant levels of employment. Tourism generates employment across a wide range of sectors, from accommodation to transportation and guiding, and at a range of levels from the unskilled to the highly trained – such as pilots. It also sustains jobs for women, the disadvantaged, the elderly and the young, as seen in the focus on employability.

FOCUS ON EMPLOYABILITY

Young workers in tourism

The International Labour Organization estimates that over 40 million people aged 18–24 years will enter the global workforce between 2017 and 2030. In 2019, the WTTC, representing leading tourism employers globally, stressed the importance and value of young people working in tourism, particularly in terms of reducing unemployment and poverty. Tourism is often a sector of choice offering flexibility, the opportunity to travel and entry-level positions which do not need prior experience. There are many benefits of tourism as a career for younger workers, including the empowerment of women, providing jobs in remoter regions and employing the disadvantaged in society. A more structured approach from larger employers includes internships, work experience and training programmes for younger workers. The skills learned in tourism jobs are transferable and can benefit employees throughout their career, in whatever sector they work.

However, the share of younger workers in tourism is declining, explained by there being more competition from older workers and the fact that many mature tourism economies have developed an employment regime that has created permanent, career-focused roles, dissuading casual or part-time younger workers who do not intend to stay within the industry.

Source: WTTC (2019) *Travel & Tourism: Generating Jobs for Youth*. London: WTTC.

Using multiplier analysis, tourism manpower planning calculates the number of jobs required to support tourism at a destination using the level of tourism expenditure. In other words, there is a threshold of expenditure required to generate each tourism job. Of course, this will depend upon the scale and maturity of the tourism industry at the destination, as well as the level of imported labour for tourism. In the Maldives, for example, levels of imported labour in the island resorts is very high.

Despite the fact that tourism is lauded for its ability to generate significant numbers of jobs quickly, there are major issues relating to the 'quality' of tourism jobs, as shown in Mini Case Study 3.2.

MINI CASE STUDY 3.2

Contemporary Tourism Employment Issues

Introduction

The International Labour Organization is campaigning for all jobs to be 'decent' jobs (www.ilo.org). One criticism of tourism employment is that the quality of the jobs is poor. This impacts upon the ability of tourism destinations to deliver the tourist experience as enterprises find it difficult not only to find employees, but also those with the right skills (Baum, 2007).

(Continued)

The Role of Tourism Employment

Tourism is a powerful instrument for development because it directly and indirectly employs large numbers of people. Employment in tourism is considerably varied and this makes the sector attractive to new entrants into the labour market and groups prone to unemployment, such as young people, women or those with minimal education. Tourism employment in the twenty-first century is, however, characterised by a range of issues.

Contemporary Tourism Employment Issues

Image and Working Conditions

The image and working conditions of tourism employment make jobs seem unfavourable. The sector suffers from high labour turnover, which comes at a cost for the employer. This is exacerbated by poor working conditions, characterised by low wages, temporary and part-time employment and anti-social hours. Naturally, employers adopt strategies to match their labour supply with the periods of demand for tourism.

To move towards 'decent' work in tourism, there is a need for the mindset of employers in tourism to change to one that values people, their skills and knowledge, develops them, rewards them and treats them as valued resources. This will demand innovative responses to human resources practice, reward systems, working conditions and skill development that are crucial to offset further supply shortages.

Understanding Tourism Labour Markets

These issues cannot be resolved if the scale and scope of the problem cannot be assessed. With the TSA methodology it is possible to understand and measure labour markets, to diagnose the problems and to act. This will allow planners to view an accurate picture of the pyramid that comprises tourism jobs. Approaches such as labour market observatories, with their local and regional monitoring of labour markets, mean that this information allows for rapid decision-making and creative approaches to manpower planning and policy.

To solve these issues, sector leadership will be required to change the image of tourism employment as being low paid and servile, and awareness programmes for communities will need to be designed to show young people the value of a career in tourism. This will help to make tourism more attractive as a career choice and help people to build a career in the sector, a sector which must be seen as offering 'decent work'.

Discussion Questions

1. Using job vacancy websites, compare the conditions and wages of a catering position with other positions in, say, IT or finance. Draw up a table comparing the jobs. In class, debate the most attractive positions.
2. As a regional manager of a large fast food franchise, draft a strategy to retain your entry-level staff.
3. Draft an outline approach to an awareness campaign showcasing the benefits of a career in tourism in a country that you are familiar with.

Sources: Baum, T. (2007) 'Human resources in tourism: still waiting for change', *Tourism Management*, 28, 1383–99; International Labour Organization (www.ilo.org); OECD (2014) *Supporting Quality Jobs in Tourism*. Paris: OECD; Riley, M., Ladkin, A. and Szivas, E. (2002) *Tourism Employment: Analysis and Planning*. Clevedon: Channel View.

Regional development

One of the major roles of tourism in an economy is for regional development, particularly in areas where other types of economic activity are difficult – such as mountainous areas or small islands. As a result, tourism development has become an important part of national economic strategies. Tourism is often used as a leading economic sector for development, to be followed by other sectors and investment. Yet the strongest lesson learned from experience around the world is that to be successful as a development option, tourism must be integrated into the rest of the economy and society and have strong public sector leadership, often through a development agency or tourism board. It is also true that the role of tourism is important in the early stages of development, but that with time this influence diminishes as the economy develops and other sectors grow.

As an economic development tool, tourism is an important agent of economic change, bringing significant advantages:

- It generates rapid injections of expenditure into the local economy.
- It is a major job creator with jobs that do not require high levels of training. Tourism can generate twice as many jobs as other economic sectors, such as oil production.
- It allows for rapid improvements in living standards and creates demand for goods and services.
- For the developing world, tourism delivers the ability to earn foreign currency.
- It creates an infrastructure and facilities of benefit to the local economy and society.
- It encourages the development of an entrepreneurial culture.
- It reduces dependence on primary economic sectors, such as mining, oil production and agriculture.
- It helps to maintain the viability of enterprises at the destination.
- It creates a stimulus for the domestic tourism industry.

These advantages are particularly valuable for two particular types of destination:

1. Those in the developing world where many countries have low incomes, an uneven distribution of wealth and high unemployment. The economies of these countries are often dependent upon the primary sector and have high levels of economic leakage to the developed world. Here, tourism can be used not only as a development tool but also for poverty alleviation (as seen in Chapter 5).

2. However, whilst the developing world is often seen as the primary focus for tourism development, it must not be forgotten that in the developing world tourism is a major contributor to the economies of peripheral coastal, mountainous and remote islands where other activities such as agriculture may be marginal – and, of course, tourism is attracted to these areas as they are often of natural beauty.

The economic costs of tourism to destinations is covered in the next section where it must be remembered that both developing country economies and those of peripheral areas tend to have structurally weak economies. Here there is a tendency for significant levels of imports, and tourism development comes with costs involved and leakages through imports of goods and labour.

THE ECONOMIC COSTS OF TOURISM

As it is the economic dimension which tends to favour tourism in any assessment, there is much less work done on the economic costs of tourism. Where research has considered these costs, it has tended to focus only upon the 'direct' costs of tourism rather than the indirect or induced effects. It can be argued, for example, that employment generated by tourism is not 'decent' work. The economic costs of tourism fall into three categories:

1. Opportunity cost;

2. Overdependence/lack of diversity; and

3. Inflation and externalities.

Opportunity cost

Any tourism development will divert labour and investment resources away from the opportunity for other developments – such as schools or healthcare. Similarly, government revenues used to enter the tourism market or to promote their destinations will not be available for other uses. This is a key issue for poorer countries justifying tourism development as a means of poverty alleviation. It explains why tourism needs to be integrated into other social and economic strategies for development to ensure a balanced approach. Finally, income spent on tourism is not available for consumers to spend on other goods – such as cars or electrical products.

Overdependence/Lack of diversity

There is always a danger that a destination will become too dependent upon tourism and therefore exposed in a downturn of demand; tourism demand is, after all, highly volatile, price elastic and prone to changes in fashion and taste. Demand in many parts of the world is also seasonal and this can mean that previously year-round economic activity becomes highly seasonal. Egyptian tourism, for example, has suffered a collapse in demand due to terrorism and political instability.

Where a country is dependent upon one or two economic sectors – such as agriculture or mining – the introduction of tourism can reduce activity in those sectors by taking labour and resources away. As a result, the addition of tourism does not help to diversify the economy but is simply a substitute for another sector.

Inflation and externalities

Tourism can be a cause of inflation in destinations where there is high demand for products. The spending power of tourists may exceed that of the locals and lead to inflation in the price of goods, property and land. This is a common issue in many areas of outstanding natural beauty or cultural heritage destinations such as national parks and heritage towns. This can eventually mean that the local community is unable to afford local housing or to purchase local goods. This has long been a problem in the English Lake District and Snowdonia national parks. In such popular tourism destinations, the externalities of tourism as an activity become evident as residents suffer from additional traffic, queues for services and competition for local goods.

SUMMARY

This chapter has mapped out the key dimensions of the economics of tourism. The chapter began by demonstrating the unique characteristics of tourism as an industry, including its highly fragmented nature, the fact that it is an 'invisible' industry and that it is produced where it is consumed. This has meant that economists have struggled to come up with accurate measurements of tourism supply and to define it. However, the development of the Tourism Satellite Account has been a breakthrough in the analysis of the supply side of tourism and is now used to measure the size and scope of the industry and to make credible comparisons with other industries.

The chapter went on to outline the economic consequences of tourism, pointing out that this work has a long history, partly because it tends to show tourism in a positive light. The chapter then outlined the concept of the tourism multiplier as an important tool for assessing the economic value of tourism to a destination. Quite simply, it is a coefficient that represents the extra income or employment earned by an injection of tourism spending into a destination. It is, however, dependent upon accurate statistics of tourism demand, a topic examined in detail in the chapter. The chapter then outlined the main areas where tourism can benefit a destination, focusing on income, employment and regional development. The chapter considered some of the economic costs of tourism, an area that has received less attention until recently. The main costs are related to the nature of tourism jobs, the risk of overdependence, inflation and opportunity cost.

All of these issues are elegantly captured in the classic paper chosen for this chapter on the economics of tourism by Sinclair et al. (2003). The chapter closes with a major case study examining approaches to evaluating the economic impact of events.

DISCUSSION QUESTIONS

1. In class, debate whether tourism is an economic force for good or evil at a destination of your choice.

2. Using UNWTO statistics, create a table of the top ten country spenders and earners from international tourism for 2019, 2005, 1995 and 1985. Highlight the changes over time and explain why these have occurred.

3. Visit the World Travel and Tourism Council website (www.wttc.org) and look at the way that they use TSA data. How credible is their approach?

4. Research the concept of opportunity cost and discuss its significance when considering tourism in a developing country of your choice.

5. Why has tourism proved so difficult to define and measure on the supply side?

ANNOTATED FURTHER READING

Dwyer, L. (2018) 'Economics of tourism', in C. Cooper, S. Volo, W.C. Gartner and N. Scott (eds), *The Sage Handbook of Tourism Management: Theories, Concepts and Disciplinary Approaches to Tourism*. London: Sage. pp. 173–92.

Excellent and comprehensive coverage of the economics of tourism.

Dwyer, L., Forsyth, P. and Dwyer, W. (2020) *Tourism Economics and Policy*. Bristol: Channel View.

Second edition of the most comprehensive text on tourism economics, already a classic.

Hara, T., Asahi, S. and Kinjo, M. (2018) 'Tourism supply side analysis', in C. Cooper, S. Volo, W.C. Gartner and N. Scott (eds), *The Sage Handbook of Tourism Management: Theories, Concepts and Disciplinary Approaches to Tourism*. London: Sage. pp. 222–39.

Excellent contemporary review of supply-side issues.

Riley, M., Ladkin, A. and Szivas, E. (2002) *Tourism Employment: Analysis and Planning*. Clevedon: Channel View.

Thorough text examining all aspects of tourism employment.

Song, H., Dwyer, L. and Li, G. (2012) 'Tourism economics research: a review and assessment', *Annals of Tourism Research*, 39 (3): 1653–82.

Advanced review of the tourism economics literature.

REFERENCES CITED

Baggio, R. (2019) 'Measuring tourism: methods, indicators and needs', in E. Fayos Soloa and C. Cooper (eds), *The Future of Tourism: Innovation and Sustainability*. Cham: Springer. pp. 255–69.

Baum, T. (2007) 'Human resources in tourism: still waiting for change.' *Tourism Management*, 28 (6): 1383–99.

Comerio, N. and Strozzi, F. (2019) 'Tourism and its economic impact: a literature review using bibliometric tools', *Tourism Economics*, 25 (1): 109–31.

Debbage, K.G. and Ioannides, D. (1998) 'Conclusion: the commodification of tourism', in D. Ioannides and K.G. Debbage (eds), *The Economic Geography of the Tourist Industry: A Supply Side Analysis*. London: Routledge. pp. 287–92.

Deloitte (2008) *The Economic Case for the Visitor Economy: Final Report*. London: Deloitte/Visit Britain.

Dwyer, L. (2018) 'Economics of tourism', in C. Cooper, S. Volo, W.C. Gartner and N. Scott (eds), *The Sage Handbook of Tourism Management: Theories, Concepts and Disciplinary Approaches to Tourism*. London: Sage. pp. 173–92.

Dwyer, L., Forsyth, P. and Dwyer, W. (2020) *Tourism Economics and Policy*. Bristol: Channel View.

Dwyer, L., Forsyth, P. and Papatheodorou, A. (2015) 'Economics of tourism', in C. Cooper (ed.), *Contemporary Tourism Reviews, Volume 1*. Oxford: Goodfellow Publishers. pp. 13–30.

Gunter, U., Önder, I. and Smeral, E. (2019) 'Scientific value of econometric tourism demand studies', *Annals of Tourism Research*, 78 (C): 1.

Hara, T., Asahi, S. and Kinjo, M. (2018) 'Tourism supply side analysis', in C. Cooper, S. Volo, W.C. Gartner and N. Scott (eds), *The Sage Handbook of Tourism Management: Theories, Concepts and Disciplinary Approaches to Tourism*. London: Sage. pp. 222–39.

Jones, C. (2013) 'Scenarios for greenhouse gas emissions reduction from tourism: an extended tourism satellite account approach in a regional setting' *Journal of Sustainable Tourism*, 21 (3): 458–72.

Leiper, N. (1990) 'Partial industrialisation of tourism systems', *Annals of Tourism Research, 7*: 600–5.

Page, S. and Connell, J. (2009) *Tourism: A Modern Synthesis*. Andover: Cengage.

Sinclair, M.T., Blake, A. and Sugiyarto, G. (2003) 'The economics of tourism', in C. Cooper (ed.), *Classic Reviews in Tourism*. Clevedon: Channel View. pp. 22–54.

Volo, S. (2018) 'Tourism data sources: from official statistics to big data', in C. Cooper, S. Volo, W.C. Gartner and N. Scott (eds), *The Sage Handbook of Tourism Management: Theories, Concepts and Disciplinary Approaches to Tourism*. London: Sage. pp. 193–201.

Wall, G. and Mathieson, A. (2006) *Tourism: Change, Impacts and Opportunities*. Harlow: Pearson.

MAJOR CASE STUDY 3.1

Evaluating the Economic Effects of Events

2007 Formula One World Championship

Source: 'IMG_0317' by moron958 is licensed under CC BY 2.0

(Continued)

Economic Evaluation in Context

As one-off occurrences, events present a unique and particular context for evaluating their consequences. In the early years of event studies (the 1980s onwards) the focus was on economic evaluation to ensure that events contributed to the destination and lived up to the expectations of both sponsors and organisers. This was particularly the case for mega events such as the Adelaide Formula 1 Grand Prix where economists were brought in to assess the economic benefits to the host city. Most studies in this period showed events in a positive light, boosting the economies of their host destinations and benefiting stakeholders commercially. However, as the subject matured into the twenty-first century, three key developments occurred:

1. Firstly, the realisation that there are many different types of events – from mega events to small local arts festivals, and that the assessment of the impact of events will therefore vary across this spectrum.
2. Secondly, it was realised that events should be evaluated in the round, including environmental impacts and the impacts on local residents (see Yolal et al., 2016). This wider evaluation of events also included their role in destination marketing and place identity. Particular effort was placed on researching the perceptions of local residents and also upon the sustainability of events from an environmental point of view. Most of these studies found that local residents viewed events positively for both themselves and the community (Scholtz, 2019).
3. Terrorist attacks on events, such as the Boston Marathon bombing, shifted the focus of event managers and researchers to the safety and security of events and the management of risk. The large crowds that are attracted to mega events, for example, pose a target for terrorism and a challenge for event managers to reassure audiences that they will be safe – especially given the exposure of such events to social media. This has resulted in a rethink in terms of the planning, staging and design of events.

Despite these developments and the fact that the focus of event evaluation has now moved away from economic impact, it is still a highly important element of any event.

Why Evaluate Events?

It is important to evaluate the economic consequences of events as often their organisers have to seek funding and sponsorship, and to do this they need to justify the benefits of the event both for its duration and its legacy. It is also important to recognise that events can have economic costs as well as benefits. These costs can be in the form of opportunity costs, revenue losses and leakages, and the reputation of the destination. As such, there needs to be thorough evaluation of the economic costs and benefits generated by an event

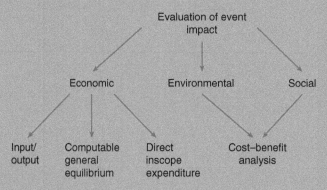

FIGURE 3.2   Evaluating the impact of an event

Source: Jago and Dwyer, 2006

to justify the funding assistance they may receive, as well as to assess their overall impact. In other words, comprehensive and robust approaches to event evaluation are important (see Figure 3.2 for a summary of the approach). Jago and Dwyer (2006) are clear: 'Economic evaluations of special events reveal important information about events to stakeholders and enable the new expenditure and employment created for the host region to be measured' (p. 2).

Economic Evaluation of Events

Economic evaluation of events has been the subject of many different, and inconsistent, methods over the years. These have often exaggerated the positive economic impact of the event, overstating the benefits by not counting the cost of staging the event, or by including expenditure that would have occurred anyway, without the event. Jago and Dwyer (2006, p. 3) include other evaluation 'myths':

- All special events create economic benefits;
- The construction of new facilities is always a benefit;
- All visitor expenditure is the same;

- Events generate substantial employment; and
- All spending by event participants counts in calculating economic benefit.

The two most common methods of economic evaluation are input–output models and computable general equilibrium (CGE) models. In a definitive report on economic evaluation, Jago and Dwyer (2006) clearly favour the CGE method. Such methods are driven by the data on expenditure at the event. This is determined by:

- the number of visitors;
- the types of visitors;
- the type of event;
- the trip duration of visitors;
- costs at the host destination; and
- spending by organisers and sponsors.

Finally, most economic evaluations of major events are economic *impact* studies rather than *evaluation* exercises, as they do not take into account the opportunity cost of resources used in staging the event (see Figure 3.3). As a result, there has been an increase in the cost–benefit analysis of events.

Total inscope expenditure attributable to the event	Economic model	Economic impact

FIGURE 3.3   The economic impact of an event

Source: Jago and Dwyer, 2006

Discussion Questions

1. Taking an event that you are familiar with, list the main categories of expenditure that would determine its economic impact.
2. As an event organiser, how would you use information about the economic 'benefits' of your event?
3. Do you think that the environmental and community consequences of events are more important than the economic impacts?

Sources: Jago, L. and Dwyer, L. (2006) *Economic Evaluation of Special Events: A Practitioner's Guide*. Altona, Victoria: Common Ground; Scholtz, M. (2019) 'Does a small community (town) benefit from an international event?' *Tourism Management Perspectives*, 31, 310–22; Yolal, M., Gursoy, D., Uysald, M., Kim, H. and Karacaoğlu, S. (2016) 'Impacts of festivals and events on residents' well-being', *Annals of Tourism Research*, 61, 1–18.

4

THE ENVIRONMENTAL CONSEQUENCES OF TOURISM

LEARNING OUTCOMES

This chapter considers the major issue of the consequences of tourism for the environment. This is a complex area as, whilst tourism is dependent upon environmental quality to attract and support visitors, it can also have a detrimental effect upon those very environments – and their climate. This chapter is designed to provide you with:

- an understanding of the historical dimensions of tourism and the environment;
- an awareness of the importance of a disciplined approach based upon carrying capacity;
- an appreciation of both the negative and positive consequences of tourism for the environment;
- an understanding of the techniques of environmental impact assessment and environmental auditing; and
- an awareness of the broader issues relating to tourism and the environment.

INTRODUCTION

This chapter adopts a broad interpretation of the environment to include not only the natural environment, but also the built environment of historic and archaeological sites and destination landscapes. In other words, the chapter considers the environment in all its forms and the ecosystems within that environment. Holden (2018) is clear on the need to maintain the integrity of ecosystems as they provide services essential to the survival of humanity, yet little is known about how much stress ecosystems can endure, or how they function. An essential component here is to understand the role of tourism within the ecosystem. We must also recognise that the consequences of tourism for the environment are substantial, but that in fact these consequences are associated with only a small percentage of the world's population – those that can afford to travel. Wall and Mathieson (2006) identify the most critical ecosystems for tourism as:

- Coastlines;
- Oceanic islands and marine ecosystems;
- Mountains;
- Polar ecosystems; and
- Tropical rainforests.

THE DEVELOPING RELATIONSHIP BETWEEN TOURISM AND THE ENVIRONMENT

Tourism is an environmentally dependent sector and the relationship is a fluid and changing one (Holden, 2018). Many tourism products depend upon the environment, and its quality, for their resource base and attractions – think, for example, of areas of scenic natural beauty such as the Canadian Rockies, or the national parks of Africa where the wildlife resources are the key draw for tourism. The environment, too, figures large in much tourism promotion and many destination images – the '100% Pure New Zealand' campaign being an obvious example here (www.tourismnewzealand.com). In the twenty-first century, it is the issue of climate change that has dominated the relationship, and there is no doubt that tourism is a 'climate sensitive' sector. Of course, tourism can also benefit the environment, not only by providing economic support and investment, but also in terms of educating tourists to understand and protect the environment. Ultimately it is the unique and special places on the earth that attract tourism, and in turn these ecosystems are the most fragile and vulnerable to change. But, as has been stressed in other chapters, it is the fact that tourists have to visit the resource itself to consume it, and that this visitation is focused in space and time, that leads to the potential pressures on the environments visited. Add to this the fact that environmental costs are rarely built into the price of tourism, and the classic conflict between the long-term horizons of sustainable development and the short-term view of developers, and the stage is set for a constant tension. Holden (2009) takes this one step further, arguing that the sustainability debate has had little impact on the practical 'business' of tourism and that, if it is to do so, then it is necessary to understand how tourism markets function. This tension is now part of a global debate on how to address climate change, where tourism and mobility have become a key part of the discussion.

The relationship between tourism and the environment is therefore a complex one and one that has evolved over time. Before 1945 the scale of tourism was such that there were few major issues, aside from hot spots of activity such as the English Lake District where, in the late nineteenth century, measures were being taken to protect it from excessive visitation. Indeed, early commentators on tourism saw it as a flawless industry – without smokestacks – that can benefit the environment. With the rise of mass international tourism in the 1960s, however, and excessive resort developments in areas such as coastal Spain, the relationship became more problematic, leading to real conflict between tourism and the environment. The full-blown development of mass tourism in the 1970s led to a wave of environmental concerns and the call for new approaches to address the situation; new models of tourism and planning were required, which eventually emerged in the form of sustainable tourism. These developments are dealt with in Chapter 6.

An important development was the promotion of alternative, responsible or eco-tourism products. Newsome et al. (2012) note that whilst there are many forms of alternative or allegedly 'low-impact' tourism, the term 'ecotourism' is the most commonly used. Ecotourism, or more strictly nature-based tourism, is often seen as the solution to negative environmental impacts. Ecotourism is seen as low-impact, encouraging responsible and 'environmentally friendly' visitors, and utilising low-impact developments and forms of transport. Ecotourism is also dominantly 'non-consumptive', that is, it does not involve killing or harming the fauna and flora; rather it is seen as having a strong educational component. A major critic of this approach is Brian Wheeller, who dismisses ecotourism as 'ego tourism', vociferously stating that all forms of tourism are damaging to the environment – ecotourism and other forms of alternative tourism are simply smokescreens for tourism developments that can be pushed through under the cloak of 'self-righteous virtue' (Wheeller, 2003). Nonetheless, ecotourism continues to grow without challenge and is legitimised through societies and organisations and a source of employment, as shown in the focus on employability.

FOCUS ON EMPLOYABILITY

Jobs in Ecotourism

Employment options in ecotourism are growing, focused around creating and promoting responsible and sustainable tourism options for the market. These jobs also have an element of environmental education and an opportunity for roles in conservation or community outreach programmes.

Jobs in ecotourism can be divided into four sectors:

1. Development and management of ecotourism projects and resorts where the roles would include managers and staff who not only have the expected hospitality skills, but are also able to provide environmental advice and education to guests. These resorts and developments also have to be constructed using sustainability principles and there are roles here for designers and architects.

2. Managing the natural environment will involve roles such as park rangers, national park managers, environmental educators, wildlife managers and conservation scientists.

3. Promotion and marketing roles include guides and interpreters, involving an in-depth understanding of the local ecosystem and culture. Marketing roles will involve developing and promoting the product.

4. The public sector and NGOs also provide opportunities in eco and nature-based tourism. There are also roles with the larger eco-certification bodies.

However, these jobs are hotly competed for. They often require prior experience (which can be gained through volunteering) and a strong educational background – sometimes up to master's degree level, as well as the usual generic competencies such as strong interpersonal skills.

The chapter now turns to the important concept of carrying capacity that mediates the relationship between tourism and the environment.

CARRYING CAPACITY

The relationship between tourism and the environment is determined by the carrying capacity of the resource in question. Quite simply, the environment becomes stressed when visitor capacity is exceeded. In recent years, this condition has been named 'overtourism'. However, whilst carrying capacity seems a deceptively simple concept, it is much more difficult to operationalise. This is because, at the end of the day, deciding upon when an environment becomes stressed is a subjective judgement. It is interesting, for example, that different groups – planners, residents and visitors – may perceive this 'threshold' of stress differently.

The concept of carrying capacity has a long pedigree. It was originally developed by resource managers in agriculture and forestry to determine the cropping levels that plots of land could sustain without nutrients and other food sources being depleted. In tourism, carrying capacity refers to the ability of a destination to take tourism use without deteriorating in some way. In other words, it defines the relationship between the resource base and the market and is influenced by the characteristics of each. One of the best definitions is by Mathieson and Wall (1982: 21): 'The maximum number who can use a site without unacceptable deterioration in the physical environment and without an unacceptable decline in the quality of experience gained by visitors'.

This definition raises three key points:

1. Carrying capacity can be managed, and there is no absolute number for any destination. For example, a beach can appear crowded with very few visitors present, while a wooded area can absorb many more visitors.

2. There are two sets of influences upon carrying capacity for any environmental system: the tourist and the resource itself, as shown in Figure 4.1.

3. Carrying capacity is determined by managers who decide when the decline in the visitor experience becomes 'unacceptable'.

Regarding environmental impact, we can think of five types of carrying capacity:

1. **Physical carrying capacity** refers to the number of facilities available, such as aircraft seats or car parking spaces. It is easy to measure and can be calculated on a simple percentage basis.

2. **Environmental or biological carrying capacity** is more difficult to measure and refers to limits of use in the ecosystem. There is increasing interest in the capacity not only of the vegetation cover to take tourism use but also of animal life, such as whale or dolphin watching, or tourism in the African game reserves.

3. **Psychological or behavioural carrying capacity** refers to the point at which the visitor feels that additional people in the environment would spoil the experience. This is less straightforward than may appear at first sight. Completely empty spaces are just as problematic as crowded ones, and the type of tourist also has an effect on perceptions of crowding.

4. **Social carrying capacity** is a measure of the ability of the host community to tolerate tourism. It is a more recent addition to typologies of capacity but is becoming an important issue and the basis of the term 'overtourism' where residents begin to feel overwhelmed by tourism and take actions against it. Here, one of the most important tests of a sustainable tourist destination is the level of involvement of the local community in plans and decisions relating to tourism development.

5. **Economic carrying capacity** refers to the point at which the investment needed to sustain environmental quality becomes prohibitive.

Carrying capacity is a pivotal concept when considering the consequences of tourism for the environment. The chapter now turns to the positive and negative consequences of tourism for the environment.

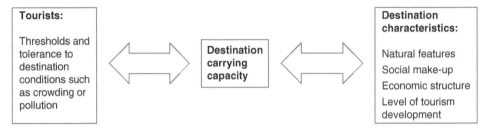

FIGURE 4.1   Influences upon carrying capacity

CONSEQUENCES OF TOURISM FOR THE ENVIRONMENT

Mutual benefit

Whilst the headlines capture the 'hotspots' of conflict between tourism and the environment, there are, in fact, three key areas where tourism can benefit the environment:

1. **Conservation.** The cause of tourism has been influential in encouraging the conservation of areas of natural beauty and their built heritage. National parks, marine reserves, historic monuments and archaeological sites all benefit economically from tourism. Tourism also encourages good practice in terms of planning and management, and drives the motivation for interpretation and visitor education which in turn help to protect fragile environments and monuments. This is practised internationally by UNESCO and locally by national governments (www.unesco.org). Indeed, tourism can be a motivation for the rehabilitation of built and natural environments – historic warehouses on the dock side in cities as far apart as Oslo and Yokohama have been saved by converting them into retail and food and beverage outlets for a dominantly tourism-driven market. Given these successes, tourism can then be used as a persuasive argument for continued protection of a site if it is threatened. It also makes the case for vibrant historic town centres beloved by the 'creative class', which leads to civic prosperity. Mini Case Study 4.1 examines how the conflict between conservation and tourism is managed in a Finnish national park.

MINI CASE STUDY 4.1

Pallas-Yllästunturi National Park, Finland

Introduction

The Pallas-Yllästunturi National Park in Finland was established in 1938 and is a classic example of managing visitation effectively. Initially, the Finnish parks were seen as primarily scientific reserves but over the years they have become increasingly used for recreation and tourism. This has the potential to lead to conflict between these two aims. Responsibility for managing the parks lies with Parks and Wildlife Finland, working cooperatively with local authorities, travel operators and businesses.

The Park receives well over 1.2 million visits annually, placing pressure on the management of the very fragile natural resources. To ensure a sustainable management regime, an advisory board has been appointed to promote the use of the park in a sustainable way. The board brings together local authorities, business organisations, the local reindeer herders' association, the Finnish Sámi Parliament and local businesses.

Tourism Products

The park is developing year-round tourism products by developing activities for each season. These include:

- Winter cross-country ski trails – over 500 kilometres of tracks;
- Summer hiking routes – over 350 kilometres of trails include the Fell Lapland trail network, connecting villages and tourist resorts;
- Mountain biking;
- Other activities including geocaching, fishing, birdwatching, foraging, canoeing, rowing, swimming and volunteering; and
- Overnight stays at designated camping sites, shelters or huts.

Management of the activities is done by the park authorities in collaboration with local businesses. These businesses work together to coordinate the transport of luggage between overnight bases for hikers, skiers and cyclists. This has the advantage of spreading the economic benefit regionally, and also promotes longer stays in the park.

Managing the Visitor

The park authorities have a range of enlightened codes and guides to ensure that the landscapes and local cultures are protected for future visitors. Advice is given to visitors who are advised to plan their visit carefully. Planning guidelines include the following:

- Pack food etc. in washable/reusable containers;
- Avoid unnecessary travel, use public transport or car share;
- Bring only the equipment and supplies needed;
- Borrow, rent or share equipment;
- Stay on marked trails to prevent erosion and other unnecessary disturbance;
- Avoid sensitive areas such as rocky ground with fragile lichen and moss cover; and
- Avoid unnecessary noise and disturbance, especially during the breeding season.

(Continued)

Restrictive visitor codes include the following:

- Litter-free hiking – biodegradable waste is composted or burnt and all other waste is carried away in hikers' rucksacks.
- Managing camping – lighting campfires is only permitted at official campfire sites and camping is permitted only in the vicinity of wilderness huts, Lapp huts and campfire sites.
- To organise events for large groups (over 50 persons) a permit is required.
- Restricted access areas have been established to preserve the area's species.
- Mountain biking is allowed on summer trails.
- Horse riding and dog-sled driving is restricted to official companies.
- It is forbidden to allow pets to run free, damage any vegetation, soil or rocks, kill, catch or disturb animals, drive vehicles or leave waste.

Discussion Questions

1. Do you think the park is managed in a negative way?
2. As a tour operator, assemble a one-week tour of adventure activities in the park.

Do you agree with the Finns' approach to opening up parks for tourism or do you think they should be kept pristine for scientific research?

Source: www.nationalparks.fi/en/pallas-yllastunturinp

2. **Environmental education.** Environmental education of visitors as a way of raising awareness of environmental values has become a major activity in many protected areas and sites of historic interest. Using the varied media of interpretation – including museums, trails, guides and new technology to curate the experience – visitors learn about the unique characteristics of their destination and can, in turn, be moved to protect it, and often police it; in other words, they behave in an environmentally responsible way. Here, the concept of 'visitor payback' works in favour of the environment with the visitor remitting monies back to the destination for conservation long after the visit. Of course, the education of visitors has a long history, with the Victorians learning about different environments and landscapes through painting and literature, but it is the contemporary, though undervalued, technique of interpretation and guiding which has made a major contribution here. Gössling (2002) observes that tourism and travel have therefore initiated changes in the relationship between humans and the environment in terms of knowledge, attitudes and behaviour. Here, the environment can be thought of as a 'social or cultural construction', such that attitudes towards the environment in Mediterranean countries, or in China, are very different to those in the Western world of, say, the USA or the UK.

3. **The built environment.** Tourism does, of course, bring a range of benefits for the built environment, some of which were noted above. Tourism use can either be integrated into destination or separated out into a tourist quarter. Where buildings and landscapes

have been designed for tourism and pleasure – such as coastal resorts or the historic landscaped gardens of the UK – tourism leaves a valuable legacy in terms of architecture, landscapes and urban detailing. Think, for example, of the resort landscapes of San Sebastian in northern Spain (www.sansebastianturismoa.eus) or of Brighton in the United Kingdom (www.visitbrighton.com). In towns and cities, tourism is prompting a process of 'heritagisation' where the buildings and values of the past create new identities and the 'placemaking' process sustains and benefits communities, landscapes and artefacts (Verbeke and Vanesste, 2018). This is often in the form of 'mixed' developments for both tourists and residents.

CONFLICT

Whilst there are many beneficial effects of tourism for the environment, the list of negative consequences is easier to draft and to describe. The scale and significance of environmental impact depends both upon the type of tourism involved and the nature of the resource. New forms of tourism are beginning to introduce new impacts – geo-tourism, for example, is seeing an increase in the collection of minerals and fossils at important geological locations. The next section of the chapter outlines the main negative consequences of tourism, beginning with possibly the most significant of all, that of climate change.

Climate change

Climate change is 'significant changes in long-term average weather patterns, which in turn shift the climatic characteristic of a region over time to new conditions' (Dwyer et al., 2007). Climate change represents the single most important challenge to the tourism sector and as such has taken a political as well as a scientific dimension. It is only in recent decades that the consequences of travel for climate change have been realised. The additional activity of transportation due to tourism increases carbon emissions, with estimates suggesting that tourism accounts for around 5 per cent of the world's total emissions, with transport generating 75 per cent of these emissions (Table 4.1). Aircraft are particularly damaging as their emissions take place at high altitude, but accommodation is also a major contributor to greenhouse gas emissions.

Climate change is a complex issue that is only now beginning to be understood. As a result, it has been realised that tourism development and activity as 'business-as-usual' are not sustainable for the environment, or for future economic development. Indeed, tourism decision-making and decision-makers are already impacted by climate change (see Buzinde et al., 2009). This means facing 'new realities' of tourism in a time of climate change, and these have begun to dominate international policy debates, fuelled by forecasts of economic and social disruption to lifestyles, health, social wellbeing and political stability – indeed destinations such as Venice, the Maldives and some Pacific islands are in danger for their very existence and will generate 'climate refugees'. Finally, central banks are increasingly concerned that the world's financial systems are too dependent upon fossil fuels, threatening the world's economic stability, and 2019 saw the first mass protests against climate change by activisits such as Extinction Rebellion (see https://rebellion.earth).

TABLE 4.1   Emissions from international and domestic global tourism
(including same-day visitors), 2005

	Carbon dioxide (Mt)
Transport	517
Other transport	468
Accommodation	274
Activities	45
Total tourism	1304
Total world	26 400
Share	4.95%

Source: UNWTO, 2007

There are two linked processes of climate change at work:

1. **Global warming.** With the accumulation of greenhouse gases in the atmosphere generated by transportation, air conditioning and other processes, solar radiation is prevented from escaping from the earth and therefore leads to a warming effect. This has consequences for tourism destinations including:

    a. Coral bleaching in iconic destinations such as the Great Barrier Reef;

    b. Retreat of the snowline for winter sports resorts in, say, the European Alps;

    c. Excessive temperatures at beach resorts;

    d. Rising sea level, threatening destinations such as the Pacific islands;

    e. More extreme weather events such as hurricanes, heavy precipitation, typhoons and heatwaves;

    f. Changing climate zones impacting upon wetlands and deserts, creating water shortages; and

    g. Changing tourism consumer decision-making and demand patterns as transport costs and taxation increase – long haul destinations in particular are vulnerable to these changes in demand patterns. This is an area that has yet to be researched in detail.

2. **Depletion of the ozone layer.** Release of certain gases into the atmosphere from devices such as air conditioning units and fridges has reduced the effectiveness of the ozone layer to filter out harmful UVB sunrays. These rays can cause eye cataracts and skin cancer and have led to many beach resorts having to adjust their products to 'beach plus' where additional products such as sports and theme parks have been developed as visitors no longer want to spend all day in the sun.

Addressing climate change

There are three key ways that the tourism sector can address climate change:

1. Offset the carbon emissions created by tourism, for example by tree planting;

2. Mitigate the impact of tourism on climate change by changing industry practices and consumer behaviour; and

3. Adapt destinations and consumer behaviour to climate change.

To address these pressing needs, the world's two leading agencies for tourism, the WTTC and the UNWTO, have both developed strategies for tourism to slow climate change.

The WTTC is committed to reducing greenhouse gas emissions and for the sector to be climate neutral by 2050. It underlines the need for partnerships between the tourism industry, consumers, employees and government. The WTTC has partnered with UN Climate Change to work towards a carbon-neutral world, with the aims of:

- Communicating the nature and importance of the interlinkages between tourism and climate change;
- Raising awareness of the positive contribution tourism can make to building climate resilience; and
- Reducing the contribution of tourism to climate change and supporting quantitative targets and reductions.

The UNWTO has held a series of meetings to discuss the issue of tourism and climate change. These began in Djerba, Tunisia in 2003 and now include side events at international climate change conferences, such as the Madrid UN Climate Change conference in 2019. One of the most significant meetings was in Davos, Switzerland in 2007. It led to the 'Davos Declaration' (UNWTO, 2009), which states that all tourism stakeholders – governments, the industry, destinations and research networks – need to harness their energies to address climate change, focusing in particular on the following points:

- Climate is a key resource for tourism and the sector is highly sensitive to climate change and global warming.
- Given the importance of tourism in the global challenges of climate change and poverty alleviation, there is an urgent need to consider policies that encourage truly sustainable tourism, reflecting a quadruple bottom line of environmental, economic, social and climate responsiveness.
- The tourism sector must respond to climate change and progressively reduce its greenhouse gas emissions. This will need action to mitigate the greenhouse gas emissions of tourism, especially from transport and accommodation.
- Tourism businesses, events and destinations must adapt to changing climate conditions, as shown in the major case study at the end of this chapter.
- Existing and new technology must be applied to improve energy efficiency.
- Financial resources to help poor regions and countries in these actions must be secured.

The UNWTO has also been involved in the global initiatives to reduce climate change, beginning with:

1. The 1997 Kyoto Protocol which determined binding emission reduction targets for 34 developed countries, but was generally agreed to have failed; and

2. The 2015 Paris Agreement which determined self-defined, non-binding targets for 187 countries and included provisions for regular reporting towards a global stock-take every five years.

For tourism, the key dimensions of the Paris agreement are mitigation, adaptation and financing emission reductions. However, international aviation emissions are omitted from the agreement and, as a result, transport has become a major stumbling block to climate change reduction. This is partly due to insufficient action on the part of the UN's aviation agency, the International Civil Aviation Organisation (ICAO). This is a serious problem for tourism, which depends on high carbon transport (Hopkins and Higham, 2018).

It is clear that tourism has to tackle climate change in tandem with other tourism-related development issues, including poverty alleviation. In order not to threaten the economic and employment benefits that tourism can bring to the developed world, greenhouse gas targets will need to be applied differentially to different parts of the tourism industry, and to different destinations so as not to jeopardise tourism-related poverty alleviation projects.

Flora

The study of the impact of visitors on vegetation has a long history dating back to work in national parks and protected areas. The dominant consequence of tourism on vegetation is through the process of 'trampling' where visitors walking on or brushing past vegetation crush and damage it. Camping, horse riding and mountain biking have similar effects. This has a number of negative effects on the local ecosystem:

- Trampling compacts soil, making it difficult for new seeds to germinate or for soil organisms to live and aerate the soil. It also reduces the effectiveness of drainage, leading to flooded paths and the natural instinct of visitors to give them a wide berth, so creating new areas of impact.
- Trampling eventually kills off the more 'sensitive' plants, leaving the 'trample-resistant' ones to thrive. This means that the presence or absence of certain plants can be used as an indicator of environmental stress. This process significantly reduces species diversity.
- Trampling means that replacement plants find it difficult to establish, and people passing by accidentally knock off flower heads and buds so exacerbating the process. This means that well-used paths or picnic sites become bare and unsightly. Re-establishment is particularly difficult in harsh environments such as the high trekking paths in the mountains in New Zealand and the Andes, or in sand-dune environments. Sand-dune environments receive many visits as they are a coastal ecosystem, often found between access roads and the beach. Here the plants that are at risk are the very ones that stabilise the dunes, so any loss of vegetation can have a severe impact. In the Netherlands, for example, these dune environments are intensively managed.

Of course, much of this damage by visitors is unintentional, as is the case for vegetation on the side of rivers, lakes and canals damaged by the wash of recreational boats or fires from campsites. Deliberate impacts come from activities such as plant collecting or deforestation of landscapes to provide timber for tourism developments as has occurred in Nepal. Here, tourists on trekking trips can use up to 5 kg of wood per day. Equally, the winter-sports industry has a major impact on delicate tundra, and high-altitude environments such as ski runs and their associated superstructure and infrastructure destroy vegetation which is slow to recover, often not before the next season. In the mountains, walkers and climbers leave spent equipment and litter on the mountains, whilst, in all ecosystems, off-road recreational vehicles, mountain bikes and horse riding can also have severe effects on vegetation, as can the contemporary technology of drones (see Focus on Technology).

FOCUS ON TECHNOLOGY

Drones

Drones, sometimes known as unmanned aerial vehicles, started life in the military but have now become an important tool for tourism and environment, facilitating, say, wildlife viewing as well as allowing for environmental monitoring. Drones are cheap to acquire, inexpensive to run, manoeuvrable and easy to use. As the technology has improved, they can be equipped with cameras or other sensors to capture high-resolution images and data such as weather conditions or wildlife population counts.

The use of drones for tourism and the environment includes:

- Environmental monitoring – using cameras and other sensors, drones are being used to monitor environmental change much more efficiently than previous methods. Drones can be used for aerial mapping to show changes in, say, coastlines, coral reefs or forests.

- Climate monitoring – drones can carry meteorological equipment to allow them to monitor weather conditions at destinations over time and provide early warning of changes in climate.

- Accessing the inaccessible – drones can allow visitors to reach inaccessible areas through video, still photography and virtual reality. These destinations include dangerous sites such as volcanoes, sensitive sites such as archaeological remains and getting close to dangerous animals.

- Defending and monitoring wildlife – thermal-imaging drones and drones with night vision are increasingly being used in African national parks to combat and deter poaching and trespassers. However, this use of drones is still at an early stage and some countries, such as Kenya, have banned their use. Drones can also be used to monitor and count wildlife populations as they can cover large areas with ease, and with minimal impact on the wildlife.

However, drones also have a downside when it comes to tourism. In Scotland, for example, police report that drones are interfering with wildlife, including seals, breeding birds and birds of prey.

Fauna

Wildlife has become a major resource for tourism, not just on land but also in marine environments, with scuba diving on reefs, whale-watching tours and activities such as swimming with dolphins or visiting loggerhead turtle nesting sites (see Mini Case Study 4.2). Demand for close interactions with wildlife is increasing, along with public concern for animal welfare (Senigaglia et al., 2020). Indeed, such is the level of concern that ethical codes now increasingly include the rights of animals. Yet, many of these activities cause unintentional stress on the fauna, an issue that is only slowly being understood.

Tourism can have intentional and direct impacts upon wildlife through activities such as hunting, poaching or trophy collecting (ivory is an example here), or indeed wildlife observation that interferes with the species being watched. There is increasing evidence in Australia, for example, that whales are migrating further from the coast to avoid the whale-watching boats and there are many stories of injuries to turtles and dolphins from boat propellers. Not enough is known about the consequences of tourism upon wildlife and it is an area in need of further research. Nonetheless, the UNWTO (2015) estimates that wildlife watching represents 80 per cent of the total annual sales of trips to Africa.

In most cases, tourists do not intend to have a harmful impact upon wildlife. Yet, it is the unintentional impacts that can be the most severe. These range from the taming of bears in Canada, who now feed on the rubbish of campsites rather than in the wild, to hand-feeding of dolphins in Queensland, Australia, through to the impact on the mating and hunting habits of predators in Africa's national parks. National park designation and resort and infrastructure development can also disrupt migration patterns and, in the case of national parks, the balance of the ecosystem can be disrupted when some species are favoured at the expense of others. Development of infrastructure such as roads through wildlife areas also increases the numbers of animals accidentally killed in road accidents, whilst beach developments and noise disrupt seabird breeding and feeding success.

MINI CASE STUDY 4.2
SEE Turtles, USA

Introduction

Sea turtles are an iconic marine species. However, they are also a vulnerable, endangered species globally due to their breeding and exposed hatching process. SEE Turtles is an organisation that has embraced ecotourism as a means to help protect the species. It was created in 2008 and is now an independent non-profit organisation based in Oregon, USA.

A sea turtle resting in the reefs of Cabo Pulmo National Park at Baja California Sur, Mexico

Source: ©Leonardo Gonzalez/Shutterstock.com

Mission

The mission of SEE Turtles is to protect endangered sea turtles by supporting community-based conservation efforts.

Programmes

SEE Turtles has five key programmes designed to fulfil its mission. Central to these are ecotourism trips and education programmes.

1. **Ecotourism trips**. The core of these trips is volunteer work with researchers to understand and conserve marine species, particularly sea turtles. Other work includes restoring habitats and working with local communities. The trips include:

    a. A Costa Rica green turtle research expedition to the Osa Peninsula rainforest to view sea turtles, dolphins and humpback whales. Participants observe the impact of deforestation and pollution on the diverse ocean life.

    b. A Baja Ocean wildlife expedition to Baja California Sur, Mexico to view sea turtles, the famous 'friendly' grey whales, whale sharks, dolphins and sea lions.

    c. A Costa Rica leatherback turtle volunteer vacation working with leatherbacks at a research station along Costa Rica's northern Caribbean coast.

    d. A Colombia nature and culture expedition to participate in sea turtle research and conservation, meeting and supporting the efforts of local communities to protect their wildlife and improve their lives.

    e. A Guerrero whale research expedition to work alongside scientists and fishermen to spot, identify and make scientific observations of humpback whales and four species of dolphins.

2. **The billion baby turtles programme** (www.seeturtles.org/billion-baby-turtles) provides support for important turtle nesting beaches and has helped save more than 1 million hatchlings. The programme supports sea turtle conservation organisations around the world, funding local residents to patrol important turtle nesting beaches, protecting turtles that come up to nest and ensuring that the eggs are protected and guiding the hatchlings to the sea. The programme has school-fundraising competitions and works with Facebook as a fundraiser.

3. **Too rare to wear** (www.tooraretowear.org) is a coalition of conservation groups and tourism businesses campaigning to end the demand for turtle shell products.

4. **School programmes** (www.seeturtles.org/schools) are designed to help teachers and students learn about sea turtles and how to protect them. This includes sea turtle student field trips as a hands-on conservation project. SEE Turtles cooperates with student travel operators. SEE Turtles also designs and makes available lesson plans on turtle conservation.

5. **Divers for turtles** (www.diversforturtles.com) is a programme designed to inspire both divers and the dive industry to support turtle conservation efforts.

Discussion Questions

1. Why do you think that school education programmes are such a key influence in SEE Turtles' mission?
2. Visit the SEE Turtles website and choose one of their ecotourism trips. Who do you think is the market for these trips?
3. Design a Venn diagram to show the interlinkage of the aims of ecotourism and volunteer tourism.

Source: www.seeturtles.org

Water supply and quality

In the twenty-first century, many parts of the world are suffering from water stress (Day and Chin, 2018; Gössling et al., 2015). As a result, tourism development will be constrained in some destinations – particularly in Africa, the Middle East, South Asia and China. Tourism development places pressure upon scarce water resources simply because tourism shifts demand for water from the tourist's origin to their destination. This is exacerbated by the fact that the tourism industry uses more water per person than the local residential population and, in particular, demands high consumption for golf courses and swimming pools.

Tourism also depends upon the water resources of lakes, the oceans, rivers and canals for many activities, yet tourist activity can have an adverse effect on water quality. This can be through:

- Developments along the shoreline, which pump waste, litter and detergents into the water, releasing nutrients and creating algal blooms, impacting upon water quality. This is particularly an issue for water bodies that are not tidal or have limited tides such as lakes or the Mediterranean. Waste also releases pathogens into the water, which kill fish and other species and reduce diversity. Cruise ships in the Caribbean, for example, deposit large amounts of waste annually.
- Petrol and oil from outboard motors and other recreational boats, which are slow to break down in the water.
- The movement of boats and jet skis that constantly stirs up water.
- Major developments such as resorts and marinas that can disrupt tidal regimes, shift currents and divert sediment flow.

Land use

Gössling (2002) sees the use and conversion of land to tourism uses as one of the major consequences of tourism globally. This is not simply for the development of resorts or attractions, but also for the supporting developments such as infrastructure. This means that the area affected by tourism is in fact significantly greater than the resort itself. Changes in land use due to tourism are a significant initiator of reductions in biodiversity and habitats. The use of land for tourism takes it out of agricultural production; clearing encourages invasive species; and deforestation reduces the area available for carbon sinks and results in soil erosion and increases in salinity.

Energy – towards a low-carbon tourism sector

Tourism is a voracious user of energy, not simply for transportation but also at the destination itself. Until the world moves to a low-carbon economy, the use of traditional sources of energy – those that are based on fossil fuel such as oil – will increase. Tourism, of course, is dependent upon transport by definition and this means that it is vulnerable to energy price rises and to taxation upon energy use. A low-carbon sector is one which has a minimal output of greenhouse gas emissions. The energy that is used by the tourism sector is predominantly based upon fossil fuels, with aviation delivering the majority of greenhouse gas emissions from tourism and motor transport almost one third. There is no doubt therefore that a transition to a tourism sector based upon low-carbon energy is needed (Eijgelaar et al., 2018). This involves a shift in energy production away from fossil fuels towards cleaner forms of energy. For tourism the biggest challenge is the transport sector, particularly aviation which needs to move to a low-emission mode and begin to use the most fuel-efficient technology possible. A further challenge is persuading the tourism sector, particularly SMEs, that they should transition towards renewable energies, despite the fact that this can reduce their costs and meet the environmental expectations of government and their customers.

The built environment

The consequences of tourism for the built environment are often glossed over, but in fact they are significant for certain environments such as resorts or historic cities and have come to prominence with concerns for 'overtourism'. Tourism can be associated with negative consequences for the built environment, not just in terms of catering for visitor needs but also in terms of poor design. These consequences can be summarised as follows:

- Tourism can be associated with congestion both within resorts or historic towns and in their route of access. Most tourists are car-borne (as seen in Chapter 10) and this brings both noise and the danger of accidents. Car-led development leads to sprawl and ribbon development around resorts – Orlando in Florida is a classic example here as development has grown around the magnet of the theme parks. Even the simple fact that many resorts have a promenade that acts as a major road artery creates a barrier between the recreational business district and the beach, as we can see in the Spanish resort of Benidorm (www.alicante-spain.com/benidorm.html).

- There is a need for traffic management at many destinations, an approach that has come late to tourism, but one that is essential to raise the overall visitor experience (see Chapter 10).

- There are many examples of inappropriate developments, often at the coast, which are out of scale with the environment and fail to use local design principles. The Mediterranean and both the Canary Islands and Balearic Islands were early culprits here.

- Catering for tourism in resorts, at attractions and in heritage towns has a reputation for attracting low-quality food and beverage outlets, tacky retailing and shambolic planning, leading to a type of 'architectural pollution'. The danger here is that these developments, often in the recreational business district of resorts, can drag down the overall environmental quality of the destination, not just for visitors but also for residents.

- Where planning has lagged behind tourism demand, the infrastructure of resorts can be overloaded, as is the case in Byron Bay in Australia where new development has been halted until the water and sewerage system can be upgraded (www.byron-bay. com). The other issue to remember is that tourism is seasonal, so any infrastructure is not fully utilised throughout the year.

- The way that many resorts and historic towns have developed means that the local population is often segregated into other parts of the town, partly because businesses in the recreational business districts do not cater for locals and partly due to the price of car parking and access.

ENVIRONMENTAL IMPACT ASSESSMENT AND AUDITING

The tried-and-tested techniques for assessing the environmental consequences of tourism developments are 'environmental impact assessment' (EIA) and 'environmental auditing' (EA). Both are effectively procedural frameworks to aid decision-making and the distinction is clear:

- Environmental impact assessment takes place before a development is begun and during its construction; and
- Environmental auditing takes place during construction and operation of the development.

Environmental impact assessment

Environmental impact assessment (EIA) is a legislative or policy-based concern for possible positive or negative effects on the total environment attributable to a proposed or existing project, programme or policy. EIA was initially formalised in US policy in the late 1960s, requiring the impacts of a development to be disclosed in an 'environmental impact statement'. At the time, it was heavily criticised as being expensive and a means to delay or cancel development, but supporters see it as a means to formalise environmental concerns into decision-making. Since its introduction in the USA, it is now used worldwide and is a major contributor to reducing the environmental impacts of tourism (Pope et al., 2019).

The main stages of an EIA are to:

1. Identify all impacts of a development, including secondary ones;
2. Measure the relevant variables, their magnitude and interactions with sources of information;
3. Interpret the findings;
4. Communicate findings to all stakeholders in a clear, non-technical style.

Approaches to an EIA vary from the very simple checklist where a tick-box method is used, through to a more complex network or matrix analysis of the relevant ecosystem to capture interactions between the environmental variables themselves.

Environmental auditing

Environmental auditing is a management tool providing a systematic, regular and objective evaluation of the environmental performance of a tourism organisation, plant, building process or product. In the twenty-first century, a key variable of these audits revolves around carbon emissions. Audits are now an important part of sustainable tourism. Normally, they are self-administered, though often externally policed, as they can lead to eco or green labels being applied to the development or organisation. As the approach has matured, a range of types of audit has evolved (Table 4.2).

There are, of course, pros and cons and issues with both approaches. On the plus side, they ensure that environmental concerns are taken seriously and can lead to cost savings for the organisation. Increasingly, the environmental credentials of a tourism organisation or development are used in promotion and both EIA and EA assist in this process. There are some problems, however, not least the fact that the environmental impact of a development does not assess the wider impact of the plan or policy within which that development plays a part. For example, in Table 4.3 whilst the EIA may assess the environmental 'footprint' of the hotel development, it does not assess the higher-level programmes, plans and policies that supported that development. The approaches also encourage the quantification of environmental variables, often using dubious methods, and there may be a minimum size of development that is required to undergo an assessment such that smaller developments escape scrutiny.

TABLE 4.2   Types of environmental audit

Type of audit	Characteristics
Activity	An overview of an activity or process which crosses business boundaries in a company such as staff travel by employees of a hotel change
Associate	Auditing of firms within the supply chain of a company – for example, tour operators' hotels and airlines
Compliance	Simple regular checks to ensure the organisation complies with current environmental regulations such as airline checking noise levels
Corporate	An audit across the whole company to ensure that agreed environmental policy is understood and carried out throughout the firm
Issues	Focuses upon a key issue such as carbon emissions
Product	Ensures existing and proposed products meet an organisation's environmental policy. For example, tour operator designs a holiday based on walking, using local, vernacular designed accommodation and services
Site	Audit directed at spot checks of buildings, plant and processes, known to have actual or potential problems – for example, hotel energy efficiencies or airport authority checking noise and emissions on take-off

Source: Goodall, 2003

TABLE 4.3   The issue of scale with EIAs

	Policies	Plans	Programmes	Projects
National plan	National tourism policy			
Regional plan		Regional tourism plan		
Sub-regional plan			Investment programme	
Local plan				Hotel development

OVERARCHING ISSUES

This chapter closes by considering some of the wider issues involved in assessing the relationship between tourism and the environment, beginning with Richard Butler's classic paper on the topic.

CLASSIC PAPER

Butler, R.W. (2000) 'Tourism and the environment: a geographical perspective', *Tourism Geographies*, 2 (3): 337–58

This paper is a classic for two reasons. Firstly, it provides an excellent review of the literature and contemporary thinking on the relationship between tourism and the environment. But more than this, the paper provides a new perspective on many elements of the 'received wisdom' of this relationship. As a result, it is a paper which is stimulating to read, but also solid in its scholarship and coverage.

Butler begins by challenging current thinking on the relationship between tourism and the environment, questioning the very dependence of tourism upon the environment as a resource. Butler says that this dependence is taken for granted, but challenges whether it is accurate in all cases – for example, much of beach tourism has little relationship with a pristine quality environment, and other forms of tourism such as VFR and business/conference tourism are only tangentially dependent upon the environment. Butler concludes that the statement about the dependence of tourism upon the environment needs to be carefully re-examined. He goes on to challenge the fact that it is actually very difficult to disentangle the environmental elements of the attractiveness of a destination from other elements; in other words, is society attracted to the destination and its environment as a whole, or to specific parts of it?

Butler then goes on to critique the tourism and environment literature. He argues that researchers should be more concerned with understanding the 'processes' of environmental change than with assigning blame for the impacts of tourism. He also rehearses the argument found in this chapter that it is sometimes difficult to disentangle the human agents of environmental change from the natural ones. The paper has an excellent section on managing the environment for tourism and Butler clearly believes that there has to be a willingness on the part of all destination stakeholders to do this if it is to be successful.

The paper concludes with some specific research issues, which Butler feels should form the future agenda for tourism and environmental research. These include:

- A better understanding of the relationship between tourism and the environment in varied settings and for a variety of forms of tourism;
- A better understanding of the elements which make up environmental attractiveness and how these change over time due to cultural perceptions;
- A stronger link between physical science research and the processes of planning and managing destinations. This will be an important issue for regions such as the Antarctic;

- More attention paid to the processes and causes of impacts rather than the end result;
- An acceptance of the need to manage the volume of tourists at destinations and a recognition of the value of carrying capacity as a concept and tool, as we discussed earlier in this chapter;
- A greater focus on less glamorous destinations, such as mass tourism resorts, rather than simply upon environmentally sensitive areas;
- An increase in funding for longitudinal studies that will allow us to understand long-term environmental change.

Butler concludes: 'The relationship between tourism and the environment in which it occurs is complex, poorly understood and should be of crucial concern' (p. 354).

There is no doubt that an imperative for researchers is to understand the structure and processes of how ecosystems work if the consequences of tourism upon the environment are to be reduced. Here it is important to consider the totality of the consequences of tourism for all elements of the ecosystem, and how these elements are related to each other. Indeed, whilst researching the relationship of tourism and the environment has come a long way since the 1960s, Wall and Mathieson (2006) identify a number of issues of concern:

- Research is uneven, with few studies examining the impact of tourism upon species such as birds or fish, whilst a huge amount of work has been done on vegetation. Similarly, research has tended to focus on the temperate climate zones and only relatively recently is research turning to the Antarctic environments, for example, or the tropics.
- Many studies do not reach the policy makers, planners or, indeed, developers who could benefit from the knowledge.
- Simply because ecosystems are so complex, research tends to focus on one aspect of the environment – fauna or flora, for example – and fails to examine the impact upon the whole ecosystem. Worse, study of the consequences of tourism tends to be pigeonholed into environmental, economic and social, with few studies looking at the interaction of these elements. In the African national parks, for example, designation has a major impact on the local population in terms of their ability to farm and hunt.
- Much research is done after the consequences of tourism have occurred, with less work examining the conditions before tourism arrived. However, with sustainable tourism indicators being developed, this situation is changing (as shown in Chapter 6). It is equally difficult to disentangle the actual effects of human intervention in ecosystems against the natural processes of environmental change.

Finally, a new strand of research is emerging, mainly due to climate change. This is based upon the impact of changing tourist behaviour, driven by environmental concerns, upon the tourism sector itself. Reduction of the desire to fly long haul, or even to fly at all, is an example here – an issue of concern to tourism authorities in long haul destinations such as New Zealand and Australia.

SUMMARY

One of the most reported issues in the world is the consequences of tourism and travel for the environment and particularly for climate change. This chapter has shown that this is a complex relationship which has developed over past decades, from a position where tourism was seen as relatively benign to one where there are real concerns about the consequences of tourism for the environment. Here there is much confused thinking about just what constitutes environmentally responsible tourism. The chapter showed that it is important to understand the underlying concepts, which include the need to consider the whole ecosystem when looking at the consequences of tourism and attempt to manage them, and to utilise tried-and-trusted concepts such as carrying capacity, EIA and EA.

Of course, the negative consequences of tourism for the environment make the headlines as with 'overtourism', but it can also be a force for good, including the economic contribution that it makes, the encouragement of conservation and environmental education and the development of attractive resort towns and landscapes. Nonetheless, tourism is problematic for the environment for many reasons, particularly in terms of carbon emissions – estimated at 5 per cent of global emissions and the consequent impact upon climate change. This issue is dealt with at length, including the approaches of the UNWTO and the WTTC in developing an agenda to address climate change. Other negative consequences are for flora and fauna, and for water energy and land use. The management of these impacts employs a range of techniques including EIA and EA. Finally, it must be recognised that the relationship between tourism and the environment is complex and we must consider issues such as whether all effects are man-made, how to disentangle tourism effects from others, and ensure that we understand the degree of change caused by tourism across the whole ecosystem.

DISCUSSION QUESTIONS

1. As a newly hired manager of a national park, draft a memo to your staff explaining the benefits of carrying capacity for managing visitors to the park.

2. In class, debate the negative and positive consequences of tourism for the environment. In two groups, come up with three key arguments on each side.

3. Take a destination which you know well and draft a checklist of the negative consequences of tourism for the environment, using the headings in this chapter.

4. Take a typical inclusive tour to a mass tourism destination and identify the 'hot spots' of environmental impact. Consider how they can be monitored by an environmental audit.

5. We know that there is confusion about terms such as ecotourism, responsible tourism and alternative tourism. Consider all of these terms and come up with your own preferred term and justify it.

ANNOTATED FURTHER READING

Fennel, D. (2008) *Ecotourism: An Introduction*. London: Routledge.

Excellent overview of the key issues of ecotourism.

Holden, A. (2018) 'The tourism–environment relationship', in C. Cooper, S. Volo, W.C. Gartner and N. Scott (eds), *The Sage Handbook of Tourism Management: Theories, Concepts and Disciplinary Approaches to Tourism*. London: Sage. pp. 393–406.

Contemporary and wide-ranging review of the tourism–environment relationship.

Holden, A. and Fennell, D. (2012) *The Routledge Handbook of Tourism and the Environment*. London: Routledge.

Comprehensive handbook covering all aspects of the relationship between tourism and the environment.

UNWTO (2009) *From Davos to Copenhagen and Beyond: Advancing Tourism's Response to Climate Change*. Madrid: UNWTO.

Authoritative and well-researched contemporary account of the thinking of the UNWTO on climate change.

Wall, G. and Mathieson, A. (2006) *Tourism: Change, Impacts and Opportunities*. Harlow: Pearson.

Excellent second edition of the key text examining the consequences of tourism.

REFERENCES CITED

Buzinde, C.N., Manuel-Navarrete, D., Yoo, E.E. and Morais, D. (2009) 'Tourists' perceptions in a climate of change: eroding destinations', *Annals of Tourism Research*, 37 (2): 333–54.

Day, J. and Chin, N. (2018) 'Tourism energy, oil and water', in C. Cooper, S. Volo, W.C. Gartner and N. Scott (eds), *The Sage Handbook of Tourism Management: Theories, Concepts and Disciplinary Approaches to Tourism*. London: Sage. pp. 466–81.

Dwyer, L., Edwards, D., Mistilis, N., Scott, N., Cooper, C. and Roman, C. (2007) *Trends Underpinning Tourism to 2020: An Analysis of Key Drivers for Change*. Gold Coast, Australia: STCRC.

Eijgalaar, E., Amelung, B., Filimonau, V., Guiver, G., and Peeters, P. (2018) 'Tourism in a low carbon energy future', in C. Cooper, S. Volo, W.C. Gartner and N. Scott (eds), *The Sage Handbook of Tourism Management: Applications of Theories and Concepts to Tourism*. London: Sage. pp. 552–66.

Goodall, B. (2003) 'Environmental auditing: a means to improve tourism's environmental performance', in C. Cooper (ed.), *Classic Reviews in Tourism*. Clevedon: Channel View. pp. 92–126.

Gössling, S. (2002) 'Global environmental consequences of tourism', *Global Environmental Change*, 12: 283–302.

Gössling, S., Hall, C.M. and Scott, D. (2015) *Tourism and Water*. Bristol: Channel View.

Holden, A. (2009) 'The environment–tourism nexus influence of market ethics', *Annals of Tourism Research*, 36 (3): 373–89.

Holden, A. (2018) 'The tourism–environment relationship', in C. Cooper, S. Volo, W.C. Gartner and N. Scott (eds), *The Sage Handbook of Tourism Management: Theories, Concepts and Disciplinary Approaches to Tourism*. London: Sage. pp. 393–406.

Hopkins, D. and Higham, J. (2018) 'Climate change and tourism: mitigation and global climate agreements', in C. Cooper, S. Volo, W.C. Gartner and N. Scott (eds), *The Sage Handbook of Tourism Management: Theories, Concepts and Disciplinary Approaches to Tourism.* London: Sage. pp. 422–36.

Mathieson, A. and Wall, G. (1982) *Tourism: Economic, Physical and Social Impacts.* Harlow: Longman.

Newsome, D., Moore, S.A. and Dowling, R.K. (2012) *Natural Area Tourism: Ecology Impacts and Management,* 2nd edn. Bristol: Channel View.

Pope, J., Wessels, J.A., Douglas, A., Hughes, M. and Saunders, A.M. (2019) 'The potential contribution of environmental impact assessment (EIA) to responsible tourism: the case of the Kruger National Park', *Tourism Management Perspectives*, 32.

Senigaglia, V., New, L. and Hughes, M. (2020) 'Close encounters of the dolphin kind: contrasting tourist support for feeding based interactions with concern for dolphin welfare', *Tourism Management*, 77.

UNWTO (2007) *Climate Change and Tourism: Responding to Global Challenges.* Madrid: UNWTO.

UNWTO (2009) *From Davos to Copenhagen and Beyond: Advancing Tourism's Response to Climate Change.* Madrid: UNWTO.

UNWTO (2015) *Towards Measuring the Economic Value of Wildlife Watching Tourism in Africa.* Madrid: UNWTO.

Verbeke, M. and Vanneste, D. (2018) 'Managing built heritage resources', in C. Cooper, S. Volo, W.C. Gartner and N. Scott (eds), *The Sage Handbook of Tourism Management: Applications of Theories and Concepts to Tourism.* London: Sage. pp. 516–36.

Wall, G. and Mathieson, A. (2006) *Tourism: Change, Impacts and Opportunities.* Harlow: Pearson.

Wheeller, B. (2003) 'Alternative tourism: a deceptive ploy', in C. Cooper (ed.), *Classic Reviews in Tourism.* Clevedon: Channel View. pp. 227–34.

MAJOR CASE STUDY 4.1

Climate Change Adaptation: The Events Sector

Introduction

Surprisingly, the event sector has not overtly addressed the issue of climate change. It can be argued that events are both a victim and a vector of climate change: there is no doubt that, as the climate warms, many events will be negatively impacted by climate change; yet, at the same time, unsustainable practices at events lead to high carbon emissions so fuelling climate change. Certain parts of the world will suffer negative impacts of a changing climate including hotter summers, droughts and extreme weather events. It is already known that climate change will create weather extremes such as high rainfall, typhoons and thunderstorms – and this is not conducive to holding successful events. Thunderstorms, for example, create a huge safety risk, not only from lightning, but also flooding and creating unstable ground from the heavy rainfall. This makes for difficult

Athletics at the 2014 Commonwealth Games

Source: 'Athletics 201 4–1–43' by Laura Ngo is licensed under CC BY 2.0

movement around the event site and logistics are interrupted.

Events are particularly vulnerable to climate change. Many events occur outdoors, often near coasts and other venues that are prone to flooding. Events represent a large investment in both finances and time, they take place over a short, limited time span and are often annual events. Therefore, if an event has to be cancelled due to weather, then the impact is severe and can bankrupt both performers and organisers. Of course, these impacts have already been observed, as for example at the 2019 world athletics event held in Doha, Qatar, where daytime temperature extremes meant that the marathon had to be held at midnight, and even then many runners did not complete the course. Even

more extreme, in 2019, Houston's annual 'Free Press Summer Fest' was forced to cancel due to adverse weather conditions in the Gulf. Cancellation of events also has a wider effect, impacting on jobs and, in the case of smaller festivals, the sense of community pride and inspiration are lost. It is therefore essential that events develop a more sustainable approach which will benefit stakeholders as well as the communities close to the event. Clearly then, events need to recognise the need to adapt to climate change.

Adaptation to climate change

Adaptation to climate change is a process by which event management aims to moderate, cope with and take advantage of the consequences of a changing

(Continued)

climate. Over and above their traditional functions of event management, managers will be increasingly expected to take on a central role in event-level climate adaptation and mitigation strategies. In terms of mitigation, this is addressed in Chapter 7 where the 'greening' of events is examined in the end-of-chapter case study.

In order to adapt events to climate change, there are two key approaches.

Firstly, on the demand side, it is important to understand the needs of the event customer. This is done through 'tourism climate indices'. Here, the relationship between weather and event activities means that different weather conditions will create comfortable, or uncomfortable, conditions for attending events or spectating. Effectively then, a tourism climate index determines the most 'ideal' weather conditions for attending an event. Future climate conditions can now be relatively easily created and these can be run through the tourism climate index model to show which regions in the world will be able to support events in the future – and which will struggle to do so (as in the Doha example above, or the hosting of the Rugby World Cup in Japan during typhoon season in 2019).

Secondly, on the supply side, events need to adjust their configuration to recognise changing weather conditions. This includes providing plentiful supplies of bottled water and free drinking taps, misting fans, shaded areas, air-conditioned zones, additional first-aid resources and water on stages. It is also essential to provide education and information to both staff and attendees of events at festivals including weather updates, advice on sun protection, hydration and appropriate clothing. This can be done through social media, onsite screens and induction of staff.

Barriers

However, recognition of the need for events to embrace climate adaptation is fraught with problems. This is a new issue for events and, for many, it involves unwelcome increases in the costs of running the event. There is also a lack both of resources to implement adaptation and expertise in these approaches. Training and awareness are needed amongst event organisers and managers, and there is a clear need for leadership to allow a sharing of expertise and good practice to foster the change management that is needed.

Discussion Questions

1. Why do you think the event sector has been slow to recognise the significance of climate change for events?
2. Taking an event that you know well, how can it begin to adapt to a warming climate?
3. Create a PowerPoint presentation to induct event staff on what needs to be done at a music festival held during a heatwave.

Source: Mair, J. (2011) 'Events and climate change: an Australian perspective', *International Journal of Event and Festival Management*, 2 (3): 245–53.

5

THE SOCIAL AND CULTURAL CONSEQUENCES OF TOURISM

LEARNING OUTCOMES

This chapter considers the social and cultural consequences of tourism and considers how these originate from the 'encounter' or 'contact' with the tourist. The chapter also outlines the theoretical frameworks which have been developed to explain these consequences. The chapter is designed to provide you with:

- an understanding of the role of the tourist, the host and the encounter;

- an awareness of the importance of the concept of the demonstration effect;

- an appreciation of the theoretical frameworks developed to understand the relationship between hosts and guests;

- an understanding of the consequences of tourism for host societies; and

- an awareness of the process and result of cultural change brought about by tourism.

INTRODUCTION

As tourism reaches out to ever more distant and exotic locations, often in lesser-developed countries, the consequence of visitation upon the host community and their culture has become an important issue. Of course, tourism can support communities economically through employment, spending and infrastructure development. However, tourism can also bring less desirable consequences for host communities, prompting both social and cultural changes within those societies. In part, this is because the contrast between affluent tourists and residents in the poorer countries of the world can be startling in terms of behaviour, language and culture – contrasts that can lead to significant, and irreversible, changes in the host society. This has been termed by the well-known travel writer Jan Morris as 'contact!' It is also important not to dismiss the impact of outbound tourism on the generating market as tourists bring back new cuisines and customs, which are slowly adopted. The issue, as with all consequences of tourism, is that societies and cultures are constantly evolving and often tourism can be a scapegoat for inevitable change that would have occurred without tourism.

This area of study is known as host–guest relationships, a research area where the methods of approach are now becoming well developed, although many of the researchers view the issues from the standpoint of their part in the developed world – as shown in Mini Case Study 1.1 on de-colonising the curriculum. To date, research on the social and cultural consequences of tourism tends to be written from a negative point of view, and certainly there is little evidence to support the rose-tinted view of earlier commentators that bringing cultures and societies together broadens people's horizons and promotes peace and understanding. Here though, on the positive side, it could be argued that tourists do become sensitised to other cultures and ways of life.

One of the most interesting aspects of this research relates back to the fundamental fact that tourists are strangers in the destination and can be the target of xenophobia. Their behaviour, language and way of dress are often significantly different from the host, leading to the idea of social or cultural distance. This means that whilst the tourist can act as a catalyst for change in the host society, the tourists themselves are vulnerable to crime and exploitation, simply by their status as strangers who are less aware of local behaviour and habits. Early commentators on these issues were Krippendorf (1987) and Emanuel De Kadt, whose paper has been chosen as the classic paper for this chapter as it covers all the key issues and is still relevant today.

CLASSIC PAPER

De Kadt, E. (1979) 'Social planning for tourism in the developing countries', *Annals of Tourism Research,* 6 (1): 36–48

De Kadt's paper is a classic because, whilst it was written in the late 1970s, it demonstrates a thorough understanding of the social and cultural consequences of tourism and links them closely to 'development' issues. As a result, the paper remains just as relevant today.

The paper begins by stressing that planners and policy makers have not addressed the social and cultural impacts of tourism in the developing world. He argues for planners to take much more account of the non-economic costs and benefits of tourism and shows how planners and policy makers act within specific socio-political contexts. These contexts and the various power relations at local and national levels influence how tourism policy is formed and plans are created. The paper is particularly forward looking here in its discussion of the role of tourism in poverty alleviation – a topic now at the top of the agenda of all tourism and development agencies. The heart of De Kadt's argument is that the usual perspectives on tourism planning have been economic and that the social and cultural costs of tourism have been ignored. He sums up these impacts clearly:

> The main 'real life' impacts of tourism are experienced by the people who live in the communities of the tourist destination areas. Some get wealthy, others do not: often all see outsiders make the richest pickings. Employment opportunities emerge, and the structure of the local labor force changes with women and young people tending to benefit most. Lifestyles come under pressure, new adjustments may have to be found to ancient concepts of hospitality. (p. 40)

De Kadt argues that community empowerment is needed to overcome some of these impacts, but at the time he was writing – the late 1970s – the notion of community-based tourism was in its infancy and barriers, both social and political, were more evident. He is accurate in his observation that these impacts will vary by destination and that rapid development tends to heighten the impact of tourism.

(Continued)

In the second half of the paper, De Kadt argues that foreign penetration into the tourism sector of developing countries through transnational enterprises is a major source of negative impacts because of their strong bargaining power at international level, their ownership, employment of expatriate labour and acculturation.

In the main areas of this paper, De Kadt's views and analysis are well ahead of his time of writing, particularly those relating to the issues of poverty alleviation and the impact of foreign ownership upon destinations. De Kadt has continued to influence the development of the sociology of tourism and this paper is clear evidence of his forward-thinking approach.

HOSTS AND GUESTS

Wall and Mathieson (2006) structure their discussion of the social and cultural consequences of tourism into three parts:

1. **Tourists** – responsible for change in the host society by 'demonstrating' their difference in terms of language, culture and affluence. The travel experience also changes both the tourist and their society.

2. **Hosts** – deliver the tourism experience at the destination and are exposed to tourists through working and living at the destination.

3. **The encounter or 'contact' between tourist and host** – when the two groups meet there are contrasts of behaviour and expectations which trigger long-term changes and consequences in both societies. In addition, the 'social distance' between the two groups and the experience during the trip will influence the tourist's attitude towards the host. Here tourism changes:

   a. The social systems of the destination in terms of value systems, individual behaviours, family relationships, lifestyles, language, religion and moral behaviour (for example, tourism is often associated with gambling and prostitution); and

   b. The culture of the destination in terms of living culture (ceremonies and events) and cultural artefacts.

Although this chapter discriminates between society and culture, in practice they do overlap.

Tourists

This part of the book has shown that the consequences of tourism can range from the beneficial to the disruptive and that this depends not only upon what happens at the destination, but also upon the characteristics of the tourists themselves. Tourists influence the degree of impact in terms of their types and number. In the past, tourists were stereotyped as wealthy, boorish and high spending, effectively the 'enemy' of the host and their culture. But these stereotypes are unhelpful and have been replaced by more analytical approaches. For example, two early attempts to classify tourists on the basis of their impact on the destination were written by Cohen (1972) and Smith (1977).

Cohen (1972) outlined four types of tourist based upon the contrast of novelty and familiarity:

1. Organised mass tourist, where the experience is structured, safe and comes with familiar home comforts.

2. Individual mass tourist, where a certain amount of control allows a degree of novelty away from the tour, but still within familiar territory.

3. Explorer, where the experience is very much off the beaten track but still retains a degree of familiar transport and accommodation.

4. Drifter, where the tourism establishment is deliberately avoided in an attempt to live like the locals.

More recent work has confirmed Cohen's approach, suggesting that there is a human gene associated with risk and sensation seeking.

Smith (1977) drew up a classification system that also attempts to link the typology with the potential impact on the host destination. Her approach considered the numbers of each type of tourist, their motivations to visit and their degree of adaptation to local norms. Although the classification was drawn up in the late 1970s, before many changes in the tourism system, it has stood the test of time (Table 5.1). Indeed, it was Smith's approach that initiated the alternative/low-impact tourism movement. If the type of tourist can be matched to appropriate types of destination, then the negative consequences of tourism will be minimised, simply because the destination and the visitor will have similar expectations (see Figure 5.1). For example, using Smith's classification, it is at the incipient mass stage that problems begin as greater numbers of visitors trigger changes and the destination has to adapt in terms of supplying facilities and standardising delivery of the experience. To ensure that Smith's classification remains relevant, 'enlightened mass tourism' can be added, representing a twenty-first century phenomenon of mass tourists sensitised to the destination by industry-led corporate social responsibility and consumer-led behavioural transformative experiences curated by interpretation and information (Weaver, 2014).

Recently, researchers have developed a broader view of the tourist as a person, recognising that tourists have a particular way of looking at the world. Urry's (1990) seminal work on the tourist 'gaze' is important here. Urry (1990) contrasts the middle classes and their 'romantic gaze' seeking authenticity with the 'collective gaze', which is more representative of mass tourism.

TABLE 5.1 Smith's classification of tourists

Type of tourist	Characteristics	Adaptation to local conditions	Numbers
Explorer	These are academics or explorers, totally accepting of local conditions and self-sufficient in terms of food and equipment. They are virtually unnoticed by the destination.	Adapt fully	Small
Elite	A group who have seen the world and are now looking for something different, such as Antarctica or the Amazon. They adapt easily to local conditions.	Adapt fully	Small
Off-beat	This group are more conventional tourists who look for some added extras to a holiday. They adapt well to local conditions. Their money is welcome and they are not disruptive.	Adapt well	Increasing numbers

(Continued)

TABLE 5.1   (Continued)

Type of tourist	Characteristics	Adaptation to local conditions	Numbers
Incipient mass	Here there are greater numbers, but they visit in small groups or as individuals – they are seeking the comforts of home but do not demand them – if they are absent then it is put down to experience. They are more dependent on the services of a tour operator. Nonetheless, it is at this stage that problems begin to emerge as expectations between the visitor and the destination differ.	Seek their own amenities	Steady flow
Mass	Here there are large numbers of tourists, bringing with them their own uncompromising values and expectations. They expect multilingual guides, their own language and their own food.	Expect their own amenities	Continuous influx
Enlightened mass	A growing group of twenty-first century tourists who are sensitised to the destination by corporate social responsibility initiatives, interpretation, guiding and information, and transformative experiences at the destination.	Sensitised to the destination community and culture	Growing numbers of arrivals
Charter	This is the full-blown, somewhat down-market, mass tourism group, arriving in large numbers, often highly seasonal but demanding of their own culture, food and facilities. They have travelled but do not want the character of the destination to interfere with their enjoyment. They are totally dependent on the services of the travel trader.	Demand their own amenities	Large numbers of arrivals

Source: adapted from Smith, 1977

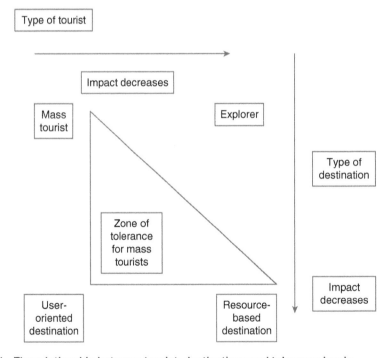

FIGURE 5.1   The relationship between tourist, destinations and tolerance levels

Hosts

Of course, hosts can be impacted by tourism even if they never come into contact with a visitor. This is because they are part of a host society that deals regularly with tourism and therefore attitudes and opinions pervade the destination. Sharpley (2014, 2018) has provided extensive reviews of how host societies perceive tourist impacts at the destination. He concludes that it is difficult to generalise about host perceptions of tourism as they are dependent upon context, and that perceptions depend upon two sets of factors – the first relate to the destination itself ('extrinsic' factors) and the second to the individual host ('intrinsic' factors).

Extrinsic factors include:

- Extent/stage of tourism development;
- Nature/type of tourism/tourists;
- Density of tourists/tourism development;
- Seasonality; and
- National stage of development.

Intrinsic factors include:

- Economic/employment dependency on tourism;
- Community attachment;
- Distance from tourism zone;
- Interaction with tourists;
- Personal values;
- Social identity/social status; and
- Demographic – age, gender, education.

The main issues of concern to the hosts are often traffic congestion, litter and overcrowding, as well as perceived impacts upon religion, crime, language and the general way of life of the destination. Residents respond to tourism through particular 'coping' behaviours in the tourism season, such as changing their shopping habits. However, equally significant is the fact that tourism can benefit host communities by helping disadvantaged groups, as shown in Mini Case Study 5.1.

MINI CASE STUDY 5.1
The TREE Alliance

Introduction

There are a number of NGOs and charitable organisations that are using tourism as a vehicle to secure the futures of at-risk and marginalised populations in many countries around the world. One stand-out organisation here is the Training Restaurants for Employment and Entrepreneurship (TREE) Alliance. The TREE Alliance represents a symbiotic, mutually beneficial relationship between the hospitality sector and an

(Continued)

NGO. It works to give a new future in the hospitality industry to former street youth, marginalised young people and adults. The TREE Alliance was established by the umbrella NGO Friends-International, in Phnom Penh, Cambodia in 2011.

The TREE Alliance is based around a collection of nine vocational training restaurants in Cambodia, Thailand, Laos, Myanmar and Ethiopia. Each restaurant trains around 200 students at any one time, and to date the Alliance has helped 32,000 young people. TREE restaurants are based upon a social entrepreneurship model which fulfils the twin objectives of delivering a high-quality product as well as securing employment for disadvantaged groups.

The Programme

The TREE Alliance seeks out at-risk groups both on the streets and in their communities, using outreach teams. There are also drop-in centres for children and young adults. Once recruited, each student has a two-year training programme. This consists of practical hospitality skills as well as social counselling, literacy/numeracy and life-skills education to provide a well-rounded education and prepare students for their future employability. The programme therefore not only provides hands-on hospitality skills, but is also designed to build confidence and act to empower students to manage their own future. After leaving the school, each student receives follow-up support for at least a year. So successful is the model that 90 per cent of graduates are in employment within one month of completing their course.

The Business Model

The basic business model of the TREE restaurants is based on the principles of social entrepreneur-ship. TREE training restaurants provide high-quality service and food. They are popular with tourists looking for (i) an authentic and meaningful hospitality experience; (ii) a connection with the country; and (iii) the chance to make a positive contribution to local communities. TREE Alliance's restaurants generate over US$ 2.6 million in sales every year and all profits are invested in the students who train there and the social programmes which support them.

Discussion Questions

1. Visit the TREE Alliance website. How might they expand their business further?
2. Design a marketing plan for a TREE restaurant.
3. Do you feel that this model could be exported to other parts of the world such as Europe or the Americas?

Source: www.tree-alliance.org

The encounter

Many of the consequences of tourism for the host community are attributable to the 'encounter' or 'contact' – when the tourists and the host meet (Sharpley, 2018). Here, the degree of impact upon the host will depend upon how the encounter occurs, the level of tourism development in the community and the social carrying capacity of the host population. Encounters commonly take place in 'organised tourism spaces' but it can be argued that when residents and tourists share the same space in crowded destinations, such as Venice, host perceptions will be negative. De Kadt (1979) states that contact can happen in a number of ways:

- Simply by being in the same place, such as in the street or on the beach;
- Through commercial transactions such as shopping; and
- Through spontaneous meeting and chatting, which is what is meant when people talk of travel broadening the mind.

If you think of your own travels you will remember that the first two encounters are the most common and have certain characteristics (UNESCO, 1976). For example, such encounters tend to be brief – being served a restaurant meal or buying souvenirs in a gift shop. This type of encounter is also temporary, something novel for the tourist that they will remember, but routine for the shopkeeper or waiter, just another encounter with another visitor. In other words, the encounter is not an equal one and is characterised by certain time and space constraints:

- On the one hand, tourists are at leisure, mobile, have money to spend and are being served whilst on holiday. The tourist has expended considerable resources to spend time at the destination and so is impatient of delays or inefficiencies.
- The host, on the other hand, is working hard, catering to the needs of the tourist, tied to their workplace and at times therefore tempted to exploit the relationship.

In contrast, a spontaneous encounter between host and tourist by, say, meeting to talk about the weather, is very rare. The encounter is more commonly a commercial transaction. There is, of course, a trade-off here as these spontaneous encounters carry greater risk than the managed, transaction-based ones. It is interesting that few studies have focused upon how hosts 'cope' with the 'encounter'. Dogan (1989) found that a host's patterns of 'coping behaviour' can include resistance to tourism through hostility to development, a retreat away from the tourism zone or maintenance of a strong boundary between themselves and the visitors. Figure 5.2 summarises the main types of encounter.

FOCUS ON EMPLOYABILITY

Tour Guides: Intervening in the Encounter

Tour guides play an essential role in tourism by acting as an intermediary between the tourist and the host population and culture. Guiding is a noble profession that contributes significantly to the management and sustainability of destinations. Whilst there are many unregistered guides, most countries now have a scheme of guide registration and training. For example, in the UK,

(Continued)

the Institute of Tourist Guiding is responsible for training and certification, and in the USA there are professional associations such as the International Guide Academy in Denver.

Guides can be either paid or voluntary and are often wrongly confused with tour directors or couriers who are responsible for the logistics and management of tours. There are specific skills and competencies needed to be a tour guide:

- Being a people person in order to understand the characteristics and needs of the audience;
- The ability to think quickly and act in an emergency. First aid training is essential;
- Being physically fit – guiding involves a lot of standing and walking whilst conducting tours of cities, landmarks, local points of interest, historical sites and other destinations;
- Being a storyteller to make facts interesting, moving and engaging; and
- Having specific knowledge of the destination.

THE DEMONSTRATION EFFECT

During the encounter, tourists often 'demonstrate' to the host that they are different by their dress, behaviour, manners and language, and come from a culture which the hosts should aspire to. This is known as the 'demonstration effect'. Effectively, the demonstration effect is about copying behaviours and transferring values from one culture to another, often in terms of economic aspirations. For it to happen, the 'social distance' between the hosts and guest has to be sufficiently different and the transfer of behaviour has to be sustainable over a long period. Fisher (2004) notes that tourists are more likely to influence the behaviour of the young generations of the host society. Of course, the demonstration effect can be positive – for example, in changing behaviour towards particular groups in society, such as indigenous peoples. It is interesting that different forms of tourism will dictate the degree of 'exposure' of the hosts to their guests. For example, low-impact, alternative forms of tourism encourage the spontaneous type of encounter where hosts and guest meet as equals, perhaps using homestay (where the visitor stays with a local family) as their accommodation – yet in some respects this type of encounter is the most damaging in terms of triggering change. In contrast, resort or 'enclave'-type tourism limits the encounters to commercial ones, with tourists travelling through the destination in a 'bubble' of hotels, escorted tours, coaches and managed, routine encounters – sometimes referred to as tourist ghettoes. Here, the local people that the tourist meets are 'culture brokers' who understand both the host and guest culture and act as a buffer between the two societies.

The notion of the demonstration effect, however, whilst intuitively attractive, has been criticised as being vague, used uncritically and at times patronising (Fisher, 2004). Fisher argues that the demonstration effect fails to recognise the other influences on the hosts, such as mass media, which can be more important than contact with tourists in changing behaviour and values.

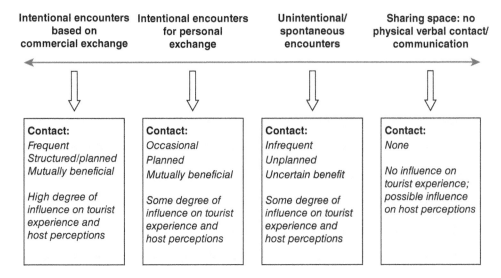

Intentional encounters based on commercial exchange	Intentional encounters for personal exchange	Unintentional/ spontaneous encounters	Sharing space: no physical verbal contact/ communication
Contact: *Frequent Structured/planned Mutually beneficial* *High degree of influence on tourist experience and host perceptions*	**Contact:** *Occasional Planned Mutually beneficial* *Some degree of influence on tourist experience and host perceptions*	**Contact:** *Infrequent Unplanned Uncertain benefit* *Some degree of influence on tourist experience and host perceptions*	**Contact:** *None* *No influence on tourist experience; possible influence on host perceptions*

FIGURE 5.2   Types of encounter

Source: Sharpley, 2014

TABLE 5.2   Doxey's irridex

The level of euphoria	People are enthusiastic and thrilled by tourist development. They welcome the stranger and there is a mutual feeling of satisfaction. There are opportunities for locals and money flows in along with the tourist.
The level of apathy	As the industry expands, people begin to take the tourist for granted. Tourists rapidly become the target for profit-taking and contact on the personal level begins to become more formal.
The level of irritation	This will begin when the industry is nearing saturation point or is allowed to pass a level at which the locals cannot handle the numbers without an expansion of facilities.
The level of antagonism	The irritations have become more overt. People now see the tourist as the harbinger of all that is bad: 'Taxes have gone up because of the tourists.' 'They have no respect for property.' 'They have corrupted our youth.' 'They are bent on destroying all that is fine in our town.' 'Mutual politeness has now given way to antagonism and the tourist is "ripped off".'
The final level	All this while people have forgotten that what they cherished in the first place is what drew the tourist, but in the wild scramble to develop they overlooked this and allowed the environment to change. What they must now learn to live with is the fact that their ecosystem will never be the same again. They might still be able to draw tourists but of a very different type from those they so happily welcomed in the early years. If the destination is large enough to cope with mass tourism, it will continue to thrive.

Source: adapted from Doxey, 1976

MODELLING THE ENCOUNTER

The consequences of the encounter will depend upon both the type of tourist and the level of development of tourism at the destination, as well as the characteristics of the host community. Sociologists have been criticised for failing to come up with analytical models of host–guest relationships, seeming rather to devise somewhat descriptive models (Wall and Mathieson, 2006). The literature provides three well-known models of the encounter:

1. The first is by Doxey (1976), who designed an index of tourist irritation (Table 5.2). Doxey's index is superficially attractive, effectively saying that the more tourists that visit a destination, the greater the level of disruption and thus irritation. However, his model suggests a one-way direction of the consequences of tourism, closely linked to the idea of Butler's (1980) tourism area life cycle.

2. Attractive though it is, Doxey's model fails to take into account the dynamics of the host community. Bjorklund and Philbrick's (1972) attitudinal model is therefore more realistic (Figure 5.3) because it recognises that at any one point in time there will be various opinions of tourism amongst the host community – and indeed these opinions and their vociferousness will change as tourism develops. Here, Strzelecka et al. (2017) found that the more a resident identified with the destination, the greater they felt politically empowered to act.

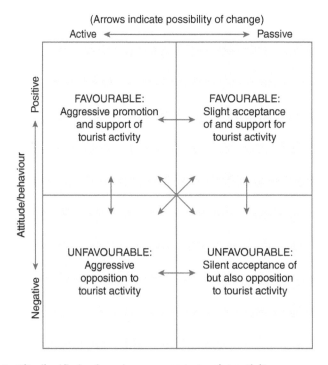

FIGURE 5.3   Host attitudinal/behavioural responses to tourist activity

Source: Bjorklund and Philbrick, 1972; Wall and Mathieson, 2006

3. Finally, MacCannell's (1973) idea of staged authenticity is based upon Goffman's idea of all daily activities being equivalent to a staged performance. MacCannell adapts Goffman's idea of a 'front and back region' for tourism:

   o The front region is the meeting place of hosts and guests and includes hotel reception areas, shops and restaurants. Here performances are staged and the host is acting out a part.

   o The back region is where the local people play out their daily lives or where the staff in the hotel relax in the canteen or staff room, out of sight of the guests. This is the intimate and 'authentic' region of the destination – the part of the destination that the 'new' tourist is most interested in.

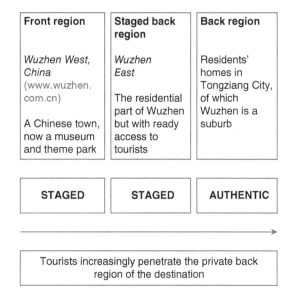

FIGURE 5.4   Levels of cultural penetration, Wuzhen, China

MacCannell argues that, in order to protect the back region from visitors, destinations design 'staged' back regions, such as creating a village to look authentic, or staging a festival as if it is part of everyday life (Figure 5.4). Here, Gao and Wu (2017) argue that the successful revitalisation of rural villages depends upon a bottom-up approach to implementation.

THE CONSEQUENCES OF TOURISM FOR THE HOST COMMUNITY

In Chapter 4 the concept of carrying capacity was introduced. Social carrying capacity relates to community acceptance of tourism – where a destination exceeds social carrying capacity, tourism development has become unacceptable, sometimes termed 'overtourism'. The consequences of tourism that can lead to this level are many and varied and demonstrate that it is misguided to dissect the consequences of tourism into economic, environmental and social/cultural factors. For example, the employment consequences of tourism would normally be thought of as economic consequences but, as shown below, they also have significant social consequences for the destination. The consequences of tourism for the host community include the following.

Social structure

When tourism is introduced to traditional societies, it can have significant consequences for social structures. For example, where coastal tourism is developed, it acts as a magnet for employment, often attracting the young and female from the rural hinterland to work in the resorts. This leads to rural depopulation and, by giving females economic independence, it can undermine traditional, male-dominated societies. This also has the effect of diverting labour from the land, and from more traditional craft-based enterprises, threatening their existence, as has happened in Corsica. Of course, it has already been shown that there are other issues linked to jobs in tourism, including (i) the quality of jobs and seasonality, and (ii) the socially divisive issue of immigrant labour.

Relocation of hosts

In some extreme cases, local people may be relocated to make space for tourism development, as has happened with the relocation of Bedouin from the historic monument of Petra in Jordan, or villagers from Ayia Napa in Cyprus.

Politics

If tourism is to be beneficial to the host community, it is important that control remains at the local level. This is best achieved if tourism grows slowly and the locals control the pace of growth so that it is kept within social carrying capacity. If this is not achieved, there is the danger of economically powerful groups emerging, as has happened in Bulgarian resorts.

As tourism grows and the destination begins to attract an international clientele, the awareness and recognition of the destination are enhanced, and both the locals and the industry will be exposed to ideas from other countries and international good practice. However, where a destination has outgrown local control and is dependent upon inclusive tours, the balance of power can shift from local decision-makers to national and international players. Quite simply, large tour operators will tend to want to deal at a higher level than with local politicians if they are seeking development or incentives, so bypassing local political groups. Decisions relating to development, marketing and promotion of the destination will be made in London, New York or Frankfurt rather than at the local or regional level, prompting the accusation of 'neo-colonialism' or 'imperialism' towards tour operators.

This means that locals are not in control of tourism at the destination and are therefore at the mercy of many of the negative consequences such as inflated prices in the shops and high land or property prices. It also implies that many of the benefits of tourism flow back to the headquarters of the tour operators and are not captured at the local level. Finally, it is possible that the local community can be manipulated to support the economic ambitions of local or national politicians in terms of tourism.

Morals

Historically, tourism has been associated with low moral standards including prostitution, crime and gambling, although of course tourism is an easy target to blame here. Away from home, tourists see themselves as anonymous and are therefore more likely to engage in these activities which, as a result, tend to be found at tourism destinations. Some destinations have legalised both prostitution and gambling – indeed the development of casinos is a classic strategy for the rejuvenation of tired destinations, expanding their tax base and attracting a new type of visitor. However, there is evidence that casinos change the nature of the destination and can attract organised crime.

Sex tourism is a controversial consequence of the fact that tourists are strangers in destinations where the moral climate of home is absent. Sex tourism is also known to spread diseases such as AIDS. Wall and Mathieson (2006) identify a number of factors that link tourism to the sex industry:

- Tourism creates spaces where sex tourism can flourish.
- Tourism employment for women liberalises them from home and they may then choose to enter the sex industry.
- Tourism is attracted to the poorer countries of the world where locals may be forced into the sex industry to survive, as shown in Major Case Study 5.1.
- Some destinations, such as Thailand, have become recognised locations for sex tourism.

Finally, there is evidence that tourism encourages crime and vandalism, partly because there are more people around the destination but also because, as strangers, tourists are easy prey to criminal activity. Residents, too, become targets and both vandalism and threats to personal safety are also an issue with tourism, creating the types of locations where these activities can flourish. In response, destinations become burdened with the extra cost of policing, often drafting in special 'tourist police' – as happens in the resorts of Spain, and in Australia during 'schoolies' weeks – and for any destination, crime is bad publicity. Finally, tourism has become the target of major crimes such as terrorism and hijackings.

Language

The demonstration effect is partly responsible for the fact that tourism can lead to the standardisation of language at destinations, threatening minority languages and driving through languages such as English and Spanish. In part, too, this is due to economic development where these languages dominate and become the language of choice of the industry, often influenced by expatriate workers. This leads to the necessity of the hosts learning the language if they are to engage with the tourism industry. Of course, in many destinations a different language is seen as an attraction with bilingual signage, as seen in Wales or the Isle of Man.

Residents' lifestyle

Much of the research into the social consequences of tourism has focused upon the impact on residents' lifestyle and quality of life. This will depend on the ratio of hosts to guests, and scales have been developed to measure this (for example, the ratio of tourists to the host population). On the positive side, tourism can foster pride in local communities and enhance community spirit and values (as, for example, in the English community of Wirksworth – www.derbyshire-peakdistrict.co.uk/wirksworth.htm – and in Tasmania) as well as assisting in community renewal (Blackstone Valley, USA, www.tourblackstone.com). Tourism brings increased opportunities to residents through festivals, events and additional facilities, and this does enhance the quality of life of the local community.

There is no doubt that tourism can be disruptive of the local way of life, whether it be through increased congestion on the roads, more people in the shops, increased crime levels, noise from entertainment at night or letting Airbnb properties in residential areas. Where tourism development has exceeded social carrying capacity, it is often through factors such as the commercialisation of local attractions and culture, loss of open space and community facilities to serve tourism, and the separation of locals from the recreational business district of the resort. The degree of disruption experienced by residents and their attitude towards tourism development will depend upon three key factors:

1. The location of their home in relation to tourist activity at the destination;

2. The length of time they have lived at the destination; and

3. Whether they work in tourism, or have close family who do so.

Resident attitude will also depend upon:

- **The type of tourism** – for example, racial tensions can arise where the cultural distances are great and there are obvious differences between host and guest, as has happened in some Caribbean islands.

- **The type of destination** – for example, in traditional mass tourism resorts much of the tourism activity takes place in and around the recreational business district and there is a separation of tourism activity and local residents. In rural areas, the consequences of tourism are more subtle as tourists are dispersed throughout the destination. Nonetheless, the consequences for local residents in rural areas can be severe, not only in terms of interference with traditional rural activities such as farming, but also through change in the level of services as shops that used to serve the local population become gift shops and tea rooms.

Here, one of the most severe set of consequences, yet one that is almost hidden, is that of second home development. Second homes deliver little economic benefit, yet their impact upon services and community spirit is severe because second homeowners are only present in the destination for a few weeks of the year. This impacts upon health, education and other services, reducing the level of support that they receive and so reducing the quality of life of the local community. Not surprisingly, it is second home development that attracts the most hostile reaction from local people, in some cases turning to violence, and has prompted authorities to attempt to limit the level of second home development in some destinations (Müller, 2014).

Tourism as an agent of poverty alleviation

Tourism has been recognised as a means of alleviating poverty. This new agenda has been enthusiastically embraced by the developing world and international agencies (including the UNWTO, UNCTAD and the World Bank) – the UNWTO, for example, has developed a 'sustainable tourism – eliminating poverty' (ST-EP) programme. Treating tourism as an agent of poverty alleviation results in increased net benefits for poor people. The critical issue is how to channel visitor spending and investment into improved income and quality of life for people in poverty (Rogerson and Saarinen, 2018).

The UNWTO state that tourism has many advantages as a sector for poverty alleviation:

- Tourism is produced where it is consumed – it brings tourists to the destination, allowing opportunities for economic gain from contact with visitors.

- Tourism is easily accessible to the poor – it is labour intensive, employs a high percentage of women and young people, and mainly comprises SMEs. It also spreads economic benefits, both geographically and to other sectors such as agriculture and handicrafts due to its 'connectivity'.

- Tourism is naturally attracted to remote, peripheral areas where other economic options are limited, and to the lesser developed countries of the world where there are significant natural and cultural attractions.

- Tourism is one of the few development opportunities for the poor and encourages entrepreneurial development.

- The infrastructure required to develop tourism benefits poor communities.

- Tourism is significant and growing in the developing and least-developed countries. These include China, Vietnam, Laos, Cambodia, Myanmar and a number of Pacific islands.

PROCESSES OF CULTURAL CHANGE

The culture of a destination has long been an attraction for visitors, dating back at least as far as the grand tour of Europe in the eighteenth century. Yet, it is interesting that whilst culture is a major attraction, it is also changed irreversibly by tourism itself, particularly as tourism often demands 'instant culture' at the destination. Brunt and Courtney (1999) view cultural impacts as 'those which lead to a longer-term, gradual change in a society's values, beliefs and cultural practices' (p. 496).

As an attraction, culture can be viewed along three dimensions:

- **Material culture**, which includes architecture, monuments, buildings, souvenirs, crafts, literature and paintings;

- **Normal daily life**, which includes local cuisine, everyday life in the destination and the lifestyle of the local people; and

- **Animated forms of culture** that include theatre, festivals and events, some of which may be re-enacted or specially staged for the visitor.

The inevitable consequence of the culture of an international tourist coming into contact with a traditional culture is the danger that the traditional culture is changed or even destroyed. Whenever there is an encounter between two cultures, the cultures tend to borrow from each other, a process known as acculturation or 'cultural drift'. In tourism, it tends to be the weaker culture that borrows the most, particularly as that culture may have to change simply to cater for the tourist. Of course, it is difficult to know just to what extent tourism is responsible for this borrowing, as in the twenty-first century most cultures are also exposed to the mass media and will evolve and change despite the influence of tourism. The danger here is that the constant process of borrowing leads to uniform cultures and destinations across the world. This is a significant issue for tourism and, despite the fact that, as we have seen, the encounter is a brief, temporary one, when grossed up, encounters with tourists lead to irreversible, permanent cultural change. At the end of the day, the degree of change will depend upon the strength and confidence of the host culture.

FOCUS ON TECHNOLOGY

Digitisation of Culture – the Death of Authenticity?

Intereg Europe (2018) defines digitisation as the process of conversion of analogue information into digital format. Technology is changing how tourists experience culture at destinations by providing (i) quality information and (ii) enhancing the experience through applications such as augmented and virtual realities. This means that cultural and heritage destinations can be made accessible to those who otherwise could not visit and the resource can be protected by re-creating it in digital form.

However, does the technology intervene unacceptably in the relationship between the visitor and the culture? For example, many feel that the apparatus of virtual reality (VR) creates an artificial barrier between the cultural resource and the visitor. Nikonova and Biryukova (2017) are clear that the technology interferes with the true reflection of memory, history and tradition and so kills the notion of authenticity as many visitors lack the historical imagination to benefit. In other words, the replacement of *real interaction* with the cultural resource to a *virtual engagement* removes authenticity and replaces it with entertainment and gamification.

Sources: Intereg Europe (2018) *Digital Solutions in the Field of Cultural Heritage: A Policy Brief from the Policy Learning Platform on Environment and Resource Efficiency.* Brussels: Intereg Europe; Nikonova, A.A. and Biryukova, M.V. (2017) 'The role of digital technologies in the preservation of cultural heritage', *Muzeológia a kultúrne dedičstvo*, 5 (1): 169–73.

Cultural change from tourism occurs as a result of:

- The demonstration effect through the intermingling of hosts and guests;
- The employment of expatriates in the tourism sector;
- The visibility of activities such as gambling; and
- The erosion of local culture and sometimes language.

The main negative consequence of tourism for culture is commercialisation, and, whilst this is prevalent in the developing world, we also observe it in the developed world – take, for example, the commercialisation of the British Royal family or of indigenous peoples in Canada or the USA, and the commoditisation of religion in many destinations where religious monuments, churches and sites have become tourist attractions rather than places of worship. Here, the contrast between the principles of some religions, such as Islam and the behaviour of visitors to countries where the religion is dominant, can be problematic.

Material culture is commonly cited as vulnerable to commercialisation through the cheap reproduction of crafts – often known as 'airport art' – where the original craft has been changed to unsophisticated and poor-quality copies. However, whilst everyone has experienced this type of souvenir, there is an argument that tourism can help to preserve these traditional crafts if tourists then seek to buy more authentic, original versions. This keeps craftspeople at work and may even revive dead crafts. The same argument can be applied to festivals, events and customs. Of course, some destinations use their culture as a marketing tool to attract visitors and to stamp a sense of identity on the destination – Australia uses its indigenous culture effectively for this purpose (www.australia.com), whilst Hawaii's culture is a key brand value in its promotion (www.hvcb.org).

Indigenous people

Butler and Hinch (1996: 9) define indigenous tourism as 'Tourism activity in which indigenous people are directly involved either through control and/or by having their culture serve as the essence of the attraction'. They are clear in their view that whilst indigenous cultures and people are a potential tourist attraction, the process is fraught with danger. The curiosity of tourists to see how others live can easily become voyeurism and there is the danger of the 'encounter' being reduced to viewing the 'savages' of, say, African tribes or South Pacific islands with hints of old colonial relationships. Even the most well-meaning of visits to see how others live can introduce subtle changes into traditional societies through the demonstration effect and the acts of the hosts to accommodate tourists. The concept of homestay, for example, ticks all the boxes of low-impact and sensitive encounters in theory, yet if the hosts are not trained and prepared for the behaviour and customs of the visitors, then it can create major changes in the host society.

Effectively, tourism reduces the 'encounter' with indigenous people to an economic transaction. Here the two words 'control' and 'attraction' are key. It is important that indigenous people are respected and not seen simply as an attraction to be gazed at, and it is important that the locus of control of the relationship lies with the indigenous community to ensure that it occurs on their terms and that the benefits are distributed fairly. If this can occur, then the economic benefit of tourism stays within the host community. Examples of successful projects here include:

- Home Valley Station in Australia, a cattle ranch owned and run by indigenous Australians and open to tourists (www.hvstation.com.au);

- Sarara Camp Kenya, a game reserve and luxury safari camp owned by the Samburu community (www.sararacamp.com); and

- Huaorani, Ecuador, guest cabins on the Amazon rainforest owned and run by the Huaorani people (www.huaorani.com).

Here, Tao and Wall (2009) have developed the 'sustainable livelihoods' approach, which shows how local populations can benefit from tourism through multiple activities rather than single jobs so that tourism complements rather than displaces existing activities. The approach is centred on people and assesses how their capabilities, activities and assets can enable them to earn a living from tourism. It is based on the idea that tourism can complement existing activities such as agriculture and hunting and that these activities themselves can grow their markets through tourism.

MINI CASE STUDY 5.2

The Social Progress Index for Tourism Destinations

Introduction

Since the 1990s, there has been a shift in how we see the development of countries, away from purely economic variables towards a more inclusive approach that includes both the environment and society. Traditional economic measures such as GDP often do not align with the progress of societies. The social dimension of development has used the social progress index (SPI) methodology which is

A tropical beach on Saona Island, Dominican Republic

Source: ©Natalia Pushchina/Shutterstock.com

used to create a common language, framework and benchmarking system for assessing the impact of development. The SPI is now being applied to tourism destinations. As such, social progress has become an important agenda on the political stage, as residents of destinations increasingly rebel against issues such as 'overtourism'.

Method

The SPI is a rigorous measure of performance on a number of social variables which allows for comparison between tourism destinations. It provides a data-driven framework for creating an agenda for policy, investment and sustainable development. For tourism, this SPI methodology provides a tool for measuring and understanding the wellbeing of the residents of tourist destinations. The SPI is often communicated as a scorecard for dissemination amongst local communities, municipalities and other stakeholders. The scorecard provides an assessment of the social strengths and weaknesses of a community compared to others, allowing for the identification of potential investments and an actionable agenda. Indicators for an SPI include:

* Nutrition and basic medical care;
* Water and sanitation;
* Shelter;
* Personal safety;
* Access to basic knowledge;

- Access to information and communications;
- Health and wellness;
- Environmental quality;
- Personal rights and freedom;
- Tolerance and inclusion; and
- Access to advanced education.

The Dominican Republic has applied the SPI methodology using 59 indicators which are grouped into themes. The indicators are designed to measure outcomes not inputs to ensure that the results are actionable. The SPI found that tourism is beneficial to 90 per cent of communities. The results include:

- **Water and sanitation** – tourist destination areas present a positive impact with regard to access to drinking water.
- **Shelter** – in general, tourist destination areas perform better than other areas, particularly in terms of overcrowding.
- **Personal safety** – tourist destination areas tend to be safer.
- **Access to information and communications** – tourist destination areas rank an average of 20 per cent higher in terms of access to ICTs.
- **Environmental quality** – tourist destination areas are strongly focused on environmental protection.
- **Access to advanced education** – tourist destination areas obtained better results than other areas.

The SPI is not used for its own sake; it is important that the results can be turned into action. For the Dominican Republic, the SPI is used to:

- Deliver sustainable social and environmental development;
- Deliver an agenda of joint social interventions and strategies to ensure the improvement of life in destinations;
- Create a roadmap of actions and social interventions;
- Promote inclusive economic growth in each destination; and
- Develop collaborative and multisectoral strategies to align social investments.

Discussion Questions

1. Why do you think that tourism has been slow to adopt the SPI approach?
2. Debate in class whether a holistic assessment of a destination (economic, environmental and social) is a better approach than singling out the social dimension.
3. Identify the policy benefits of taking an SPI approach.

Source: Social Progress Imperative (2019) *Social Progress Index 2019*. Washington, DC: Social Progress Imperative.

ASSESSING THE SOCIAL AND CULTURAL CONSEQUENCES OF TOURISM

Whilst the methodology of assessing both the economic and environmental consequences of tourism are well developed, much less work has been done on developing methods to assess the social and cultural consequences of tourism on the quality of life of the local people. In part, this is due to the difficulty of 'quantifying' these consequences and often the lack of agreement at local level as to just what is 'acceptable change'. The social progress index is a new methodology, showcased in Mini Case Study 5.2. It is a breakthrough approach to assessing the impact of tourism on local communities. Of course, environmental impact assessments now take into account social and cultural impacts, but often the local population is excluded from the process and the SPI is an approach to get around this issue. Similarly, recent work on the development and monitoring of sustainability indicators (discussed in Chapter 6) has gone some way to assist in this approach. There are also tried-and-tested techniques of surveying local communities as to their views of tourism development and the degree of change they are prepared to accept due to tourism development. This also has the advantage of assessing acceptable levels of change before tourism develops, rather than the more common approach of assessing consequences after the event.

SUMMARY

This chapter has outlined the social and cultural consequences of tourism for the host population. It began by outlining the tripartite framework needed to analyse these consequences, namely the tourist, the host and the encounter or 'contact'. The chapter has shown that the social and cultural consequences of tourism depend upon the type of tourism development and its pace, as well as the type and number of tourists and the characteristics of the local population at the destination. The concept of social carrying capacity was introduced to explain how destinations might suffer from excessive development in the eyes of the local population – or overtourism. The chapter stressed the importance of the 'encounter' with the tourist and how this encounter occurs in different ways and has certain characteristics. An important aspect of the encounter is the 'demonstration effect' – a process whereby the hosts may copy the behaviour and values of the tourist. Theoretical frameworks to help understand these processes were then outlined, namely those of Doxey, Bjorklund and Philbrick, and MacCannell.

The chapter went on to outline the various social consequences of tourism for the host destination and examined influences upon the hosts' perception of tourists and tourism development. The main social consequences were identified as impacts upon the political and social structures of the destinations, negative impacts on moral behaviour through crime, gambling and sex tourism, the impact upon language and negative host attitudes brought about by changing lifestyles through experiencing crowding and congestion at the destination. Finally, the chapter considered processes of cultural change brought about when a dominant tourism culture comes into contact with a host culture. Here the process of acculturation, or 'borrowing', was identified. Cultural consequences of tourism include the commoditisation of culture and the impact on indigenous peoples. The chapter closed by considering frameworks for assessing the social and cultural consequences of tourism.

DISCUSSION QUESTIONS

1. In class, debate the proposition that there is little evidence to support the rose-tinted view that bringing cultures and societies together promotes peace and understanding.

2. For a destination with which you are familiar, draw up a balance sheet of positive and negative social consequences of tourism.

3. Analyse the process of the 'encounter' from your own holiday experience – how accurate is the statement that true 'equal' encounters between host and guest are rare?

4. Assess the impact of tourism on the host culture of a destination with which you are familiar.

5. Taking a destination with which you are familiar, map the various interest groups onto Bjorklund and Philbrick's matrix.

ANNOTATED FURTHER READING

De Kadt, E. (1979) *Tourism: Passport to Development?* Oxford: Oxford University Press.

Classic coverage of the social and cultural consequences of tourism.

Krippendorf, J. (1987) *The Holidaymakers: Understanding the Impact of Leisure and Travel.* Oxford: Butterworth-Heinemann.

One of the first books to raise concerns about the social and cultural consequences of tourism.

MacCannell, D. (1973) 'Staged authenticity: arrangements of social space in tourist settings', *American Journal of Sociology*, 73 (3): 589–603.

Classic and highly influential paper.

Sharpley, R. (2018) 'The host community: perceptions of and responses to tourism', in C. Cooper, S. Volo, W.C. Gartner and N. Scott (eds), *The Sage Handbook of Tourism Management: Applications of Theories and Concepts to Tourism*. London: Sage. pp. 537–51.

Contemporary review of host and guest relationships.

Smith, V. (1977) *Hosts and Guests: The Anthropology of Tourism*. Philadelphia, PA: University of Pennsylvania Press.

A further classic text examining hosts and guests through anthropological eyes.

REFERENCES CITED

Bjorklund, E.M. and Philbrick, A.K. (1972) *Building Regions for the Future*. Quebec: Department of Geography, Lowal University.

Brunt, P. and Courtney, P. (1999) 'Host perceptions of sociocultural impacts', *Annals of Tourism Research*, 26 (3): 493–515.

Butler, R.W. (1980) 'The concept of a tourist area cycle of evolution', *Canadian Geographer*, 24: 5–12.

Butler, R. and Hinch, T. (1996) *Tourism and Indigenous People*. London: Routledge.

Cohen, E. (1972) 'Toward a sociology of international tourism', *Social Research*, 39 (1): 164–82.

De Kadt, E. (1979) *Tourism: Passport to Development?* Oxford: Oxford University Press.

Dogan, H. (1989) 'Forms of adjustment: sociocultural impacts of tourism', *Annals of Tourism Research*, 16 (2): 216–36.

Doxey, G.V. (1976) 'When enough's enough: the natives are restless in old Niagara', *Heritage Canada*, 2 (2): 26–7.

Fisher, D. (2004) 'The demonstration effect revisited', *Annals of Tourism Research*, 31 (2): 428–46.

Gao, J. and Wu, B. (2017) 'Revitalizing traditional villages through rural tourism: a case study of Yuanjia Village, Shaanxi Province, China', *Tourism Management*, 63: 223–33.

Krippendorf, J. (1987) *The Holidaymakers: Understanding the Impact of Leisure and Travel.* Oxford: Butterworth-Heinemann.

MacCannell, D. (1973) 'Staged authenticity: arrangements of social space in tourist settings', *American Journal of Sociology*, 73 (3): 589–603.

Müller, D. (2014) 'Progress in second home tourism research', in A.L. Lew, C.M. Hall and A.M. Williams (eds), *The Wiley Blackwell Companion to Tourism*. Chichester: Wiley. pp. 389–400.

Rogerson, C.M. and Saarinen, J. (2018) 'Tourism for poverty alleviation: issues and debates in the global south', in C. Cooper, S. Volo, W.C. Gartner and N. Scott (eds), *The Sage Handbook of Tourism Management: Applications of Theories and Concepts to Tourism*. London: Sage. pp. 22–37.

Sharpley, R. (2014) 'Host perceptions of tourism: a review of the research', *Tourism Management*, 42: 37–49.

Sharpley, R. (2018) 'The host community: perceptions of and responses to tourism', in C. Cooper, S. Volo, W.C. Gartner and N. Scott (eds), *The Sage Handbook of Tourism Management: Applications of Theories and Concepts to Tourism*. London: Sage. pp. 537–51.

Smith, V. (1977) *Hosts and Guests: The Anthropology of Tourism*. Philadelphia, PA: University of Pennsylvania Press.

Strzelecka, M., Boley, B.B. and Woosnam, K.M. (2017) 'Place attachment and empowerment: do residents need to be attached to be empowered?' *Annals of Tourism Research*, 66: 61–73.

Tao, C.T.H. and Wall, G. (2009) 'Tourism as a sustainable livelihood strategy', *Tourism Management*, 30 (1): 90–8.

UNESCO (1976) 'The effects of tourism on socio-cultural values', *Annals of Tourism Research*, 4 (1): 74–105.

Urry, J. (1990) *The Tourist Gaze: Leisure and Travel in Contemporary Societies*. London: Sage.

Wall, G. and Mathieson, A. (2006) *Tourism: Change, Impacts and Opportunities*. Harlow: Pearson.

Weaver, D.B. (2014) 'Asymmetrical dialectics of sustainable tourism: toward enlightened mass tourism', *Journal of Travel Research*, 53 (2): 131–40.

MAJOR CASE STUDY 5.1

Sisterhood of Survivors Programme, Nepal

A Nepalese woman doing laundry by hand in a mountain village in the rural Himalayas

Source: ©Gekko Gallery/Shutterstock.com

(Continued)

The Issue

Nepalese women and girls are vulnerable to human trafficking and other abuse, including human slavery and sexual exploitation. For example, it is estimated that 30,000 Nepalese girls suffer in this way every year. These girls, often aged from 12 to 19 years old, are poorly educated, illiterate, have no income and therefore no employment prospects. Many live in remote rural villages and an estimated 7000 women and girls are trafficked to countries such as India. Unfortunately, prosecutions are few and far between and cases are rarely reported. In 2013, the Nepal Human Rights Commission estimated that:

- 250,000 to 270,000 Nepalese people are trapped in slavery;
- these victims are mainly teens, between 12 and 19 years old; and
- each day an estimated 54 Nepalese women and children are trafficked.

The Response: SASANE

In response to this situation, SASANE was established in 2008 by former female victims of human trafficking. It is a not-for-profit organisation with the aim of empowering survivors of human trafficking to break the cycle of corruption in Nepal under the slogan 'Let's protect ourselves'. SASANE believes that 'every human trafficking survivor can achieve her individual dream and potential'. In other words, the philosophy is that survivors have the potential to combat human trafficking and drive social change. SASANE trains survivors as paralegals and they become the first point of contact for other victims. SASANE works in the remote rural villages of Nepal, where the paralegals educate communities and raise awareness as a means of prevention. By 2018, SASANE had provided job opportunities to 371 female survivors and it receives 200 applications from survivors to become paralegals, but there are only 45 places available. In response to this high level of demand, SASANE established a programme in tourism as a second outlet for survivors – the Sisterhood of Survivors programme.

Sisterhood of Survivors Programme

SASANE's initiative in tourism is called the Sisterhood of Survivors (SOS) programme. The SOS programme was created with support from the tourism social enterprise Planeterra Foundation and the company G Adventures. The objective of the programme is to teach survivors skills in the tourism industry, so that they can have a sustainable income and means of support, gain self-confidence and not need to return to being trafficked or abused.

The programme trains survivors in trekking and tour guiding as well as how to be successful hospitality staff and so gives them access to the tourism sector in Nepal. The training includes:

- Conversational English;
- Culinary skills;
- Accounting;
- Food and beverage management; and
- Tour and trekking guide skills, certified through the Nepal Tourism and Training Centre.

The programme also includes training in traditional cuisine, including dumplings, where survivors demonstrate their skills to tourists from G Adventures with authentic Nepali 'thali' cuisine served for lunch. In 2017/18, 3404 tourists visited SASANE as a part of the SOS programme. This initiative helps to provide facilities and infrastructure in the villages and uses the income from tourism to train more 'sisters', as well as to provide income for local people. To date, the SOS programme has trained 43 survivors in tourism skills, and with money earned from tourism SASANE has sent ten sisters for guide training. A further aim of the programme is to educate travellers about the human trafficking issue.

Trekking – Unique Educational Cultural Exchanges

As noted above, it is the rural villages suffering from poverty that are most vulnerable to human trafficking. G Adventures directs treks and tourism into these areas and arranges homestays to provide economic independence for the villagers. This means that travellers seeking an authentic, immersive experience in Nepal can join treks and tours to support the SOS and SASANE programmes. These treks are off the beaten track and allow for engagement with local people and culture. The treks include:

- a 25-day trekking programme in Ghyangfedi where priority is given to the local Tamang lifestyles and traditional Nepali food, and travellers are given the opportunity for sightseeing and interaction with the local villagers; and
- a 25-day trekking programme in Ghyangfedi around Nuwakot, regarded as one of the trafficking-prone villages of Nepal – the trek highlights the scenic beauty of the village.

In summary, through a responsible tourism model, the SASANE and SOS programmes allow the survivors of human trafficking to gain self-respect, become role models for young Nepali girls, and provide hope and inspiration to other survivors.

Discussion Questions

1. Draft a human trafficking awareness campaign for travellers to Nepal.
2. Design a marketing plan for trekking in Nepal associated with the SOS programme.
3. How can the culinary aspect of the SOS programme be scaled up to provide sustainable incomes across rural Nepal?

Sources: www.gadventures.co.uk; https://planeterra.org; https://sasane.org.np

6

SUSTAINABLE TOURISM

LEARNING OUTCOMES

This chapter considers the background and approaches to sustainable tourism as an organising concept for tourism in the twenty-first century. It outlines the evolution of the concept and shows how it can be effectively implemented. The chapter is designed to provide you with:

- an understanding of how the idea of sustainable tourism has evolved;
- an awareness of the various concepts and definitions of sustainable tourism;
- an appreciation of the different types of sustainable tourism;
- an understanding of the underpinning principles of sustainable tourism; and
- an awareness of contemporary approaches to implementing sustainable tourism.

INTRODUCTION

As tourism continues to grow across the world, reaching ever more remote and sensitive places, it has placed increased pressure upon the environment and host communities of those destinations – as shown in the previous three chapters. A pioneer of sustainable tourism, Jost Krippendorf (1982: 135) states the matter clearly: 'Unrestricted tourism growth could lead to the positive economic effects of tourism being outweighed by significant social and environmental disadvantages'.

Tourism is unusual in that its core product depends upon the successful management of the resources upon which tourism depends. To respond to the challenges that this implies for tourism in the twenty-first century, there is an imperative for the sustainable development of tourism, even though it could be argued that the goals of development and environmental protection are irreconcilable (Higgins-Desbiolles, 2018). The challenge includes four key priorities:

1. To plan and manage tourism growth to minimise negative impacts and promote the positive impacts of tourism. This is particularly important for vulnerable destinations such as coasts, wetlands, mountains, deserts, the polar regions and areas of significant cultural heritage.

2. To use tourism to help alleviate poverty in the world.

3. To take action on climate change, as climate change will impact upon tourism in two ways – firstly, demanding adaptation on the part of destinations and, secondly, shifting patterns of demand by stressing tourists' individual responsibility for their behaviour, including the choice of 'to fly or not to fly'.

4. To ensure that sustainability is financially attractive by developing new ways of operating as a sector, including public–private partnerships, embracing the principles of the 'green economy' and developing environmental accounting techniques.

Here contemporary thinking is based upon two principles:

1. Scientists accept that ecosystems are complex adaptive systems, with natural, social and economic elements. For tourism, this means that it is essential to take a 'whole of destination' approach to sustainability, managing the system by determining thresholds of acceptability and monitoring the system through the use of indicators (which are dealt with later in the chapter). The systems approach embraces the concept of 'resilience' – the ability of a system to withstand change and retain its essential function. This is a core idea for sustainability at destinations as they respond to the challenges of climate change and other threats (Hall et al., 2018). Indeed, some now use the term 'resilience' as an alternative to 'sustainability'.

2. The challenge of sustainability is closely linked to economic development. As such, not only should the issue of tourism's sustainable development be considered, but also the means by which tourism itself can contribute to sustainable development in economies across the world. Indeed, the challenges posed by sustainability are allowing the tourism sector to be both innovative and adaptive to rethink the way that it operates (Fayos Sola and Cooper, 2019). This is known as the 'higher level approach' to planning and contrasts with the 'lower level approach' based upon property development. The 'higher level approach' has been driven by the imperatives of climate change, environmental pressures and demands from the consumer.

BACKGROUND TO SUSTAINABILITY

The concept of sustainability itself has a long pedigree, rooted in resource management and agriculture dating back to ancient times, and reflecting shifting priorities in society. It is also a concept that continues to evolve (Fennell and Cooper, 2020). From the 1960s onwards there was a growing interest and concern for the environment, fuelled by media coverage, the emergence of 'green' consumerism and the establishment of powerful NGOs. For tourism, the concept has come late, growing in awareness throughout the 1980s, supported by international conventions, declarations and initiatives that reflected the mood of the times (see Table 6.1). It is interesting, for example, that in the UN's Earth Summit in Rio the word tourism did not appear, yet in the next decade, in the second Earth Summit in Johannesburg and Rio+20 in 2012, tourism was seen as an important player with its own section of the report. Sustainable tourism has also matured over the decades, moving from idealism to reality. Examples here include the way that leading companies such as Accor and Tui are showing leadership in sustainability. However, Buckley feels there are still exceptions and that the sector is not yet mature in this regard, relying on regulation rather than the market for sustainable initiatives (Buckley, 2012).

The concept of sustainability has evolved, and continues to do so, in a process of re-balancing away from a sole concern with the environment to a broader concern for society. Here, the development of the United Nations 'Millennium Development Goals' (MDGs) in 2000 was pivotal in broadening the agenda (www.undp.org/mdg). The goals include targets for poverty reduction, increasing education levels, empowering women, reducing child mortality and combating diseases such as HIV/AIDS and malaria (see Saarinen et al., 2012). The MDGs are important as they act as the framework for the development agencies of the developed world to intervene in the developing world. However, by 2012 the UN's Conference on Sustainable Development, Rio+20, supported the redevelopment of the MDGs into Sustainable Development Goals (SDGs) to redress the criticism that the MDGs neglected the environment. As the debate has matured, it has moved from a position of tourism being either sustainable or not, to one where the effort is focused upon moving all forms of tourism towards sustainability (Clarke, 1997). Here, the idea of 'relative' and 'absolute' sustainability is helpful. Tourism will never reach a position of 'absolute' sustainability, but will always be 'transitioning' towards it. Miller and Twining-Ward (2005) see this process as the 'sustainability transition', where sustainable tourism evolves to adapt to society and its particular sites and destinations. Essentially, sustainable tourism can be viewed as a continuous process of improvement that has become the organising concept for much of tourism.

TABLE 6.1   Milestones of sustainable tourism development

Date	Initiative
1962	Publication of Rachel Carson's *Silent Spring*
1968	Publication of Hardin's *Tragedy of the Commons*
1972	Club of Rome Report *Limits to Growth* UN Stockholm Conference on the Human Environment – no mention of tourism
1973	Publication of Schumacher's *Small is Beautiful*
1980	World Conservation Strategy published by the International Union for the Conservation of Nature (IUCN)
1987	Brundtland Report, *Our Common Future*, published
1992	Rio Earth Summit – very much with *environment* as the focus: Agenda 21 UN Commission on Sustainable Development
1993	Establishment of the *Journal of Sustainable Tourism*
1999	UNWTO Global Code of Ethics for Tourism
2000	Tour Operators' Initiative for Sustainable Tourism Development Millennium Development Goals
2002	Johannesburg World Summit on Sustainable Development developed idea of Agenda 21 – shifting the emphasis from *environment* to *people* International Year of Ecotourism Quebec Declaration on Ecotourism
2003	European Commission Tourism Sustainability Group established
2006	Marrakech Task Force on Tourism Sustainable Development
2007	UNESCO/UNWTO Collaboration for World Heritage Davos Processes on Climate Change

Date	Initiative
	Global Sustainable Tourism Criteria
	Publication of European Union's 'Action for a More Sustainable European Tourism'
2008	Sustainable Tourism Stewardship Council
2009	Copenhagen Climate Conference aiming to deliver a holistic framework to stabilise global warming by 2050
2010	UN Framework Convention on Climate Change, Cancun, Mexico
2012	Rio+20, Rio, Brazil, shifting the emphasis from MDGs to Sustainable Development Goals (SDGs) to re-address environmental concerns
	UN Climate Change Conference, Qatar
2015	UN Climate Change Conference, Paris where agreement on carbon emission targets was reached
2017	UNWTO International Year of Sustainable Tourism for Development

THE PILLARS OF SUSTAINABILITY

There are three key pillars that support the triple bottom-line approach to sustainability (Figure 6.1). These pillars are interlinked and mutually reinforcing:

1. **Economic sustainability** revolves around the concept of the enterprise supporting jobs and delivering income to communities in the long term. Without this, destinations and their communities cannot survive. Increasingly, environmental considerations will impact upon the economy as there is a move to 'greening' the economy.

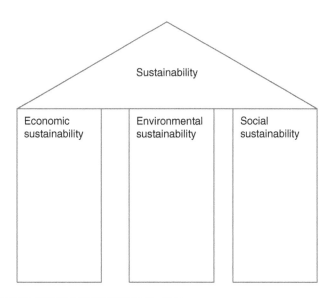

FIGURE 6.1   The three pillars of sustainable tourism

2.   **Social sustainability** focuses upon sharing benefits fairly and equitably and respecting the quality of life of communities and of human rights. It will increasingly involve 'living within our means'.

3.   **Environmental sustainability** focuses upon stewardship of resources and managing and conserving the environment, and will involve the notion of 'limits to growth'.

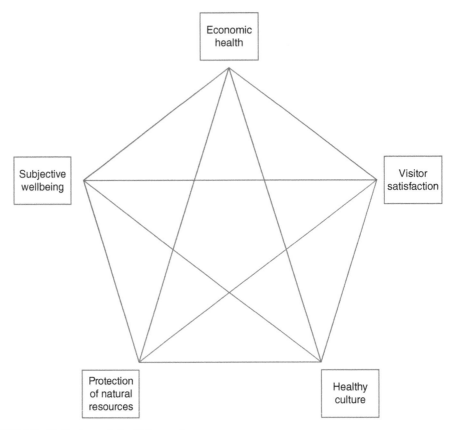

FIGURE 6.2   Muller's sustainability pentagon

Source: Muller, 1994; Miller and Twining-Ward, 2005

There is also an increasingly accepted view that there should be a fourth pillar based upon carbon. Tourism is a key player in each of these pillars, not only as a private sector activity, but also as one that impacts upon destination communities and utilises the environment as a resource to attract tourism. At the same time, it is in a strong position to educate the tourists themselves about the imperative for sustainable development and appropriate behaviours, as shown in the Eden Project case study. There is therefore a delicate balance to be struck between the pillars, as environmental damage to a destination will reduce visitation and so jeopardise the viability of local enterprises that depend on it. The Great Barrier Reef in Australia is a good example here (www.gbrmpa.gov.au). Muller's (1994) conceptualisation of sustainability is useful as it diagrammatically illustrates the 'pillars' of sustainability, and in his pentagon, he extends them to five (Figure 6.2). The centre of the pentagon represents a harmonious situation of balanced development where all forces are balanced – for destinations this is easier said than achieved!

MINI CASE STUDY 6.1

Education for Sustainability: The Eden Project, UK

Introduction

The Eden Project is located in the south-west of England in the county of Cornwall. It was fully opened in 2001, built on a reclaimed china clay pit. The project has two iconic domes containing plants from desert and Mediterranean environments. The domes are constructed of hexagonal and pentagonal inflated plastic cells on steel frames. They are surrounded by other gardens and features, including a wildlife garden, shop and restaurant. The Eden Project is an educational charity and social enterprise with the mission to 'promote the understanding and responsible management of the vital relationship between plants, people and resources leading to a sustainable future for all'.

The project has been hugely successful, with estimates suggesting that it has contributed over £1 billion to the Cornish economy. The Eden Project receives over a million visitors annually and employs around 40 core staff, an additional 500 staff in the summer and a further 150 volunteers.

Education for Sustainability

What sets the Eden Project apart from other, similar initiatives is the focus on sustainability education at all levels from kindergarten – with Little Eden, an outdoor club for under-5s – to degree programmes and employee development. There is a range of school activities including visits, activities and lesson plans, attracting over 50,000 children each year.

This is all based around the 'Core' which opened in 2005, providing the Eden Project with an education facility, including classrooms and exhibition spaces designed to help communicate Eden's central message about the relationship between people and plants.

The Eden degree programmes range from plant science to festival management and are developed with and awarded by the University of Plymouth, Falmouth University and Anglia Ruskin University. The degrees are overtly vocational with a focus on contemporary practice and take place in the unique learning environment of the Project's environment and collections, so providing a world-class study platform.

The project also offers short, intensive leadership programmes in business and creativity, as well as women's creative leadership retreats. These courses are designed for emerging leaders who want to be agents of change and a force for good in their businesses, organisations and communities. The learning is inspired by the project's founder, Tim Smit and the Eden environment – which acts as an inspirational classroom.

Outreach – Eden Project International

To spread the educational philosophy internationally, the Eden Project has set up Eden Project International to drive the establishment of other Edens around the world. These include three projects in China, a project on a former mine site in Australia, a social enterprise attraction in the earthquake zone of Christchurch, New Zealand and an outdoor classroom in the California redwoods, USA.

(Continued)

CONCEPTS AND DEFINITIONS

Confusion and lack of agreement remain over exactly how to conceptualise and define sustainability, sustainable development and sustainable tourism – indeed the terms are used rather loosely and interchangeably. Generally, the most commonly cited definition for, and accepted thinking about, sustainable development is from the 'Brundtland' World Commission on Environment and Development (1987). It defines sustainable development as 'a process that meets the needs of the present without compromising the ability of future generations to meet their own needs'. The Brundtland report neatly linked the concept of economic development with the notion of environmental and social sustainability, concluding that it is impossible to separate them. The Brundtland definition comprises three parts:

1. **Development** – here the issue is the compatibility of sustainable development with economic growth;

2. **Needs** – focusing around issues of equity and distribution of resources; and

3. **Future generations** – where the issue is that the income of future generations should not be less than that of current generations, and that current generations have a responsibility of stewardship for both social and natural 'capital'.

At the heart of the Brundtland Commission's concept of sustainable development was the apparent paradox between economic development and environmental quality. The Commission has been highly influential in subsequent thinking on sustainability and its report has shaped the agenda. It stated that sustainable development should address the maintenance of ecological integrity and diversity, meet basic human needs, address the needs of future generations, reduce injustice and increase self-determination. In stating this, the Commission laid the early bases for the UN MDGs.

There continues to be a debate over just what sustainable tourism encompasses and how it should be defined. For example, some commentators confuse it with ecotourism or nature-based tourism, or feel that it is only about small-scale, niche forms of tourism. This is not the case; sustainable tourism encompasses all forms of tourism and, indeed, is as much a process as an approach, as shown above. The UNWTO (2005) developed a set of paragraphs to act as a conceptual definition:

> Sustainable tourism development guidelines and management practices are applicable to all forms of tourism in all types of destinations ... Sustainable tourism principles

refer to the environmental, economic and socio-cultural aspects of tourism development and a suitable balance must be established between these three dimensions to
guarantee its long term sustainability ... Sustainable tourism development requires
the informed participation of all relevant stakeholders as well as strong political leadership to ensure wide participation and consensus building. Achieving sustainable
tourism is a continuous process and it requires constant monitoring of impacts, introducing the necessary preventive and/or corrective measures ... Sustainable tourism
should also maintain a high level of tourist satisfaction ... raising their awareness
about sustainability issues. (p. 11)

This definition can be shortened to 'Tourism that takes full account of its current and future
economic, social and environmental impacts, addressing the needs of visitors, the industry,
the environment and host communities' (p. 12).

The key sentiment here is collaboration between stakeholders (see UNWTO, 2010).
Saarinen (2006) draws heavily on the idea of carrying capacity for his elegantly simple
definition: 'The scale of tourism that can occur in a spatial unit without doing any
serious harm to the natural, economic and socio-cultural elements at destinations'
(p. 1126).

TYPES OF TOURISM SUSTAINABILITY

Hunter (1997) maps out four different types of tourism sustainability, showing that there
are different levels of both sustainable commitment and also permissible tourism development. His typology can be seen as a continuum, where tourism is strong at one end and
sustainability is strong at the other (Figure 6.3).

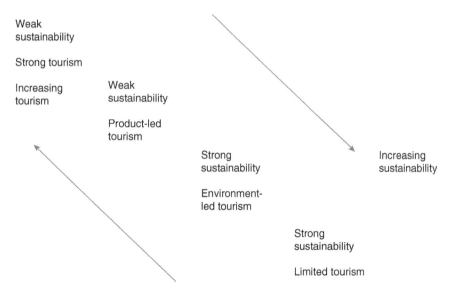

FIGURE 6.3 A continuum of sustainable tourism

Source: after Hunter, 1997

1. **Very weak sustainability/strong tourism imperative.** Here the emphasis is on satisfying the demands of the tourism sector and tourists, sometimes at the expense of destination resources. Often, this occurs in the early stages of tourism at a destination where growth is encouraged.

2. **Weak sustainability/product-led tourism.** This scenario is where tourism remains dominant and sustainability secondary to the development of new products, although the need for resource conservation and the management of growth is recognised.

3. **Strong sustainability/environment-led tourism.** This is a familiar type of sustainable tourism where environmental management lies at the heart of destination management and niche tourism products include ecotourism.

4. **Very strong sustainability/limited tourism.** Here, tourism activity is small in scale, and in places discouraged if it could cause environmental damage. The use of both renewable and non-renewable resources is limited through the use of environmental management techniques. The general view is against economic growth.

Clarke (1997) has classified approaches to sustainable tourism into four positions from early ideas of polar opposites, to mass tourism, moving to convergence where all tourism should be sustainable (Table 6.2). These approaches reflect the thinking of the times (Table 6.3). For example, the contemporary viewpoint is one of 'convergence', where sustainable tourism takes an interdisciplinary approach combining both natural and social science. This has replaced the earlier 'product-based' approach where sustainable tourism is seen as the polar opposite of mass tourism. The UNWTO is a strong advocate of the convergence position, stressing that sustainable development of tourism should apply to all forms of tourism, not simply special interest and nature-based forms of tourism, but also mass tourism. Here, Spanish destinations such as the Balearic Islands have led the way (see, for example, the Calvia strategy for integrated sustainable development at www.calvia.com). The Calvia example is interesting because it opens up the debate as to whether regeneration projects for 'tired' mass tourism destinations are as useful as, say, small-scale rural or green tourism projects. In the classic paper for this chapter, Hunter's (1997) pivotal contribution to the sustainability debate is selected.

TABLE 6.2 Sustainable tourism positions

Position	Features
Polar opposite	In the early 1990s, sustainable tourism was seen as the polar opposite of mass tourism, and different forms of alternative tourism, including ecotourism, were seen as the answer to sustainability.
Continuum	During the 1990s, the polar opposite position was rejected as being too simplistic and replaced by the idea of a continuum of tourism approaches from mass tourism to sustainable tourism.
Movement	Eventually, it was recognised that all forms of tourism should be sustainable, including the movement of mass tourism towards a sustainable model, rethinking scale and applying ideas to achieve this.
Convergence	All tourism should be sustainable – very much the goal of the UNWTO's sustainable tourism unit.

Source: Clarke, 1997

TABLE 6.3 The evolution of the sustainability concept in the tourism literature

Platform	Characteristics
Advocacy, 1950s and 1960s	Tourism seen uncritically as an economic benefit and solution to growth in the developing world and encouraged by international agencies.
Cautionary, 1970s and early 1980s	The negative effects of tourism development are exposed and the value of tourism begins to be questioned.
Adaptive, mid-1980s to early 1990s	Realisation that alternative forms of tourism can be developed and that sustainable tourism can be managed.
Knowledge based, mid-1990s onwards	Recognition that sustainability concepts need a factual or knowledge underpinning, including the development of sustainability indicators.

Source: Jafari, 1990

CLASSIC PAPER

Hunter, C. (1997) 'Sustainable tourism as an adaptive paradigm', *Annals of Tourism Research*, 24 (4): 850–67

Hunter's paper was influential in changing the thinking on sustainability, marking the turning point from the rather narrow 'product led' approach of tourism which saw sustainable tourism simply as another form of tourism at the other end of the spectrum from mass tourism. In doing so, his intention was to open up debate as to how sustainable tourism can be seen in a different light. Hunter's paper draws the tourism debate into the mainstream of sustainable development thinking, and he is critical of previous 'tourist-centric' approaches, which fail to encompass the wider and complex systems of which destinations are a part. As a result, he states that tourism can learn much from the wider literature on sustainable development. The main lesson of Hunter's paper is that 'Sustainable tourism should not be regarded as a rigid framework, but rather as an adaptive paradigm which legitimises a variety of approaches according to specific circumstances' (p. 851).

Hunter then goes on to outline a 'theoretical array' of sustainable tourism which allows for individual circumstances of particular destinations and situations, situations which allow for differences across host communities and their desire for participation, tourism demand, tourism supply and various environmental impacts. This allows for trade-offs between sustainability and development at different stages of destination evolution, but above all encourages informed and transparent decision-making. Hunter's array comprises four categories:

1. **Sustainable development through a tourism imperative.** This type of tourism is concerned with satisfying the needs of tourists and developers and does not prioritise environmental concerns or planning. Hunter suggests that this form of tourism could occur in three situations – (i) where tourism is a priority for poverty alleviation, (ii) where tourism replaces an environmentally degrading activity such as open cast mining, and (iii) where the development of tourism can prevent the development of other, environmentally degrading activities.

(Continued)

2. **Sustainable tourism through product-led tourism.** Here, the development of new products and expansion of the distribution channels through the use of intermediaries take precedence over environmental concerns except where they can be seen to sustain the development of tourism products. This situation can occur in well-developed tourism destinations where the economic benefits of tourism sustain the local community.

3. **Sustainable tourism through environment-led tourism.** Here concerns for the environment and host community move more to the centre of the stage in tourism development, often in areas where tourism is being newly introduced, or where tourism is highly dependent upon the quality of environmental resources to be successful.

4. **Sustainable development through neotenous tourism.** In this approach environmental concerns are paramount, and tourism may be actively discouraged or heavily managed through, say, the use of access permits. The exploration or involvement stage of the tourism area life cycle would be an appropriate stage for this type of development. Hunter debates this approach at length and voices concerns that such an 'extreme' management approach is open to criticism on the basis of elitism.

These four types of sustainable tourism development illustrate Hunter's notion of an 'adaptive paradigm capable of addressing widely different situations and articulating different goals in terms of utilisation of natural resources' (p. 864).

He ends with a challenging question: 'Who decides on the most appropriate approach for a destination?'

PRINCIPLES OF SUSTAINABLE TOURISM

Sustainable tourism began to gain considerable acceptance amongst the tourism community from the 1990s onwards (Butler, 2018). Since then, it has moved along the path from concepts, definitions and typologies towards elucidating the principles of sustainability and how it can be implemented.

The UNWTO (2005, p. 18) has been influential in shaping the sustainable tourism agenda. It states that sustainable tourism comprises two elements:

1. The ability of tourism to continue as an activity in the future, ensuring that the conditions are right for this; and

2. The ability of society and the environment to absorb and benefit from the impacts of tourism in a positive way.

They go on to outline that the principles of sustainable tourism are to:

*   Ensure that all forms of tourism are sustainable – sustainable tourism is not a discrete type of tourism; all tourism should be sustainable;
*   Take a long-term view;

- Take a 'whole of destination' approach – this ensures balanced development and that one element of the destination mix does not surge ahead of the others. It is important not to take a tourist-centric approach as was done in early debates on sustainable tourism;

- Balance global and local impacts – for example, local initiatives to reduce carbon emissions will have a positive global impact;

- Ensure tourists are aware of the issue and pursue sustainable consumption;

- Make optimal use of environmental resources;

- Develop cultural richness of the destination by respecting the socio-cultural integrity and authenticity of host communities;

- Conserve tangible and intangible heritage;

- Ensure that businesses are economically viable over the long term;

- Involve all stakeholders at the destination;

- Ensure community wellbeing such that communities benefit from tourism; and

- Provide a high-quality tourist experience to maintain high levels of tourist satisfaction.

There should be two additions to this list:

1. The need for tourism to transition towards a low-carbon economy and to minimise its carbon footprint; and

2. The need to incorporate values into sustainable tourism, covering areas of stewardship, professionalism and ethics (see, for example, www.besteducationnetwork.org).

By adhering to these principles, the aims of sustainable tourism can be articulated as triple bottom-line sustainability – environmental, social and economic (Figure 6.1). These aims are also about balancing the negative impacts of tourism with the positive benefits that it can bring, particularly to communities (through, say, poverty alleviation), economies and environmental protection. This delivers a strategy for long-term destination competitiveness along five key dimensions:

1. Influencing the location and form of tourism development through land use planning, design control, building codes and planning regulation;

2. Empowering local communities through ensuring participation in decision-making, building local tourism expertise and capacity through training, and ensuring the economic viability of local businesses through financial assistance where necessary;

3. Ensuring a high-quality tourist experience by managing the destination elements of safety, access, information and interpretation;

4. Conserving and managing destination heritage by site and visitor management techniques; and

5. Integrating environmental management into tourism facilities including energy, water and waste management, and strategies for minimising carbon emissions and a move towards a low-carbon economy.

The importance of delivering a high-quality experience is central to any sustainable tourism strategy. This dimension of visitor fulfilment must not be neglected in any consideration of sustainable tourism. As the sector and the activity of tourism have matured, the market has become experienced and sensitised to the potential damaging effects of tourism. As a result, the tourism market now is concerned for the social and environmental wellbeing of destinations, and particularly where this impacts directly upon their own experience. This is compounded by the fact that tourists are increasingly attracted to unique and special places which are vulnerable to visitation and their authenticity and integrity are placed at risk. As a result of these issues, and the growing awareness of climate change, tourists are expressing concern about their own actions of, say, flying long haul, and are prepared to pay more for the experience, whether it be through increased charges, taxes or carbon offsetting. Here, British Airways' 'One Destination' responsible air travel programme recognises that tourists need to be 'confident that together we are acting responsibly to take care of the world we live in' (www.britishairways.com/en-gb/information/about-ba/responsible-flying). The issue here is one of visitor education and awareness to ensure that decisions are taken on a reasoned basis. Of course, codes of conduct for visitors and guidelines for ethical behaviour play an important role here (see, for example, the WWF codes of conduct for the Mediterranean and also for Arctic tourists – https://arcticwwf.org/newsroom/publications/code-of-conduct-for-arctic-tourists; and guidelines for tourists to Africa at www.roveafrica.net, or the Middle East at www.kasbahdutoubkal.com). Another initiative is 'clean up tourism', based on the notion of 'enhancive sustainability' where the aim is to leave the destination in a better state than when the tourist arrived (see, for example, initiatives for the Nile and Botswana).

MINI CASE STUDY 6.2

Biosphere Expeditions

Introduction

As the concept of sustainable tourism has taken hold, specific products have been developed to cater for the market. A standout example here is Biosphere Expeditions, a tour organiser with impeccable environmental and social credentials. The company claims to be:

Arabian oryx in the Dubai Desert Conservation Reserve, UAE

Source: 'Gemsboks (Oryx gazella)' by berniedup is licensed under CC BY-SA 2.0

an award-winning, non-profit-making organisation offering hands-on conservation volunteer work expeditions as an adventure …
Biosphere Expeditions bridges the gap between scientists at the forefront of conservation work in need of funds and helpers, and enthusiastic laypeople, who in their holiday time, through their hands-on assistance and with their expedition contribution want to support them.

Biosphere Expeditions aims to deliver a worthwhile volunteering experience that achieves tangible benefits. It counsels its customers against some volunteer-focused companies that are profit driven and do little for local wildlife or communities. The organisation aims to bridge the gap between the voluntourist and scientists and conservationists working in remote areas trying to study and manage the most endangered species.

Biosphere Expeditions Products

Examples of the products are:

- Study of Arabian oryx, Gordon's wildcat and other iconic desert species in the Dubai Desert Conservation Reserve, UAE;

- Survey of whales, dolphins and turtles around the Azores Archipelago;

- Direct conservation action on critically endangered leatherback turtles in Costa Rica;

- Conservation of wolves in Lower Saxony, northern Germany;

- Big Five and African biodiversity protection in the Maasai Mara, Kenya;

- African biodiversity survey of cats, elephants, primates and others in Malawi;

- Diving expedition studying coral reefs and whale sharks of the Maldives;

- Survey of leopards, caracals and Cape biodiversity in the fynbos Cape mountains, UNESCO World Heritage Site, South Africa;

- Monitoring brown bear in the woodlands of Dalarna province, Sweden;

- Conservation of elephants in the Himalayan foothills, northern Thailand; and

- Survey of snow leopards in the Tien Shan mountains, Kyrgyzstan.

Operations

The organisation is now ramping up its sustainability agenda, with guidelines on activism and behaviour change to reduce climate change and develop a policy on flying. It has policies on offsetting and carbon emissions. It also has a sponsorship policy, refusing to take donations from organisations with services or products that come with a persistent and large-scale negative impact on the environment, society or who behave unethically. Biosphere Expeditions produces an expedition report from each trip which is used by scientists and conservationists. The organisation also works closely with local communities, providing them with opportunities to work on the project.

Discussion Questions

1. In what ways do you think voluntourism can be abused?
2. Visit the Biosphere Expeditions website and examine their pages on activism and behaving 'green'. Is this an example of 'mission drift' or are they right to diversify into this area?
3. Is it risky to allow 'amateurs' to get involved in scientific projects?

Source: www.biosphere-expeditions.org

IMPLEMENTATION OF SUSTAINABILITY

The concept of sustainable tourism is intuitively appealing but one that is more difficult to implement in practice. In part, this is because tourism is part of complex social and environmental systems. This means that any initiatives to implement sustainable tourism development have to recognise that tourism is just one part of these complex systems and so has to 'adapt' as such. The earlier approaches to address sustainable tourism through a 'tourism-centric' approach were not successful because they failed to address this issue and saw tourism as separate. One feature of the implementation of sustainability in the tourism sector has been the degree of voluntary and industry-led initiatives, including the concept of certification which acts to quality assure tourism businesses. These certification schemes audit the environmental performance of tourism organisations, assess product quality and assess corporate social responsibility initiatives. Examples include Green Globe (www.greenglobe.com), Ecotel for accommodation operators, the UNEP Green passport (www.unep.fr/greenpassport), the Rainforest Alliance (www.rainforest-alliance.org) and Australia's Eco Certification programme (www.ecotourism.org.au). In part, these initiatives were started to avoid strong government involvement and regulation in tourism and to some extent they have succeeded. They have also shown that a strong business case can be made for sustainability. Table 6.4 lists the main instruments that can be used to implement the sustainable development of tourism.

Here, there are two general principles that have to be adhered to in the implementation of sustainable tourism:

1.   Recognise that it is the local, or destination, level where initiatives will be the most effective; and

2.   Initiatives will only be effective if all destination stakeholders are involved. Table 6.5 maps the stakeholders involved in many destinations.

TABLE 6.4   Instruments of tourism sustainability

Type of Instrument	Examples
Command and control	Legislation regulation and licensing
	Land use planning and development control
Voluntary instruments	Certification schemes and self-declarations
Private sector	Guidelines and codes of conduct
	Reporting and auditing
	Certification and ecolabels
	Awards
	Private sector policies and associations
Economic instruments	Taxes and charges – particularly through the 'polluter pays' principle
	Financial agreements and incentives

Type of Instrument	Examples
Supporting instruments	Infrastructure provision and management
	Capacity building
	Marketing and information services
Measurement and monitoring instruments	Indicators
	Benchmarking
	Carrying capacity

Source: UNWTO, 2005

TABLE 6.5   Stakeholder mapping for sustainability

Sector	Stakeholders
Public	Local authorities and officials
	National, regional and local agencies and officials
	Management agencies for cultural and natural heritage
Private sector companies – here the issues are not simply profit but also public image and corporate social responsibility and their impact upon the environment	Intermediaries
	Accommodation, food and beverage
	Transportation
	Producers and suppliers
	Trade organisation and chambers of trade
NGOs	Environmental and conservation groups
	Community development groups
Communities, who are concerned to protect their quality of life	Local environmental and conservation groups
	Property owners
	Consumer associations
Tourists are seeking quality experiences, but also safe environments and reassurance about destination stewardship	Tourists
	Tourism pressure groups

Source: UNWTO, 2005

THE ROLE OF GOVERNMENT IN IMPLEMENTING SUSTAINABLE TOURISM

Traditionally, government has taken a leading role in implementing sustainable tourism development, although of course it is the responsibility of all stakeholders to ensure sustainability. The public sector, particularly at the local level, is critical to the coordination, regulation and facilitation of sustainable tourism. In tourism, the role of government is important because:

- The sector is fragmented and a coordination role is needed;
- The sector lacks leadership and this is a role that government can play;

- There is often a need for some public funding of sustainability initiatives, for example in terms of overseeing eco labelling as with the European Commission's eco labelling scheme (http://ec.europa.eu/ecat/hotels-campsites/en);

- Many vulnerable elements of the destination – coasts, wetlands, small islands or the built heritage – are in public ownership (see, for example, the UN's COAST initiative); and

- Government has the mandate to regulate, plan and legislate.

Government was slow to act in addressing sustainable development in tourism until the 1992 UN Earth Summit in Rio. A key outcome from Rio was Agenda 21, signed by over 180 governments (www.un.org/esa/sustdev/agenda21.htm). Agenda 21 was a commitment on the part of governments to address the issue of development and the environment across a range of activities. For tourism, an important feature of Agenda 21 is the focus on implementation at the local destination level, through local government, with international coordination of initiatives provided by the Earth Council Alliance (www.earthcouncilal-liance.org). Although criticised for potentially curtailing individual choices, the principles of Agenda 21 were re-affirmed at Rio+20. Agenda 21 reflects contemporary thinking on sustainable development in two ways:

1. Whilst tourism is the focus of many Agenda 21 plans in, for example, resorts, small islands and heritage towns, tourism also forms an integral part of other Agenda 21 initiatives stressing the need for 'whole of destination' management.

2. Projects involve not only government but also NGOs (such as the WWF) and the private sector stressing the need for all stakeholders to be involved, as shown in the major case study at the end of this chapter.

More recently, the private sector, in the shape of large multinational companies, has taken the lead in terms of sustainability. These companies include Accor, Tui, P&O and Whitbread, but smaller family-run companies are also leading on sustainable initiatives.

FOCUS ON EMPLOYABILITY

How Can Human Resources Contribute to Sustainability?

The ILO's concept of 'decent' jobs has been cited as a way for tourism to contribute to sustainability across the sector, but in fact, human resources (HR) can play a wider role in promoting sustainability in tourism organisations. When an organisation decides to embrace sustainability in its operations, it is essential to ensure that everyone is on board, from the CEO to the employees. Here the role of HR is key. For example, recruitment can be used as a way to change culture and this can then be followed up through communication and training in sustainable practices in the workplace, such as eliminating paper and plastic from offices, reducing flying and increasing recycling. Sustainability can be integrated into HR performance reviews linked to clear incentives and rewards such as offering volunteering opportunities. In this way, HR acts as an architect of culture change across the organisation and enables strategic alignment of the organisation's work with sustainable values.

CONTEMPORARY TOOLS OF SUSTAINABLE TOURISM
Visitor management and interpretation

Sustainable tourism demands not only that the visitor receives a satisfying and high-quality experience but also that the destination is sustainable. These twin objectives of sustainable tourism can be achieved if innovative and effective tools of sustainable tourism are utilised. One such approach is the application of visitor management techniques to tourism. Visitor management is a tool of sustainable tourism as it ensures that the increasingly experienced and discerning 'new tourist' does indeed receive a high-quality experience, while also sustaining the destination for future generations (Harrison, 1994; UNWTO, 2011).

Visitor management is an approach that was developed in natural areas, particularly national parks and sensitive natural reserves, where there was a need to manage visitation. Here, the real innovation of visitor management approaches is the focus on positive planning and provision rather than negative restrictions and prohibition. In so doing, visitor management provides a true focus on the visitor and recognises that each visitor is different, bringing to a destination or site his or her own prejudices, needs, preferences and ignorances. After all, a group of teenage friends visiting a destination will be seeking very different benefits from, say, a family group.

The objectives of visitor management are therefore transparent and straightforward. On the part of the visitor, it:

- Enhances the visit experience;
- Increases the chances of repeat visitation;
- Encourages higher spending; and
- Induces greater sympathy for the cause of, say, wildlife conservation or historic preservation at a destination.

At the same time, visitor management provides a flow of benefits to the destination:

- It allows visits to be spread in both space and time.
- It encourages a longer length of stay (or dwell time).
- It reduces the environmental impact of visitation through effective management.
- There is increasing evidence that visitor management, and particularly interpretation techniques, foster a sense of civic pride and sense of ownership amongst the host community.
- It creates revenue streams that can be used for conservation (the International Union for the Conservation of Nature (IUCN) estimates that 80 per cent of national parks are under-funded worldwide – www.iucn.org). This can be done through a variety of mechanisms:
  o Government funding;
  o Visitor revenue – entrance fees, parking, special events, donations and visitor payback;
  o Business revenue – concession fees (accommodation, equipment rental, food and beverage, retail); and
  o Other forms of revenue – licensing images, publications.

To be effective, visitor management should be integrated into the management of every destination but to date it tends to be viewed as an approach that can be added in at the end. In one sense, this recognises the lack of exposure to the technique on behalf of tourism planners and consultants. Visitor management is very much a practitioner-based approach with few manuals of good practice or well-documented case studies of its positive effects. And yet there are a number of leading attraction companies – such as the Disney Corporation – which are very skilled in the art.

Figure 6.4 shows the outline approach that may be adopted for visitor management of a site, destination or region. For a museum, for example, the critical unit will be the rooms housing the displays and the pathways between them. The technique will ensure visitors move freely between each room and get the best out of the experience. However, for a theme park it will be the themed areas and their links that form the unit of analysis, while for a region the approach will be based on sub-areas or resorts.

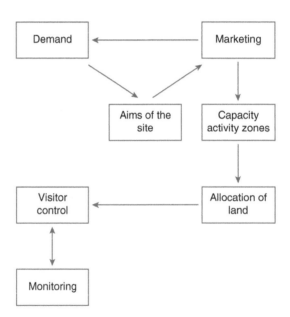

FIGURE 6.4   A model of visitor management

Approaching visitor management

Destination objectives

Determination of objectives is critical for the sustainable management of any destination. The simple question to be asked is – why do we want to attract visitors to this destination? Of course, the obvious answer may be an economic one of profit or return on investment. Other reasons, however, are also possible, including educational reasons (for a wildlife reserve, say) or propaganda (as in show sites in socialist republics). The visitor management process demands that the destination is very clear on these objectives since they drive the whole management process.

Destination demand and marketing

A second key variable is demand – the profile and numbers of visitors attracted to the destination. It is important that marketing communicates clearly the objectives to ensure that appropriate types of visitor are attracted. The most common management problems occur when the wrong type of visitor is attracted to a destination. If these problems do arise, then it is the role of marketing constantly to adjust the visitor profile to the objectives of the destination. This can be done in subtle ways such as through the choice of merchandising in the shops, the type and price of food and beverage in the cafés, or communication strategies adopted in the marketing campaign and social media.

Capacity and activity zones

At this stage of the visitor management process, decisions are taken as to the intensity of visitation at each part of the destination, and also the type of activity to be scheduled there. For greenfield sites, the planner has a relatively free hand, but for sites such as museums or historic houses then it is probable that the use of rooms and displays will be fixed. Nonetheless, there are two important principles involved at this stage:

1. **Determination of capacity.** Here, planners have to determine the volume of visitors that can be sustained in each part of the site. The key question is then: do you manage a site for its peak capacity, or a percentage of that capacity?

2. **Avoidance of conflicting uses in the same area.** For example, the use of motorised vehicles or trail bikes where children are likely to congregate, or allowing motorboats and bathing in the same area of water are both examples of conflicting uses and should be avoided.

Visitor control

To achieve a sustainable destination, it is important to ensure that visitors are managed in such a way as to ensure capacity levels in each area are not exceeded, and therefore that both the quality of the experience and integrity of the destination are maintained. Influencing visitor movement and behaviour is a subtle science and can be seen as a selection from a menu of options along a continuum from hard management to soft management (Table 6.6):

TABLE 6.6   Visitor management options

Hard management	Soft management
Negative signing	Interpretation, guiding and use of information on mobile devices
Fencing	Marketing
Charging	Landscaping and planning
Zoning	Signing
Security measures	Location of facilities

- Hard visitor management can be problematic as neither destination manager nor visitor is satisfied because both recognise the severity of the measures adopted. There are occasions, however, where hard management is inevitable. Guarding valuable sites, or where there is potential danger to visitors, are cases in point.

- Soft management, on the other hand, is perhaps the most effective form of visitor management. The visitor is influenced without knowing it and the manager is effective because the destination is running smoothly. There are many well-known examples of soft management. In theme parks where one area is over capacity and another is under capacity, managers assemble a cast of their characters playing in a band and walk them through the busy area. Visitors all follow and are led into the under-used area – perfect and unobtrusive visitor control. At sites where there are 'pinch points' (areas where too many visitors congregate in small areas, preventing an even flow around the site), it is common to provide a commentary of the object or display in question. Once the commentary is complete and begins again, visitors naturally move on to the next display. Interpretation and information are increasingly favoured approaches. Here, the destination is displayed to the visitor using a variety of techniques such as guiding, trails, apps on mobile devices and signboards.

Monitoring

There is no point in developing sophisticated visitor management approaches without a means of monitoring their success. There are a variety of options here:

- A formal questionnaire with the visitor to elicit their level of enjoyment;
- Monitoring of social media;
- The more cost-effective approach of debriefing of destination staff on a regular basis to check all is well; or
- Many of the larger theme parks have constant monitoring through devices including electronic eyes and turnstiles.

There is much to be said for the technique of visitor management as a contemporary tool of sustainable tourism to deliver many of the benefits sought by both visitor and destination alike. It neatly ties together the nature of the destination, elements of the new demand and approaches to both planning and marketing at the destination level.

However, the approach could be seen as controversial and does raise a number of important questions:

- Is there a danger of becoming too scientific and organised in the development of tourist destinations and thereby losing some of the magic?
- Are techniques such as interpretation taking away the spontaneity and moment of discovery if everything is labelled and sanitised?
- Is the marketing and management of destinations becoming too slick?
- Are some places just too 'busy' with information, signboards and hi-tech interpretive equipment?
- Who decides on the information to be given or displayed to the visitor and is this 'gatekeeper' role one that we can safely entrust to planners and interpreters, or should the local community be more involved?

FOCUS ON TECHNOLOGY

Wildlife Viewing Apps

It is clear that technology is opening new horizons in visitor management, and the use of apps not only to enhance the experience, but also to educate and interpret is a growing trend. One area receiving attention and delivering sustainability is wildlife viewing apps which allow tourists to use a smartphone to both locate and identify wildlife, flora and other features. The apps are really focused on identification but some of them also allow tourists to upload photographs, share sightings with others on social media, upload sightings to help with conservation and wildlife research, download guides before the trip and also report any abuse such as poaching. These apps have become particularly popular in the safari sector. Some of the popular apps include:

- Africa: Live App
- African Safari Wildlife Guide
- Audubon African Wildlife
- eTrees
- Latest Kruger Sightings
- ParkSpotter Africa
- Roberts Multimedia Birds of SA
- Sasol eBirds of Southern Africa
- Snakes of Southern Africa
- The David Sheldrick Wildlife Trust
- The Kingdon Guide to African Mammals
- Tracking the Wild
- Where is the Wildlife

SUSTAINABLE TOURISM INDICATORS

A vital, but previously neglected, issue in terms of sustainable tourism is that of measurement and the development of indicators of sustainability. Clearly, it has to be possible to measure and monitor the degree of sustainability at the destination, by the tourists themselves and in the enterprises (see Agyeiwaah et al., 2017 for an account of indicators for enterprises). Delivery of accurate information for decision-makers is therefore critical and the UNWTO is developing an international network of sustainable 'tourism observatories' to gather and report sustainability data. Indicators are the key building blocks and tools for developing sustainable tourism. Quite simply, by developing credible indicators of sustainability and monitoring them on a regular basis, destinations receive early warning of potential problems and can take remedial action (Figure 6.5). The UNWTO (2004) defines sustainability indicators as 'Information sets which are formally selected for a regular use to measure changes in key assets and issues of tourism destinations and sites' (p. 5).

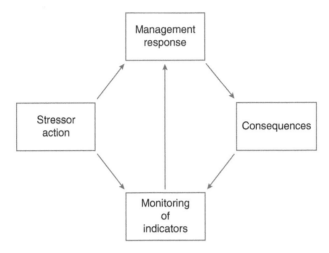

FIGURE 6.5 The role of indicators in monitoring sustainability

Source: Miller and Twining-Ward, 2005

Indicators can be used to measure:

- Changes in tourism at the destination itself;
- Changes in the external environment which impact upon the destination; and
- Impacts caused by tourism at the destination.

To be effective, indicators must be readily accessible and relatively straightforward to measure – the UNWTO is integrating indicators with other forms of data collection to provide an international benchmark; they must be relevant and responsive to changes in the tourism system and they must be credible. Table 6.7 provides a list of commonly used indicators.

Here there a number of issues to be considered. Firstly, how the indicators are selected to be representative of destination sustainability – and this is not straightforward. Increasingly, indicators are chosen with the agreement of the host community at the destination and, rather than treating indicators as simple thresholds to trigger action, decisions are taken as to an 'acceptable range' for each indicator and only when measurements fall outside that range is action needed. Secondly, it is important to consider how these indicators will be utilised by managers. Often a traffic light system is used: green – everything is running well; amber – the indicator is showing that intervention may be needed; and red – the indicator shows that remedial action is needed to bring the destination back on track. This 'early warning' system is effective as it allows managers to intervene before the problem has become too severe. This approach demands stability and consistency in measurement and that the results are clearly communicated to managers on a regular basis. One of the first approaches to achieve this was the TOMM planning approach for Kangaroo Island in South Australia. Here a major research exercise identified the key indicators, the community was consulted as to the levels of 'acceptable change' that they would tolerate in terms of tourism, and the indicators were monitored on a regular basis and communicated to the community and managers.

TABLE 6.7 Types of sustainability indicators

Type of measurement	Indicator
Quantitative	Data – number of tourists, bed nights, carbon emissions
	Ratios – ratio of tourists to residents
	Percentages – occupancy levels, trained staff, change in tourist numbers
Qualitative	Category indices – level of protection
	Normative indicators – existence of recycling plan, yes or no
	Nominal indicators – ecolabelling, certification
	Opinion-based indicators – level of satisfaction of tourists, residents' tolerance of tourists

Source: UNWTO, 2004

It is possible to use existing data as indicators and so reduce the cost of collecting data, but many destinations have now embarked on comprehensive research exercises for indicators (www.sectur.gob.mx). Indicators can also be envisaged at different levels and therefore will nest. For example, national levels of indicators will detect broad levels of change in, say, tourism employment; at the regional level, finer-grained indicators can be used for reliable planning whilst, at the local level, specific indicators can be tailored for destinations, sites or companies.

Good tourism sustainability indicators will:

- Facilitate better decision-making;
- Involve the host community;
- Identify emerging issues at the destination;
- Identify tourism impacts;
- Facilitate performance measurement of plans or strategies by providing KPIs and clarity;
- Reduce the risk of poor decisions;
- Allow for greater accountability;
- Facilitate constant monitoring; and
- Provide a catalyst for future action.

Of course, there are some problems associated with the development of indicators of sustainability. These include: lack of consistency in measurement between different destinations and poor coordination across different agencies; the fact that there may be gaps in the indicators and key elements of sustainability are missed; many destinations do not have the qualified staff – or the budget – to monitor indicators; and, finally, indicators are often not collected nor communicated to encourage effective decision-making.

SUMMARY

This chapter has analysed the deceptively simple concept of sustainable tourism. The chapter began by outlining how the idea of sustainable development has evolved and the various important milestones along the way. It showed that tourism came late to the debate, not really being seen as significant until the Rio Earth Summit. The chapter then discussed the various approaches to defining sustainable development and sustainable tourism, concluding that many of the terms are used loosely and that the UNWTO has moved the debate forward with a set of statements and definitions. The tourism community has adopted a range of underpinning principles of sustainability, including the idea of triple bottom-line sustainability with equal consideration of the environment, the economy and the community. It has been shown that different types of sustainable tourism approaches can be identified, ranging from the early approach where sustainable tourism was seen as the polar opposite of mass tourism, to the contemporary approach of 'convergence' where all forms of tourism should transition to being sustainable. Hunter's 'classic paper' showed how he contributed to this debate. Finally, the chapter outlined contemporary approaches to implementing sustainability, highlighting the significance of managing visitors and developing a system of indicators to warn against potential problems at the destination.

DISCUSSION QUESTIONS

1. Why is sustainable tourism so difficult to define?

2. Table 6.2 provides a range of positions that have been taken with regard to sustainable tourism. Do you agree that the tourism sector has now embraced the idea of the final position of 'convergence'?

3. Table 6.4 outlines the main instruments of sustainable tourism development. Match each one with an example and make a judgement as to which instruments are the most effective.

4. Taking a destination with which you are familiar, map out up to 20 indicators of sustainability that you feel would accurately reflect the character of the destination. How easy would these be to measure?

5. Take a tourist site with which you are familiar – such as a theme park or museum – and revisit it with the eyes of a visitor manager. Make your own evaluation – does the site work in terms of visitor movement and rhythms, is the experience enhanced and did you enjoy it?

ANNOTATED FURTHER READING

Butler, R. (2018) 'Sustainability and resilience: two sides of the same coin?' in C. Cooper, S. Volo, W.C. Gartner and N. Scott (eds), *The Sage Handbook of Tourism Management: Theories, Concepts and Disciplinary Approaches to Tourism*. London: Sage. pp. 407–21.

Lively and informative account of sustainability and resilience.

Fennell, D. and Cooper, C. (2020) *Sustainable Tourism*. Bristol: Channel View.

Contemporary and all-embracing text on sustainable tourism.

Hall, C.M., Prayag, G. and Amore, A. (2018) *Tourism and Resilience*. Bristol: Channel View.

Excellent advanced text on tourism and resilience.

Krippendorf, J. (1987) *The Holidaymakers: Understanding the Impact of Leisure and Travel*. Oxford: Butterworth-Heinemann.

One of the first books to map out a sustainable tourism agenda.

Miller, G. and Twining-Ward, L. (2005) *Monitoring for a Sustainable Tourism Transition: The Challenge of Developing and Using Indicators*. Wallingford: CABI.

Comprehensive approach to sustainable tourism indicators.

REFERENCES CITED

Agyeiwaah, E., McKercher, B. and Suntikul, W. (2017) 'Identifying core indicators of sustainable tourism: a path forward', *Tourism Management Perspectives*, 24: 26–33.

Buckley, R. (2012) 'Sustainable tourism: research and reality', *Annals of Tourism Research*, 39 (2): 528–46.

Butler, R. (2018) 'Sustainability and resilience: two sides of the same coin?' in C. Cooper, S. Volo, W.C. Gartner and N. Scott (eds), *The Sage Handbook of Tourism Management: Theories, Concepts and Disciplinary Approaches to Tourism*. London: Sage. pp. 407–21.

Clarke, J. (1997) 'A framework of approaches to sustainable tourism', *Journal of Sustainable Tourism*, 5 (3): 224–33.

Fayos Sola, E. and Cooper, C. (2019) *The Future of Tourism: Innovation and Sustainability*. Cham: Springer.

Fennell, D.A. and Cooper, C. (2020) *Sustainable Tourism*. Bristol: Channel View.

Hall, C.M., Prayag, G. and Amore, A. (2018) *Tourism and Resilience*. Bristol: Channel View.

Harrison, R. (1994) *A Manual of Heritage Management*. Oxford: Butterworth-Heinemann.

Higgins-Desbiolles, F. (2018) 'Sustainable tourism: sustaining tourism or something more?' *Tourism Management Perspectives*, 25: 157–60.

Hunter, C. (1997) 'Sustainable tourism as an adaptive paradigm', *Annals of Tourism Research*, 24 (4): 850–67.

Jafari, J. (1990) 'Research and scholarship: the basis of tourism education', *Journal of Tourism Studies*, 1 (1): 33–41.

Krippendorf, J. (1982) 'Towards new tourism policies: the importance of environmental and sociocultural factors', *Tourism Management*, September: 135–48.

Miller, G. and Twining-Ward, L. (2005) *Monitoring for a Sustainable Tourism Transition: The Challenge of Developing and Using Indicators*. Wallingford: CABI.

Muller, H. (1994) 'The thorny path to sustainable tourism development', *Journal of Sustainable Tourism*, 2 (2): 131–6.

Saarinen, J. (2006) 'Traditions of sustainability in tourism studies', *Annals of Tourism Research*, 33 (4): 1121–40.

Saarinen, J., Rogerson, C.M. and Manwa, H. (2012) *Tourism and the Millennium Development Goals: Tourism, Local Communities and Development*. London: Routledge.

UNWTO (2004) *Indicators of Sustainable Tourism*. Madrid: UNWTO.

UNWTO (2005) *Making Tourism More Sustainable: A Guide for Policy Makers*. Madrid: UNWTO.

UNWTO (2010) *Joining Forces: Collaboration Processes for Sustainable and Competitive Tourism*. Madrid: UNWTO.

UNWTO (2011) *Communicating Heritage: A Handbook for the Tourism Sector*. Madrid: UNWTO.

World Commission on Environment and Development (1987) *Our Common Future*. Oxford: Oxford University Press.

MAJOR CASE STUDY 6.1

The Roatan Marine Park, Honduras

A healthy coral reef, Honduras

Source: ©blue-sea.cz/Shutterstock.com

Introduction

This case study showcases the sustainability initiatives of a small voluntary organisation in Honduras. The case shows how a focused set of programmes can revitalise previously degraded reef environments.

The case is based on Roatan, the largest of the Honduras Bay of Islands. It is a marine tourism destination well known for its reef and inner lagoon. The island sits on the exposed coral reef; it is quite remote and so development is on a small scale. However, even on this scale, tourism development, deforestation and overfishing have begun to severely damage the reef.

The RMP

In response, the Roatan Marine Park (RMP) was created in 2005 by a consortium of dive operators and local businesses and was given official non-governmental organisation status in 2008 by the Honduras government. The RMP is a not-for-profit, community-based organisation with the aim of halting the reef degradation in the Sandy Bay-West End Marine Reserve (SBWEMR) – the reserve was given marine protected area status in 1988.

Since its establishment in 2005, the RMP has expanded the scope of its environmental efforts through the addition of other programmes to protect Roatan's natural resources, including patrols and infrastructure, education, conservation and public awareness; as well as to prevent over-exploitation through unsustainable fishing practices.

Funding of the RMP comes from a variety of sources:

- Sale of merchandise;
- Dive equipment rentals;
- The RMP voluntary 'user fee';
- Donations; and
- Grants from organisations such as WWF, USAID, PADI Project AWARE.

RMP Programmes

The programmes of the RMP can be grouped into four main categories:

Research

Through the Roatan Institute of Marine Science, research is conducted to help conserve the island's natural resources. The Institute is also a teaching institution and receives visits from other universities and colleges. The research done by the institute is a fundamental basis for conserving the reef, as well as informing the education programmes undertaken by the RMP.

Community Development

The RMP has prioritised 'bottom up' community development programmes. These represent an innovative approach to alternative livelihoods by offering alternative sources of income to local communities to offset their dependence upon extracting Roatan's natural resources. This includes three programmes:

1. **Protect our Pride (POP)** trains locals to be dive professionals, allowing them to earn an income while protecting the reef and sharing their knowledge with the rest of the community.
2. **The Corozal Association of Apicultural Producers** is a programme which supports local communities through the production and sale of honey products. This has created an alternative livelihood which does not depend on illegal fishing practices or placing pressure on the reef. The project funds the local production of honey, equipment, building structures and training.
3. **Community outreach**, which focuses on promoting the Bay Islands Sustainable Sea Food Guide at local restaurants and hotels.

Education

The RMP recognises that education is the key to changing behaviours. It has a schools programme which reaches over 3000 children every year. It focuses on visiting schools, organising beach clean-ups and

(Continued)

re-planting mangroves. In terms of the mangroves, the children learn how to manage and restore these fragile environments. The mangroves are essential to the reef ecosystem. The Junior Park Ranger and other programmes engage young people to interact with and protect the reef and the island's natural resources. The RMP also works with the private sector to educate and engage in conservation practices, including reduction of single use plastic by using alternatives such as paper cups and paper straws. Education also includes a set of RMP rules and regulations and guidelines on reef etiquette which are intended to conserve the reef for the future.

Marine Infrastructure

The commercial development of tourism around the island has increased the incidence of mechanical damage to the reef through anchoring on the reef and collision of vessels. The RMP's marine infrastructure programme is a community service provided to all boat owners. It includes the following:

- Over 230 dive and snorkel moorings reduce damage caused by anchoring on the reef and fuel being dumped directly on these ecosystems.
- The RMP's 80 channel markers demarcate the exit and entry points of the majority of the traffic areas around Roatan, increasing the safety of

navigating through Roatan's narrow channels and reducing the occurrence of collisions.

- The RMP patrol programme helps to enforce Honduran environmental laws, regulations and best practices. There are five patrol boats, each manned by an RMP ranger and two members of the Honduran Navy. The patrols keep the reef healthy by protecting key species such as corals, turtles, sharks, conch, lobster and parrot fish.

Impact of the RMP Programmes

The implementation of the RMP's focused set of programmes has led to divers reporting an increase in sightings of turtle, conch and lobster and to one of the highest indicators of a 'healthy reef' in the region.

Discussion Questions

1. The RMP focuses on education – do you feel this should be extended to educating tourists and the growing numbers of cruise visitors?
2. How effective is the alternative livelihoods programme by the RMP, do you think?
3. Is it right that a consortium of dive operators and businesses should set up the RMP, or is it the role of government?

Source: www.roatanmarinepark.org

PART 3
TOURISM SECTOR ESSENTIALS

This part of the book considers the tourism sector, made up of both private and public organisations. The private sector includes attractions, hospitality, transportation and intermediaries – tour operators and travel agents. But it is important not to neglect governments as they have a major stake in tourism in most destinations, not only in terms of planning and regulation, but often they own many key attractions such as coastlines, national parks and the built heritage.

Tourism is often described as one of the world's largest industries, as has already been stated, with large figures quoted for the value of the tourism industry and the numbers it employs. The tourism sector sprawls across many parts of the economy, and commentators agree that it does not form a coherent industry from an economic point of view. This is because many industries are involved such that tourism is in fact only partially an industry as governments, communities and others are involved in delivering the product.

Together, tourism businesses form the contemporary tourism sector, the machinery of tourism production which manipulates and permits the tourist experience to happen. As shown in the following chapters, in recent years the sector has become global in scale and restructured in response to technology, changing consumer demand, increasing concentration in the industry, and the demands of flexible specialisation which creates integrated networks of supply and destinations. Technology, in particular, has had a major impact upon tourism businesses, particularly intermediaries, whilst the carbon debate and 'wild card' events such as terrroism attacks and natural disasters have impacted upon the sector.

This part of the book also shows that the tourism industry is highly diverse and fragmented and made up predominantly of small businesses and entrepreneurs. This has implications for the level of management competence in tourism as well as for the ability of the sector to both innovate and invest in new products and ideas.

7

VISITOR ATTRACTIONS AND EVENTS

LEARNING OUTCOMES

This chapter considers visitor attractions and events as the key element of the destination, motivating the visit and energising the total tourism system. The chapter outlines approaches to defining and classifying attractions and events before considering how they are managed and what their future holds. The chapter is designed to provide you with:

- an awareness of the issues surrounding definitions of visitor attractions and events;

- an understanding of the various approaches available to classify visitor attractions and events;

- an appreciation of the economics of visitor attractions;

- an understanding of the key management issues and approaches for visitor attractions; and

- insights into the future of visitor attractions and events.

INTRODUCTION

Visitor attractions and events are the raison d'être for tourism; they generate the visit, give rise to excursion circuits and create an industry of their own. As such they are the main motivator for travel, energising the tourism system and providing tourists with the reason to visit a destination. Indeed, such is the power of attractions that they can transform a destination from the mundane to the spectacular as, for example, with Dubai. Clare Gunn (1972) puts it well, describing attractions as 'lodestones for pleasure'.

It is therefore important from the outset to understand the distinction between visitor attractions, the motivators of the visit, and support services, such as accommodation, transport and retail, that facilitate the visit. There are, of course, exceptions to this rule in destinations such as Las Vegas where support services such as hospitality are an integral part of the attraction in their large themed casinos. Both visitor attractions and events appeal to different visitor audiences from international and domestic tourists, through to day visitors, local residents and those visiting friends and relatives.

Visitor attractions have a long history, featuring strongly in grand tour itineraries, for example. They have developed hand-in-hand with transportation, particularly since the advent of the railway in the mid-nineteenth century and then the boom in tourism demand following the Second World War, when purpose-built attractions were further developed and grew. This long pedigree has left a heritage of custom and practice in managing visitor attractions that has survived from the past and is still in use today.

DEFINING VISITOR ATTRACTIONS

Definitions of visitor attractions are difficult because the environment within which they operate is so dynamic in terms of both the market and product innovation – a definition today may seem dated in ten years' time (Leask, 2010). It is nonetheless important to define attractions for statistical measurement purposes and to allow comparison of, say, performance. In part, the lack of an accepted definition is due to the fact that research into attractions and their management is not as developed as in other parts of tourism. This makes the comparison of visitor attraction statistics difficult internationally. Leask (2018) defines visitor attractions as 'natural, cultural or built assets that have been created or converted into a permanent visitor experience where visitor interpretation and engagement with the asset is the core purpose of the development and management of the site' (p. 301). In this chapter, a simplified definition is preferred – anything that has sufficient appeal to 'attract' a visit.

Defining visitor attractions is made more difficult by the fact that they come in a variety of forms, including fixed points such as museums, linear attractions such as heritage railways, or temporary attractions such as events – indeed one of the constant debates is whether events are, in fact, 'attractions'. They can be distinguished from the broader concept of a destination by virtue of their smaller size and the fact that they are based upon a key feature. However, the link between attractions and the destination is an intimate one, and there is a clear synergy between the success of a destination and its attractions. Here, Leiper's (1990) classic paper on attraction systems analyses how attractions can be single nuclei or dispersed across a destination. Finally, destinations are finding it increasingly difficult to compete in the visitor economy and increasingly use visitor attractions and events as one means to differentiate their appeal to the market.

CHARACTERISTICS OF VISITOR ATTRACTIONS

There are five main characteristics of visitor attractions:

1. **Cultural appraisals**. Visitor attractions are a tourism resource, and this means that what is attractive to one tourist may not be to another. The sector, and indeed the tourist, therefore has to recognise that an attraction is of value before it can become an attraction and draw visits. For example, until the eighteenth century, mountains were viewed by most people in the West as places to be feared rather than as scenic attractions. Similarly, until sunbathing became fashionable in the 1920s, the combination of sun, sand and sea was not seen as a valuable attraction. People's perceptions of the beach holiday are beginning to change again due to fears of skin cancer. In other words, the core product of the attraction has to be seen to have a utility for the tourist and so be worth the visit. An interesting example here is the concept of 'dark tourism' where sites such as battlefields or concentration camps become attractions, but only after an acceptable interval of time has passed. Attractions are therefore inherently dynamic and can pass into and out of favour. New technologies also allow attractions to come to life – wet suits, for example, have lengthened the surfing season at many coastal destinations, whilst virtual reality makes the inaccessible – the peak of Everest, say – accessible to many.

2. **Multiple use**. Many visitor attractions are not used exclusively by tourists. Apart from resort areas or theme parks, where tourism is the dominant use, natural and built heritage attractions are shared with other uses such as agriculture, forestry, religion or residents using local services. In national parks, for example, tourism is a significant use but rarely the dominant one, and this can lead to conflict with tourism, as a latecomer, being 'fitted in' with other users. This is known as *multiple use* and needs skilful management and coordination of users to be successful. The same is true of events such as the Australian Formula One Grand Prix, for example, which is held in a public Melbourne park.

3. **Perishability**. Visitor attractions are perishable in two senses. Firstly, they can suffer from intensive use, with daily and seasonal peaking and the consequent pressure upon the attraction. This means that they need effective visitor management. Secondly, in common with many service industries, attractions are also perishable in another sense. Visitor days or ride seats in theme parks are impossible to stock and have to be consumed when and where they exist. This has led to the development of techniques such as differential pricing and timed tickets to maximise the use of the attraction. It has also led some attractions such as museums and zoos to allow visitors to visit at night to maximise the available time for income generation.

4. **Economic significance**. Visitor attractions, including events, play an important part in the visitor economy of a destination, generating income, jobs and competitiveness for the destination. Although they motivate the visit, attractions themselves do not receive the majority of tourists' expenditure, which tends to be upon accommodation and transportation. However, attractions and events often form the centrepiece of regional development and civic regeneration schemes, providing an anchor for both tourism and residents' visits.

5. **Ownership**. Perhaps surprisingly, the visitor attractions sector is not dominated by large corporations such as Disney, although they do dominate in terms of good practice. Instead, the operation and ownership of attractions are fragmented across a variety of organisations, including the private sector, the public sector and voluntary organisations such as charities. Indeed, one of the reasons why attractions have been a late entry into serious academic research is the fact that the sector is dominated by small attractions, often with limited resources and development potential. Charities include the National Trust in the UK (www.nationaltrust.org.uk), which operates a large number of properties, and the National Trust for Historic Preservation in the USA (www.preservationnation.org). The public sector is heavily involved in owning attractions because it is the guardian of the historic, cultural and natural heritage of many countries. Mini Case Study 7.1 shows the innovative approach of a private ownership attraction in the Philippines.

MINI CASE STUDY 7.1

The Masungi Georeserve, Philippines

Background

The Masungi Georeserve is a geological park located in the upland area of Baras, Rizal in the Philippines. The limestone region is 45 kilometres from the capital, Manila and therefore has the potential to attract large visitor numbers. The reserve represents a renaissance of a part of the Philippines that had suffered from illegal logging, land speculation and quarrying. In 1996 the Philippines

The Masungi Georeserve, Philippines

Source: 'Masungi Georeserve' by francesbean is licensed under CC BY-ND 2.0

government recognised the destruction that was occurring to the region and, with private sector partners, restoration was begun by managing the landscape in a sustainable way. The Masungi Georeserve Foundation was established in 2015 with the aim of delivering education and a sustainable financial management regime for the reserve. In 2017 the government expanded the conservation area from 400 hectares to almost 3000 hectares. The impact of the reserve on the local economy is now estimated at US$1 million annually.

The Georeserve

The Masungi Georeserve is a privately led conservation area with gardens, offering adventure and education activities. The reserve is based upon low-impact structures and trail experiences and is carefully managed to a set of specific conservation policies. These policies reflect the reserve's mission to be 'a sanctuary and home for animal and plant life in the Philippines' (www.masungigeo reserve.com).

The policies apply to visitors and staff and are based upon respect for the natural resources of the reserve. Specifically, they state:

- Access to the reserve is for end-use, private groups only, booked in advance;
- No littering;
- No smoking – to reduce air and health pollution. Smoking materials are to be surrendered at the reserve entrance;
- All plastic packaging and loose objects such as sunglasses must be secure and not left behind;
- Noise is not permitted;
- Feeding or touching wildlife is not permitted; and
- Removal of flowers, rocks and other specimens is prohibited.

The Reserve Trails

Visitors can experience three different trails in the reserve:

1. The Discovery Trail is based on the limestone karst landscape through winding paths, rope courses and uniquely designed stops. It includes a night-time experience in the rainforest and a campfire.
2. The Legacy Trail is based on the conservation work to restore the forest landscape. It includes food prepared by the local community at the Amihan floating huts.
3. The Garden Stroll involves a walk around the rock gardens and water cascades.

In addition, the reserve has the Silayan Dining Room with views of the Manila skyline and local and indigenous ingredients are on the menu. Visitors can also take scenic helicopter flights from Manila and see the reserve from the air as they arrive.

(Continued)

CLASSIFYING VISITOR ATTRACTIONS

There are many approaches to classifying visitor attractions – some obvious, others simplistic and some that offer real insights into the core of the attraction and its management. Leask (2018) has neatly encapsulated the many approaches into one diagram (Figure 7.1). Her contemporary approach uses the term 'experiences' to replace the traditional term 'product', 'assets' to replace the term 'resources' and an all-encompassing environment of the attraction's stakeholders.

One of the oldest and most useful approaches is that of Clawson (Clawson and Knetsch, 1966). It was designed for the broader categories of recreational resources, but it works well for attractions and provides insights into their management and operation. Clawson views attractions as forming a continuum from intensive theme park development at one extreme to wilderness attractions at the other. His scheme therefore incorporates the core of the attraction itself, the marketplace and management issues. Clawson's three basic categories are:

1. **User-oriented attractions** of highly intensive development close to population centres. This would include theme parks, zoos, museums and many events – in other words, attractions designed specifically with a particular market in mind and located strategically to attract that market. Here, management issues relate to managing large numbers of visitors.

2. **Resource-based attractions** where the core product determines the market, but the location is determined by the product itself – examples include significant natural attractions such as the Grand Canyon and cultural icon attractions such as the Taj Mahal. Here, management issues are more concerned with managing visitation and protecting the attraction from damage.

3. **An intermediate category** where access is the determining factor and the market is more regional or local. Examples include local arts festivals and regional forest parks.

Table 7.1 relates a selection of recreation activities to Clawson's classification.

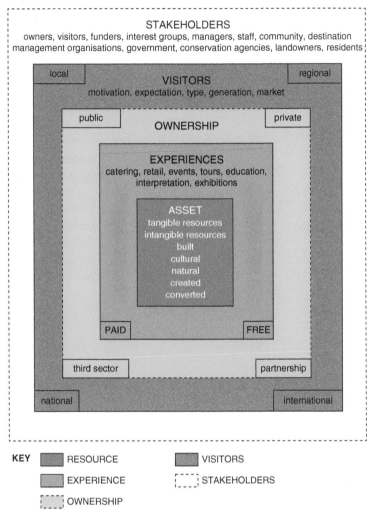

FIGURE 7.1   Classification of visitor attractions

Source: Leask, 2018

TABLE 7.1   A classification of recreational resources

Use-orientated	Intermediate	Resource-based
Based on resources close to the user	Best resources available within accessible distance to users	Outstanding resources based on their location, not that of the market Primary focus is resource quality
Often artificial developments (city parks, stadiums, etc.)	Access very important	
Highly intensive developments	Natural resources more significant than user-orientated facilities, but these experience a high degree of visitor pressure	Often distant from user, the resource determines the activity
Activities often highly seasonal, closing off-peak		

(Continued)

TABLE 7.1   (Continued)

Use-orientated	Intermediate	Resource-based
Reproducible	↔	Non-reproducible
Activity paramount	↔	Resource paramount
Artificiality	↔	Naturalness
	←Intensity of development→	
Proximity	←Distance from user→	Remoteness
Examples of activities:	**Examples of activities:**	**Examples of activities:**
Golf	Yachting	Sightseeing
Tennis	Windsurfing	Mountain climbing
Spectator sports	Boating	Trekking
Visits to theme parks, zoos, resorts	Camping	Safaris
	Hiking	Expeditions
	Angling	Surfing
	Field sports	Whitewater rafting
	Downhill skiing	Canoeing
	Snowboarding	Potholing
		Scuba diving
Typical resource:	**Typical resource:**	**Typical resource:**
Theme park	Heathland	Unique historical monument
		National park

Source: Boniface et al., 2016

Another way of thinking about attractions, related to Clawson's ideas, is to distinguish reproducible attractions (those which can be replaced, such as theme parks) from non-reproducible attractions which, if lost, are irreplaceable, such as elements of the natural and cultural heritage.

Other approaches to classifying attractions include the following:

- **By the size of the attraction**. Page and Connell (2014) quote analysts who classify attractions by visitor numbers:

  o Fewer than 50,000 visitors annually counts as a small attraction and would include a local museum;

  o 50,000–300,000 visitors annually, a medium-sized attraction; and

  o 300,000 visitors or more per year, a large attraction, such as The Smithsonian Museum in Washington, DC (www.si.edu).

- **By the 'pulling power' of the attraction or event** (Figure 7.2). Iconic attractions are few in number but act as a magnet for tourists from all over the world, due to their status as national 'icons'. Second-order attractions might be visited as part of an excursion circuit focusing on one or two major 'sights'. Then there are a host of minor attractions which draw their visitors from within the immediate region.

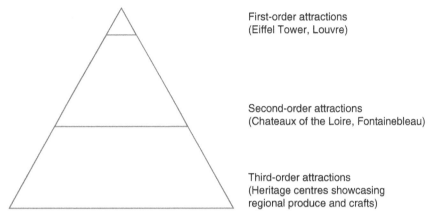

First-order attractions
(Eiffel Tower, Louvre)

Second-order attractions
(Chateaux of the Loire, Fontainebleau)

Third-order attractions
(Heritage centres showcasing
regional produce and crafts)

FIGURE 7.2   A hierarchy of tourist attractions

Source: Boniface et al., 2016

- **By primary attractions**, which generate the visit, and secondary attractions, which enhance the experience but do not necessarily motivate people to visit the destination.
- **By the pricing regime of the attraction**, whether it is free or charges an admission fee, or has a combination of the two, with free entry but an extra charge for special exhibitions.
- **By ownership of the attraction**.

However, by far the most common approach to classifying visitor attractions is by the nature of their core product. Like Clawson's approach, this too has a long pedigree, dating from the USA's Outdoor Recreation Resources Review Commission in the early 1960s. It has since been adapted by a number of authors including Swarbrooke (2001). The basic approach makes a simple division between natural attractions (such as wilderness areas and national parks) and man-made ones (cultural or human-made attractions such as theme parks, townscapes, museums and national monuments).

This division is problematic, however, given that all visitor attractions are inherently cultural appraisals. Indeed, a decision to set aside an area as a national park is as much of a reflection of culture as it would be to farm the same area of land. The classification also omits attractions such as events. Clearly then, the simple twofold classification needs to be developed further as follows (Swarbrooke, 2001):

1. Natural attractions;

2. Man-made visitor attractions;

3. Man-made and purpose-built visitor attractions; and

4. Event attractions.

Natural attractions

Natural attractions include rivers, lakes, beaches, caves, scenic features such as the Victoria Falls, flora and fauna, national parks, wilderness areas and forests. These are often, though not exclusively, in public ownership and demand strict management regimes to protect them from tourist use. These attractions would be classified as resource-based attractions by Clawson.

Many such attractions are not commercially viable in terms of the investment costs and the operating budgets needed to establish and maintain them. They are therefore in public ownership because it is unlikely that the commercial market could sustain them. Public ownership secures such attractions for the population and helps to conserve and manage their natural beauty, flora and fauna. In the USA, for example, the vast majority of outdoor recreation areas, such as national parks, are owned by the government. Here, the first US national park, Yellowstone, was created in 1872 (www.nps.gov/yell), whilst in the UK they came later with the 1945 National Parks and Access to the Countryside Act – indeed national parks are still being created in the UK.

Man-made visitor attractions

Man-made visitor attractions that were not originally designed to attract tourists include historic houses, castles and cathedrals. This category includes heritage attractions, archaeological attractions, such as Stonehenge (www.english-heritage.org.uk/visit/places/stonehenge), and battlefields including First World War sites in northern France. Many heritage attractions have been built around existing towns, villages or settlements such as Colonial Williamsburg in the USA (www.colonialwilliamsburg.com), or complexes of buildings in conservation areas and city centres such as the rebuilt old city of Warsaw. In Northern Europe, North America, Australia and New Zealand, these heritage attractions are conserved and protected. Elsewhere in the world, however, this is not the case and many are lost to development – Singapore, for example, has lost the majority of its old buildings and in other countries historic buildings and monuments are poorly maintained. Archaeological remains are even more difficult to protect; often they are in the centre of cities and destroyed by developers, or in remoter rural areas. Equally they can be sensitive to the environment, as with the prehistoric caves at Lascaux where an artificial version has now been created to deflect visitation (www.lascaux.culture.fr). These attractions, and others such as heritage and visitor centres, have been criticised for overly commercialising or even patronising history by turning it into a commodity to be consumed and purchased by the tourist.

Industrial and transport attractions also belong in this category. They are interesting because they exemplify the notion of resources that become attractions by virtue of the market wanting to visit. They include wineries, factories and industrial archaeology. The marketing of industrial heritage as an attraction is very powerful and is exemplified by the Blackstone Valley in the USA (www.tourblackstone.com), or by Ironbridge Gorge in the UK (www.ironbridge.org.uk). Some companies have leveraged from the demand to visit by creating a themed attraction alongside the factory, as has happened at Cadbury World in the UK (www.cadburyworld.co.uk). In terms of transport, heritage railways and tramways create linear attractions, whilst iconic destinations such as the departure and arrival point of immigrants to the USA are popular. Historic ships are also being created as attractions as with the Cunard's Queen Mary moored in Long Beach California. Other attractions in this category include backstage tours, theatre tours, tours of TV and film locations and behind-the-scenes visits to famous sporting venues such as the Melbourne Cricket Ground (www.mcg.org.au).

Man-made and purpose-built visitor attractions

Man-made and purpose-built visitor attractions are created with the purpose of attracting tourists. They include museums, art galleries, exhibition centres, casinos, theme parks, aqua-parks, zoos and aquaria. Zoos, menageries and aquaria have a long history and are now reinventing themselves as foci of conservation to deflect the criticism of cruelty and stress to animals, as shown in Mini Case Study 7.2. Artificial environments, such as the UK's Eden Project in Cornwall (www.edenproject.com; see Mini Case Study 6.1), or indoor rainforests in the USA, such as the Lied Jungle in Nebraska (www.omahazoo.com), are now being created alongside existing attractions. Safari parks are, of course, the staple attraction of southern African countries.

Museums and galleries are now shrugging off their old-fashioned image and developing technologically driven displays and special exhibitions, again in a bid to reinvent themselves to appeal to new audiences. Many iconic museums such as the Guggenheim in New York (www.guggenheim.org) and Bilbao, the Smithsonian in Washington and the British Museum in London (www.britishmuseum.org) are significant attractions in their own right.

Other attractions in this category include recreation attractions such as swimming pools, golf courses and major shopping venues. Whilst shopping can be thought of as mainly a support facility, it can be an attraction in its own right such as the giant duty-free centre on the old US naval base at Subic Bay in the Philippines (https://visitsubic.org). In the future, as large numbers of Asian tourists travel overseas, shopping will become an important part of the experience. Factory outlet shopping centres and large shopping malls such as the West Edmonton Mall in Canada (www.wem.ca) are attractions in their own right. Shopping, too, is a major attraction for cross-border tourism and capital city tourism.

MINI CASE STUDY 7.2

Animals and Visitor Attractions

Introduction

In the past, animals were an important part of many visitor attractions, including zoos, aquariums and event attractions such as circuses. However, as the views of society have changed, attitudes have hardened against the exploitation of animals in visitor attractions. This has given rise to codes of practice and a change in behaviour by both intermediaries and the attractions themselves.

Codes of Conduct

The UK Farm Animal Welfare Council (www.gov.uk/government/groups/farm-animal-welfare-committee-fawc#assessment-of-farm-animal-welfare---five-freedoms-and-a-life-worth-living) has developed five freedoms of animal welfare:

1. Freedom from hunger;
2. Freedom from discomfort;

(Continued)

3. Freedom from pain, injury and disease;
4. Freedom to express normal behaviour; and
5. Freedom from fear and distress.

The Association of British Travel Agents (ABTA) encourages attractions and destinations to satisfy the following six areas (ABTA, 2015):

1. To understand the scope of tourism's impact on animals;
2. To raise awareness of animal welfare best practice with customers, suppliers and governments;
3. To assess and improve performance within the tourism supply chain;
4. To review and report on actions;
5. To set targets for improvements; and
6. To influence and encourage governmental policy around animal welfare and tourism.

Thomas Cook launched its animal welfare policy in 2016 (Thomas Cook Group, 2018). Its state-of-the-art policy contains the following procedures (as noted in the media release by the Born Free Foundation (Born Free, 2016)):

- All animal attractions must be fully compliant with the ABTA Global Welfare Guidance for Animals in Tourism;
- A decision to no longer sell or promote any new attractions or hotels keeping wild animals in captivity that do not comply with industry minimum welfare requirements;
- Ensuring that existing facilities keeping captive wild animals, contracted by Thomas Cook, meet the highest animal welfare standards;
- Agreeing to phase out practices that are known to severely compromise the welfare and survival of animals; and
- Supporting attractions and excursions that safeguard the welfare and protection of animals.

Behaviour Change

Examples of behaviour change include:

- TripAdvisor has stopped selling tickets to many of the world's cruellest tourism activities;
- A number of zoos and aquaria work closely with charities, universities, government agencies, conservationists and stranding networks to conserve and rescue threatened or damaged species; and
- Australia's Taronga Zoo has adopted a 360-degree approach to conservation and rescue to inspire and educate visitors and the community.

Discussion Questions

1. A recent innovation has been the banning of visits to theme parks that use captive animals or mammals. Debate the pros and cons of this in class.

2. Is it the role of tourist attractions to protect and conserve the world's wildlife?

3. How can attractions educate their visitors to care about the world's wildlife?

Sources: ABTA (2015) Animal welfare. Accessed January 12, 2018 at: https://abta.com/working-with-the-industry/animal-welfare; Born Free (2016) Thomas Cook calls on the travel industry to better protect animals in tourism. Accessed January 12, 2018 at: www.bornfree.org.uk/news/news-article/?no_cache=1&tx_ttnews%5Btt_news%5D=2381; Thomas Cook Group (2018) A new approach to animal welfare in tourism. Accessed January 12, 2018 at: www.thomascookgroup.com/a-new-approach-to-animal-welfare-in-tourism

Event attractions

Event attractions have been neglected as a category until recently. They include the whole range of events from small community festivals to major 'hallmark' events such as pop festivals. Event attractions differ from other attractions because they occur only periodically and, in some cases, change venues. Major hallmark events include sporting occasions, notably the Football World Cup, the Commonwealth Games, Formula One Grand Prix and both the Summer and Winter Olympics. Hallmark events present unique opportunities to promote the host country and have a spin-off effect encouraging other attractions nearby. They also require considerable investment in buildings and infrastructure, planning and organisation to safeguard the health, safety and security of visitors and participants. Cultural event attractions of major international significance would include Rio de Janeiro's Carnival and the Edinburgh Festival.

A destination system of visitor attractions

Of course, whilst it is useful to classify attractions, it is often a combination of attractions that motivate a visit – a theme park combined with a casino as in Sun City, South Africa, for example (www.sun-city-south-africa.com). Excursion itineraries are also important in allowing the visitor to see a number of attractions over a period of a few days – the golden triangle in India is a classic example, with Delhi, Jaipur and the Taj Mahal at Agra all on the circuit. This allows us to begin to think of a destination system of attractions with the associated support facilities, signage and transport necessary to sustain tourism at the destination (Leiper, 1990; Weidenfield et al., 2016). Some destinations have adopted this system and cluster attractions together for marketing purposes to create critical mass and to attract visitors, including multiple pass tickets. Of course, this can be a problem where one or two attractions dominate and smaller satellite attractions suffer, as in the case of Orlando, Florida (www.visitorlando.com). Clustering does assist destinations in fostering a sense of cooperation. As a result, forward-thinking tourism authorities have created strategies to support both fixed and event attractions in their destination.

SPECIFIC TYPES OF VISITOR ATTRACTION

Theme parks

Sometimes known as amusement parks, theme parks have a long history of entertaining visitors, dating back to the sixteenth century with the development of pleasure gardens in

Copenhagen, and more recently iconic theme parks such as the UK's Blackpool Pleasure Beach (www.blackpoolpleasurebeach.com) and New York's Coney Island, site of the first roller coaster, the Gravity Pleasure Switchback in 1884 (www.coneyisland.com). The industrial revolution saw a demand for amusement parks coincide with the development of engineering technology that enabled the rides to be constructed. The industry came of age in 1955 with the opening of Disneyland in California (https://disneyland.disney.go.com), followed by other parks in the USA, France, Japan and Hong Kong, and the extension of the concept to studios and wildlife conservation. Disney transformed the concept of the amusement park into the theme park by extending the range of activities, not only to rides but also to parades, themed restaurants and accommodation and the sheer professionalism of the corporation. Theme parks are increasingly based upon entertainment and media stars such as Elvis Presley or stars of computer games. This is reflected in the contemporary parks of film studios, such as Universal Studios (www.universalorlando.com) and Disney, which now dominate the industry both in size and expertise. The resulting theme park industry is therefore complex. Holloway and Humphreys (2019) classify theme parks into three types:

1. **Local parks** focused on the day trip market such as Adventure Wonderland in Dorset, UK;

2. **Flagship attractions** such as the Tivoli Gardens in Copenhagen (www.tivoli.dk/composite-7438.htm); and

3. **Iconic parks** which attract a worldwide market such as the Disney parks.

As the industry has grown, it has created a range of industry associations to support it. These include:

• The Association of Leading Visitor Attractions (ALVA) in the UK (www.alva.org.uk);
• The International Association of Amusement Parks and Attractions (IAAPA), a global trade association (www.iaapa.org); and
• The Themed Entertainment Association (TEA) in the USA (www.themeit.com).

Theme parks are classic 'user-oriented' attractions in Clawson's classification. They tend to locate close to large conurbations, as in Japan, or close to large holiday areas such as the parks on Australia's Gold Coast, or the US parks in Florida and California. Most theme parks, though not all of them, have a family market, appealing to children. They tend to be designed to a particular formula which includes the pay one price (POP) concept, meaning that the admission price pays for all the rides and activities. They also tend to be designed around a series of themed 'zones' or 'lands', often with a main thoroughfare or 'main street' linking the zones with a spine of restaurants and other facilities. In recent years, hybrids of the parks have developed with water parks, safari lands, shopping and accommodation all on the site.

Theme parks are also characterised by their sophisticated marketing and use of technology. But, like all attractions, they must constantly reinvent themselves with new and refreshed rides, signature rides unique to a particular park, new products and merchandising – often based upon media celebrities or TV programmes. Here, there is a recognised life cycle of visitation with a rise in visits as the attraction becomes known, followed by a fall-off in visits after the first five years as the park reaches market saturation, as without innovation in the product, attractions are not sustainable. The industry also faces threats such as competition from destinations like Las Vegas. In response, the globally significant parks in central Florida now cooperate on marketing and other activities and are using technology to enhance the experience (as shown in Chapter 14).

Globally, the Disney theme parks and studios dominate the industry but, of course, there are other popular theme parks:

- Everland, South Korea (www.everland.com)
- Lotte World, South Korea (www.lotteworld.com)
- Yokohama Hakkeijima Sea Paradis, Japan (www.seaparadise.co.jp/english)
- Parc Asterix, France (www.parcasterix.fr)
- Legoland, Denmark (www.legoland.dk)

Event and festival attractions

Festivals and events are attractions that are time constrained. They are rarely permanent, although they can re-occur on a regular basis on the same site. They are not only used to attract visitors to a destination but can also be used to extend the season (as with Blackpool's illuminations) and to target particular market segments. Event attractions have become increasingly important to building destination success and their features are summarised by Getz and Page (2016: 597):

- Events can attract visitors who otherwise might not visit a destination, generate economic benefits through spending, help reduce seasonality, and spread tourism spatially.

- Events can create positive destination images and help brand or re-position destinations and as such are a key tool of destination marketing.

- Events animate cities, resorts, parks, urban spaces and venues of all kinds, making them more attractive and liveable.

- Event tourism acts as a catalyst for other forms of development, thereby generating a long-term or permanent legacy.

FOCUS ON EMPLOYABILITY

The Event Manager of the Future

Event management education is booming, yet there is a debate as to exactly what constitutes an effective foundation for the event manager of the future. This debate is heightened by discussion as to whether event management is a true 'profession'. There are many views here:

(Continued)

- Whitford (2019) is clear that educators should be creating 'citizen scholars' who are well-rounded managers with both the generic business skills of, say, finance and marketing, and the specific skills needed to manage events.
- Employers also have a view and are clear that they are seeking students who have had industry experience of managing events 'at the sharp end' as well as possessing the personal characteristics of negotiation, creativity and good communication.

These views certainly move the debate forward from the early days of event education when the focus was on designing a set of essential knowledge for event management. But it also begs a more fundamental question: What is the knowledge base that is needed by event managers of the future?

Festivals and events have their roots in medieval travelling fairs, and more recently in the huge mega events created by sports such as the Football World Cup, the Olympics and Formula One Grand Prix, or in hallmark events such as the Calgary Stampede. Indeed, early festivals and events were delivered by amateurs but the sector is now professionalised and has become the realm of entrepreneurs and corporations as events have emerged as an industry in their own right in the twenty-first century. These events are estimated to generate huge economic benefits for their host destinations, as well as acting to place the destination on the world map.

Hallmark events demand huge investment from the host destination (as shown in Chapter 3), but it is not simply the benefits of the event whilst it is being held that are important. The 'legacy' effects of hallmark events are, if anything, more important. This is not only in terms of the facilities constructed, but also the social and environmental benefits. The Olympic Games in both Atlanta and Barcelona generated major urban renewal projects, for example. The London Olympics regenerated run-down parts of London, created new green spaces, stimulated improved airport gateways and a convention centre in London (UK Government and Mayor of London, 2014). An event such as the Festival of Britain now has the legacy of the South Bank in London. Finally, major events are increasingly focusing on the security of their visitors following the Boston Marathon bombing in 2013, the first major terrorist attack on a major event. In the classic paper for this chapter, Ritchie outlines a comprehensive approach to assessing the impact of hallmark events.

CLASSIC PAPER

Ritchie, J.R.B. (1984) 'Assessing the impact of hallmark events: conceptual and research issues', *Journal of Travel Research*, 23 (1): 2–11

This paper is a classic because not only was it written at least ten years before the realisation of the significance of events for tourism and the consequent boom in event management literature, but also because it displays the author's characteristic insights into how tourism works and his thoroughness in coverage.

The paper begins with a definition and characterisation of hallmark events as: 'Major one-time or recurring events of limited duration, developed primarily to enhance the awareness, appeal and profitability of a tourism destination in the short and/or long term' (p. 2).

Such events are classified as world fairs, unique carnivals and festivals, major sporting events, significant cultural and religious events, historical milestones, classic commercial and agricultural events and major political personage events. To quote Brent Ritchie: 'previous discussions of the impact of hallmark events have tended to be largely one-dimensional … a broader analytical framework is both useful and necessary' (p. 4). The paper examines these major events, not simply in terms of economic, environmental and socio/cultural consequences, but instead Ritchie takes a broader approach including political, commercial and psychological consequences.

The article discusses the difficulties associated with measuring each of these consequences of holding a hallmark event. Ritchie rightly views the economic dimension as the most developed in terms of practice and methodology; this is in contrast to the tourism/commercial impacts. This includes the impact of sponsorship, which boosts the attractiveness of the destination generally and for investment purposes. Of course, the consequences are difficult to measure in the short term and often the benefits are intangible, exemplified by the issue that has arisen in Australia with debate over the real benefits of the State of Victoria's significant sponsorship of the Melbourne Formula One Grand Prix.

The remainder of the paper is devoted to a consideration of the research and measurement challenges of each of the six consequences of holding a hallmark event.

The paper concludes that the field is young (as indeed it was when this pioneering article was written) and that it is hoped that the paper will stimulate further work in the field. That has certainly been the case and Brent Ritchie's paper set the research agenda for event management over the ensuing decades; hence it is a truly 'classic' paper.

Of course, not all events are on the scale of hallmark events, and worldwide there are many local-scale arts festivals, music events and sporting activities. Many smaller events in the past were targeted at local residents, but the popularity of events now means that many small festivals attract visitors from outside the area. Getz and Page (2016) have designed a contemporary classification of events and festivals (Figure 7.3).

For the large events, government is often a major sponsor, but festivals and events also need to attract other sponsors. They are often run by volunteers, particularly community and charity-run events, with a small professional team of managers. Page and Connell (2014) distinguish between event tourism as a strategic approach to utilising events in destination management, where many destinations now have their own event strategy, and event management as the approach to designing, producing and managing events (Getz, 2012). The events industry also has its own professional organisation – the International Festivals and Events association (IFEA, www.ifea.com/p/about/ifeaglobalaffiliates/ifeaeurope).

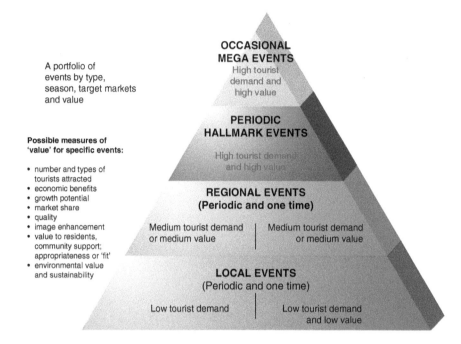

FIGURE 7.3   Classification of events and festivals

Source: Getz and Page, 2016

Iconic attractions

As already shown, some attractions have come to be widely regarded as icons by virtue of the large numbers of people who visit them. As a result, they are closely associated with the destination's image – think of the Eiffel Tower and Paris, for example, or Table Mountain and Cape Town. For a destination to be competitive, it is important to have an iconic focal point. These icons were often not designed with tourism in mind, however; indeed, it is difficult to create such icons deliberately.

UNESCO has designated many such iconic attractions as World Heritage Sites on its World Heritage List (http://whc.unesco.org/en/list). The list includes 1121 properties which are part of the global cultural and natural heritage, considered by the World Heritage Committee as having outstanding universal value. The list includes:

- 869 cultural sites;
- 213 natural sites; and
- 39 sites which are 'mixed' – both natural and cultural.

However, the committee also lists 53 World Heritage Sites that are in danger.

MANAGING VISITOR ATTRACTIONS

The majority of visitor attractions operate as businesses and have a set of key performance indicators (KPIs) associated with them against which their management is measured. These

KPIs include visitor numbers, visitor revenue and both gross and net profit. However, by far the most important KPI is visitor numbers. Visitor numbers drive the overall performance of the attraction and the rest of the attraction's business – catering, retail and special events. Visitor numbers can be formally recorded by ticket sales, through questionnaire surveys, automatic counters or observers. Surveys at attractions are common to determine not only numbers of visitors, but also their demographic and visit profile, their spending and their likes and dislikes. Figure 7.4 summarises the key factors involved in managing effective visitor attractions.

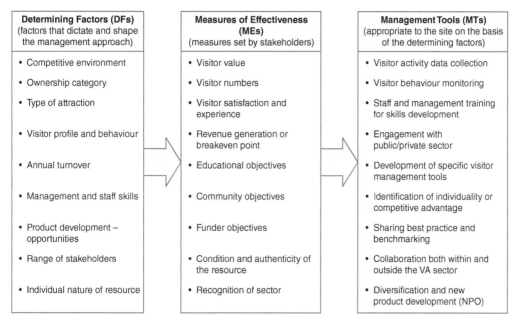

FIGURE 7.4   Key factors for effective attraction management

Source: Leask, 2010

Economics of visitor attractions

The economics of managing attractions are ably described by Wanhill (in Fyall et al., 2008). Most attractions are characterised by a very high ratio of fixed to variable costs, simply by virtue of the considerable capital investment needed to establish an attraction. This means that attractions tend to require a relatively high number of visitors to generate revenue before they can break even and begin to make a profit. Of course, this means that the marketing of the attraction (often approaching 10 per cent of costs) and its location close to large population catchment areas is even more important.

Attractions therefore have to diversify and secure a range of income streams – from tickets, merchandise, catering and event functions to car parks – if they are to be successful. There are a number of ways to achieve this, including diversifying into educational or corporate markets, persuading visitors to stay longer (dwell time), and so spend more, or seek commercial sponsorship. Table 7.2 demonstrates the breakdown of costs and revenue for a 1.5 million visitor theme park. The table shows that with discounts it is usual to achieve 70–80 per cent of the ticket price. Aside from investment, the highest costs are mainly for seasonal and salaried labour.

TABLE 7.2   Income breakdown for a 1.5 million visitor theme park

Item	Revenue percentages
Revenue	
Admissions (a)	55.6
Catering	22.2
Merchandising	16.7
Miscellaneous (b)	5.6
Total	**100.0**
Cost of sales	
Catering	8.9
Merchandise	8.3
Total	**17.2**
Gross profit	**82.8**
Other income (c)	**9.0**
Total income	**91.8**
Controllable expenses	
Payroll	32.4
Marketing	10.2
Administration	4.3
Maintenance	3.1
Operating supplies	2.5
Utilities	4.3
Insurance	3.1
Total	**59.9**
Cash flow	**34.9**
Capital expenses	
Attraction replacement and renewals	14.7
Occupation costs (d)	5.7
Total	**20.4**
Net income before tax	**11.3**

(a) Adult admission is $US45, giving an average discount (after sales tax) of 30.2%

(b) Includes rentals, arcades and vending machines

(c) Sponsorship, corporate hospitality and rental of facilities

(d) Rental provision for site and premises

Source: Fyall et al., 2008

In terms of revenue, the type of pricing policy adopted by the attraction is critical. Simply to receive the cost of the initial fixed investment in an attraction means that the price of entry has to be set well above the operational cost of supplying the facilities and labour for each visit. So critical is this decision that attractions are now adopting a yield management approach to ticketing where they achieve the best price possible for a ticket for each day and each time of day. Strategies include 'pay one price' for admission, which is good for families, can be used in marketing and is cost-efficient for the attraction.

There is, of course, a fierce debate about whether the public sector should charge admission to, say, museums or galleries. It could be argued that local people have already subsidised the museum through their taxes, but of course this does not apply to tourists. As a result, some countries, such as Finland, have a differential charging policy.

Management approach

Good visitor attraction management focuses on positive planning and provision rather than negative restrictions and prohibition. Attraction management is also very much a practitioner-based approach with few manuals of good practice or well-documented case studies. Yet, as already noted, there are a number of leading attractions companies – such as the Walt Disney Corporation – which are very skilled in the art.

The visitor management approach (see Chapter 6 and Figure 6.4) is commonly used at attractions, and the following elements relating to attractions can be identified:

- **Management objectives.** Determination of management objectives is critical for the successful management of any attraction at the outset as they will determine the overall management strategy. Here, some attractions struggle to determine their true objectives – think of St Paul's Cathedral in London, for example, which is an iconic tourist attraction, but also a place of worship. For some attractions the answer is easy – an economic objective or one of profit or return on investment. Other objectives, however, are also possible. These include educational reasons (for a wildlife reserve, say) or propaganda (as in show sites in socialist republics). The management process demands that attractions have to be very clear on these objectives since they drive the whole process.

- **Demand.** A second key variable is demand – the profile and numbers of visitors attracted to the attraction. It is important that marketing communicates clearly the objectives of the attraction to ensure that appropriate types of visitor are attracted. The most common management problems occur when visitors with objectives that conflict with the site are attracted. If these problems do arise, then it is the role of marketing to constantly adjust the visitor profile to the management objectives. A key consideration here is the determination of approaches for resource-based and user-based attractions.

- **Capacity.** At this stage of the visitor management process, decisions are taken as to the intensity of visitation at each part of the site, and also the type of activity to be scheduled there. For greenfield sites the planner has a relatively free hand, but for sites such as museums or historic houses it is probable that the use of rooms and displays will be fixed. Here attraction managers have to determine the volume of visitors that can be sustained in each part of the site. This is done using the concepts of:

  o **annual physical capacity** (APC), which is the number of users that can be sustained in one year; and

○   **sustained physical capacity** (SPC), which is the maximum number of visitors that can be accommodated at any one point in time without deterioration in the condition of the site.

The calculation is then: APC = SPC x number of periods open. This is a useful approach as it allows planners to build in seasonality effects – industry norms for theme parks mean that the park is designed on the basis of 80–90 per cent of the peak number of visitors expected.

*   **Visitor management.** Once a decision has been made for the attraction to open, it is then important to ensure that visitors are managed in such a way as to ensure capacity levels in each area are not exceeded, and therefore that the quality of experience is maintained. Influencing visitor movement and behaviour is a subtle science and can be seen as selection from a range of options along a continuum, from hard management to soft management (as shown in Chapter 6).
*   **Monitoring.** There is no point in developing sophisticated management approaches without a means of monitoring their success. This includes administering formal questionnaires, debriefing front-line staff, monitoring social media posts or monitoring through the use of electronic eyes, turnstiles or other technology.

MANAGEMENT ISSUES

Seasonality

A key issue for attractions is the seasonal nature of tourism. Whilst this is often put down to climate, in fact there are institutional reasons for seasonality too, such as school and other holidays from the demand side and supply-side reasons such as labour supply and transport access. Goulding (2008) identifies a range of issues for attractions stemming from the inherent seasonality of demand. These include:

*   Staffing, where the skills developed by seasonal workers are lost in the off season;
*   Poor use of the attraction's capacity with crowding at peak times, leading to congestion and poor visitor experience; and
*   Perishability of the unit of production such that revenue-earning opportunities are lost.

Goulding (2008) maps a range of management responses to the issue of seasonality, including developing yield management systems, prioritising staffing at peak times to ensure revenue is maximised, diversifying to less seasonally sensitive markets such as corporates, flexible pricing strategies which are sensitive to seasonal variation, and extending the attraction product to, say, events, or developing new facilities. For destinations it is important to develop a portfolio of attractions, some of which will be weather resistant. Seasonality impacts on the profitability and operation of the attraction and demands particular strategies – museums, for example, mount special exhibitions, or differential pricing to encourage local people or schools to visit at off peak times.

Marketing

Creating and managing a memorable visitor experience is the key to successful attraction marketing. This involves designing a memorable set of activities and experiences and putting in place quality assurance across the whole experience. One poor aspect of the visit – such as catering – can influence the whole memory and desire to return.

Attractions are competing for expenditure across the leisure sector, including entertainment and white goods as well as other attractions and destinations. Changing patterns of leisure, an increasingly competitive marketplace and technological innovation mean that consumer expectations are rising. The challenge for attractions is to create products to satisfy these new patterns of demand with their media and entertainment-driven expectations. Here, there is no doubt that smaller attractions are vulnerable as they cannot access the investment required to meet the market's expectations. However, as Leask (2018) notes, there is an increasing trend for attractions to cooperate across a destination, as in the case of the Association of Singapore Attractions which was established to exchange knowledge and encourage collaboration. Voase (2008) examines the needs of the 'new tourist' when it comes to attractions. He characterises the new tourist as being more demanding and sophisticated, identifying two key types:

1. **The thoughtful consumer** – seeking a more active involvement from the attraction and a learning experience; and

2. **The smart consumer** – accepting commoditisation of attractions, and seeing the visit as more of a transaction.

It is therefore vital for attractions to understand visitor motivation in targeting their market. Quite clearly, different target markets are attracted to different types of attraction. Theme parks attract the family and the younger market, whilst heritage attractions tend to attract a more mature market. The target market then determines all the aspects of the attraction's marketing mix. For attractions, promotion through word of mouth is important, and surprisingly, the sector still uses old-fashioned promotional techniques such as leafleting.

Sustainability

Both visitor attractions and events generate consequences for the environment, society and economy, particularly in terms of water and energy, waste and relations with neighbouring communities (see Andersson and Lundberg, 2013). They therefore have to embrace sustainability in all its forms, from the type of transport used to reach them, through the management of local community relationships, to the notion of ethical trading in shops and restaurants. Sustainable attractions management demands not only that the visitor receives a satisfying and high-quality experience, but also that the destination is sustainable. Here, the major visitor attractions corporations such as the Walt Disney Company in the USA and Village Roadshow in Australia have embraced sustainability overtly in the management of their parks. Major Case Study 7.1 examines approaches to sustainable event management.

THE FUTURE OF VISITOR ATTRACTIONS

As the visitor attraction sector matures, a number of trends are becoming evident. Greater professionalism is developing across the industry with a more strategic approach to staff and their training, as well as more professional management approaches to the attractions themselves. In part, this is driven by competition. Here, attractions are increasingly compared to the entertainment and media sector and this has led to new product development, in particular the innovative use of technology. In the future, immersive experiences, virtual reality and combined experiences with other parts of tourism, such as accommodation, dining and cruising, will be part of the attractions landscape. This has led one industry commentator to predict a new generation of multifaceted, all-inclusive destinations that will appeal to many markets and provide a sound return on investment (Stevens, 2000).

Attractions, and events too, will have to embrace sustainability in all its forms, from the type of transport used to reach them, through the management of local community relationships, to the notion of ethical trading in shops and restaurants, as shown in Major Case Study 7.1. Smart tourism demands not only that the visitor receives a satisfying and high-quality experience, but also that the destination is sustainable. Innovative application of visitor management ensures that the increasingly experienced and discerning new tourist does indeed receive a high-quality experience, while also sustaining the destination for future use. Here, innovative engineering such as that used in the Grand Canyon Skywalk Lookout – a horseshoe-shaped, glass-floored walkway over the canyon – is leading the way (https://grandcanyonwest.com/explore/west-rim/skywalk-eagle-point), whilst technology based upon the Internet of Things is helping to 'curate' the visitor experience. Closer matching of market segments with product development is already evident. Leask (2018) gives the example of night-time and sleepover visits to zoos and museums to appeal to a gen Y audience (see Taronga Zoo's 'roar and snore' programme – https://taronga.org.au/sydney-zoo/accommodation/roar-and-snore). Other attractions are introducing gamification – the Super Nintendo World theme park opens in 2020 at Osaka's Universal Studios in Japan. And finally, visitor attractions have to safeguard their audiences against terrorism, whilst at the same time remaining welcoming and open to all.

FOCUS ON TECHNOLOGY

Virtual and Augmented Reality

In the future, technology will uncouple attractions from physical space. In other words, they will no longer be locationally constrained as visitors will be able to access them virtually through the use of VR technology.

VR creates an artificial environment that visitors can interact with using technology. It has many advantages for attractions – it can be used to provide a virtual alternative for fragile resource-based attractions such as the Galapagos Islands; it can be used to provide rich visitor information about the attraction as well as enhancing the experience of the visit; it allows those who would otherwise never have the chance to visit, say, the Great Wall of China, to do so – the disabled, the elderly or the sick; and it can be used as a simulated training environment for staff.

But there is criticism of VR, saying that it poses a barrier between the attraction and the visitor, something that can be solved by augmented reality (AR). In AR the real environment is overlaid with visuals and information. For attractions, AR is already used to augment intepretation and information without coming between the visitor and the resource.

SUMMARY

This chapter has analysed visitor attractions and events, and outlined key elements of their management. Clearly, visitor attractions motivate the visit to a tourism destination and in so doing energise the tourism system. It is important to distinguish attractions from support facilities at the destination, although both are needed for tourism to function effectively. Defining attractions is fraught with difficulty but any definition must be based on the ability of a facility to attract visitation. Classifying attractions can be done simply by listing different types – such as natural or cultural attractions – or, and more usefully, they can be classified according to an approach that assists in management decisions, as was done by Clawson. Specific types of attraction demand different management approaches. Events, for example, are time-limited attractions and are often run by a core of professionals supported by many volunteers. Theme parks, on the other hand, have a long history and are very professionally managed. Natural attractions are often owned by the public sector and their management is more about conservation and protection of the resource. The management of attractions also depends on a keen understanding of their economics, particularly the significant up-front investment costs, and it also demands a clear identification of management objectives which then determine the remaining management decisions. The future of attractions will be dominated by technology, a demand for sustainability, a focus on security, and a closer linkage of attractions with other aspects of tourism in order to create multifaceted, all-inclusive destinations that will appeal to many markets, and provide sound return on investment.

DISCUSSION QUESTIONS

1. Design a survey to assess visitor profile and visitor satisfaction for an attraction that you are familiar with. Limit the number of questions to 20 or less.

2. Take a tourist attraction with which you are familiar – such as a theme park or museum – and re-visit it with the eyes of a visitor manager. Does the attraction work in terms of visitor movement and rhythms, is the experience enhanced and did you enjoy it?

3. In class, discuss the advantages and disadvantages of a city government sponsoring a hallmark event such as a Formula One Grand Prix.

4. Take the example of a local museum or religious building that attracts a significant number of visitors – is it managed as a visitor 'attraction'? If not, should it be?

5. Debate whether attractions in the public domain – national parks, museums, etc. – should be free, or should charge visitors an entrance fee.

ANNOTATED FURTHER READING

Getz, D. and Page, S. (2016) 'Progress and prospects for event tourism research', *Tourism Management*, 52: 593–631.

Contemporary and thorough review of events as attractions.

Leask, A. (2018) 'Contemporary perspectives on visitor attractions', in C. Cooper, S. Volo, W.C. Gartner and N. Scott (eds), *The Sage Handbook of Tourism Management: Applications of Theories and Concepts to Tourism*. London: Sage. pp. 299–314.

Excellent contemporary review of visitor attractions.

Swarbrooke, J. (2001) *The Development and Management of Visitor Attractions*. Oxford: Butterworth-Heinemann.

User-friendly text with thorough coverage of visitor attractions.

Weidenfeld, A., Butler, R. and Williams, A. (2016) *Visitor Attractions and Events: Locations and Linkages*. Abingdon: Routledge.

Innovative volume exploring the relationship between attractions and events and geography.

Whitford, M. and Fredline, E. (2018) 'The growth and development of leisure events and festival tourism', in C. Cooper, S. Volo, W.C. Gartner and N. Scott (eds), *The Sage Handbook of Tourism Management: Applications of Theories and Concepts to Tourism*. London: Sage. pp. 360–79.

Thorough review of event and festival issues and research.

REFERENCES CITED

Andersson, T.D. and Lundberg, E. (2013) 'Commensurability and sustainability: triple impact assessments of a tourism event'. *Tourism Management*, 37 (C): 99–109.

Boniface, B., Cooper, C. and Cooper, R. (2016) *Worldwide Destinations: The Geography of Travel and Tourism,* 7th edn. London: Routledge.

Clawson, M. and Knetsch, J. (1966) *The Economics of Outdoor Recreation*. Baltimore, OH: Johns Hopkins University Press.

Fyall, A., Garrod, B., Leask, A. and Wanhill, S. (2008) *Managing Visitor Attractions: New Directions*. Oxford: Butterworth-Heinemann.

Getz, D. (2012) *Event Studies Theory, Research and Policy for Planned Events*, 2nd edn. London: Routledge.

Getz, D. and Page, S. (2016) 'Progress and prospects for event tourism research', *Tourism Management*, 52: 593–631.

Goulding, P. (2008) 'Managing temporal variation in visitor attractions', in A. Fyall, B. Garrod, A. Leask, and S. Wanhill (eds), *Managing Visitor Attractions: New Directions*. Oxford: Butterworth-Heinemann. pp. 197–216.

Gunn, C.A. (1972) *Vacationscape: Designing Tourist Regions*. Austin, TX: Bureau of Business Research.

Holloway, J.C. and Humphreys, C. (2019) *The Business of Tourism*. London: Sage.

Leask, A. (2010) 'Progress in visitor attraction research: toward more effective management', *Tourism Management*, 31: 155–66.

Leask, A. (2018) 'Contemporary perspectives on visitor attractions', in C. Cooper, S. Volo, W.C. Gartner and N. Scott (eds), *The Sage Handbook of Tourism Management: Applications of Theories and Concepts to Tourism*. London: Sage. pp. 299–314.

Leiper, N. (1990) 'Tourist attraction systems', *Annals of Tourism Research*, 17: 367–84.

Page, S.J. and Connell, J. (2014) *Tourism: A Modern Synthesis*. Andover: Cengage Learning.

Stevens, T. (2000) 'The future of visitor attractions', *Travel and Tourism Analyst*, 1: 61–85.

Swarbrooke, J. (2001) *The Development and Management of Visitor Attractions*. Oxford: Butterworth-Heinemann.

UK Government and Mayor of London (2014) *Inspired by 2012: The Legacy from the Olympics and Paralympic Games*. London: Cabinet Office.

Voase, R. (2008) 'Rediscovering the imagination: meeting the needs of the "new" visitor', in A. Fyall, B. Garrod, A. Leask and S. Wanhill (eds), *Managing Visitor Attractions: New Directions*. Oxford: Butterworth-Heinemann. pp. 148–64.

Wanhill, S. (2008) 'Economic aspects of developing theme parks', in Fyall, A., Garrod, B., Leask, A. and Wanhill, S., *Managing Visitor Attractions: New Directions,* Oxford: Butterworth-Heinemann. pp. 59–79.

Whitford, M. and Fredline, E. (2018) 'The growth and development of leisure events and festival tourism', in C. Cooper, S. Volo, W.C. Gartner and N. Scott (eds), *The Sage Handbook of Tourism Management: Applications of Theories and Concepts to Tourism*. London: Sage. pp. 360–79.

Weidenfeld, A., Butler, R. and Williams, A. (2016) *Visitor Attractions and Events: Locations and Linkages*. Abingdon: Routledge.

MAJOR CASE STUDY 7.1

Greening the Event Industry

Southbank Centre Winter Market, London. An outdoor, global street food market focused on sustainable and artisan produce.

Source: ©Alena Veasey/Shutterstock.com

Introduction

The event industry is not exempt from the imperative to deliver a sustainable industry and reduce carbon emissions. Whatever the scale of an event, from the football world cup final to a local festival, the gathering together of audiences will impact upon local resources, create extra waste and can disrupt the way of life of local communities (Goldblatt and Goldblatt, 2011; Raj and Musgrave, 2009). Yet, creating a sustainable event industry is challenging

simply because of the large number of organisations involved in delivering an event. These range from audiences, through organisers, suppliers, communities and partners. This means that delivering sustainable events involves all stages of the event supply chain (ISO, 2012) including:

- Event organisers;
- Event owners;
- Event workforce;

- Event caterers;
- Constructors;
- Transport companies;
- Participants;
- Attendees;
- Regulatory bodies; and
- Local communities.

There is a dedicated international standard to guide organisers to deliver a sustainable event – the ISO International Standard – ISO 20121 (ISO, 2012). The standard provides guidelines and operational advice for event sustainability management systems to ensure that events contribute to the three dimensions of sustainability – economic, environmental and social.

The Copenhagen Case

An excellent example of how sustainable events can be delivered is provided by the Copenhagen Business School (2019). The school has written a guide to sustainable event operation based on its experience of organising the Sustainable Consumption Conference in 2018. The guide provides intelligent, smart and innovative solutions to sustainable event delivery and details practical solutions. The guide provides the following advice:

- **Food and catering**. The school compared vegetarian and meat-based menus for the conference including food ingredients, transportation, cooking processes and waste treatment. The analysis showed that by adopting the vegetarian option for the conference, the environmental footprint of the conference's catering was reduced by 44 percent compared to the meat-based menu. The analysis also identified sustainability 'hotspots' where the import of food was not environmentally sound. This included importing berries to Denmark from the USA. For conference dinners and dining out, the conference chose 'local' restaurants that provided organic food and vegetarian food, not only to reduce the environmental footprint of the

conference, but also to promote the non-meat food concept to delegates.

- **Water supply**. There are a variety of ways to supply water to a conference and it is important to match this with the number of attendees and the length of the event. For the Copenhagen conference, three options were analysed:
  - Reusable glass bottles;
  - Single-use cardboard cartons; and
  - Single-use plastic bottles.

    The analysis showed that glass bottles are more sustainable for a four-day event where it would be used many times compared to both the cardboard and plastic options. This result is interesting when compared to the drive to replace single-use plastic cups in coffee shops with cardboard ones.

- **Procurement**. A variety of sourcing decisions were made by the conference to ensure enhanced sustainability. These included renting pot plants which are then returned to the rental company; ensuring the purchase of organic cotton products for t-shirts and bags; and giving sustainable gifts to speakers.

- **Waste reduction**. The conference made sure that all waste was sorted and disposed of correctly. Waste was also reduced where possible by a number of smart initiatives:
  - Using re-useable tableware such as porcelain or ceramic plates instead of the conventional wisdom of using disposable products;
  - Delegates were encouraged to return nametags and lanyards for later reuse;
  - Paper use was reduced; and
  - Food waste was minimized by carefully planning portions and donating any leftover food to charities and homeless shelters.

- **Participants**. The conference carefully considered the environmental implications of where

(Continued)

they sourced their speakers, preferring locally based presenters who did not need to travel far. Similarly, they encouraged delegates to avoid flying (although this can be difficult if a conference is to be truly international). In terms of delegate and speaker accommodation, participants were encouraged to choose a sustainable accommodation option and to think of ways to reduce their environmental footprint during their stay. Finally, the conference was keen to showcase sustainable businesses and their products, encouraging delegates to share their experiences on social media. This creates a forum and triggers conversations about sustainability to inspire delegates and others.

The Advantages of a Sustainable Approach to Events

There are clear advantages of taking a sustainable approach to delivering events. In particular, organisers can leverage from the approach to gain reputational advantage and to show how they have acted. It can also reduce costs such as insurance and shows that the event complies with regulatory guidelines on, say, noise. Adopting a sustainability approach also allows event organisers to identify the key environmental challenges of their individual event so that they can devise solutions, set targets, create action plans, monitor and evaluate the results and so begin a process of continual improvement. The process can also be extended to the supply chain and external stakeholders. Finally, event organisers who adopt the ISO 20121 guidelines can gain certification to act as independent verification of conformity to ISO requirements.

Discussion Questions

1. Taking an event that you are familiar with, map out the stakeholders involved and determine the sustainability challenges of each group.
2. In terms of sustainability, what are the different challenges of running a mega event compared to a local community festival?
3. There is a paradox in creating a green, but international, event whilst also allowing delegates the flexibility to travel by air. How can this be solved?

Sources: Copenhagen Business School (2019) *Sustainable Event Guide: An Inspirational Guide to Making Your Event More Sustainable*. Copenhagen: Copenhagen Business School; Goldblatt, S. and Goldblatt, J. (2011) *The Complete Guide to Greener Meetings and Events*. New York: Wiley; ISO (2012) *Sustainable Events with ISO20121*. Geneva: ISO; Raj, R. and Musgrave, J. (2009) *Event Management and Sustainability*. Wallingford: CABI; www.cbs.dk/sustainability/resources

8

HOSPITALITY

LEARNING OUTCOMES

This chapter focuses upon a key industry of the tourism sector, that of hospitality. Hospitality partly defines the tourism industry as it services the overnight stay of the visitor. This chapter is designed to provide you with:

- an understanding of the scope and definitions of hospitality;
- a disciplined approach to analysing the sectors of the hospitality industry;
- an awareness of the different approaches to managing the hospitality industry;
- an understanding of the key operational aspects of hospitality units;
- clarity on the role of occupancy, pricing and yield management in the hospitality industry; and
- awareness of the environmental consequences and responses of the hospitality industry.

INTRODUCTION

The provision of overnight accommodation, food and beverage for tourists partly defines the tourism industry and is an integral part of Leiper's (1990) destination region. It is also the one that delivers the most significant economic benefits and spend to the destination when compared to, say, a day visitor. Hospitality comes in many different forms, ranging from condominiums through resorts and conference centres to guest-houses, homestay, visiting friends and relatives, Airbnb, and restaurants and bars. It is the hospitality industry that provides the welcome and delivers the food, flavours and local colour at the destination. As a result, it is important that the industry has a good strategic fit with the destination, providing appropriate products for the visitor – it could, for example, be argued that the Victorian accommodation buildings of many UK seaside resorts are inappropriate for twenty-first century expectations. Here, we can see that hospitality is an important part of the tourism product, but it must be remembered that it is unusual for hospitality to be the motivation for the visit. Of course, there are exceptions, such as a stay at a landmark hotel such as the Raffles in Singapore (www.raffles.com) or the iconic Burj-Al-Arab Hotel in Dubai (www.jumeirah.com/en/hotels-resorts/dubai/burj-al-arab).

DEFINITIONS AND SCOPE

Definitions of the hospitality industry and the traditional focus of the literature have been dominated by the hotel industry, its management and business – partly because of the size and dominance of the hotel industry in tourism. Indeed, the scope of just what is meant by the hospitality industry has been at the heart of the debate about defining tourism from a supply-side perspective. In the late twentieth century, emergence of satellite account methodology clarified the debate (as shown in Chapter 3). More recently, definitions of hospitality have broadened from the purely commercial aspect of providing accommodation, food and beverage to include the social and cultural aspects of host and guest relationships and 'gastronomy', where the geography and culture of food and wine become important (Lynch et al., 2011). Along these lines, Lashley (2000: 14) has broadened definitions of hospitality to: 'contemporaneous human exchange, which is voluntarily entered into and designed to enhance the mutual well being of the parties concerned through the provision of accommodation and/or food and drink'.

This definition implies that hospitality is not a purely commercial transaction, but includes human interactions, cultural considerations and exchange. Lashley and Morrison (2000) have taken this further by identifying three domains of hospitality, each representing a particular aspect of hospitality. Their overlap is where hospitality management is performed (Figure 8.1). These domains are:

1. **The private domain** – relating to the host–guest relationship and fulfilling physiological and psychological needs;

2. **The commercial domain** – relating to services provided for profit, clearly linked to the economics of the marketplace; here, the host–guest relationship is commoditised; and

3. **The social domain** – providing hospitality for strangers in an act of generosity and the social space in which this occurs.

These definitions and domains are contentious, however, and authors such as Slattery and Brotherton have joined the debate, arguing that Lashley and Morrison's approach firstly overlooks the 'relationship' aspect of hospitality, that between the host and the guest, and secondly, underplays the 'corporate' element of hospitality that has emerged since industrialisation (see Jones, 2004, for a good summary of the debate).

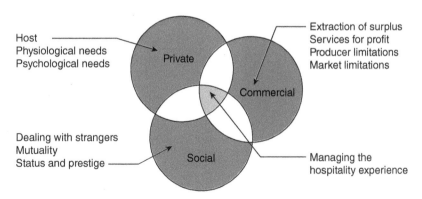

FIGURE 8.1   The three domains of hospitality

Source: Lashley, 2019

HISTORY OF THE HOSPITALITY INDUSTRY

The concept of hospitality dates back to ancient times when communities took strangers into their homes to provide food, drink and accommodation. Hospitality developed into one of the earliest forms of business with guest quarters provided in monasteries and inns, particularly as the Roman and Greek empires expanded internationally. Whilst the Grand Tour demanded that hospitality was provided for tourists throughout Europe, it was not until the nineteenth century that hotels as we know them developed. They initially grew in Europe, partly in response to travellers' needs as the railways developed. Indeed, there has always been a close link between the development of hospitality and both transportation and economic growth. The nineteenth century saw changing working patterns and the growth of transport infrastructure encouraged the provision of food, drink and hospitality, particularly at the focus of new destinations such as coastal resorts. In the twentieth century, the development of the motor car and associated infrastructure led to an expansion of accommodation and hospitality, including dedicated facilities for motorists such as motels and drive-in restaurants. After the Second World War, the focus of accommodation trends moved to the USA where American-style hospitality management developed to include the standardisation of provision and service, and a strong emphasis on marketing and branding – for example, as observed in Hilton (www.hilton.com), Hyatt (www.hyatt.com) and Holiday Inn (www.holidayinn.com). The most recent development has been the disruption to the sector caused by peer-to-peer accommodation sites such as Airbnb. By 2020, the hospitality industry is estimated to comprise 500,000 hotels and 10 million restaurants and to employ 100 million people. (www.ih-ra.org). The industry is concentrated in the leading destination regions of the world, particularly Europe, North America and increasingly in Asia. For the future, investment and growth are occurring in emergent destinations such as the Middle East, India and China.

STRUCTURE OF THE HOSPITALITY INDUSTRY

The characteristics of supply of the hospitality industry polarise into many small businesses, which dominate in terms of numbers of establishments, and very large companies, such as Hilton, Marriott (www.marriott.com) and Airbnb, which dominate in terms of practice and the profession. Between these two extremes lie a myriad of different businesses and hospitality concepts – so many in fact that it is difficult to generalise and encapsulate the hospitality industry. A key supply-side trend is increased concentration with a decline in small and independent hotels and an increase in franchise and chain properties. This means that medium-sized companies are vulnerable to takeover or failure as they do not have the market strength, productivity and economies of scale of the large chains, nor the identifiable niche of the small hotel.

Serviced accommodation

Serviced accommodation comes in many forms, not only including hotels and guest houses, but also campus accommodation, medical accommodation such as the spas of the former

Eastern Europe, and of course cruise ships and other forms of transport such as sleeper trains where accommodation is provided.

Hotels

Hotels are a key element of the accommodation stock of most destinations, ranging in size from the boutique hotel to the large 'bed factories' found in resorts such as Las Vegas. In fact, many commentators mistake hotels as surrogate for the whole accommodation industry, and even tourism itself, as they are such a visible and often iconic part of the destination. Of course, there are many landmark properties such as the Savoy in London (www.fairmont. com/savoy-london), but in fact within the hotel industry there is huge variation.

The vast majority of hotels are small family-run businesses. Here estimates vary, but a good rule of thumb is that 80 per cent of accommodation establishments have a capacity of less than 50 rooms; the accommodation stock in France, for example, predominantly comprises small hotels. These small, family-run hotels come in a number of forms – many are 'lifestyle businesses' where the owners buy a property in an attractive destination and run it as a small hotel; others are boutique hotels, seeking a niche in the market, such as spas or lifestyle retreats, to compete with the larger companies on personalised service.

The small hotels contrast with the large, professional, heavily branded style of operation demonstrated by the household names of Hilton, Marriott or Intercontinental (www. intercontinental.com). Many of these larger companies also operate hotels on management contracts whilst others operate franchises. The large chains bring the advantage of scale to their operation with their own reservations systems, marketing, training, technology expertise, including the use of social media, and leverage over suppliers. They are also integrated with tour operators and transport companies to provide a seamless product for the tourist.

The hotel sector is very varied. For example, hotels often form part of the national heritage as with the Palace hotels in India, and governments actively encourage conversion of heritage properties into hotels – see, for example, the 'paradores' in Spain (www.paradores-spain.com) or the 'pousadas' in Portugal (www.pousadas.pt). Budget hotels represent a significant growth industry with companies such as 'Travelodge' (www.travelodge.co.uk) and 'Days Inn' (www.daysinn.com) that are heavily branded and operate to strict standards so that the guest knows exactly what to expect in terms of service and the room. Originally developed in North America, budget hotels are now found across Europe in major resorts and cities and also on transport routes at airports, rail stations and motorways. It is a growth sector of the Chinese accommodation industry, and new 'disruptor'-style budget hotels are emerging which offer 'affordable luxury' aimed at the young market. These properties offer shared workspaces, café-style dining and minimalist rooms (see www.citizenm.com). Across the globe, this sector of the hotel industry has grown at the expense of the more variable quality of the bed and breakfast market.

Specialist provision of serviced accommodation in the form of resorts, condominiums and holiday camps exists in major tourism destinations. Early examples include the Butlins holiday resorts established in the UK in the 1930s (www.Butlins.com), which morphed into the Center Parcs resort concept in the late 1960s (www.centerparcs.com). This part of the hotel industry tends to offer accommodation 'plus' other activities. These might include organised activities as well as leisure facilities such as sports, swimming pools and extensive grounds. Many also provide an 'all-inclusive' tariff where food and drink are included. We look at the future of the hotel in Chapter 14, a future which includes a social conscience, as shown in Mini Case Study 8.1.

MINI CASE STUDY 8.1
Lemon Tree Hotels, India

Introduction

This chapter demonstrates that the hospitality sector has firmly embraced environmental principles and has adopted sustainable ways of operating – this is shown clearly in Mini Case Study 8.2, which focuses upon the Accor Group. However, there has been less attention paid to social issues. This case demonstrates the sector-leading work of Lemon Tree Hotels in India, a mid-priced hotel chain that has embraced principles of social sustainability.

Lemon Tree Hotels

Lemon Tree Hotels was founded in 2004. It is India's largest hotel chain in the mid-priced hotel sector, and the third largest hotel chain overall. So, this is not a niche company but a mainstream provider of hotel rooms in India, with 52 hotels and over 5300 rooms. It has plans to expand to over 8000 rooms by 2021.

Lemon Tree Hotel in Ahmedabad, Gujarat, India

Source: ©AjayTvm/Shutterstock.com

Social Inclusion

Lemon Tree Hotels' core mission is to give deprived Indians a route into employment, believing that the brand should not just be about profit. The company has created a socially inclusive workplace, such that by 2018 21 per cent of employees had some form of social disadvantage.
Lemon Tree Hotels' mission commits them to:

- Ensuring the wellbeing and self-worth of our colleagues, who are of the utmost importance to us.

- Contributing to the community we live in and to India in general.

- Delighting our guests, whose comfort, safety, security and wellbeing are our main reason for being.

- Rewarding our stakeholders, whose trust motivates us to excel further.

- Maximising the efficiency of our processes, to enable us to be the most cost-effective brand offering the greatest value, which our customers have every right to expect.

The company believes that persons with disabilities should be provided with work opportunities. This has involved creating a supportive environment to mainstream 'opportunity-deprived Indians' into its workforce. These groups include:

- Employees with a disability such as a physical disability, a speech and hearing impairment, or an orthopaedic disability;
- Acid survivors;
- The visually impaired and those with low vision; and
- Those with an intellectual disability including Downs Syndrome and autism.

In addition, Lemon Tree Hotels is mainstreaming people into the workforce who belong to marginalised sections of society, including those living below the poverty line, are widowed or abandoned/battered/destitute/divorced women, orphans/abandoned girls, individuals from economically weak families, and those from communities who do not get education and employment opportunities easily such as those in remote rural areas.

The social inclusion initiative began in 2007. Early on in the programme, these employees were employed in areas where guest interaction was minimal. Later on, the programme was extended to the restaurant areas by re-engineering the service process.

Lemon Tree Hotels also support tribal art and are the largest buyer nationally of tribal art from some states. This enables the group to support poor tribal craftsmen and allows the chain to showcase its art extensively across its hotels. The company also has a policy of adopting a stray dog in each of its properties, naming the dog, inoculating it and feeding it.

Discussion Questions

1. Why do you think few hotel companies have adopted a far-reaching social inclusion programme?
2. Draft a marketing plan for the company based on the USP of social inclusion.
3. What are some of the downsides of this approach from a hospitality operations point of view?

Source: www.lemontreehotels.com

Bed and breakfast/Guesthouses

Long the source of many jokes as standards and quality can be variable, the guesthouse industry predominantly comprises small businesses which are often owner occupied and come in many forms such as farm stay as well as the traditional small bed and breakfast establishment. The size of establishment and the facilities on offer distinguish guesthouses from hotels, with guesthouses often having only a few bedrooms. Typically, the traditional owner-occupied guesthouse may lack the management expertise and investment to compete with more professional companies. Here, the response has been the highly professional development of lifestyle and luxury guesthouses (see, for example, www.numberone blackpool.com). The major advantage of guesthouses is that they provide a genuine feel and flavour of the destination in a way that the five-star chain hotels fail to do. However, it is still the case that family-run businesses often do not have the expertise to manage a property to its full potential.

Homestay

Homestays, sometimes known as home hosting, are increasingly popular and are a variant on the guesthouse concept. Here tourists stay in the homes of the host community with local families. Homestays can be organised by government tourism organisations as in Malaysia, by individuals as in Bali or by community organisations at the destination. Homestays are viewed as a low-impact form of tourism, allowing tourists to understand local ways of life, cuisine and culture.

Self-serviced accommodation

Self-serviced accommodation does not provide any form of food or beverage and typically comprises rental apartments which are common across the pleasure periphery of Europe and throughout North America, and includes the suites and motels found in North America and Australia. Other forms of self-catering accommodation are timeshare, which we deal with below, the use of university accommodation for tourists in vacation periods or house rental such as the 'gite' concept in France. There is no doubt that this type of accommodation has grown since 1945 and has taken market share from the serviced accommodation industry. There are also blended forms of accommodation that have taken the elements of both serviced and self-serviced accommodation, such as all-suite hotels.

Timeshare

The Resort Development Organisation (RDO) defines timeshare as 'a form of ownership interest that may include an estate interest in immovable property and which allows use of the property on a recurring annual basis for a fixed or variable time period' (https://rdo.org/what-is-timeshare). Effectively, timeshare allows ownership of a holiday property for multiples of weeks and also the opportunity to exchange time in that property for time in another. The timeshare concept began in Europe in the 1960s as an innovative way of increasing and diversifying the tourism offer and it has developed significantly since then. It does, however, have a reputation for pressure selling, and in response the European Union has implemented the timeshare directive to regulate the industry. Traditionally, timeshare properties were concentrated in North America, the Caribbean and Europe, but they are growing in Asia and the former countries of Eastern Europe. It is interesting that many timeshare properties were purchased by the baby boomer generation and it is not certain that their children will want to continue with the arrangement.

Camping, caravans and motor homes

Camping has a down-market image, but this contrasts with the concept of luxury camp-sites in, say, the safari parks of Africa or the notion of up-market camping – 'glamping'. In countries such as Australia and the USA, camping is a popular domestic holiday option, and campsites are well equipped with electricity, water, entertainment and Internet access. Caravans and motor homes provide 'mobile' accommodation for the owners, and these vehicles can also be rented – to travel across North America or Australia, for example. Caravan sites provide for both 'static' and 'mobile' caravans but have been criticised on the basis of their impact on the landscape.

Conventions and meetings

The conventions and meetings market is an important part of the hospitality industry. Often facilities are provided within hotels, but it is also common for destinations to have their own dedicated convention centre. The conventions and meetings industry is a major generator of revenue for companies and destinations, with delegates typically spending more than the leisure tourist, although the length of stay tends to be shorter. Competition for conferences and meetings is fierce and, whilst the major international conferences attract the headlines, it is the smaller domestic meetings that are the mainstay of the industry.

Peer-to-peer accommodation

The second decade of the twenty-first century saw the rise of peer-to peer accommodation as a major disruptive innovation in hospitality. This variant of hospitality uses a website or app to put people who are seeking accommodation in touch with those who have accommodation available, often in private homes or apartments. The most well known of these companies is Airbnb, which is dealt with in Major Case Study 8.1.

Non-commercial forms of accommodation

This chapter is mainly concerned with the commercial side of the hospitality industry, but it must be remembered that there is a considerable non-commercial industry when it comes to tourism accommodation. The visiting friends and relatives (VFR) market, for example, is well known, but it is important also to consider tourists' use of their own properties, such as second homes, boats for overnight accommodation or exchanging homes with tourists from another destination (Müller, 2014). Visiting friends and relatives is often overlooked as an accommodation type, and surveys of bed nights in destinations frequently undercount because they fail to survey VFR. In recent years, destination management organisations have realised the value of the VFR market for attractions and the economic benefits it delivers to the destination.

Food and beverage

Food and beverage is essential to the tourism product, but it is also increasingly complex as new concepts emerge and traditional boundaries between product types become blurred. For example, traditionally in the UK, pubs were in the beverage industry but increasingly they are a major force in food retailing. Rather like accommodation, food and beverage is one of the earliest commercial industries with provision of food and drink for strangers. Of course, a large proportion of the food and beverage market is local residents, but many food and drink outlets also have a significant percentage of turnover from tourists (as shown when discussing the tourism satellite account in Chapter 3). This is particularly the case in major destinations such as Orlando in Florida or Australia's Gold Coast.

Food and beverage outlets can be classified in many ways, but the most common approach is to think of them as restaurants, fast food outlets, bars, cafeterias, clubs and canteens. Here, fast food outlets have seen the most rapid growth, built upon a robust business model which delivers high levels of productivity, low costs and use of the franchise model, although concerns for healthy eating and carbon emissions have meant that they have had to make menu adjustments, including offering vegan products. Two key issues for the food service industry are:

1. Labour supply and the quality of jobs on offer (as shown in Chapter 3); and

2. Its sensitivity to economic conditions for demand.

The future of the sector is examined in Chapter 14.

Gaming

With historic roots in destinations such as Monte Carlo (www.monte-carlo.mc), gaming has now become a major economic phenomenon in destinations such as Las Vegas (www.visitlasvegas.com) and Macau (www.macautourism.gov.mo). Legalisation of gambling in the latter half of the twentieth century allowed companies to tap into considerable latent demand and created a sub-sector of the hospitality industry based upon casinos, often within large themed hotels. Here, resorts such as Las Vegas have cleverly integrated gaming with other attractions such as big-ticket entertainment events and cabaret. Casinos are used by governments as a source of revenue to revitalise run-down resorts (as at Scheveningen in the Netherlands) and as a means to further develop tourism. Gaming as an activity is often opposed by local residents, who link the activity with crime and the social consequences of gambling addiction. The future of gaming linked to tourism may be constrained by the increased availability of Internet gaming, and the increased legalisation of gaming means that gamblers will not need to travel to find a casino.

Hospitality organisations

At the international level, the International Hotel and Restaurant Association (IHRA – www.ih-ra.org) was founded in 1946 in Paris and is the peak industry body, providing industry information and research for the industry as well as lobbying in bodies such as the UNWTO.

At the national level, each country has its own set of organisations. The two major trade associations in North America are the American Hotel and Lodging Association (www.ahla.com) and the National Restaurant Association (www.restaurant.org). They provide a range of support for their members including publications, lobbying and advice on industry practice. In the UK, the major trade association is UK Hospitality which provides services for its members (www.ukhospitality.org.uk).

At the destination level, there are many organisations representing the hospitality industry; indeed, some argue that this has led to fragmented representation of the industry in many destinations. For example, a destination may have separate trade associations for guest houses, hotels and for restaurants.

MANAGING THE HOSPITALITY INDUSTRY

The hospitality industry is large and complex, demanding particular management approaches. These approaches focus upon management, marketing and quality management.

Management approaches

At the strategic level, there is increasing pressure upon large hospitality businesses to deliver a return on investment for their owners and investors. Traditionally, the hospitality industry has been characterised by low rates of return on investment, and this explains the fact that many investors enter the hospitality industry for the long-term gains of property value and business goodwill rather than short-term considerations of profitability. A strategy of growth has meant that in the hotel sector, for example, there is a trend to larger and larger hotels. With this trend, new management options have emerged as often owners of hospitality businesses are now companies such as financial institutions that do not have the expertise needed to run the business. As a result, there is a trend towards increasing concentration in the hospitality industry. This is due simply to the advantages that can be leveraged by larger organisations. Indeed, globally the hotel industry is dominated by a small group of large companies. Economies of scale for hotels are found in increased purchasing power, economies of centralising services such as laundry, reservations or marketing, the ability to raise finance and lower administration and training costs.

International strategy

These trends are set against the background of a global marketplace, the rise of e-intermediaries and the Internet, which is encouraging the development of online review sites such as www.tripadvisor.com (as detailed in Chapter 13). For market and revenue growth, hospitality businesses look beyond domestic markets to international expansion. This has led to two contrasting approaches:

1. Development of standardised products, operating procedures and properties across the world – here there is a danger of all destinations becoming similar with identikit Hiltons, Marriotts and fast food outlets; or

2. Development of locally sensitised products and locally designed hotels and products tailored according to the destination, often by companies that specialise in particular regions of the world, such as the Taj group in India (www.tajhotels.com) – the issue here is for companies to balance the need for international quality standards with local delivery in indigenously designed properties with local decor and culture.

Of course, the disadvantage of either approach for the destination is that profits may be repatriated to the home country head office. The Maldives is a good example of a destination that suffers in this way.

Management strategies

Strategic options for hospitality businesses focus upon creating market and revenue growth. These options include:

- **Management contracts**. Management contracts are common in the hospitality industry, particularly in larger properties at the upper end of the market. Here, a professional management company manages the property on behalf of the owner, bringing guaranteed operating standards and good practice. Knowles (1998: 73) defines a management contract as 'a written agreement between the owner and the operator of a hotel ... by which the owner employs the operator as an agent to assume full responsibility for operating and managing the property'.

  Management contracts benefit owners of hotels who may not have an expertise in hospitality or a desire to operate the property, and they benefit the managing company which does not have to have large capital commitments in property. In other words, the owner supplies the fixed assets including the property and grounds, whilst the operator undertakes operation of the property for an agreed management fee. Contracts vary in their arrangements, but all have up-front expectations of performance in terms of income and profitability.

- **Franchising**. Franchising is a common strategy in the hospitality industry as it avoids expensive fixed investment costs. It is found in both accommodation companies (especially in the budget market) and food service companies (such as McDonalds – www.mcdonalds.com, and Pizza Express – www.pizzaexpress.com). Franchising operates by the *franchisor* granting the rights to a product format – such as a fast food restaurant – to a *franchisee,* and the right to distribute its products or services. Franchising brings significant benefits for both sides – the franchisor can grow their concept rapidly using investment from the franchisee, whilst the franchisee has access to an established product and support network such as market and product knowledge, allowing access to the industry for small businesses. Normally the franchisee pays an upfront fee and then a percentage of turnover to the franchisor. However, franchising can provide problems for the franchising group, particularly in terms of maintaining quality and standards.

- **Consortia.** One issue for small hospitality businesses is their lack of marketing and purchasing power. This has led to the development of 'consortia' of businesses where resources are pooled for purchasing and marketing. As a result, the businesses are often marketed under one brand name, even though they are each independently owned. The Best Western Group is an example of a successful consortium (www.bestwestern.com).

- **Contract catering.** The hospitality industry has a poor image as an employer and there is a perennial shortage of skilled labour such as chefs. For the industry, use of contract caterers to provide 'cook chill' meals is a common solution as it cuts out the need for skilled functions. As a result, it has been accused of encouraging de-skilling.

Marketing approaches

Sophisticated hospitality marketing began in the USA in the post-war period with the strong development of brands such as Holiday Inn. As a service, the hospitality product is produced where it is consumed. It is therefore important for hospitality managers to understand where their customers come from, and to raise awareness of their premises to boost the flow of customers. The hospitality product itself comprises both tangible elements, the bedroom or the food, and intangible elements such as the ambience of a hotel, or the service in a restaurant. For accommodation, Medlik and Ingram (2000) have developed five features which impact upon the market and the marketing of a property:

1. **Location** is a primary influence upon the market, whether by the geographical location of the hotel within the destination, or the destination itself. Resort hotels will experience annual seasonality, whilst city hotels will experience weekly peaking of demand, busier during the week and with less demand at the weekend; hence they offer cheaper leisure-based packages for Friday and Saturday night.

2. **The mix of facilities** in terms of public rooms, leisure centre, WiFi access, restaurants or conference halls is an important influence. The mix will depend upon the particular market served – for example, demand for accommodation itself tends to be from national and international markets, whilst demand for restaurants will be more localised.

3. **Image** in terms of formality and how it is presented to the market, particularly in terms of websites and presence on social media.

4. **The type of service** provided, including the level of staffing.

5. **Price** is also influenced by the factors above – for example, location and the level of facilities and services all impact upon the price charged. Hotels will also vary their prices according to season and market segment.

The larger hospitality companies lead the way in terms of marketing thinking, especially in terms of market segmentation and distribution strategies.

Market segmentation has grown in significance in the hospitality industry, particularly in the accommodation sector. In the early years of hospitality marketing, segmentation was crudely based upon segments such as leisure, business or convention groups. However, with increased competition in the industry, segmentation has become more sophisticated and includes preferences and motivations for stay. For example, the larger chains offer different products for different segments from budget to luxury formats. As a result, many of the larger chains have diversified their branding to meet the particular needs of market segments, to develop brand loyalty (through, for example, loyalty schemes such as IHG 'Rewards Club') and to clarify their product offering in the face of confusion over accommodation grading. Here, development of budget brands is a common response. A useful example is the Accor group which has developed luxury properties marketed as Sofitel or Novotel, whilst their budget brands are the Ibis and Formule 1 brands (www.accorhotels.com). This allows Accor to closely target the hotel product to the particular market segment through pricing, facilities and marketing.

In terms of distribution, the larger hotel chains and consortia have access to computer reservation systems and keep in close touch with tour operators, both the airlines and their computer reservations systems (CRS) and the coach companies. With Internet distribution many hospitality companies not only have their own website, but they also provide their room stock to last-minute booking sites such as www.lastminute.com and www.wotif.com. For smaller accommodation units, public sector tourist boards also provide a source of bookings for a commission.

Managing quality

To be a successful hospitality business it is vital to be customer focused and to understand the needs of the guest at each 'touch point' with the unit and its personnel. Here, the concept of the 'guest cycle' is useful (Figure 8.2). The hospitality industry has embraced the concept of quality in terms of service-oriented strategies (Solnet, 2015). In other words, the heart of a hospitality business is anticipating and serving customer needs. Solnet (2015) identifies the key dimensions of this approach:

- **The service encounter** can be defined as the interaction between a guest and a hospitality operation through its frontline employees. If the encounter is successful, it builds loyalty and creates satisfaction. To quote Solnet (2015: 106) 'At the heart of service management is the unavoidable fact that a significant proportion of tourism experiences are delivered by people (tourism employees, managers, owners). From the tourist's perspective, the most immediate evidence of service quality is the service encounter itself.' Customer contact employees are a hospitality organisation's primary interface with customers and, as such, employees are often perceived by the customer as being the product itself, although the situation is changing, as shown in this chapter's Focus on Technology.

FOCUS ON TECHNOLOGY

Service Delivery by Robots

The falling costs of technology have allowed the manufacture of robots to replace humans in the hospitality service delivery environment. Where robots are already used – such as in the 'Weird' Hotel in Japan (www.h-n-h.jp/en), robots are proving to be a novelty with family travellers, increasing guest satisfaction with their entertaining operation and allowing children to take 'robot selfies'. In other words, robots not only perform dirty and dull work but now can interact with and entertain guests as they have become more approachable and less frightening. Robots can collect data whilst they are operating and free up human staff for other duties.

Of course, traditionalists say that robot service lacks the warmth and charm of human contact but, in fact, evidence is quite the contrary. So, hospitality is vulnerable to the use of robots and artificial intelligence because tasks are routine and the operating environment is stable. Estimates suggest that up to 30 per cent of current jobs will be obsolete by the early 2030s and that robots, particularly in the hospitality sector, will be the norm by the mid-2020s, replacing blue collar jobs. Applications of robots and artficial intelligence in tourism are dealt with in more detail in Chapter 14.

- **Customer satisfaction** is difficult to measure but generally when customers are satisfied, they become loyal, often repeat their visit, will recommend and become less price sensitive. Indeed, so important is this concept to the service approach that many operations now aim to 'delight' rather than merely 'satisfy' the customer.
- **Service quality** has been defined as a cognitive evaluation of a performance by a service provider (Parasuraman et al., 1988) and its broad dimensions include some degrees of

reliability, responsiveness, tangibles, empathy and assurance (Solnet, 2015). Measuring service quality is particularly difficult, because different people rate individual dimensions of service in different ways and with different weightings of importance.

There are two distinct models of service quality:

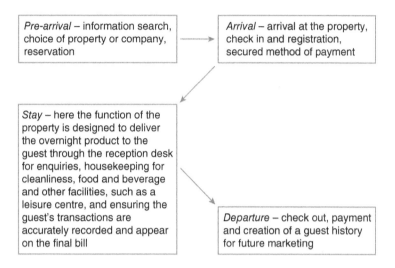

FIGURE 8.2 Guest cycle for an accommodation unit

- SERVQUAL, where service quality is measured using five dimensions, evaluating the guest's actual experience with their expectations (Parasuraman et al., 1988 – this paper has been chosen as the classic paper for this chapter); and
- the Nordic Model, which has two dimensions – an 'outcome' dimension, such as providing a meal, and a 'process' dimension – how the meal was prepared and served.

Linking service quality and business performance has emerged as an important driver of hospitality businesses. Here, hospitality operations develop quality management programmes to overtly boost financial performance through building customer satisfaction and loyalty.

CLASSIC PAPER

Parasuraman, A., Berry, L. and Zeithaml, V. (1988) 'SERVQUAL: a multiple-item scale for measuring consumer perceptions of service quality', *Journal of Retailing,* **64 (1): 12–40**

This paper has become a classic, is frequently cited and has spawned a set of literature of its own, focusing upon their particular model of service quality.

(Continued)

As a result, there are many interpretations, debates and controversies surrounding their SERVQUAL model. Nonetheless, there is no substitute for returning to their original paper and reading it before forming a view.

The paper introduces the concept of service quality and takes the view that the consumer defines service quality, seeking certain benefits from any service that is performed on their behalf. The article then identifies five 'gaps' that may be experienced by the consumer when the service delivered does not come up to expectations Their model has subsequently become known as the service quality 'gaps' model, labelled by the three authors as 'SERVQUAL'.

The basis of SERVQUAL is five dimensions of service:

1. **Reliability** – accurate and dependable service;
2. **Responsiveness** – prompt and helpful service;
3. **Empathy** – caring and personalised attention;
4. **Assurance** – knowledgeable and trustworthy; and
5. **Tangibles** – appearance of physical facilities.

These dimensions are used in the pre- and post-evaluation of a service in order to compare the variance between expectation and actual performance.

The SERVQUAL model is known as a 'gaps' model because of its measurement of the variance between expectations and performance. The paper goes on to develop a measurement approach to five gaps between expectation and performance:

1. **Gap between management perceptions and consumer expectations** – the company does not understand its market and the service is not aligned with what the customer expects.
2. **Gap between management perceptions and service specification** – this may occur when the company is trying to reduce costs and so fails to deliver a service that meets expectations.
3. **Gap between service quality specification and service delivery** – here it is at the point of delivery that the service fails to satisfy, often due to poor training of frontline staff.
4. **Gap between service delivery and external communications** – effectively this means that the company has overpromised in terms of service delivery and the reality has not met the promise.
5. **Gap between expectations and perceptions** – the totality of the service delivery does not meet customer expectations.

As mentioned above, SERVQUAL has generated controversy, particularly in terms of its measurement approach and the difficulty of applying it across different types of service, from hospitality to banking.

Classification and grading

An important aspect of controlling the quality of hospitality businesses is the classification and grading of accommodation and food service outlets. It is done for quality control purposes, legislation and consumer information. An added benefit is that it encourages owners to invest in their properties, raises standards and provides a means of comparing across properties in similar price and quality bands. It also provides properties with differentiated positioning for marketing purposes. Classification and grading is a controversial issue and competing organisations are involved in the process:

- In some countries, registration for classification and grading purposes is compulsory to gain a licence to operate – schemes are often run by tourism ministries or boards and some argue that this approach generates red tape and inhibits innovation.
- Private organisations are also involved and include the Automobile Association with its star rating of accommodation (www.theaa.com) and Michelin (https://guide.michelin.com/gb/en).
- Public industry organisations such as tourist boards also classify and grade accommodation for legal purposes.

It is important to distinguish between 'classification' (which allocates properties to a particular class on the basis of their features and services – in other words, it is a descriptive approach) and 'grading' (which looks not only at the facilities but also at a range of verifiable features and services, such as the time room service is available, to deliver a 'grade' for the property). Both grading and classification schemes operate on an inspection basis.

The very many different schemes and lack of agreement mean that, for the consumer, classification and grading schemes can be both confusing and misleading. They have also been criticised for being too subjective, based upon an inspector's judgement, as well as only relating to the particular point in time when the inspection is done.

HOSPITALITY OPERATIONS

At the heart of any hospitality operation are the human resources involved and their ability to deliver a high-quality service. This is essential in the concept of service marketing where the staff not only influence perception and evaluation of the hotel stay or the meal experience but are also closely involved in the 'co-creation' of the hospitality experience. Of course, this process must deliver a profitable business for the company. As a result, the role of a hospitality manager in a pub, restaurant, hotel or resort is complex, involving a thorough understanding of all elements of the business. These elements are outlined below.

Finance

Most hospitality businesses, and particularly accommodation properties, require major investment in the fixed plant of a destination. As a result, hotel and resort financing and investment have attracted considerable literature and interest. The level of investment in accommodation at a destination can act as a major constraint upon tourism development, or as a stimulus. In Australia, for example, the opening up of new budget airline routes to regional airports prompted a considerable investment in accommodation in 'new' destinations.

Location is an important consideration for accommodation investors. This is not only due to the importance of location in relation to the market, but also because the bulk of investment in accommodation units is in the land and the buildings. In other words, the up-front investment required is considerable and this impacts upon pricing decisions as the revenue streams from the unit have to contribute to very high fixed costs, whilst the variable costs of each extra guest are low. This means that accommodation units have to achieve high levels of utilisation. Of course, here the classic dilemma of services is at play, as an unsold room can never recoup the lost revenue – hence the importance of techniques such as yield management to maximise revenue, and of understanding the various market segments for the accommodation unit.

The hospitality industry is characterised by a high ratio of fixed costs to operating costs – quite simply, the fixed costs in developing and building an accommodation unit, for example, are very high and are therefore subject to an extensive feasibility study.

The main elements of hotel balance accounts are as follows (also see Figure 8.3):

- Rooms revenue – depends on the rate charged and the occupancy level;
- Food and beverage revenue – partly dependent upon occupancy, but also upon the local market and includes revenue from functions and events; and
- Other revenue.

The relative importance of each of these three sources will vary according to the size, location and market for the hotel.

The operating costs for a large hotel can be classified as:

- Labour;
- Marketing and administration;
- Energy and maintenance; and
- Food and beverage.

Of these costs, labour is by far the highest, and for five-star hotels the number of employees per guest is substantially higher than for budget hotels. As a result, some companies are experimenting in the use of robots to provide service, as in the Weird Hotel in Tokyo, Japan, and robot bars on cruise ships (see the Royal Caribbean Lines' *Anthem of the Seas*), as shown in the technology box in this chapter. The ratio of staff per guest also varies in different parts of the world where, for example, unemployment may be high and wage costs low. Both revenue and costs are captured in an accounting system that is unique to the industry, known as the 'uniform system of accounts', developed to allow the accounts of different properties to be compared. In addition to the economic cost of labour, we also have to consider the human cost, as shown in the 'Focus on employability'.

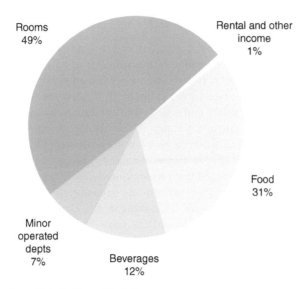

Rooms
49%

Rental and other
income
1%

Food
31%

Beverages
12%

Minor
operated
depts
7%

FIGURE 8.3   Percentage distribution of hotel revenue

Source: Knowles, 1998

FOCUS ON EMPLOYABILITY

Human rights and modern slavery in hospitality

The nature of the hospitality workforce, with temporary, part-time and shift work, lends itself to the exploitation of vulnerable employee groups. As a result, many larger hospitality companies have introduced diversity and inclusion in their operations and in the supply chain. Some, such as Marriott, are now leading the sector in this area and have gone further by adopting human rights principles into their HR operations. This includes being aware of the dangers of modern slavery and human trafficking (Marriott, 2017). The company has a training programme for human rights and a reporting process for issues such as suspicion of modern slavery. Marriott has developed three key goals in this area:

1. By 2025, 100 per cent of associates will have completed human rights training, including on human trafficking awareness, responsible sourcing and recruitment policies and practices.

2. By 2025, Marriott will enhance and embed human rights criteria in recruitment and sourcing policies and work with the sector to address human rights risks in the construction phase.

3. By 2025, Marriott will have invested at least $500,000 in partnerships that drive, evaluate and elevate tourism's role in cultural understanding.

Source: Marriott International (2017) *Sustainability and Social Impact Goals*. Bethesda, MD: Marriott International.

Occupancy and yield management

The concepts of occupancy and yield management are important tools for the hospitality manager. Occupancy is a simple measure of the number of rooms or beds occupied as a percentage of the total available. It is also used in the food service industry with 'covers' as the measure. Average accommodation occupancies worldwide are around 65 per cent, but across Asia and in many world cities such as London, New York and Milan they are considerably higher. In most European capitals, the average room rates are also high. In contrast, destinations in decline, such as some cold-water resorts, experience a marked seasonal peaking of occupancy that brings down the overall average.

Yield management is a technique used to maximise the revenue achieved per room by managing occupancy. Ideally, hotels will achieve the full, advertised price for the room (rack rate) but more commonly they will vary their rates in a trade-off between occupancy and yield per room. Accommodation has adapted the concept of yield from the airline industry and the larger companies have sophisticated yield (or revenue) management systems designed to cope with peaks and troughs in demand. This has given rise to the notion of late booking where consumers can book a room at the last minute for a cheaper price, as the property discounts the room to make a contribution to fixed costs. Specialist websites such as lastminute.com, LateRooms.com and Wotif.com have taken advantage of this trend.

Hospitality management

Managing a hospitality unit is an increasingly complex task, and managers in the twenty-first century are expected to possess a wide range of competencies and knowledge. For accommodation, most establishments have a management structure that distinguishes between:

- revenue-earning activities such as restaurant, accommodation and other functions such as a leisure centre; and
- service activities such as marketing and reservations.

These functions are normally divided into departments – such as front of house, to allow for accurate accounting and cost control. The following are the major operational departments in a hotel:

- **The rooms department** includes all those functions related to the overnight stay of the guest and will include reception/front office and housekeeping.
- **The food and beverage department** is concerned with the production of food and beverage service on the property, from ordering and receipt of goods, menu design and kitchen operations through to managing the various food and beverage outlets in the property. In recent years, this department has become the focus of a major new branch of legislation – food safety – partly in response to a rise in the number of food poisoning cases. Here, technology is increasingly being used in menu design and cost control.
- **The administration department** is the main servicing area for the property's business and includes functions such as accounts, marketing and reservations, human resources, engineering and maintenance, and one function which has become increasingly

important – security and risk management. This area, along with the front office, has seen the greatest impact of technology. Indeed, technology has transformed the hospitality industry through online services for guests, social media and the use of software marketing, reservations, managing properties and cost control.

ENVIRONMENTAL ISSUES

Environmental issues for the hospitality industry have come to the fore since the 1990s and are of increasing concern to consumers (Fennell and Cooper, 2020). Surprisingly, the accommodation industry is a significant source of carbon emissions, as well as being perceived as a heavy user of energy and water. Major accommodation developments have to undergo an environmental impact assessment, whilst many properties adopt environmental auditing of their operations. Of course, there is controversy over how the industry has addressed these issues, with some using 'green' initiatives as a major marketing point of differentiation. Accor, for example, has state-of-the-art environmental management systems and publishes its green credentials in its annual report, as shown in Mini Case Study 8.2. Of course, a related major issue is that most hospitality enterprises are SMEs and this brings its own challenges in terms of sustainability. There are a number of initiatives which have been established to promote sound environmental behaviour by hotels:

- The International Tourism Partnership (www.tourismpartnership.org) provides advice to accommodation companies on responsible business, including energy consumption and greening the supply chain.
- Hotel Energy Solutions is an energy management toolkit available for accommodation properties supported by international agencies including the IHRA and the UNWTO (www.hotelenergysolutions.net). The initiative deals with energy strategies, including saving energy costs and advice on installing renewable energy systems, claiming savings of 20 per cent on energy costs with simple operational changes.
- The Global Sustainable Tourism Council is an independent and not-for-profit organisation that publishes a set of criteria for sustainability in the tourism sector, including hospitality-specific criteria.
- The Considerate Group (https://considerate group.com) is an association of independent hoteliers that encourages and supports good, socially responsible environmental policies and practices in their properties. Initiatives include publications on 'green sourcing' and saving energy costs.

These initatives have encouraged a range of sustainable practices in hospitality, including:

- Corporate social responsibility;
- Dedicated sustainable management systems for properties;
- Adoption of green supply chain practices;
- Resource conservation – particularly energy and water; and
- Reduction in pollution and waste.

MINI CASE STUDY 8.2

The Accor Group – Research Leadership in Sustainability

Introduction

Accor is one of the world's major international hotel chains. The company leads the sector in terms of its thinking and operations in sustainability. At Accor, sustainability is wired into key performance indicators, reporting and every aspect of the company's operation. It is not treated as an add-on or as 'greenwashing'. Accor's commitment to sustainability dates back to the mid-1990s, but it is the more recent initiatives and research which mark the company out as a leader in the field, particularly the research underpinning its five-year sustainability strategy.

Accor aims to 'create a virtuous circle that benefits its ecosystem – comprising employees, customers, partners, local communities, in which hotels are implanted … creating value for its operations' (Accor, 2011, p. 2). In other words, all stakeholders are involved, including hotel guests and suppliers, which is essential if Accor is to reduce its environmental impact. But also, and perhaps more importantly, Accor is honest in its statement that it is involved in this field to boost its 'competitiveness'.

Accor's 'Sustainable Development Department' initiates sustainability projects and assists in the implementation of sustainable development for both accommodation operations and support services (such as HR, purchasing or marketing) through the communication of good practice and development of projects.

Accor has developed a new sustainability strategy (Accor, 2016c) underpinned by its 'earth guest research'.

Earth Guest Research

In 2011, Accor released its groundbreaking research into the environmental and socio-economic footprint of its guests and the company Earth Guest Research. The research is the basis for communication to the rest of the industry and for training and e-learning modules, clearly demonstrating Accor's leadership in this field. Three reports were released:

1. *Sustainable Hospitality* is a study of guest attitudes to sustainability (Accor, 2011). The key idea is to understand the impact of its guests from booking to checking out and beyond.
2. *The Accor Group's Environmental Footprint* is a multi-criteria life cycle analysis (Accor, 2016a). The study set out to assess the impact of the Accor group on the environment and, by focusing on the total life cycle, it looks back to the impact of suppliers – such as dairy farms – on the environment.
3. *Accor Hotel's Socio-economic Footprint* (Accor, 2016b) researches the social and economic impact of the group's hospitality operations and its value chain across 92 countries. As the businesses in this value chain play a decisive role in creating financial value for Accor, the research provides a broader picture of its business model.

Discussion Questions

1. How would you communicate Accor's leadership in sustainability to a hotel guest in the property?
2. Why do you think Accor has invested so much in research and development for sustainability?
3. How would you communicate the environmental imperative to a small, family-run guest house?

Sources: Accor (2011) *Sustainable Hospitality: Ready to Check In*. Paris: Accor; Accor (2016a) *The Accor Group's Environmental Footprint*. Paris: Accor; Accor (2016b) *Accor Hotel's Socio-economic Footprint*. Paris: Accor; Accor (2016c) *Planet 21 Season 2*. Paris: Accor; www.accorhotels.com/gb/sustainable-development/index.shtml

SUMMARY

This chapter has analysed the hospitality industry as a key element of the tourism system as it provides the overnight stay. The industry is significant in economic terms and scale globally, though it comprises predominantly small businesses. In the past, it has been narrowly defined as the commercial part of the industry, but contemporary approaches now view hospitality more generally as including all transactions and the space in which they occur. The chapter showed that the hospitality industry is complex, comprising many sectors such as serviced and self-serviced accommodation, food service outlets, non-commercial activities such as visiting friends and relatives, and new segments such as Airbnb (see Major Case Study 8.1). Managing the hospitality industry is complex, and there are a number of approaches that have been used to minimise investment, including management contracts and franchising as well as upgrading properties. The industry has become adept at marketing too in recent years, closely matching, say, accommodation products with market segments and embracing digital marketing and social media. This is particularly true of the larger companies. Of course, the heart of hospitality is providing service, and we have seen the various approaches to service quality and its management. The chapter then considered the operational aspects of hospitality management and closed with an overview of the environmental issues facing the sector and some of the responses to these issues, including a case study of Accor's sustainability approach.

DISCUSSION QUESTIONS

1. The dominance of small businesses in hospitality means that it will be difficult to improve environmental practice. How true is this statement?

2. Taking a large hotel chain of your choice, examine the various brands that it uses to market its group of properties and draft a customer profile for each brand.

3. As the CEO of a major restaurant chain, draft a memo to your board explaining the advantages of franchising your concept to achieve growth.

4. Examining a recent hospitality experience, how 'customer centric' was the experience?

5. Design in outline a training scheme for prospective small businesses wishing to enter the guesthouse industry.

ANNOTATED FURTHER READING

Dolnicar, S. (2019) 'A review of research into paid online peer-to-peer accommodation: launching the *Annals of Tourism Research* Curated Collection on peer-to-peer accommodation', *Annals of Tourism Research*, 75: 248–64.

Authoritative, comprehensive overview of peer-to-peer accommodation.

Hawkins, R. and Bohdanowicz, P. (2011) *Responsible Hospitality*. Oxford: Goodfellow.

Accessible and contemporary account of sustainability and CSR.

Lashley, C. (2019) 'Hospitality management', in C. Cooper, S. Volo, W.C. Gartner and N. Scott (eds), *The Sage Handbook of Tourism Management: Applications of Theories and Concepts to Tourism*. London: Sage. pp. 328–43.

Contemporary coverage of all the key issues and literature in hospitality.

Lashley, C. and Morrison, A. (eds) (2000) *In Search of Hospitality: Theoretical Perspectives and Debates*. Oxford: Butterworth-Heinemann.

Landmark volume challenging traditional thinking about hospitality as a subject and an industry.

Solnet, D. (2015) 'Service management and tourism', in C. Cooper (ed.), *Contemporary Tourism Reviews, Volume 1*. Oxford: Goodfellow. pp. 91–128.

Contemporary and practitioner-based account of service management approaches.

Wood, R. (ed.) (2015) *Hospitality Management: A Brief Introduction*. London: Sage.

Thorough review of all aspects of hospitality management by renowned authors.

REFERENCES CITED

Fennell, D. and Cooper, C. (2020) *Sustainable Tourism: Principles, Contexts and Practices*. Bristol: Channel View.

Jones, P. (2004) 'Finding the hospitality industry or finding hospitality schools of thought', *Journal of Hospitality, Leisure, Sport and Tourism Education*, 3 (1): 33–45.

Knowles, T. (1998) *Hospitality Management: An Introduction*. Harlow: Longman.

Lashley, C. (2000) 'Towards a theoretical understanding', in C. Lashley and A. Morrison (eds), *In Search of Hospitality: Theoretical Perspectives and Debates*. Oxford: Butterworth-Heinemann. pp. 1–17.

Lashley, C. (2019) 'Hospitality management', in C. Cooper, S. Volo, W.C. Gartner and N. Scott (eds), *The Sage Handbook of Tourism Management: Applications of Theories and Concepts to Tourism*. London: Sage. pp. 328–43.

Lashley, C. and Morrison, A. (eds) (2000) *In Search of Hospitality: Theoretical Perspectives and Debates*. Oxford: Butterworth-Heinemann.

Leiper, N. (1990) *Tourism Systems*. Auckland: Massey University Department of Management Systems, Occasional Paper 2.

Lynch, P., Molz, J.G., Mcintosh, A., Lugosi, P. and Lashley, C. (2011) 'Theorizing hospitality', *Hospitality & Society*, 1 (1): 3–24.

Medlik, R. and Ingram, S. (2000) *The Business of Hotels*. Oxford: Butterworth-Heinemann.

Müller, D. (2014) 'Progress in second home tourism research', in A.L. Lew, C.M. Hall and A.M. Williams (eds), *The Wiley Blackwell Companion to Tourism*. Chichester: Wiley. pp. 389–400.

Parasuraman, A., Berry, L. and Zeithaml, V. (1988) 'SERVQUAL: a multiple-item scale for measuring consumer perceptions of service quality', *Journal of Retailing*, 64 (1): 12–40.

Solnet, D. (2015) 'Service management and tourism', in C. Cooper (ed.), *Contemporary Tourism Reviews, Volume 1*. Oxford: Goodfellow. pp. 91–128.

MAJOR CASE STUDY 8.1

Airbnb – Redefining Hospitality

Airbnb is part of the sharing economy

Source: 'Airbnb Office' by Open Grid Scheduler/Grid Engine is licensed under CC0 1.0

(Continued)

The Sharing Economy

Airbnb is part of the sharing economy which operates by mobilising assets with idling capacity – in this case properties or rooms. As such, it bypasses traditional regulation, distribution and ownership models and, as a result, has sparked furious opposition. Hospitality is particularly vulnerable to this type of 'disruptive innovation' and Airbnb has taken advantage of this by providing a website that connects people who have space to share with those who are looking for a place to stay (Dolnicar, 2019).

Background

The Airbnb concept traces its roots back to 2007 when a US website offered private accommodation for conference delegates. It was launched as airbedandbreakfast.com in 2008, based on bed and breakfast in private homes using air beds in bedrooms and living rooms. By 2009 the concept was spreading across the USA and it was renamed Airbnb; by 2011 Airbnb was acquiring competitors internationally and began opening new offices – initially in Paris, Milan, Barcelona, Copenhagen, Moscow and São Paulo to add to its existing offices in San Francisco, London, Hamburg and Berlin. Expansion continued into Asia, and by 2019 Airbnb estimates suggest Airbnb will take over 500 million bookings/night by the early 2020s. The scale of the company is impressive with over 4 million listings in 2019.

The Concept

Airbnb is a perfect example of innovation in the hospitality sector with a very new concept and way of doing business – effectively a technology company morphing into a hospitality company. It is also an example of the growth of the 'sharing economy'. The concept is clear: 'Airbnb is an online marketplace for vacation rentals that connects users with property to rent with users looking to rent the space' (www.airbnb.com).

The concept is a simple one, bringing together 'hosts' who have spare rooms or space in their property, or indeed a spare property to rent, and 'guests' who are seeking accommodation in the particular location.

Hosts

The Airbnb website gives very clear guidance for those thinking of acting as hosts: 'We encourage hosts to think carefully about their responsibilities. Hosting offers rich experiences, but it comes with a certain level of commitment' (www.airbnb.com).

Guests

Guttentag et al. (2017) have researched five motivating factors that drive guests to book on Airbnb – interaction with the destination, home away from home, novelty, the sharing economy ethos and local authenticity. Cheng and Jin's (2019) research identified three straightfoward reasons for booking – location, amenities and the host.

The Business Model

The Airbnb concept is innovative whilst being simple and clear. The key features of the business model are:

- Airbnb provides a secure payment method for the transaction – Airbnb's primary source of revenue comes from service fees from bookings;
- Both hosts and guests must register with Airbnb and pay a fee per booking;
- There is an almost zero marginal cost to add a room or property to the system, unlike for traditional suppliers. Airbnb does not own any rooms or properties;
- Both hosts and guests have profiles which include features such as user reviews and shared social connections to build reputation and trust in the Airbnb marketplace;
- Airbnb provides a secure messaging system for hosts and guests to communicate;
- Airbnb provides insurance against such things as damage and theft;
- Airbnb is now diversifying its offer and includes:

  o 'Airbnb experiences' and 'Airbnb adventures' including a Kenyan warrior camp and cliff camping in Colorado;

o Airbnb Plus, a collection of homes that have been vetted for quality of services, comfort and design; and

o Beyond by Airbnb, which offers luxury vacation rental properties.

- Airbnb's operation is data-driven, constantly collecting and analysing its market – a lesson for traditional providers. It uses this data to power algorithmic management strategies;

- Airbnb has developed a social networking system, particularly using Facebook; and

- Airbnb has developed a 'neighbourhoods' product which acts as a guide to the locality.

For the future, Airbnb is looking at acquiring other parts of the tourism business, including tour operators, whilst traditional accommodation suppliers are now cloning the product. Marriott, for example, has launched a home-sharing website where properties are vetted and quality controlled (Homes & Villas by Marriott International, https://homes-and-villas.marriott.com).

Issues

Airbnb is a good example of a disruptive innovation, by creating new sources of demand and supply in the accommodation market. However, this innovation has brought with it some negative issues and criticism:

- A number of US authorities do not allow this type of renting out of rooms or are attempting to restrict it. These include New York and ironically the city where it began, San Francisco;

- Airbnb properties are, by definition, often away from the recreational business district of the destination, spreading tourism into residential areas and angering local residents;

- There is a quality issue in terms of the product as it is impossible for Airbnb to control the quality of the accommodation;

- Hosts are exposed to risk of property damage and theft;

- Airbnb itself has been accused of tax avoidance; and

- The concept is open to abuse by being used by commercial accommodation operators and property developers rather than individuals with a spare room. They use the site to avoid paying taxes and charges.

Discussion Questions

1. Airbnb is growing rapidly – is there a danger that it will outgrow its roots?
2. Airbnb is an example of a disruptive innovation – what other examples can you identify in the hospitality sector?
3. How can the traditional hotel sector respond to Airbnb?

Sources: Cheng, M. and Jin, X. (2019) 'What do Airbnb users care about? An analysis of online review comments', *International Journal of Hospitality Management*, 76: 58–70; Dolnicar, S. (2019) 'A review of research into paid online peer-to-peer accommodation: launching the *Annals of Tourism Research* Curated Collection on peer-to-peer accommodation', *Annals of Tourism Research*, 75 (24): 8–26; Guttentag, D. (2013) 'Airbnb: disruptive innovation and the rise of an informal tourism accommodation sector', *Current Issues in Tourism*, 18 (6): 1–26; Guttentag, D., Smith, S., Potwarke, L. and Havitz, M. (2017) 'Why tourists choose Airbnb: a motivation-based segmentation study', *Journal of Travel Research*, 1–18; www.airbnb.com

9

INTERMEDIARIES

LEARNING OUTCOMES

This chapter considers intermediaries – tour operators and travel agents, both physical and virtual – as a key element of the tourism distribution channel and of the tourism sector. The chapter is designed to provide you with:

- an understanding of the role and behaviour of distribution channels in tourism;
- clarity on the role of intermediaries – tour operators and travel agents – in the distribution channel;
- an appreciation of the role and significance of integration within the distribution channel;
- an understanding of the way that technology has re-engineered the tourism distribution channel; and
- insights into the future of intermediaries.

INTRODUCTION

In the past, distribution was the unglamorous part of tourism but is now seen as critical to the profitability and competitiveness of both organisations and destinations. Distribution forms the 'place' aspect of the classic 4 Ps of the marketing mix and is a strategic decision (see Chapter 13). Yet for tourism, distribution is so critical because not only is the consumer physically distant from the product itself, but also the product itself is highly fragmented and therefore coordination across suppliers is essential. Distribution therefore acts to link supply and demand, producer and consumer, and to allow the consumer to obtain information about a product and to book it. In other words, it provides access to the product and facilitates its purchase. In order to do this, the system depends upon efficient flows of information (Zhang et al., 2009). The distribution process is achieved through channels – the means by which the tourism product is delivered to the customer. The distribution channel in tourism can be complex, involving a number of organisations and stages. Typically, the channel will involve:

- A tourism supplier such as an airline or a hotel;
- A tour operator who buys in bulk and packages together elements of supply;
- A travel agent acting as a point of sale; and
- The customer.

Here, the elements of supply represent the 'core' tourism products of transport, accommodation and attractions and these are distributed by 'intermediaries'. Intermediaries include tour operators or wholesalers, travel agents and increasingly e-intermediaries, as the Internet has changed the traditional supply chain pattern significantly. But here, as Cavlek (2018) notes, the distribution system is highly resilient – companies established in the nineteenth century are still trading.

TOURISM DISTRIBUTION CHANNELS

Models and diagrams of tourism distribution channels tend to show single direction transactions, outward from suppliers to the consumer (see Figure 9.1). This, however, masks just how complex the relationships can be between the various players in the channel. In reality, distribution channels in tourism are complex behavioural systems with many different products and segmented markets (Pearce, 2007). This means, as Pearce and Schott (2010) stress, that we should take a broader view of tourism distribution by considering not only the needs of tourism suppliers and intermediaries, but also the needs of the tourists themselves. Li and Petrick (2008) take this further, stating that the role of distribution in the service-dominant logic paradigm of marketing should focus on transactions, the consumer and the complex networks of consumers and suppliers (see Chapter 13). This is captured in Stern and El-Ansary's (1992: 1–2) comprehensive view of a channel as: 'sets of interdependent organisations involved in the process of making a product or service available for use or consumption'. They go on to say that channels both satisfy and stimulate demand: 'therefore channels should be viewed as an orchestrated network that creates value for the user or consumer through the generation of form, possession, time and place utilities'. For tourism, we can modify this definition to define a distribution channel as: 'An operating structure, system or linkages of various combinations of travel organisations through which a producer of travel products describes and confirms travel arrangements to the buyer' (Goeldner and Brent Ritchie, 2009: 182).

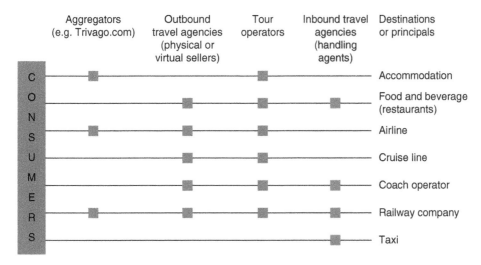

FIGURE 9.1   Tourism distribution mechanisms

Source: Buhalis and Laws, 2001; Page and Connell, 2009

What is clear from this discussion is that we cannot ignore the end user in the distribution process – the tourist. Indeed, technology is transforming the role of the intermediary from being an agent of the supplier to being an agent of the tourist, as we see later in this chapter. Distribution after all is one part of the marketing mix and the starting point for the mix is to identify the target market of consumers. Ultimately, it is the consumer who determines the level of service required – for example, do they require simply a booking service or a full travel counselling service? Understanding customer needs is therefore critical to a successful distribution strategy in a service industry such as tourism. Baby boomers, generation X and generation Y will each require a different level of service from the members of the distribution channel and channel members therefore have to design their strategy accordingly.

DISTRIBUTION STRATEGY, POWER AND RELATIONSHIPS

The fact that the tourism product is both a service and is distant from the consumer has two important implications:

1. The product is a service and cannot be stored – intermediaries such as travel agents therefore do not hold any stock; and

2. Intermediaries therefore have no reason to be loyal to a particular supplier and can therefore be influential in the purchase – the intermediary is not impartial.

Tourism organisations face a number of choices in their distribution strategy. Here, it is important that distribution conforms to the overall objectives of the marketing strategy and ties in with other elements of the marketing mix. It would not, for example, be expected that mass-market inclusive tours be sold through highly exclusive retail outlets. Mill and Morrison (1985) outline three basic distribution options for a supplier:

1. **Intensive** – where the plan maximises exposure of the product through all available channels;

2. **Exclusive** – where a limited number of channels are chosen to distribute the product, carefully mapping onto the supplier's marketing strategy; and

3. **Selective** – where a combination of the two above approaches is adopted; not every channel is used but instead a wide selection of appropriate channels are chosen, often targeting particular market segments.

As we have already seen, there are a number of players in the distribution channel, each of whom plays a particular role, but all of whom are dependent upon each other. This has led to both conflict and cooperation in the channel. In tourism, in the past, channel relationships were adversarial, with members striving to gain market share and channel power from other members. Tour operators, for example, had an adversarial relationship with hoteliers in terms of squeezing them on price. Kotler et al. (2020) term this 'vertical conflict' in the channel, whilst 'horizontal conflict' occurs between channel members at the same level – for example, between travel agents vying for market share. Of course, this conflict can be viewed as healthy competition but, increasingly, channel members have realised the importance of striving towards the same objectives in the channel. Channel members are dependent upon each other for success and any change by one reverberates through the channel; this means that the selection of partners in the channel has to be carefully done. For example, a tour operator selecting a travel agent would use a variety of criteria, including economic considerations. Equally, considerations of control are important if a franchise operation is being considered (Kotler et al., 2020). Finally, channel members are dependent upon the overall health and competitiveness of their destinations.

TABLE 9.1   The basis of power in the distribution channel

Sales and profit	Increased sales of a tour operator's products through a specific travel agent or their network means that the agent can place pressure on the operator for greater commission.
Role performance	Agents will favour those operators who regularly communicate and build a business-to-business relationship.
Specific assets	Tour operators who invest in IT systems and install them in favoured travel agents will 'lock in' those agents to their sales.
Trust	The greater the degree of trust that develops between organisations in the channel, the more likely it is that favourable financial deals will be done.

Source: Ujma, 2001

Power in the channel is exercised when the actions of one channel member lead to a change in behaviour of another. Each player in the channel has a 'base' of power that is exercised by their size, ownership of other members of the channel or contractual relationships (Ujma, 2001). Some channel members are so powerful that they are known as 'channel leaders' who formulate policy for the complete channel (Table 9.1). This has led Mill and Morrison (1985) to define three types of channel on the basis of power:

1. **Consensus** – no member exercises power over another – instead they work together for the common good;

2. **Vertically integrated** – producers and retailers are owned by the same organisation or managed by them; and

3. **Vertically coordinated** – where members are related through a contract or franchise arrangement rather than ownership.

Finally, as shown in this chapter, there are two basic approaches to understanding distribution channels – the economic approach and the behavioural approach (Ujma, 2001). The economic approach covers transactions and the costs and benefits of distribution, whilst the behavioural approach looks at how organisations within the channel behave, their relationships and how they compete for channel power. Mini Case Study 9.1 outlines a bold new move by airlines to influence the travel distribution channel and reassert their power.

MINI CASE STUDY 9.1
New Distribution Capability

Introduction

In a bold new move, the International Air Transport Association (IATA) is working to reduce the cost of distribution for airlines by developing a 'new distribution capability' (NDC) model of retail operation. There are four main aims of the NDC:

A lineup of colorful aircraft tails at Frankfurt Airport, Germany

Source: ©Markus Schmal/Shutterstock.com

1. To create efficiency in the distribution channel;
2. To allow airlines to sell more product;
3. To allow customers to be able to see airline offerings in a transparent way; and
4. To allow airlines to move away from the monopoly of the global distribution systems (GDS).

Operation of the NDC

The NDC model is designed to address the way that airline products are sold to both the travel industry and the traveller. Structured around seven distribution-related functions, the NDC approach provides the opportunity to address the end-to-end airline distribution process from searching to booking, and to deliver enhanced customer experiences. It particularly addresses current weaknesses in the distribution channel, which include:

- Difficulties in displaying product differentiation;
- Slow time to market;
- Lack of access to the full range of airline products' content;
- Transparency in pricing; and
- Lack of standardisation across different platforms.

Whilst the NDC incorporates the travel trade – tour operators and travel agents – it represents an aggressive move by airlines to dominate in the distribution channel by reducing the influence of these intermediaries.

Addressing Content Fragmentation in the Channel

The NDC goes some way to address the issue of content fragmentation in the distribution channel. Both travellers and the travel trade are confronted with a large amount of content and choices for tourism products, including airline tickets and tours. This is a perennial problem even for technologically experienced travellers, as unlike in the retail sector for, say, white goods, there is no consistency or transparency of choice and pricing. And, of course, this is made worse by the fragmentation of the tourism product where it is normal to book flights, accommodation and a rental car on different platforms.

The NDC is a step towards addressing this issue, although it is certainly not the complete solution. For example, Amadeus – a computer reservation system that sells tickets for many different providers – is also working towards addressing content fragmentation with its 'Amadeus Travel Platform', where content from travel providers is aggregated and normalised from multiple sources so it can be searched and compared by both the travel trade and travellers across all touch points in the purchasing process in a complete and personalised experience (Amadeus, 2019).

Finally, there is concern that the roll-out of the NDC will take many years and effectively will operate alongside existing traditional systems, in other words we remain in the hybrid stage of distribution.

Discussion Questions

1. What do you understand by the term 'content fragmentation'? Give examples from the tourism distribution channel.
2. Is the launch of the NDC an aggressive move in the channel by the airlines?
3. How transparent is the current airline pricing system?

Sources: Amadeus (2019) *Content Fragmentation: The Most Pressing Issue in Travel Distribution Today*. Madrid: Amadeus Insights; IATA (2019) *NDC: Together, Let's Build Airline Retailing Fact Sheet*. Montreal: IATA.

INTERMEDIARIES

It is important to recognise the importance of intermediaries and intermediation in the tourism distribution channel. Intermediaries include tour operators who bundle together two or more elements of supply (say an airline seat and accommodation) and sell it to the public. Suppliers and tour operators are known as 'principals'. Because it is not practical for a principal to have a sales office in every city in the world, they use a second type of intermediary to access the market – travel agents. Agents are found in the high street and in cyberspace and are paid commission for sales. According to Fyall and Wanhill (2008), the roles played by intermediaries in the distribution channel include:

* Making markets by matching buyers and sellers;

* Transferring risk owned by a supplier, such as a hotel, to a tour operator who purchases their hotel bedstock in bulk;

* Reducing marketing costs for the principal by finding buyers and communicating with the marketplace;

* Passing on knowledge and price advantage;

* Acting as a one-stop shop for many products for the consumer;

* Acting as a cheaper source of products because intermediaries can negotiate and purchase in bulk and pass on the savings; and

* Helping improve the competitiveness of destinations that leverage from the intermediary's extensive marketing network – there is a danger here, however, as destinations can become overly dependent upon, say, tour operators to deliver tourists and so lose control of their own markets, as has been the case for some Mediterranean islands.

Intermediaries: Tour operators

The nature of the tourism product as a fragmented set of services has created an important role for tour operators, bridging elements of supply with the consumer. Effectively, tour operators bundle together two or more elements of supply and sell them for a single price. They make contracts in bulk with hotels, airlines and ground transport companies and assemble them into 'inclusive tours' communicated to the market through print brochures or the Internet. Tour operators therefore act as 'wholesalers', as they are known in North America, passing on the savings to the traveller that they have made by contracting in bulk. Their core product is the inclusive tour, assembled by the operator, easy to purchase, competitively priced and distributed traditionally through travel agents but increasingly via the Internet.

Tour operators are historically significant to tourism and have shaped the way that the industry has developed. Most commentators agree that the historic roots of tour operation date back to Thomas Cook's UK tours in the nineteenth century, later followed by his expansion internationally and its unfortunate demise in 2019. However, it was after 1945 that tour operation really came into its own, responding to pent-up demand for holidays and taking advantage of the availability of cheap air travel.

Types of tour operator

It is possible to classify tour operators in a number of ways, though the most basic distinction is between domestic, outbound and inbound operators:

- **Domestic operators** tend to focus on particular markets such as the youth/student market or the elderly, and upon particular tour formats such as coach holidays, city breaks or short-break holidays.

- **Outbound operators** have grown substantially since 1945, taking advantage of the growth in demand for international travel. They normally package together flights, accommodation and transfers into a well-tried inclusive tour format. Initially focused on the short haul market, outbound operators are increasingly expanding into long haul travel. The incentive here is that long haul tours tend to have a high yield as opposed to the low yield for short haul.

- **Inbound operators** are often overlooked yet they play a significant role for the destination. They tend to contract transfers, accommodation and attractions/events and are normally appointed by a tour operator or an organisation to handle the ground-based aspects of a tour. They are often small operators with substantial destination-based expertise (Buhalis, 2001).

Operators can also be classified by the type of transport they use (such as rail-based operators), by accommodation type (such as villa holidays by market segment – for example, the elderly), by type of tourism (such as adventure specialists), or by particular destinations. These specialist operators have more flexibility in their operations and can command higher prices. Other types of tour operator include brokers and consolidators who purchase air tickets in bulk and distribute them at a substantial discount, often working closely with airlines to sell off excess capacity. Increasingly too, operators will be classified by their level of destination stewardship. The example of Intrepid Travel – a Benefit Corporation is provided as Major Case Study 9.1.

Regulation and the consumer

The knife-edge economics of tour operation, dealt with below, has led to a number of high-profile company failures. These failures have stranded tourists overseas and meant that many prospective travellers have lost money. In response, the tour operation sector has been the subject of significant government legislation to protect the consumer. In Europe, legislation developed in the 1960s and took the form of government bonding schemes. In the UK, this was managed by the Civil Aviation Authority (www.caa.co.uk) and the trade association, the Association of British Travel Agents (ABTA) (www.abta.com). This was followed by intervention by the European Commission in 1990 with an extensive piece of consumer protection legislation, the Package Travel Directive. The Package Travel Directive is not simply a response to the economics of tour operation, however. It recognises the rise of the empowered consumer and sets standards of quality and operation against which operators are measured. This recognises that relationships within the distribution channel are changing and that the consumer is gaining channel power. In the USA, tour wholesaling industry associations dealing with these issues include the National Tour Association (NTA – www.ntaonline.com) and the US Tour Operators Association (USTOA – www.ustoa.com). An additional regulatory constraint that will likely impact upon tour operators is that of carbon management, as shown in Mini Case Study 9.2.

MINI CASE STUDY 9.2

CARMACAL – Carbon Calculator for Tours

Introduction

Research has uncovered the 'hidden' greenhouse gas emissions of inclusive tours, a situation which is now being addressed by a new application – CARMACAL (Filimonau et al., 2013). CARMACAL is an easy to use application which allows tour operators to measure the carbon footprint of their tour packages and look for ways to make them more carbon efficient. It is both a practical and a strategic tool, as we see below. The idea to implement carbon management in the global management of a tour operator, travel agency or destination management organisation is entirely new for the tourism sector. The application was developed in the Netherlands and is web based with an English interface.

The objectives of CARMACAL are:

- To open the way for the tourism and travel sector to apply serious carbon management, giving a large range of options to improve the carbon footprint of products;

- To provide data that are unique and of high academic standards;

- To make it easy to use for businesses;

- To become the world standard for carbon footprinting, and potentially carbon labelling; and

- To apply CARMACAL-based carbon management to reduce product portfolio carbon footprints.

(Continued)

Operation of CARMACAL

CARMACAL will calculate the carbon footprint of a short break to, say, Venice and contrast it with a short break to Dublin. This encourages the integration of a carbon management system into the operation of a tour operator. CARMACAL works by combining CO2 data with volume and financial data. It allows the tour operator to choose accommodation, transport modes (down to choice of aircraft as well as airline) and transfers that have the lowest carbon footprint. This integrated feature of CARMACAL is unique as most carbon calculators simply have carbon data for transport modes. For example, the variance in carbon footprint for different accommodation units was done in combination with bookdifferent.com. This involved creating a listings database with 700,000 estimated footprints based on the characteristics of the accommodation.

CARMACAL's approach to carbon management will stimulate management thinking about the product portfolio development of tours and encourage innovation. For example, replacing an Antarctica cruise with an Arctic cruise will cut emissions by over 50 per cent. However, the challenge here will be to make the alternative choice attractive to customers. Indeed, CARMACAL can be used with customers, showing them the different carbon footprints of their choices and encouraging them to behave differently.

Benefits of CARMACAL

CARMACAL generates direct economic benefits to the tour operator. This can be by savings on energy consumption, carbon taxes and carbon trading costs. Indirectly it will help to make product development more innovative because of the added constraint of minimising the carbon footprint.

The environmental benefits are also considerable. CARMACAL says that on a flight between London and Athens, a choice of the airline Thomsonfly instead of Aegean Airlines will save almost 40 per cent on carbon emissions per passenger.

Discussion Questions

1. As a tour operator, how would you sell the benefits of CARMACAL to your customers?
2. Why should tour operators care about the carbon footprint of their suppliers – surely that is the business of the supplier, not the operator?
3. Research the idea of carbon labelling. How might it be applied in the travel sector?

Sources: Filimonau, V., Dickinson, J., Robbins, D. and Reddy, V.M. (2013) 'The role of "indirect" greenhouse gas emissions in tourism: assessing the hidden carbon impacts from a holiday package tour', *Transportation Research Part A: Policy and Practice*, 54: 78–91; www.cstt.nl/carmacal; www.youtube.com/watch?v=RSTbFJjGVYI

Tour planning and economics

It is important to understand the economics of tour operation as this has driven developments in the industry. For all but the specialist operators, inclusive tours are sold in high volume and competitively on price. This means that the profit per passenger tends to be very small because competition keeps profit margins low, and so bearing down upon costs and efficient capacity utilisation are critical to success.

The economics of tour operation is based upon the marginal cost principle. Once the fixed costs of offering the tour are covered by revenue, each extra passenger above this 'break even' point is almost pure profit. For any tour, fixed costs are high and will include accommodation and transport costs. Once these have been covered for the tour, then the cost to the operator of carrying an extra passenger is simply the variable cost associated with that person – say the airline meal. Clearly, the reverse applies – for every passenger below break-even the operator makes a substantial loss (Table 9.2). It is these 'knife edge' economics that have led to failures in the tour operation sector.

The economics of tour operation have a number of implications for how the industry operates. These include:

- The adoption of yield management to facilitate constant changes in pricing – this allows operators to combat the trend towards late booking, and to dump late unsold capacity and achieve the best possible price for each tour.
- Effective capacity management and utilisation of aircraft to achieve high load factors. Here, operators reserve the right to consolidate flights as the fixed capacity of planes means that demand is lumpy. The Boeing 737 is often viewed as the ideal size of aircraft to provide flexibility in tour operation.
- Tour prices are competitive and have to be set for each market – to cover costs, achieve a return on investment and match competitors. The fact that some tours will be more profitable than others means that operators allocate their overheads across their whole portfolio of tours rather than by individual tours. Operators can also charge additional supplements for elements of the tour, such as single rooms. Other pricing decisions include differential pricing for the low and shoulder season as well as pricing by market segments, such as for the elderly, the youth market or group travel.

TABLE 9.2   Mass market tour operator pricing

	Flight costs in euros	Package cost (including flight costs) in euros
Flight cost based on 15 holiday departures (back to back) on Boeing 737–800 189 seat aircraft at €20,725 per flight	621,750	
Plus one empty leg each way at beginning and end of season:		
Out	20,725	
Home	20,725	
Total flight cost	663,200	
Total cost per flight:		
(€663,200 divided by 15 holiday departures)	44,213.33	
Cost per seat at 90% occupancy (170 seats) i.e. €44,213.33 divided by 170		260.08

(Continued)

TABLE 9.2 (Continued)

	Flight costs in euros	Package cost (including flight costs) in euros
Plus passenger charges (e.g. airport fees at outbound and inbound airports, airport taxes, security fees)		40
Net hotel cost per person, 14 nights half board		245
Resort agent's handling fees and transfers, per person		10
Gratuities, porterage		5
Total cost per person		560.08
Add mark-up of approx. 30% on cost price to cover agency commission, marketing costs (including brochure production, advertising, etc.), head office administration and profit		168.02
Selling price (rounded up)		730

Source: Holloway and Humphreys, 2019

- Use of the Internet and reservation systems means that operators can bypass traditional travel agent intermediaries, saving on commission and providing more flexibility on pricing.
- Operators can also boost their profitability by hedging on foreign exchange.

Planning an inclusive tour can take 18 months to two years (as shown in Table 9.3). Whilst the core inclusive tour product has not changed for over a hundred years, aspects of the planning process have changed substantially. This is very true for the issue of seasonality, and how operators communicate and distribute to the market:

- **Seasonality.** Given the importance of capacity utilisation, any seasonal variations in demand will damage an operator's profitability. The European market, for example, is highly seasonal compared to the long haul market, with prices varying by up to one-third between peak and low season. In the immediate post-war period, operators were predominantly operating in the summer season and so created a demand for winter sun to utilise their spare capacity. This has since been supplemented by sophisticated market segmentation and product development to ensure year-round operation.
- **Communication and distribution.** Until the 1980s, the norm was for tour operators to have an expensive and comprehensive brochure for their products and to distribute it through the high street retail travel agent. Technology, however, has changed these practices substantially. Tour operators' brochures are usually full-colour representations of their product portfolio and therefore expensive to produce. Today, the Internet allows operators to cut significantly the costs of the printed brochure and also provides a much more flexible means of communicating with the market. It is, for example, easy to post price changes. In many ways, the operators' websites can communicate the same features as a brochure. As Holloway and Humphreys (2019) demonstrate,

the brochure or website must show visual images of the resort and accommodation, describe the product with dates and departures, show the prices and provide terms and conditions.

TABLE 9.3   Typical timescale for planning a summer tour programme

Research/ planning	Year 1	Summer	First stages of research. Look at economic factors influencing the future development of package tours. Identify a likely selection of destinations.
		September/ December	Second stages of research. In-depth comparison of alternative destinations.
	Year 2	January	Determine destinations, hotels and capacity, duration of tours, departure dates. Make policy decision on size and design of brochure, number of brochures to print, date for completion of print.
Negotiation		February/March	Tenders put out for design, production and printing of brochures. Negotiate with the airlines for charter flights. Negotiate with hotels, transfer services, optional excursion operators.
		April/May	Typesetting and printing space booked with printer, copy for text commissioned. Illustrations commissioned or borrowed. Early artwork and text under development at design studio, with layout suggestions. Contracts completed with hotels and airlines, transfer services, etc.
		June	Production of brochure starts.
Administration		July	Determine exchange rates. Estimate selling prices based on inflation, etc. Galley proofs from printer, corrections made. Any necessary reservations staff recruited and trained.
		August	Final tour prices to printer. Brochures printed and reservations system established.
Marketing		September/October	Brochure on market, distribution to agents. Initial agency sales promotion, including launch. First public media advertising, and trade publicity through press, etc.
	Year 3	January/March	Peak advertising and promotion to trade and public.
		February/April	Recruitment and training of resort representatives, etc.
		May	First tour departures.

Source: Holloway and Humphreys, 2019

Operators are also questioning the value of the retail travel agent, as we see below. This is because technology has provided an alternative. Of course, many operators still utilise retail agents as part of their distribution strategy. Here, operators are keen to keep distribution costs down by carefully selecting their agents and rewarding the productive ones.

Intermediaries: Travel agents

Travel agents act as distributors of individual elements of tourism supply or inclusive tours. For principals, they act as a convenient network of sales outlets and/or websites, whilst for the public they provide advice and a location for booking products, saving the consumer search time and money. As intermediaries, they do not carry stock and act for principals such as airlines or tour operators. Travel agents therefore simply make products from tourism suppliers available and so are cheap to establish and, unless they are part of a larger organisation, they carry no loyalty to any particular supplier. This is unusual in other distribution channels. Agents carry a large range of products including tours, tickets, currency, insurance, accommodation, and tickets for attractions.

The history of travel agents has many parallels with tour operators. They too have a long and influential pedigree, dating back to the late nineteenth century, and they developed quickly following the advent of air travel: airlines needed a network of sales offices, whilst the main modes of travel before them – shipping and rail – had city centre terminals and offices and no need of travel agents.

Types of travel agent

Travel agents can be clearly classified into three main types:

1. Leisure travel agents tend to be located in the high street because location is critical to this very competitive market where high turnover is needed to generate profit. This sector of the agency market has been subject to substantial concentration through takeovers and mergers, as we explore further below. Leisure travel agents also demonstrate the benefits of integration in the channel with many owned outright by mass-market tour operators.

2. Business travel agents such as American Express tend to be located in cities or close to concentrations of industry such as industrial estates or universities. Some agencies also 'in-plant' themselves within large companies to provide an exclusive service. This travel agency sector tends to be specialised and demanding, and is changing as e-tickets have become the norm for airlines and the traditional role of the agent is bypassed.

3. The home-based independent is a rapidly growing sector in North America where the key success factor is product knowledge. A dedicated qualification – the certified travel counselor (CTC) – is now available for this sector.

Regulation and industry bodies

As travel intermediaries, agents are subject to extensive government control and bonding. In many Asian countries, for example, agents have to be registered with the relevant government department. In the UK, both travel agents and tour operators have a strong industry association – ABTA. ABTA pioneered and now manages the fund established by government to protect consumers in the event of the failure of an agent or operator. In the USA, the American Society of Travel Advisors (ASTA) represents the sector and is the largest industry association for travel agents in the world, promoting professional standards, acting as an information resource and lobbying on behalf of the industry (www.asta.org).

Economics and trends

For mass-market travel agents operating in the leisure sector, turnover has to be high because the profit margin on each transaction is very small. In terms of costs, staffing takes up a significant proportion, which underlines the importance of investment in good training. For business travel and the more specialist agencies, margins are higher.

Economics have driven the shape of development of the travel agency sector. The fact that the tourism distribution channel is so dependent on intermediaries such as agents has meant that it is vulnerable to external factors such as the development of the Internet. Travel agents in particular have found that many of their traditional functions are being replaced by e-intermediaries or by principals going direct to the public with their own websites. Innovations in the tourism sector, such as the web-based operation of low-cost airlines (see Chapter 10), have accelerated this trend as the consumer is actively discouraged from booking in any other way than through the airline's own website. It is also true that principals are constantly seeking ways to reduce their costs and cutting out intermediaries, and either reducing or capping their commission is one way to do this. It also allows principals to control communication with their customers.

As a result, travel agents have had to reinvent their role in the channel. This is happening in a number of ways. For example, the home-based independent role in North America is based upon specialist advice to the consumer, advice that is difficult to extract from the chaos of the Internet. At the same time, traditional agents are establishing their own e-intermediary operations, and with the concept of 'dynamic packaging' (dealt with below) they can also become tour operators and develop a new income stream. Agents are also re-engineering their processes in order to update their offering, improve customer satisfaction and remain competitive. This re-engineering will involve consideration of customer relationship management and their gradual integration with loyalty schemes (Buhalis, 2003). Of course, reinventing travel agencies may require new staff skills and competencies, and as the role becomes more demanding, pay and training will have to be enhanced. At the end of the day, travel agencies will have to provide added value to the consumer to survive.

FOCUS ON EMPLOYABILITY

The Changing Workplace of the Travel Agent

Technology has transformed the way that travel agents do business, but it has also changed the working environment for those already in the business, and for those who aspire to join a travel agency. So, what does a twenty-first century travel agent do – and is it so different from what was done, say, 40 years ago? The main job functions are as follows:

- Arranging flights, insurance and accommodation;
- Using booking systems;
- Collecting and processing payments;
- Advising clients on travel arrangements, visas, insurance and passports;

(Continued)

- Dealing with complaints or refunds;
- Promoting and marketing the business, including preparing materials;
- Dealing with customer queries and complaints;
- Recruiting, training and supervising staff; and
- Managing budgets, statistics and financial records.

So, has the profile of a travel agent changed over the years? Interestingly, the importance of generic personal skills has not changed. These skills include:

- Interpersonal skills to deliver excellent customer service;
- Numeracy and accuracy with figures;
- Verbal communication skills;
- 'Active' listening skills;
- Organisational skills and the ability to multi-task and manage time;
- Attention to detail with, say, spelling names and recoding dates of birth;
- Empathy with customers to understand their needs;
- Patience – for example, when dealing with complaints;
- Good problem-solving skills;
- Commercial awareness; and
- Ability to work with colleagues and in teams.

But, of course, there are the technical aspects of travel agency to master and it is here that the changes are found. The twenty-first century agent needs to understand the contemporary distribution environment (navigating booking websites, for example) and its regulation (such as passports, visas and insurance). In particular, they need to be computer literate, with good keyboard skills but, more importantly, have excellent IT skills and be able to learn new systems quickly.

However, all those who enter the sector must have a passion for travel and the industry.

INTEGRATION IN THE DISTRIBUTION CHANNEL

The difficult economics of intermediaries, allied to the fact that the distribution channel comprises many different organisations, has led channel members to forge close alliances. These alliances allow organisations to control the costs of distribution as, typically, distribution is an activity external to the organisation, performed by intermediaries for a fee. By integrating with other organisations in the channel through ownership or contracting, these costs can be minimised. Effectively, this internalises the otherwise 'external' distribution cost to the organisation.

This process is known as 'integration', an economic concept to describe formal linking arrangements between one organisation and another. Not only does integration reduce distribution costs, but it also allows enterprises to be in control of how their product is represented and to more closely match distribution channels to particular market segments.

In an increasingly competitive marketplace, integration has become one way to be more efficient and to compete. We are also beginning to see integration across international boundaries, particularly as trading blocs such as the European Union harmonise regulations. The Internet is, however, reducing some advantages of integration because it has reduced the number of links in the channel and so the cost saving is lower. Integration is either horizontal or vertical within the channel.

Horizontal integration

Horizontal integration occurs when alliances are forged between enterprises of similar type in the channel, for example a tour operator links with another tour operator. This has been common in both the tour operator and travel agency sectors for the simple reason of gaining economies of scale through increasing size. This creates large organisations within the channel that command channel power, buying power and deliver cost efficiencies because they can sell more units and the fixed costs of each unit are correspondingly lower. A further benefit may be to extend the geographical reach of, say, a travel agency chain by merging with one in another region or country, developing powerful branding to gain market profile and deliver quality assurance. There are clear benefits of increased size for organisations within the channel:

- Securing supplies and increasing buying power – for example, larger retail agency chains can leverage better commission from principals, and principals, too, often prefer to deal with larger organisations;
- Increased market profile and presence;
- Increased geographical representation;
- Assured consumer confidence through quality control of processes;
- Greater investment capability and revenue streams;
- Higher Internet traffic and lower customer acquisition costs; and
- Improved yield per transaction.

Vertical (diagonal) integration

Vertical integration occurs when an enterprise within the channel links along the production process with an enterprise closer to suppliers (backward integration), or closer to the market (forward integration). For example, a tour operator may purchase a hotel chain or an airline in an example of backward integration in a bid to secure supply and reduce contracting costs. On the other hand, a tour operator may purchase a travel agency chain or website to secure sales as an example of forward integration to the market. These linkages can take place in the form of ownership, contracts, alliances or franchising. The benefits of vertical integration are similar to those of horizontal integration – economies of scale, securing supply and internalising costs that would otherwise go to an external organisation. There are also benefits through enhanced channel power. Holloway and Humphreys (2019), for example, speak of 'directional selling' where travel agents give preference to the sale of products of their parent tour operator.

REACTIONARY STRATEGIES

Of course, because of the creation of larger organisations within the channel through integration, other channel members become vulnerable and have to devise defensive strategies. There are a number of strategies that have been devised to counter the threat of large organisations exercising channel power:

- The small size of independent travel agencies means that they risk loss of market share and so, in response, have grouped together to form consortia in order to strengthen their negotiation power in the distribution channel. This is often facilitated by trade associations such as ASTA and ABTA.

- Independent agents can also adopt strategies of differentiation through niche marketing and specialising in particular markets or destinations, enhancing service to consumers through, say, travel counselling and an ability to deal with barriers that increase with consolidation, most notably in the form of price wars.

- 'Dynamic packaging' is an option for smaller agents and operators, where they allow consumers to assemble their own package using flexible elements of supply.

- Destinations, too, are concerned about the domination of the channel by large organisations, not only because it gives them enhanced bargaining power with, say, a destination's hotels, but also because it removes control of marketing from the destination.

- Whilst the consumer will benefit from the trend to integration within the channel, there is no doubt that it is impacting upon industry structure. Buhalis (2003), for example, suggests that the result will be a future where tour operators will fall into two distinct groups: multinational, large and vertically integrated operators with economies of scale, wide distribution and a global network, taking a high-volume, low-profit approach; and small, niche, differentiated operators focusing on particular destinations or products, taking a low-volume, high-profit approach.

And, of course, it will be technology that drives the future of intermediaries. Before turning to consider the impact of technology, the classic paper for this chapter by Buhalis and Licata provides a useful introduction.

CLASSIC PAPER

Buhalis, D. and Licata, M.C. (2002) 'The future of eTourism intermediaries', *Tourism Management*, 23 (3): 207–20

This classic paper tackles one of the key issues facing the tourism sector in the first two decades of the twenty-first century, namely how information communication technologies impact upon the distribution process. This chapter has already shown that technology has initially led to a process of 'disintermediation' as the Internet has replaced the traditional functions of tour operators and travel agents. However, this classic paper examines the next stage of the process – the 're-intermediation' process – as operators and agents reinvent themselves and define their core competencies.

The paper surveys expert opinion leaders in the UK about the future of e-tourism intermediaries, the new breed of companies that have moved into the tourism distribution channel. The survey found that 'the use of new distribution channels and the launch of value-added services features across all ePlatforms and distribution channels [are] ... the main factors affecting the competitiveness of all tourism intermediaries' (p. 218). In other words, the intermediaries have acted as an innovation that has impacted upon the total distribution channel and all its members. Even here, there are new e-intermediaries developing which are challenging the older model of e-intermediaries, particularly through the use of mobile commerce and interactive television and the convergence of these technologies with the Internet.

However, the survey did identify the fact that many of these newer e-intermediaries lack experience in tourism, do not have a robust business model and their links with suppliers are not secure. An issue here is that the investment needed is considerable and many do not expect to break even for four or five years, and as a result they need to quickly establish themselves and their brands in the marketplace and secure a significant level of bookings. Of course, building relationships with suppliers will be important, as many suppliers, such as the airlines, already have done. Finally, of course, it will be vital to deliver a personalised service and value to the customer through building relationships online.

In terms of global distribution systems (GDS), the survey found that experts felt that they could become sophisticated hosts for inventory and connections between suppliers, and so will be enablers rather than intermediaries, supporting e-intermediaries rather than actually doing the booking. Other experts felt that a GDS also had the potential to serve the business market.

The paper concludes that 'flexible and dynamic e-intermediaries will use both old and new ePlatforms to survive and expand in the future ... the only winner in the future will be the consumer' (p. 219).

TECHNOLOGY

Cavlek (2018) identifies three major eras of technology influence on intermediaries:

1. Global distribution systems;

2. The Internet era; and

3. The hybrid era.

Global distribution systems

An early development of technology in the channel was the 'global distribution system' – 'large and sophisticated travel reservation systems in use throughout the world' (Goeldner and Brent Ritchie, 2009: 194). Global distribution systems (GDS) have been hugely influential in the distribution channel. They were created in the post-war period when the major airlines developed their own automated 'computer reservation systems' (CRS), facilitated by the growth of the processing power of computing and the transmission speed of communication technology. By the late 1970s, airlines began to share their systems with other suppliers, offering a comprehensive range of services and products, and today airlines such as Air Canada are leaders in the field (www.aircanada.com). They also installed terminals in travel agents' offices to ensure that their system was used. This saw the gradual shift from CRS to GDS and, as the systems matured and merged, three major global distributions systems resulted – Amadeus (www.amadeus.com), Sabre (www.sabre.com) and Travelport (www.travelport.com).

The Internet era

The Internet influences every aspect of the contemporary tourism business and has changed the culture and behaviour of how people purchase, search and communicate (Buhalis and Soo, 2011). It connects companies, customers and governments at low cost and without constraints of time or space, and as such is a paradigm-breaking marketing tool and a 'disruptive innovation'. This is because it has significant advantages over traditional communication media, such as reach, low cost, richness, speed of communication and interactivity. Significantly, technology has shifted power from suppliers and intermediaries to the traveller, facilitating access to information and the ability to manage reservations and itineraries.

As technology develops, it is having a profound impact upon how distribution channels operate in tourism, and how other elements of the marketing mix such as promotion and pricing are done. For the tourism sector, technology provides the opportunity for direct communication with customers and other channel members, as well as interactivity, massive data storage, processing power, speed of communication and the ability to build, track and maintain relationships. Technology also provides a medium for consumers to gather information, communicate with each other through social media and make purchasing decisions.

Through technology, a new branch of tourism marketing has developed – e-marketing. E-marketing is ideally suited to tourism and has allowed the emergence and rapid development of electronic intermediaries. Specifically, technology has brought the following innovations to the channel:

- Information communication technologies (ICTs) facilitate the exchange of information that is critical in the distribution channel.

- For tour operators and suppliers, technology allows the development of online brochures that can deliver rich multimedia content, which blends text, images, sound and video into multimedia documents to deliver the ability to 'test drive' the product, and overcomes its intangible nature.

- It allows suppliers to instantly change dates, prices and availability online, so saving on expensive brochure reprints.

- It delivers significant cost savings through the electronic processing of bookings (such as e-tickets and electronic confirmations) and other transactions, reducing labour costs and office space. This encourages suppliers and intermediaries to go 'paperless' and allows customised messages to facilitate relationship building with suppliers and customers.

- Electronic distribution works well for tourism where the product is fragmented and web portals allow companies to provide and deliver a dynamic assembly of all of the elements of the product (Expedia – www.expedia.com – is a good example here).

- The Internet gives smaller suppliers such as independent hotels a degree of global market reach previously unheard of, and allows them to bypass the marketing muscle of intermediaries.

- It provides a powerful tool for an increasingly computer-literate consumer to search for and book tourism products. It also makes direct sales possible and gives power to the consumer to manipulate their own travel.

- It encourages customer-driven distribution through blogs and websites (www.tripadvisor.co.uk).

Buhalis (2003) confirms that a major impact of technology has been upon the tourism distribution channel:

> As a result of developing information marketplace and electronic commerce, new opportunities and challenges emerge. Although it is not clear who will be the final winners and losers of this process, it is quite apparent that the internet bridges the gap between consumers and suppliers and provides opportunities for dis-intermediation and re-intermediation. (p. 39)

There is no doubt that electronic distribution has decimated traditional intermediaries such as 'bricks and mortar travel agents', though after the initial shock of disintermediation, intermediaries are successfully reinventing themselves (Holland and Leslie, 2017). By 're-engineering' the channel, traditional power relationships are changing, with the role of intermediaries weakening and that of suppliers and the consumer strengthening. As a result, distribution channels have changed significantly since the 1990s, with the growth of 'eTailing' and 'e-intermediaries' leading to 'dis-intermediation' (Buhalis, 2003). In other words, technology has replaced the old way of distributing the tourism product with a 'merchant model' of suppliers, who can sell direct to the customer and control suppliers' inventory (Page and Connell, 2009). E-intermediaries do their business through powerful websites – Orbitz (www.orbitz.com), Expedia (expedia.com) and Travelocity (www.travelocity.com) are examples here. The airlines soon followed this trend once the benefits became clear – low-cost airlines, for example, financially penalise customers who do not book online. The US airline Southwest Airlines was the first to develop a fully functioning website and e-tickets in the mid-1990s (www.southwest.com).

The hybrid era

As shown above, tour operators and other intermediaries are responding to technology by reinventing themselves. Indeed, all members of the channel have had to redefine and evaluate their core competencies – tour operators, for example, now have the ability to 'dynamically package' the product and to deal directly with their customers and will increasingly design services across the whole of the value chain, specialising in both market segments and products. A sad example of the power of the hybrid era was the bankruptcy of the world's oldest tour operator, Thomas Cook in 2019, an example of an analogue business model failing in a digital age. Travel agents will increasingly act as travel counsellors or develop their own electronic presence (cyber-mediation), though here the response is variable globally, with some countries retaining their reliance on bricks and mortar agents. And to add to this complexity, the emergence of two innovations will further stress the system: peer-to-peer channels such as Facebook and aggregator websites such as Booking.com and trivago.com.

Constraints

Despite the obvious advantages of its use, technology does bring with it certain constraints when used in the distribution channel. For example, for the tourist trying to book a vacation, consumer technology skills are highly variable and many have concerns over the sheer chaos and lack of quality standards on the Internet, with doubts over the security of financial information and personal identity as well as question marks over the credibility of some websites such as those promoting individuals' second homes for rent. In addition, most websites are in English, so creating a barrier to access, and in some countries access to the Internet comes at a high cost.

Yet, despite these issues, intermediaries have to embrace technology. The following Focus on Technology showcases an innovative approach that also acts as a good link to the future of intermediaries.

FOCUS ON TECHNOLOGY

Blockchain Technology

Blockchain technology has the potential to transform the way that the travel industry does business. Blockchain creates a digital ledger whereby every transaction is stored as a series of blocks across many computers. This allows for the security of the transaction and builds trust in the network (Amadeus, 2018). Blockchain is therefore particularly relevant for tourism intermediaries where inventory is stored, and supply chains are used.

So far there is a view that the full potential of blockchain technology has yet to be realised. Tourism, too, has been slow to adopt the technology, despite the fact that it simplifies the transactions in the supply chain by integrating all users – hotels, airlines and transfer companies, into one network where all the transactions are secure and transparent. Examples in tourism include the following:

- TUI uses it to manage hotel bed inventories in real time in a system called BedSwap;
- Winding Tree has a decentralised inventory system for hotel stock;
- Trippki is developing a loyalty programme through a token system which is registered in the blockchain;
- Etherisc is an app that uses a blockchain platform to automate the underwriting and payouts of flights;
- Civic is a start-up helping people to secure their identity;
- Loyyal is a company that is simplifying loyalty schemes; and
- Avinoc is a booking platform for optimising empty flight seats.

Source: Amadeus (2018) *Blockchain: Harnessing Its Potential in Travel*. Paris: Amadeus.

FUTURE TRENDS

The very nature of the distribution process in tourism means that it will always be under threat from somewhere. For example, the fact that enterprises are increasingly trying to control their distribution costs through, say, cuts in commission threatens agents, whilst innovation from outside the system – from the Internet or disruptors – stimulates change in the channel. Nonetheless, intermediaries have proved resilient as they reinvent themselves in the twenty-first century to cope with new trends. These trends include:

- **Innovation and technological trends in the tourism system**. This includes the complexity of airline retailing; the continued growth of the low-cost airline model where Internet bookings cut out intermediaries; and the rise of gatekeepers such as Google and Facebook in acquiring Internet traffic. There is also an increase in independent travel and demand from the 'new tourist', which means that intermediaries have to be more responsive to customer needs and creative with their products.

- **Trends in technology** as e-intermediaries begin to outperform the overall market. For example, the product planning cycle of traditional tour operators means that they cannot compete with the flexible and responsive model used by online operators. The trend towards e-intermediaries will also be reinforced as mobile technologies are adopted. Digital convergence will lead to overlapping and all-pervasive use of computer systems with other devices such as entertainment systems, tablets and mobile phones in the move towards a hybrid distribution system. In addition, the Internet has enabled the sharing economy and peer-to-peer models, and here the car hire and accommodation sectors will be impacted (LSE, 2016).

- **Trends in consumer behaviour** which mean that intermediaries will need to be much more aware of different tourist segments and their needs, catering, for example, to the 'new tourist' who seeks a more individualised experience, flexibility and choice, and will opt for companies that behave in a sustainable and ethical way. Here, intermediaries will be able to create opportunities for added value, such as high levels of customer service by resort representatives. Of course, dynamic packaging also provides a tool to allow intermediaries to cater for and focus upon satisfying the needs of the new tourist, using sophisticated segmentation and tight quality control.

- **Trends in corporate social responsibility** which will see intermediaries changing their behaviour to embrace sustainability by building 'green supply chains', act responsibly towards destination communities (see Schott and Nhem, 2018) and lock in ethical behaviour and environmental audits with other suppliers in the distribution channel. Here, the Tour Operators' Initiative for Sustainable Tourism Development was established in 2000 as a voluntary, non-profit organisation, open to all tour operators. In 2015 it merged with the Global Sustainable Tourism Council, representing the tour operator sector on the Council (www.toinitiative.org and www.gstcouncil.org). The initiative builds sustainability into the distribution channel and focuses on stewardship of the destinations that tour operators use.

SUMMARY

Distribution is critical to the profitability and competitiveness of both tourism organisations and destinations. It forms the 'place' aspect of the classic 4 Ps of the marketing mix and for tourism is critical because the consumer is physically distant from the product itself. Distribution therefore acts to link supply and demand, producer and consumer, and to allow the consumer to obtain information about a product and to book it. The channel is a complex behavioural system with various players who vie for power. In tourism, distribution is performed dominantly by intermediaries. These are tour operators who bundle the various parts of the tourism product together for sale to the consumer, and travel agents who provide physical or virtual points of sale in convenient locations for tour operators, airlines and other 'principals'. However, power in the tourism distribution channel has been redistributed by two developments: integration within the channel which has created large powerful intermediaries, and the innovation of the Internet. The Internet provides a means for consumers to seek out tourism products and to make a reservation. As a result, traditional intermediaries have had to reinvent themselves. Technology will drive the future of the travel distribution channel and intermediaries. They will need to be more consumer focused, demonstrate concern for destinations and adopt principles of corporate social responsibility, redefining their core competencies and function.

DISCUSSION QUESTIONS

1. This chapter has stressed the significance of technology, and particularly the Internet. In class, draw up a checklist of the advantages and disadvantages that this brings to the tourism consumer.

2. Draft an Internet strategy for consideration by the board of a traditional 'bricks and mortar' travel agent.

3. Explain why integration in the distribution channel is a good thing for intermediaries, destinations and the tourism consumer.

4. Explain what is meant by 'dynamic packaging' and identify the main beneficiaries of the approach.

5. Write a newspaper article on 'the tour operator of 2025'.

ANNOTATED FURTHER READING

Buhalis, D. and Soo, H.J. (2011) *Tourism and Technology: Contemporary Tourism Reviews*. Oxford: Goodfellow.

Thorough and enlightening review of IT and tourism. A must-have book that provides thorough coverage of the development of e-intermediaries.

Cavlek, N. (2018) 'Tourism distribution and intermediaries', in C. Cooper, S. Volo, W.C. Gartner and N. Scott (eds), *The Sage Handbook of Tourism Management: Applications of Theories and Concepts to Tourism*. London: Sage. pp. 268–85.

Contemporary coverage of the literature on tourism distribution.

Holland, J. and Leslie, D. (2017) *Tour Operators and Operations: Development, Management and Responsibility.* Wallingford, Oxfordshire: CABI International.

Covers all aspects of tourism distribution and intermediaries.

LSE Consulting (2016) *Travel Distribution: The End of the World as we Know it?* London: LSE Consulting.

Excellent report on the future of travel distribution and intermediaries.

Pearce, D. (2007) 'A needs-functions model of tourism distribution', *Annals of Tourism Research*, 35 (1): 148–68.

Excellent paper showing how channels can incorporate the needs of the consumer.

REFERENCES CITED

Buhalis, D. (2001) 'Tourism distribution channels: practices and processes', in D. Buhalis and E. Laws (eds), *Tourism Distribution Channels: Practices Issues and Transformations*. London: Continuum. pp. 7–32.

Buhalis, D. (2003) *eTourism: Information Technology for Strategic Tourism Management*. Harlow: Pearson Education.

Buhalis, D. and Laws, E. (eds) (2001) *Tourism Distribution Channels: Practices, Issues and Transformations.* London: Continuum.

Buhalis, D., and Soo, H.J. (2011) *Tourism and Technology: Contemporary Tourism Reviews*. Oxford: Goodfellow.

Cavlek, N. (2018) 'Tourism distribution and intermediaries', in C. Cooper, S. Volo, W.C. Gartner and N. Scott (eds), *The Sage Handbook of Tourism Management: Applications of Theories and Concepts to Tourism*. London: Sage. pp. 268–85.

Fyall, A. and Wanhill, S. (2008) 'Intermediaries', in C. Cooper, J. Fletcher, A. Fyall, D. Gilbert and S. Wanhill (eds), *Tourism Principles and Practice*. Harlow: Prentice Hall. pp. 372–403.

Goeldner, C.R. and Brent Ritchie, J.R. (2009) *Tourism: Principles, Practices, Philosophies*, 11th edn. Hoboken, NJ: John Wiley & Sons.

Holland, J. and Leslie, D. (2017) *Tour Operators and Operations: Development, Management and Responsibility.* Wallingford, Oxfordshire: CABI International.

Holloway, J.C. and Humphreys, C. (2019) *The Business of Tourism*. London: Sage.

Kotler, P., Bowen, J., Makens, J. and Baloglu, S. (2020) *Marketing for Hospitality and Tourism*, 7th edn. Harlow: Pearson.

Li, X. and Petrick, J.F. (2008) 'Tourism marketing in an era of paradigm shift', *Journal of Travel Research*, 46: 236–44.

LSE Consulting (2016) *Travel Distribution: The End of the World as we Know it?* London: LSE Consulting.

Mill, R.C. and Morrison, A.M. (1985) *The Tourism System: An Introductory Text*. Englewood Cliffs, NJ: Prentice Hall.

Page, S. and Connell, J. (2009) *Tourism: A Modern Synthesis*. Andover: Cengage.

Pearce, D. (2007) 'A needs-functions model of tourism distribution', *Annals of Tourism Research*, 35 (1): 148–68.

Pearce, D. and Schott, C. (2010) 'Tourism distribution channels: the visitor's perspective', *Journal of Travel Research*, 44: 50–63.

Schott, C. and Nhem, S. (2018) 'Paths to the market: analysing tourism distribution channels for community-based tourism', *Tourism Recreation Research*, 43 (3): 356–71.

Stern, L.W. and El-Ansary, A. (1992) *Marketing Channels*. Englewood Cliffs, NJ: Prentice Hall.

Ujma, D. (2001) 'Distribution channels for tourism: theory and issues', in D. Buhalis and E. Laws (eds), *Tourism Distribution Channels: Practices, Issues and Transformations*. London: Continuum. pp. 33–52.

Zhang, X., Song, H. and Huang, G.Q. (2009) 'Tourism supply chain management: a new research agenda', *Tourism Management*, 30: 345–58.

MAJOR CASE STUDY 9.1

Intrepid Travel – a Benefit Corporation

Benefit Corporations

Benefit corporations represent a significant shift in corporate thinking towards the environment and indeed inclusivity and sustainability more generally. A benefit corporation is a type of for-profit corporate entity that includes positive impact on society, workers, the community and the environment – in addition to profit – as its legally defined goals. Benefit corporations are proud of their values and use them in their marketing. Directors of a benefit corporation have to consider the impact of the actions of the corporation on employees, customers, the community, and the local and global environment, as well as shareholders. These impacts are reported in an annual benefit report using a respected third-party standard.

Intrepid Travel

Intrepid Travel is a significant tour operator, deserving of this major case study. It is not only the largest

adventure travel company globally, but it has also become a 'benefit corporation'. Intrepid Travel was founded in Australia in 1989. Its scale is impressive:

- Over 1000 employees;
- Revenue of over US$300 million;
- Over 250,000 passengers carried every year; and
- Over 1000 itineraries offered across Asia, Latin America, North America, Europe, the Middle East, Africa, Australasia and Antarctica.

Intrepid Travel has a number of brands that contribute to its overall operation. These include Intrepid Travel, Peregrine, Geckos Adventures, Adventure Tours Australia, Urban Adventures, Peak DMC (which includes 20 destination management companies), and the Family Adventure Company travel brands. The company has also established a not-for-profit organisation – The Intrepid Foundation. By 2016, the

Intrepid Travel structures its activities around the UN's Sustainable Development Goals (SDGs)

Source: ©YanLev/Shutterstock.com

Foundation had distributed more than US$6 million in grassroots projects including healthcare, education, human rights, child welfare, animal welfare and environmental conservation in the destinations that it visits. This included significant support for the Nepal earthquake relief campaign in 2016.

Intrepid Travel is also a champion of gender equality, both within the business and in the value chain, and had doubled its number of female leaders by 2019.

Responsible Travel Vision

Intrepid's vision is 'to change the way people see the world'. It achieves this by structuring its activities around the UN's Sustainable Development Goals (SDGs) and acting responsibly towards the destinations that it visits. It has identified eight of the 17 SDGs

that it can contribute to most as a tourism business and so ensure a strong commitment to areas where the business can make the most difference and be a company with a purpose beyond profit – a benefit corporation. The company is a signatory to the 'United Nations Global Compact'– the world's largest corporate sustainability initiative.

Principles of Responsible Travel

The Intrepid Group recognises the need to establish principles of responsible travel:

- Respect: the destination including its culture, religion and customs;

- Support: local people and the local economy;

(Continued)

- Preserve: the environment through its operations, as well as the attractions visited;
- Protect: vulnerable people (including women, children and minority groups) as well as animals and wildlife; and
- Give back: through partnerships with local, non-government organisations.

Responsible Tour Construction

Quite clearly, Intrepid Travel is a purpose-driven tour operator, determined to act responsibly in terms of both environmental and social sustainability. It does this in many ways, including:

- Operating beach clean-ups in the Caribbean;
- Offering carbon-offset tours;
- Running vegan tours;
- Being the first tour operator to ban elephant riding and other cruel activities such as lion walks;
- Campaigning to end orphanage tourism in the travel industry;
- Reflecting its sustainable mission in the way that Intrepid Travel assembles its tours – using public transport, local food and locally owned lodging.

Carbon-neutral Business

Intrepid Travel became a carbon-neutral business in 2010, a process that began in 2006. The aim was to have zero net CO_2 emissions for assessed activities. Since 2010 Intrepid Travel has offset over 200,000 tonnes of carbon emissions from tours and offices worldwide. This has been achieved through the company's Carbon Management Plan, which helps it operate its business in a sustainable manner, addresses its environmental commitments under the United Nations Global Compact and outlines its carbon-offsetting initiatives. The plan has a number of features – it seeks less carbon-intensive alternatives where possible and then balances the remaining emissions by purchasing internationally certified carbon credits. Various approaches are used to decrease the carbon emissions generated from the firm's trips, such as staying in locally owned accommodation and eating at locally owned restaurants where the food has been locally sourced. Although most of the carbon emissions are generated from tours, Intrepid also uses carbon-reduction strategies across its offices and stores around the world. As a result, the company has 42 carbon-neutral offices and offers over 2000 carbon-offset trips.

Reporting

As we saw above, a key part of the philosophy behind the benefit corporation approach lies in its approach to reporting. Intrepid Travel now recognises that successful business growth should be linked to sustainability. As a result, it has integrated its sustainability reporting with its financial results to show how being a responsible business not only results in short-term value, but also long-term value for stakeholders.

The integrated report brings together standard annual reports with the company's progress report for the United Nations Global Compact. The report provides full accountability and visibility of Intrepid Travel's worldwide business operations, including performance and vision in the following areas:

- External environment;
- Responsible business practices;
- Financial performance;
- Customer satisfaction;
- Employee engagement;
- Employee wellbeing;
- Relationship with destination communities; and
- Corporate governance.

Discussion Questions

1. Why do you think that benefit corporations have been slow to take off in the travel sector?
2. Visit Intrepid Travel's website. In class, debate whether the firm's strong values may reduce or enhance its profitability.
3. Intrepid Travel is a carbon-neutral company. Why is this important in tourism?

Sources: https://bcorporation.net; www.intrepidtravel.com

10
TRANSPORT

LEARNING OUTCOMES

This chapter considers transport for tourism as the element of the tourism system that links the market with the destination. The chapter outlines the general principles of transport before considering the various modes available to the tourist. The chapter is designed to provide you with:

- an understanding of the principles of transport for tourism;
- an awareness of the role of network analysis in transport for tourism;
- an appreciation of the public and private sector management principles of transport for tourism;
- an awareness of the environmental impacts of transport for tourism; and
- an understanding of the various modes of transport available to the tourist.

INTRODUCTION

Tourism and transport are inseparable. Tourism is about being elsewhere and, in Leiper's tourism system, transport bridges the gap between origin and destination. As a result, tourism cannot happen without transportation, although there are many forms of transport that do not involve tourism (such as cargo operations), whilst others are used by residents and local businesses as well as by tourists (such as ferries in the Greek islands). When studying tourism, it is important to consider transport for these reasons:

- In a historic sense, transport has developed hand-in-hand with tourism. Improvements in transport have stimulated tourism and, in turn, tourism demand has prompted transport developments such as the growth of low-cost carriers to serve the leisure market.

- Transport can be a tourism attraction in its own right, as, for example, with cruising, where two of the elements of Leiper's tourism system are combined and transport becomes the attraction. This illustrates that whilst transport is sometimes seen as secondary to tourism, in fact it should be integrated into the product – as, for example, with heritage railways.

- New transport provision can create new tourism demand as well as diverting demand from other modes or routes. Transport facilitates tourism and we can see that innovations have made tourism accessible to new markets. Here too, the falling real cost of transport has lowered the cost of the tourist product and widened the market.

- Transport and tourism companies are increasingly combining their resources through 'integration' to deliver a seamless tourist experience.

- Transport renders tourist destinations accessible to their markets in the tourist-generating areas. All tourism depends on access: indeed accessibility, or the lack of it, can make or break a destination – islands are particularly vulnerable here.

- Transport is a major sector of the tourism industry in terms of employment, investment and revenue generation: accessibility underpins inward investment and business productivity for destinations.

- Transport has significant environmental implications – particularly in terms of carbon emissions – and it is important that tourists understand the consequences of their transport choices. It is now recognised that tourism transport accounts for around 5 per cent of the world's carbon emissions. However, it is estimated that approximately 80 per cent of these emissions are caused by around 20 per cent of all trips, and that these are mostly long haul trips (Peeters et al., 2007).

TRANSPORT NETWORKS

Transport networks play a key role in the development of destinations, especially through accessibility and connectivity to markets (Lohmann and Duval, 2015). Each transport network is made up of a series of links (along which flows take place) and nodes (terminals and interchanges). There are three factors necessary for flows to take place between nodes in a transport system:

1. **Complementarity** means that places differ from each other, and that in one place there is the desire to travel and in the other the ability to satisfy that desire.

2. **Intervening opportunities** mean that there may be other destinations (nodes) in between a tourist's origin and their intended destination.

3. **Friction of distance** refers to the cost (in time and money) of overcoming the distance between two places.

Duval (2007) demonstrates how the study of networks is fundamental to tourism transport:

- Networks determine flows, as the configuration of a network will affect the operation, pricing and demand for transport. It will also place some destinations in a better competitive position to receive tourists.

- Patterns and intensities of flows determine the viability of networks: 'thick' routes between, say, Washington and New York are more viable than 'thin' routes across New Zealand's South Island.

- Regulations govern network operations because governments can influence the operating characteristics of a route through pricing and demand for frequency of the service (the public sector obligation clause).

ELEMENTS OF A TRANSPORT SYSTEM

For flows to take place within a transport network, a transport system will be needed. There are four key elements in any transport system, each of which is found in different combinations to create a transport 'mode':

1. The way;

2. The terminal;

3. The carrying unit; and

4. Motive power.

The way

The way is the medium of travel along which transport vehicles travel. A way can be artificial, including roads, railways, tramways and cableways; natural, including airspace or water; or it can be a combination of the two, such as inland waterways. The way has a number of important features:

- A natural way is effectively free, whilst if the way has to be provided artificially – roads, for example – a cost is incurred.
- If the user shares the way with others (for example, inland waterways) costs are shared, whereas if the carrier is the only user, then they bear all the costs.
- Vehicles on roads and boats on inland waterways are controlled almost exclusively by their drivers or operators. In contrast, the movement of aircraft, trains and to some extent shipping is subject to traffic control, signalling or other navigational aids.
- Organisations independent of the carriers usually manage the way.
- Transport routes do not occur in isolation from the physical and economic conditions prevailing in different parts of the world. For example, mountains, the locations of major cities and political boundaries influence the way, although not all modes of transport are equally affected by these factors.
- Some modes of transport have a restricted 'way', which automatically channels movement. For natural ways, movement is also channelled, and movement does not take place across the whole available surface of, say, the sea.

The terminal

Terminals, hubs and gateways are important for access to destinations. A terminal gives access to the way for the users and acts to limit the capacity of routes through, for example, airport 'slot' control. Terminals can also act as interchanges between different transport modes, allowing travellers to transfer. Terminals vary considerably in size, layout and the amenities they provide, as these are determined by the length and complexity of the journey, and the expectations of passengers. Airports are increasingly showpieces of contemporary architecture, often privatised as, for example, at Brisbane in Australia, and offer a wide range of services including accommodation, food and beverage, and retail.

The carrying unit

Each type of way demands a particular type of carrying unit – aircraft for the air; boats for waterways; cars, buses/coaches and other vehicles for the roads; and rolling stock for the railways. Each carrying unit has distinctive costs and specifications, as well as environmental impacts – aircraft, for example, have to be designed to particularly high specifications to ensure safety, and are therefore costly. Aircraft, ships and road vehicles are flexible to operate compared to trains, monorails and trams, where breakdowns on the track cause extensive delays.

Motive power

The historical development of motive power technology is closely linked to tourism development. Motive power combines with the way and the carrying unit to determine the speed, range and capacity of the transport mode in question.

Through the twentieth century, motive power for most transport modes was dependent on either coal or oil as the energy source. However, in this century, realisation of the consequences of carbon emissions has led to the search for alternative sources of motive power such as hydrogen, biofuels and electricity.

A key consideration for the economics of any transport system is 'capacity'. Here, the trick is to find the optimum combination of carrying unit and motive power that can hold the maximum number of passengers whilst still allowing sufficient utilisation of the transport system. Here, size is not always the most efficient option – for example, large aircraft such as the Airbus A380 require reconfigured airport access and large numbers of passengers to break even. This highlights the two very different approaches taken by Airbus and Boeing: Airbus sees the future as long haul travel using large aircraft, whilst Boeing sees the future as one of shorter, point-to-point journeys.

FOCUS ON EMPLOYABILITY

Women Railroaders

The image of railway workers is often one of male engineers and trackside workers moving heavy machinery. However, the Canadian National Railway Company (CN) has brought a twenty-first century approach to jobs on the railroad by empowering women railroaders. They have been guided by the UN's Sustainable Development Goal 8, which is focused around 'decent work'. The company therefore aims to 'provide a safe, supportive, and diverse work environment where our employees can grow to their full potential and be recognized for their contribution to our success' (CN, 2017: 36).

This is achieved through four key approaches:

1. Attracting a diverse and inclusive workforce;
2. Ensuring productive employment through competitive wages and benefit packages;
3. Improving work–life balance by engaging in collaborative partnerships with union partners and employees; and
4. Developing employees to increase their engagement, retention, business knowledge and leadership capabilities.

(Continued)

CN is particularly focused on attracting and developing women railroaders. CN empowers women through two key schemes:

1. The 'Women in Operations Internship Program'; and
2. Providing women with training, development and mentorship opportunities to help them understand opportunities for personal and professional growth within CN; further develop their operational skills; and build strong partnerships with fellow employees and communities along the tracks.

Source: Canadian National Railway Company (2017) *Delivering Responsibly: 2016 Sustainability Report*. Montreal: Canadian National Railway Company.

Transport modes

Boniface et al. (2016) state that each transport mode has different operational characteristics, based on the different ways in which technology is applied to the four elements of a transport system. Technology determines the appropriateness of the mode for a particular type of journey. Of course, some modes overlap in their suitability for the needs of travellers, and this may lead to competition between, say, airlines and surface transport operators on some routes, such as London to Paris. In other cases, transport modes are complementary – for example, the road or rail links between airports and city centres.

Transport integration

An important issue for transport planners is to provide smooth transfers between transport modes. It is more common to find a lack of integration between modes in terms of poor coordination between operators, timetables and the physical siting of terminals. Integrated transport systems are therefore an ideal solution, though in practice they are expensive to deliver.

MANAGING TRANSPORT SYSTEMS

Demand

Demand for transport is *derived demand,* created for the transport operator because a tourist desires to get to the destination. In most cases, transport per se is not the tourist's real motivation for the trip. Incomes are the principal driver of travel demand, but are moderated by the cost of travel, the time taken, the distance travelled and the characteristics of the tourist. Of course, different purposes of visit demand different levels of transport provision:

*   Business travellers demand instant and flexible availability and can command a premium price.
*   Leisure travellers are able to book further ahead and are often flexible in terms of dates. They therefore seek the lowest price and their demand is highly price elastic.

- Common interest travellers lie somewhere between the two – a student has to travel for the beginning of semester but has a degree of flexibility in how and when they travel.

The trend in all transport modes is for fares to match distinctive market segments, each of which has its own travel requirements. Here too, fares can be manipulated to increase traffic in the off-peak; indeed, managing seasonality of demand is an important part of transport planning.

Lumsdon and Page (2004) provide a continuum of tourist transport using the type of experience sought – with, at one extreme, taxis or city buses which have a low intrinsic value as an experience; at the other extreme are, say, steam railways and ballooning which have a high intrinsic value as a tourist experience. Here, transport can deliver both the utilitarian aspect of tourism by getting the visitor from point A to B, and additional motivations such as romance on the Orient Express.

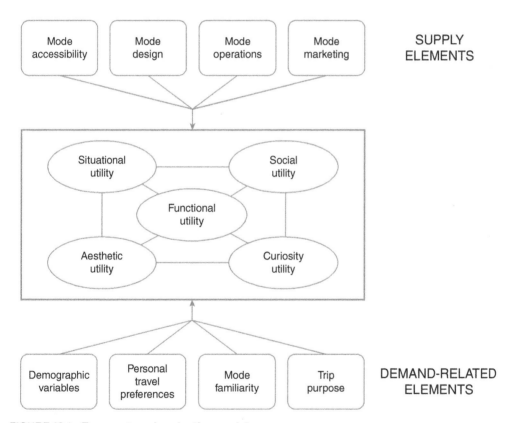

FIGURE 10.1   Transport mode selection model

Source: Mill and Morrison, 1985

It would be expected that particular tourism trips, and particular tourism products, will influence modal choice. This involves considering the tourist's original motivation for travel. For some trips, the tourist has no choice but to travel on, say, a scheduled airline, but this can then be fine-tuned in terms of the tourist's ability to pay and their desire for different levels of ticket flexibility and comfort. In terms of their choice of transport mode, the tourist will be influenced by a variety of factors, including distance and time, status and comfort, services offered, speed, competition, frequency and convenience, reliability, comfort, environmental considerations and safety. Mill and Morrison (1985) summarise this process of decision-making clearly (Figure 10.1).

Transport costs and pricing

Transport costs and pricing are fundamental to the successful operation of a transport system. The elements of each transport mode deliver a distinctive cost structure which both influences consumer choice and determines the volume of traffic on a route. Boniface et al. (2016) identify two types of transport cost:

1. **Social and environmental costs.** These costs are not paid for by the transport operator or user but are borne by the community. An example would be the environmental cost of aircraft carbon emissions.

2. **Private costs.** Transport operators pay private costs which are then passed on to the customer as fares.

Here, it is important to understand the distinction between fixed and variable costs:

- Fixed costs, also known as overheads, are incurred before any passengers are carried or indeed before a carrying unit moves along the way. These costs are 'inescapable' and include items such as interest on capital invested in the system and depreciation of assets. The most important feature of fixed costs is that they do not vary in proportion to the number of passengers carried or the distance travelled.

- Variable or running costs depend upon the level of service provided, the distance travelled and the number of passengers carried. These costs include fuel, crew wages and maintenance. Variable costs are 'escapable' because they are only incurred when the transport system is operating and can be avoided by cancelling services.

Of course, in reality the distinction between fixed and variable costs is blurred – for example, costs of staffing and equipping a terminal may increase with the volume of traffic. These costs are known as 'semi-fixed'.

Because each mode has a different ratio of fixed to variable costs, the distinction is a very important one:

- Railways, for example, have to provide and maintain a track as the 'way' and this is an expensive fixed cost. This means that the cost per passenger-kilometre decreases rapidly for rail. Railways are uneconomic if they are only carrying a few passengers, as each one has to make an unacceptably large contribution to fixed costs.

- Roads are much more competitive as the greater part of the costs is variable, and fleets of, say, coaches can be deployed more readily to meet changes in demand.

- For air transport, the success of low-cost carriers (LCCs) is down to an understanding of these principles. The LCC business model is designed to reduce fixed costs whilst also reducing variable costs such as free catering on board.

There are five further key issues related to transport pricing. Firstly, compared to many activities, transport has a *high proportion of fixed costs*. The product is also perishable, because if a seat is not sold on a flight it cannot be stored to be sold later. This means that operators must achieve a high utilisation of their systems as idle carrying units do not make a contribution to fixed costs. Finally, it is important to achieve a high *load factor* (the number of seats sold compared to the number available).

Secondly, the link between load factor and pricing is clearly illustrated by the *marginal cost principle.* For LCCs, for example, marginal cost is the additional cost incurred by carrying one extra passenger. The carrier determines a load factor that covers the fixed costs of the journey and the variable cost of each passenger carried. If the flight is budgeted to break even at a load factor of 80 per cent, then every passenger carried over this level will incur a small marginal cost, but because variable costs are low this represents a substantial profit for the LCC. Of course, exactly the opposite also applies – for every passenger below the 80 per cent level, a loss will be incurred.

Thirdly, a related problem is the fact that tourism demand tends to be *highly peaked* on a daily, weekly and annual basis. This means that airline fleets may only be fully utilised at certain times of the year. Both in Europe and North America, one solution to this was the creation of the winter holiday market in the late 1960s to utilise idle aircraft and make a contribution to fixed costs. Another solution is to use *differential pricing,* offering low fares for travel in the off-peak period to increase traffic.

Fourthly, *yield management* is now universally used to optimise the profitability of transport systems. These are effectively sophisticated computer models that match market demand in real time for a service with availability and fares. They optimise profitability because the passenger pays the maximum price achievable on a route at a particular point in time.

Finally, transport operators are not immune to the external economic environment. For example, they respond in a variety of ways to economic downturns. In 2008, for example, airlines saw their passenger numbers fall, particularly in the premium sector as businesses cut back on costs. Resultant strategies were a combination of business and marketing approaches and included:

- Closely managing capacity on routes with some cutbacks;
- Reducing fares;
- Pursuing premium passengers;
- Mergers and alliances;
- Hedging fuel and currency; and
- Seeking new markets.

The public sector

The transport sector is one part of the tourism system where the public sector is heavily involved. This is not only for passenger safety and security reasons, but also because governments are involved in international negotiations over routes and environmental issues. The public sector also has a role in protecting the public, and other operators, against unfair business practices and monopolies. Of course, some transport modes are more heavily controlled by government than others – air transport, for example, is heavily regulated whilst cruising has to date escaped significant government control. Governments, too, provide the funding for transport infrastructure development and national transport planning. This implies that transport planning cannot be achieved in isolation of other economic sectors, including tourism, whilst at the destination scale transport should be 'designed in' as part of the leisure environment – the monorail serving Darling Harbour in Sydney is a good example here. Nonetheless, high-quality transport infrastructure is a key driver of destination competitiveness – compare, for example, the relatively poor infrastructure in Africa with that of the Asia/Pacific region.

Regulation

Duval (2007) identifies a range of reasons why regulation of transport is important:

- Markets are not perfect and intervention is sometimes required in the public interest.
- Regulation can prevent monopoly situations on routes.
- Regulation is necessary to ensure safety and security standards.
- Regulation is necessary to maintain a particular level of service on an otherwise unprofitable route.
- Regulation can deal with externalities such as noise or carbon emissions through legislation and taxation.
- Regulation assists in national transport planning.

Economic regulation

Economic regulation of transport is where government controls pricing and competition through market access to routes. Since the 1960s, the trend has been towards deregulation of transport, as seen in the airline sector as 'open skies' policies. This was led by the USA and followed by the European Union before spreading to other regions of the world – including Asia. However, with the turbulent environment of the twenty-first century's economic crises and terrorism, deregulation has not progressed as far as some countries and regions (such as the EU) intended.

Whilst other transport modes, such as shipping and coaching, are also closely regulated, it is the air transport sector where there has been the greatest activity. Back in 1944, the Chicago Convention defined five freedoms of the air that are put into practice by bilateral agreements between pairs of countries (Figure 10.2). These freedoms are:

- The privilege of using another country's airspace;
- To land in another country for 'technical' reasons;
- The third and fourth freedoms relate to commercial point-to-point traffic between two countries by their respective airlines; and
- The fifth freedom allows an airline to pick up and set down passengers in the territory of a country other than its destination.

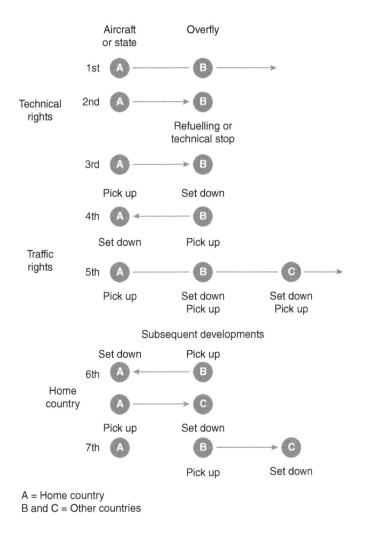

FIGURE 10.2 The five freedoms of the air

Source: Boniface et al., 2016

As the sector has developed, these freedoms have been extended, partly as commercial considerations such as hub-and-spoke operations have become more important. The sixth and seventh freedoms allow an airline to pick up in a country other than the country of origin, take passengers back to its home base or 'hub' and then take them on to another destination. This hub-and-spoke operation has encouraged the development of hub airports at a regional and intercontinental scale.

International agreements are becoming less important with the deregulation of the air transport system. This means that it is more difficult for governments to control routes, fares and volumes of traffic on flights within and across their borders. Boniface et al. (2016) summarise the features of deregulation as:

- Encouraging competition among airlines;
- Leading to the building of strategic alliances between airlines;
- Encouraging the growth of regional airlines and regional airports; and
- Favouring the development of LCCs on busy routes because it not only allows competition on the routes, but also opens up the possibility of using smaller regional airports.

However, many countries have yet to agree to an 'open skies' policy for reasons of military security, or to protect the national 'flag-carrier' – usually state owned and heavily subsidised – from foreign competition.

Non-economic regulation

- **Safety and security**. Any form of passenger transportation carries a risk of injury or death, whether through accident or malicious intent. Since 9/11, the railway bombings in London and Madrid and the use of vehicles as terrorist weapons, safety and security have become paramount in transport operations and governments have had to take a lead on this. Everyone is aware of the restrictions now placed on airline passengers as they pass through the airport. The key here is to ensure that these procedures are done with a 'human touch'. Security has required major reconfiguration of the layout and operation of airports as well as innovations in aircraft design.

  For surface transport, these types of checks are much more challenging and the networks are more reliant upon passenger vigilance. Of course, safety and security are now an important part of tourists' decisions about transport – in the wake of the London Underground bombings, many people decided against travelling on the Underground and, of course, we saw a huge fall in air traffic post 9/11. Marine transport, too, is now vulnerable given attacks on cruise liners by pirates and hijackers, as well as the publicised incidents of food poisoning on cruise ships.

- **Taxation.** Air passenger taxes are added to fares to offset the externalities of travel. They have become a source of competition, with the Netherlands, for example, abolishing them in an attempt to divert passengers from other airports.

- **Infrastructure.** It is important for governments to provide a high-quality transport infrastructure, which is an important determinant of destination competitiveness, connecting destinations to markets across the world. This is particularly the case for less developed countries such as those in Africa, although there are also severe capacity constraints on the air transport network of Europe due to inadequate airport development.

- **Environment.** Governments and international agencies are pressing to make transport more sustainable. Government response is through legislation to encourage cleaner technologies, particularly electric and hydrogen-based transport, in the face of dwindling oil reserves. Passengers using the bullet train in Japan, for example, receive a note of their carbon emissions, comparing it to less environmentally friendly forms of transport such as flying.

CLASSIC PAPER

**Dubois, G., Peeters, P., Ceron, J.P. and Gössling, S. (2011)
'The future tourism mobility of the world population: emission
growth versus climate policy', *Transportation Research Part A:
Policy and Practice*, 45 (10): 1031–42**

This paper is classic because it contributes to an issue that strikes at the very
heart of the future of tourism and its sustainability – indeed it questions the very
acceptance of the sector. Mobility through tourism generates carbon emissions,
yet the current structure of green taxes does not affect tourism as aviation fuel –
kerosene – is not taxed. Both Peeters and Gössling have pioneered a scientific
approach to calculating the greenhouse gas emissions of various forms of tourism transport. This paper is one of their most far reaching. They unpack the fact
that tourism emissions globally are estimated at around 5 per cent of overall CO2
emissions by examining future scenarios of the carbon emissions of various forms
of transport. They contrast air with surface travel and examine the policy implications. They conclude that it is clear that future environmental policy will favour
lower-emission surface public transport and penalise air transport. As a result,
the current pattern of how tourists travel, who travels, and if indeed travel is still
possible, will change substantially as tourism moves into a low-carbon society.

TRANSPORT MODES FOR TOURISM

Air transport

Whilst surface modes of transport carry much greater volumes of traffic than the airlines, air
transport has had the most impact upon the nature of international tourism and the structure of the travel industry since 1950. Few parts of the world are now more than 24 hours
flying time from any other part, and it is estimated by the UN World Tourism Organization
that around 20 per cent of international tourists use air transport.

Air transport took off in the early 1920s with aircraft that were noisy, unpressurised and
without toilets! At this time, flying was an expensive pursuit for the elite and it was not until
the 1950s that pressurised aircraft crossed the Atlantic. Even so, air travel remained for the
privileged. Tourist fares were only introduced in 1952 and economy class in 1958. The real
revolution in air transport came with the jet engine giving aircraft speed and range, as well as
allowing more passengers to be carried, opening up the skies, and destinations, to mass tourism.

More recently, LCCs have opened up new routes and made air travel accessible to
many more people than would otherwise be able to afford to fly. Nonetheless, despite the
apparent success of LCCs, the economics of air transport are precarious, characterised by
a transport mode that demands high levels of capital investment in a volatile market with
low returns (Graham, 2009).

The traditional distinction between air carriers has been between *scheduled airlines*
operating to a timetable and flying whatever the number of passengers and *chartered*

airlines that operate on behalf of a third party such as a tour operator. However, with the rise of the LCCs, this distinction has become blurred and Duval (2007) provides a more contemporary classification:

- **Network carriers** have extensive route coverage, regular schedules and are often part of international alliances and codeshares.
- **Regional airlines** ply geographical niche markets such as India and are smaller carriers with route networks that feed the network carriers' routes.
- **LCCs** serve niche markets in geographic regions (for example, Virgin Australia in Australia and the Pacific – www.virginaustralia.com). Low-cost carriers are featured in the major case study at the end of this chapter.
- **Charter carriers** serve pre-booked tours.

The traditional network carriers are now facing fierce competition for their routes and they have responded by forming alliances. The three major alliances are the 'One World Alliance' (www.oneworld.com), 'Skyteam' (www.skyteam.com) and the 'Star Alliance' (www.staralliance.com). This allows a passenger to book with, say, British Airways from Vancouver to London and then on with Iberia to Madrid, using a codeshare. Alliances bring efficiencies in operation, reduce costs, give passengers a greater choice and, above all, allow an airline access to an expanded route network.

Boniface et al. (2016) identify the main advantages of the air transport mode as:

- The way allows the aircraft a direct line of flight unimpeded by natural barriers such as mountain ranges, oceans, deserts or jungles.
- Superior speeds can be reached in everyday service, giving aircraft both range and reach for tourism destinations.
- Air transport has a high passenger capacity and is ideally suited to journeys of over 500 kilometres, travel over difficult, roadless terrain, and journeys between groups of islands.

However, air transport does also have disadvantages:

- It needs a large terminal area that may be some distance from the destination it serves and increasingly there is local opposition to new airports.
- It is relatively expensive due to the large amounts of power expended and the high safety standards demanded.
- It has significant negative environmental impacts, both internationally through its contribution to climate change, and locally through impacts on noise and air quality. The true cost of air travel for the airlines and their passengers has been masked by the fact that the airlines, unlike other business enterprises, have been exempt from certain taxes although, as already mentioned, this situation is changing with the onset of passenger and environmental taxes. The continued growth of air traffic, particularly long haul, may not be sustainable, given aircraft emissions (see, for example, klm.com/flyresponsibly). In response, in order to reduce emissions, the International Air Transport Association (IATA) has devised a fourfold approach:

1. Improved technology, including the deployment of sustainable, low-carbon fuels;

2. More efficient aircraft operations;

3. Infrastructure improvements, including modernised air traffic management systems; and

4. A single global market-based measure to fill the remaining emissions gap.

Air routes

The nature of the way has a significant impact upon global air routes. For example, air routes can utilise the shortest distance between origin and destination, with the improvements in range and technical performance that have been achieved since 1950. Aircraft can also fly 'above the weather' in extremely thin air, uniformly cold temperatures and cloudless conditions of the stratosphere. In middle latitudes, routes take advantage of jet streams in the stratosphere that attain high speeds, reducing the flying time from California to Europe by over an hour compared to the journey in the opposite direction.

Despite the apparent freedom of the way, air routes are influenced by a number of factors:

- Operational characteristics of aircraft;
- Safety and security factors which mean that routes are channelled to avoid, say, city centres;
- The level of demand for the route;
- The extent of infrastructure on the ground for passenger handling; and
- International agreements.

As a result of these factors, most of the world's air traffic is concentrated in the three regions of Eastern USA, Western Europe and East Asia. This is due partly to market forces and partly because of the strategic location of these areas. The 'air bridge' between Europe and North America across the North Atlantic is the busiest intercontinental route, linking the two largest generators of international tourism and significant international destinations globally. On this route, the capacity provided by wide-bodied jets and vigorous competition between the airlines has brought fares within the reach of many tourists.

Air routes, too, have been influential in opening up tourism regions and are utilised by governments to stimulate tourism development. This has been especially the case since the development of the jet engine brought the developing world within range of the Western traveller. In turn, the establishment of international routes into a region then stimulates the development of domestic air services and inward investment into the tourism sector.

Of course, not all air routes are long haul and for short sightseeing trips, heli-hiking and heli-skiing helicopters are used, whilst for novelty short trips tourists can also go ballooning (for, say, game watching), or take trips in a glider or microlight.

Airports

Although the aircraft is the real star of air transport, the importance of airports must not be underestimated. Airports act as the primary gateway to a destination for tourists.

As the volume of air traffic has grown, so too have the size and complexity of airports, particularly given the twenty-first century demands of security checks. Airports not only have passenger terminals, but also hotels with conference facilities, transport interchanges and large car parks. Major airports such as Heathrow are akin to small cities, sustaining thousands of jobs and taking up large land areas, but also, of course, having large environmental footprints.

The accessibility of the airport to the tourism destination is critical. Many are within a transfer distance of 20 to 30 kilometres but newer airports, as in Milan or Kuala Lumpur, are much further away, necessitating dedicated train connections. Whilst these are examples of newer airports, in many parts of the world airports and the air traffic control systems are reaching capacity. Yet, despite their importance for tourism and the national economy, proposals for new airports, or for airport expansion, are fiercely opposed due to concerns about noise and land use.

Land transport

The nature of the way for land transport immediately places a number of constraints on routes and access. Land transport is by far the most common form of tourism transport for domestic travel and for short international trips. The forms of transport available can be viewed as:

- **Personal** – such as the car or private pleasure boats; or
- **Supplied** – services provided by rail or coach operators, for example.

From a security point of view, land transport was perceived as safe following 9/11, but this changed with the bombings of the rail networks in Madrid and London, the use of vehicles as terrorist weapons, and marine piracy, as for example, around the horn of Africa.

Road transport

As the most important form of tourism transport, the car has been neglected by tourism transport experts. Yet, the car has many advantages for tourism. It can provide comfort, privacy, flexibility in timing, choice of itineraries and door-to-door service – travel by other transport modes almost invariably begins and ends with a road journey. This, combined with the fact that road vehicles can only carry a small number of passengers and have a relatively low speed, makes them particularly suitable for short- to medium-distance journeys. Also, the development of recreational vehicles (RVs) such as campervans and caravans allows a form of motorised accommodation. Finally, the car rental sector is a major part of the tourism sector, generating significant revenues.

The main disadvantage of road transport is that many users share the way and this can lead to congestion at periods of peak demand, such as in France during school holiday periods or China during the peak annual holidays. In some destinations such as Florida or Queensland, the demands of the private car have resulted in a tourism landscape of motels and other drive-in facilities dedicated to personal mobility.

Since the 1950s, the car has become the dominant transport mode for most types of tourism, while coach travel accounts for a much smaller share of the holiday market. Coach operations differ from scheduled bus services in that they are very much part of the tourism industry and provide higher standards of comfort and service. Coach travel not only provides a transfer service at airports and other terminals, but is also used for excursions from resorts and for touring holidays as a product in its own right. The coach has undergone a resurgence in popularity with increased levels of quality and service and a perception that it is a more sustainable form of transport than the car.

Innovations in road transport for tourism include specialised touring services and innovative park and ride schemes – the US national Scenic Byways programme is an example here. Roads designed especially for sightseeing have been built in scenically attractive coastal and mountain areas, encouraging 'drive tourism'. Car ownership is already static across Europe, the USA and Australia and car use can be further reduced at destinations in a number of ways. This can be done through 'park and ride', by improving access to bus, tram and train services, and through disruptive innovations such as 'ride sharing' (see Waze and Zipcar for examples of car sharing). In some cities, measures to limit car use include road pricing or congestion charges, whilst the development of autonomous (self-driving) vehicles will reduce congestion and pollution, and indeed they are predicted to lead the next transport revolution (Prideaux, 2018; Cohen and Hopkins, 2019). The environmental cost of road transport is increasingly understood and governments in some countries are taxing cars according to their carbon emissions, whilst manufacturers now offer 'zero' emission electric or hybrid cars.

Of course, the most sustainable forms of land transport are walking, cycling and horse riding and, for niche products such as ecotourism, these forms of transport are becoming increasingly popular with dedicated suppliers.

FOCUS ON TECHNOLOGY

Uber Air

Uber, the taxi disrupter company, is developing a fleet of autonomous aerial taxis – Uber Air. The scheme is part of Uber's strategy to become a frictionless hub for all kinds of connected transport, from driverless cars to electric bikes and existing public networks.

The Product

The Uber Air product will be a network of small electric aircraft that take off and land vertically to deliver rapid, reliable transportation between suburbs and cities and, ultimately, within cities (Uber, 2016). This is possible because vertical-take-off-and-landing aircraft (eVTOLs) do not follow one-dimensional routes, travelling independently of any specific path and complementing existing ground networks in cities.

Uber Air's autonomous eVTOLs will transition from vertical to horizontal flight after a helicopter-like lift-off. The infrastructure will include repurposed roofs of parking garages, existing helipads and brownfield sites near highway interchanges for a distributed network of 'vertiports' or single-aircraft 'vertistops'. The infrastructure will have cost advantages over heavy-infrastructure approaches, such as roads, rail, bridges and tunnels.

(Continued)

It is likely that the cost of an eVTOL ride will eventually be comparable to current Uber rideshare prices and will avoid traffic congestion. The launch of Uber Air is planned for Los Angeles and Dallas Forth Worth in the USA and Melbourne, Australia.

The Barriers

The main barriers to success will be:

- Safety – autonomous vehicles are still not judged to be safe;
- Air space regulation – air regulators will have to avoid the risks of a sky full of low-flying autonomous aircraft and Uber Air will come under regulatory bodies such as the Federal Aviation Authority in the USA; and
- The current lack of lightweight, long-range, fast-charging battery technologies.

Source: Uber Elevate (2016) *Fast-Forwarding to a Future of On-Demand Urban Air Transportation*. San Francisco: Uber.

Rail transport

In contrast to the road, the way used by rail – the railway track – is not shared and extra carriages can be added or removed to cope with demand. In the past, this was useful at peak times in holiday areas where special trains could be run. In addition, specialised carrying units such as dining cars or viewing cars can be provided on scenic routes. The railway's main disadvantage is that the track, signalling and other equipment have to be maintained and paid for by the single user of the way. Providing railway track is particularly expensive as the motive power can only negotiate gentle gradients. This means that engineering work for cuttings, viaducts and tunnels is a major cost consideration, especially on long routes and in mountain regions. Railways are therefore characterised by high fixed costs and a need to utilise the track and rolling stock very efficiently to meet these high costs. The fact that terminals are relatively limited in number, combined with the railway's speed and capacity to move large numbers of passengers, make it suitable for journeys of 200–500 kilometres between major cities.

The steam engine was vital in the development of the railways in the nineteenth century, revolutionising transport and allowing cheap mass travel for domestic tourism. In the UK, the first modern passenger railway was opened in 1830, and from the 1840s onwards, railway companies grew rapidly, encouraging entrepreneurs such as Thomas Cook to develop excursions. As the great trans-continental railways were built before 1914, when there was no serious competition from other modes of transport, the train was the mode that people used to travel long distances across continents. Iconic trains, such as the Orient Express, date from this period (www.orient-express.com).

From the 1950s onwards, rail travel went into decline, facing competition from airlines for long-distance traffic and from the private car for short journeys. New railway construction virtually ceased in most countries, but improvements were made to tracks, and steam was replaced as motive power by diesel fuel or electricity. The decline in passenger rail transport has been greatest in the Americas.

Environmental pressure, combined with technological innovations such as high-speed trains, are allowing rail to compete with air on short to medium haul routes. Eurostar, for example, is marketed as the 'green' alternative to flying (www.eurostar.com), whilst in France, China and Japan there has been considerable government investment in applying new technology (such as electric trains and maglev – magnetic levitation – technology) to the development of high-speed trains and upgrading the trunk lines between major cities. In Western Europe, the Channel Tunnel between England and France has encouraged the development of rail-based tourism products such as the 'Eurostar' service between London and Paris/Brussels/Amsterdam, in response to the European Union's development of an integrated rail network.

MINI CASE STUDY 10.1

Tren Ecuador

Introduction

There is a large market for nostalgia-based rail travel. This includes luxury travel on, say, the 'Blue Train' (www.bluetrain.co.za) or the 'Ghan' (https://journey-beyondrail.com.au/journeys/the-ghan) as well as the proliferation of private steam railways as in the UK. Yet, amongst these products, Tren Ecuador stands out as a visionary approach to train travel, built around responsible tourism and concern for the communities on its route. With Tren Ecuador (the commercial brand of the Ecuadorian Railway Company, which operates heritage tourist trains along 500 kilometres of restored tracks) tourists are not cocooned on the train viewing passing landscapes and communities remotely – instead the train journey takes them through a series of 'experiences', partnering with local enterprises and handicrafts to sustain the communities on the route.

Social Responsibility

Tren Ecuador has created a model of 'social co-responsibility' in which local communities and natural heritage are built into the train experience. Along the route, Tren Ecuador works with 23 station-cafes, 13 local museums, two lodges, nine folklore and historical recreation groups and community-based tourism operations. This network creates and maintains more than 5000 jobs in local communities along the railway. All partners are carefully selected and receive technical support, training and fixed contracts compliant with fair-trade principles.

Experiences

Tren Ecuador's product is a series of one-day train rides to well-known Ecuadorian tourist attractions including the Otavalo area, Nariz del Diablo and the Avenue of Volcanoes. Examples of these experiences include:

- A visit to Alausí – a 'train town' between the Andes and the coast. The town only exists because of the railway, which arrives through a series of 'switchbacks'.

(Continued)

- Artisan squares located around 14 restored railway stations across the country. Here crafts are made and sold by more than 100 artisans. Their crafts are based on different ancestral techniques including loom and hand weaving, embroidering, leatherwork, jewellery, woodcarving, ceramics, lute-making, brocade, filigree and stonework.

- A visit to the last ice merchant of Chimborazo is based on the dying craft of climbing mountains to harvest ice which was sought after for food preservation and for hand-made ice creams. However, technology has rendered the role redundant. Tren Ecuador allows travellers to recreate the steps of the ice merchants and provides employment for those otherwise redundant.

- Mural recovery in Salinas de Ibarra is an experience based on the technical skills of the Tren Ecuador and a local university. Travellers visit the murals and have guides to explain their social history and relationship with the train since the 1950s.

To sum up, it is the involvement of local communities and their leading role in the product that is the real innovation in Tren Ecuador's approach.

Discussion Questions

1. Is there a danger that the local communities become mere actors on the Tren Ecuador stage?
2. Tren Ecuador has cleverly used the network approach to move travellers along a link and then provide experiences at a node – is this a model that other modes of transport could use?
3. Visit the websites of other iconic railway routes – are they also using the principles of responsible tourism in the design of their tours?

Source: http://trenecuador.com

Waterborne transport

It was water transport rather than rail that was the first to use steam power. Waterborne transport is slow compared to air travel, and by the late 1960s most of the long haul market on the North Atlantic routes had been lost to the airlines. Boniface et al. (2016) identify the main advantages of the mode as:

- Ships expend relatively little power.
- Ships can be built to much larger specifications than land vehicles or aircraft – they can also provide a high degree of comfort, the basis of the cruise market.
- Ships can be designed as roll-on roll-off ferries, accommodating large numbers of motor vehicles – in effect 'floating bridges'. This has led to marketing directed at motorists using the short sea routes, such as travelling the coast of British Columbia.

Technological innovations are overcoming some of the natural disadvantages of sea transport. These include hydrofoils where the hull is lifted out of the water, allowing much higher speeds to be attained. Hydrofoils, however, are dependent on good weather and have relatively small capacity. Wave-piercing catamarans have proven to be more versatile than hydrofoils on some routes. And the environmental costs of shipping are being addressed by the development of alternative fuels such as hydrogen.

Sea routes

There is a clear distinction between long haul shipping routes, the short sea routes served by ferries and cruising.

Short sea routes

Passenger traffic on the short sea routes is increasing rapidly around the world. The Indonesian and Ionian archipelagos, for example, host many ferry services, whilst in Western Europe the popularity of motoring holidays and the growth of trade between the countries of the European Union has boosted ferry traffic. The introduction of roll-on roll-off facilities has enabled ports on these routes to handle a much greater volume of cars, coaches and trucks, and most ferries now operate throughout the year with greatly improved standards of comfort and service. In Scandinavia, the large ferries plying between Finland and Sweden, for example, are now equivalent to cruise liners with the associated amenities as we see the two product offerings beginning to merge. There are, however, increased safety concerns for ferry services following major accidents.

Long haul routes

By 1890 iron ships with steam turbines were crossing the Atlantic, heralding the era of the ocean liner on long haul routes. This era lasted from 1900 to the late 1950s as ocean liners had no competition on long-distance voyages until the jet engine appeared.

Cruising

In the 1920s, cruising was for the elite, with voyages lasting for several months. The sea voyage, often undertaken for health reasons, was more important than the places visited. Faced with increasing competition from the airlines in the 1950s, ship owners diversified from operating passenger liners into cruising, although this was not an easy transition as the ships were often unsuitable. The introduction of fly-cruising in the 1960s was important as it allowed the cruise ship to be based at a port in the destination region, so that clients no longer had to make a long, possibly stormy, voyage from a port in their home country.

Since 1980, the cruise market has undergone a renaissance, with massive investment in large, purpose-built cruise ships, over 300 vessels now carrying over 28 million passengers on the seas and waterways. Many of these ocean-going ships are huge, some with up to 6000 beds. As well as a high standard of service and accommodation, a variety of sports, activities and entertainment, including gambling, are available. At the same time, prices have fallen and new markets have begun to cruise – there are more passengers in the younger age groups, so that cruising is less of a 'grey market' than in the past. Themed and special interest cruises are increasingly promoted as the ship provides an ideal viewing platform. For example, there is a growing number of cruises to Antarctica and the Arctic Ocean.

The majority of cruise ships are based in the USA, and around 50 per cent of cruise tourists are American, although the European market is growing. The Caribbean is the most popular cruising destination, due to its location close to the North American market, the warm climate and the wide variety of scenery offered by the islands. The two other main cruising destinations are the Mediterranean and the Far East/Pacific.

In the future, larger ships will be built to benefit from economies of scale, there will be greater differentiation in the cruise offerings and new itineraries will be developed to avoid crowded routes such as the Caribbean. Cruising, too, will take its environmental and social responsibility more seriously, as it has had a poor environmental reputation (see Wozniak, 2018). Initatives include being more transparent on environmental practices, acting as stewards for fragile destinations such as Venice and ensuring that cruise workers are fairly treated. Examples here include P&O which launched 'fathom' where passengers worked alongside NGOs and locals on environmental and social projects , whilst the Holland America Line has been a pioneer of sustainable cruising.

Inland waterways

Natural waterways and artificially constructed canals provide linear tourist attractions as well as a recreational transport system. Tourists can hire boats for touring and waterbuses are used in destinations with an extensive river or canal system such as Amsterdam. Personal craft are common on inland waters as well as inshore around coasts. Cruises on major rivers such as the Rhine, the Nile, the Danube, the Volga and the Yangtze are important tourism products. However, the environmental credentials of river cruising are being questioned, as shown in Mini Case Study 10.2.

MINI CASE STUDY 10.2
Sustainable River Cruising

Introduction

The river cruise sector has grown in popularity in the twenty-first century. By 2016 an estimated 1.4 million passengers were cruising in Europe, representing over 80 per cent of the world's market. The product is also available in Asia (on the Mekong), the Americas (on the Columbia and Mississippi rivers) and Australia (Prideaux, 2018). The Danube and the Rhine are the world's most popular rivers for cruising, whilst terrorism and political activity have reduced the demand for cruising on the Nile.

A cruiseship on the Mekong river

Source: 'RV Mekong Pandaw' by Traveloscopy is licensed under CC BY-ND 2.0

River cruising vessels are small as they have to accommodate the demands of shallow rivers and low bridges. This impacts on the facilities available on board.

River Cruising Trends

Whilst river cruising is a relative newcomer to the tourism industry, it is growing rapidly as both capacity and awareness increase. River cruising displays a number of trends (GfK Group, 2015). These include:

- Construction of larger boats with more facilities, such as swimming pools and larger cabins with balconies;
- Diversification to rivers such as the Seine, Rhône and Douro;
- Diversification of markets to include younger passengers such as Gen-Z;
- A greater range of on-land activities;
- Sophisticated marketing stressing the benefits of purchasing a highly priced product; and
- Theming, such as Christmas market cruises.

River Cruising and Sustainability

River cruising lags behind other tourism sectors in terms of its approach to sustainability. The sector has prioritised growth over concerns for river ecosystems and communities on shore (Jones et al., 2016). Here the Travel Foundation (2013) has published a guide to sustainable river cruising based on ten principles:

1. Establish environmental monitoring systems to continuously provide feedback on performance.
2. Reduce energy use and generate energy from non-renewable fuel.
3. Reduce water consumption by using the best technology available and creating awareness about water-saving practices.
4. Limit on-board waste production and liaise with shore-based operations on waste disposal.
5. Foster a sustainability culture through training.
6. Environmental considerations and criteria should be systematically integrated into standard operating procedures and clear responsibilities assigned to staff.
7. Increase cooperation with other river cruise companies to exchange experiences, lobby for better port facilities and negotiate with common suppliers.
8. Work with the entire supply chain to minimise impact on the environment.
9. Incorporate state-of-the-art technology in the fleet.
10. Focus on efficiency with sustainability indicators – for example, 'waste produced per guest night'.

Discussion Questions

1. What are the benefits of adopting a sustainable approach for river cruise companies?
2. What shore-based activities can river cruises become involved in to minimise impact on local communities and maximise economic benefits?
3. Visit the website of a leading river cruise operator. How evident are their sustainability credentials?

Sources: GfK Group (2015) *Future Opportunities of River Cruising*. London: GfK; Jones, P., Comfort, D. and Hillier, D. (2016) 'European river cruising and sustainability', *International Journal of Sales, Retailing and Marketing*, 5 (1): 61–71; Travel Foundation (2013) *Environmental Sustainability for River Cruising: A Guide to Good Practice*. Bristol: Travel Foundation.

SUMMARY

This chapter has introduced the transport sector as an essential part of the tourism system, linking tourism markets and destinations. Tourism and transport have developed hand-in-hand, and breakthroughs in transport have tended to benefit tourism. Transport forms transport networks with nodes as terminals and links as routes. This allows analysis of the efficiencies and the development of transport systems. These systems comprise four main elements – the way, the terminal, the carrying unit and motive power. A distinctive mix of each of these elements is found in each of the major modes of transport – air, land and sea.

The chapter went on to analyse demand for transport and, in particular, how tourists make the choice between transport modes. An analysis of transport pricing showed the importance of distinguishing between the fixed and variable costs of transport, and that the ratio of the two varies by transport mode. The public sector is intimately involved in transport systems through planning and regulation, as well as in environmental and security initiatives. Major issues are the deregulation of transport systems and increasing concern for the environmental consequences of travel.

The chapter then considered each of the major transport modes for tourism, beginning with air transport and concerns for carbon emissions. For surface transport, whilst the car is the major mode used for tourism, it is neglected, despite the great potential for developing tourism routes. Rail travel is undergoing a renaissance fuelled by environmental concerns and technological innovations that have allowed the development of high-speed trains. Finally, waterborne transport is also seeing a resurgence through cruise tourism.

DISCUSSION QUESTIONS

1. Draw up a balance sheet for the environmental consequences of air travel versus rail travel.

2. Draft a briefing note to your transport minister, outlining the benefits of deregulating your national air transport system.

3. Create a short PowerPoint presentation for training purposes, explaining the marginal cost principle.

4. Using a timeline, explore the link between transport developments and tourism.

5. Draft a checklist of the key benefits of the car for tourism.

ANNOTATED FURTHER READING

Boniface, B., Cooper, C. and Cooper, R. (2016) *Worldwide Destinations: The Geography of Travel and Tourism*, 7th edn. London: Routledge.

Comprehensive text covering tourism transport development in every country in the world, now in its 7th edition.

Gross, S. and Klemmer, L. (2014) *Introduction to Tourism Transport*. Wallingford: CABI.

Good introductory text.

Lohmann, G. and Duval, D.T. (2015) 'Tourism and transport', in C. Cooper (ed.), *Contemporary Tourism Reviews, Volume 1*. Oxford: Goodfellow. pp. 129–82.

Contemporary and thorough review of transport for tourism.

Prideaux, B. (2018) 'Tourism and surface transport', in C. Cooper, S. Volo, W.C. Gartner and N. Scott (eds), *The Sage Handbook of Tourism Management: Theories, Concepts and Disciplinary Approaches to Tourism*. London: Sage. pp. 297–313.

Contemporary and thorough review of the literature on surface transport.

Spasojevic, S. and Lohmann, G. (2018) 'Aviation and tourism', in C. Cooper, S. Volo, W.C. Gartner and N. Scott (eds), *The Sage Handbook of Tourism Management: Theories, Concepts and Disciplinary Approaches to Tourism*. London: Sage. pp 314–33.

Contemporary and thorough review of the literature on air transport.

REFERENCES CITED

Boniface, B. and Cooper, C. (2009) *Worldwide Destinations: The Geography of Travel and Tourism*. London: Heinemann.

Boniface, B., Cooper, C. and Cooper, R. (2016) *Worldwide Destinations: The Geography of Travel and Tourism*, 7th edn. London: Routledge.

Cohen, S.A. and Hopkins, D. (2019) 'Autonomous vehicles and the future of urban tourism', *Annals of Tourism Research*, 74 (1): 33–42.

Duval, D. (2007) *Tourism and Transport: Modes, Networks and Flows*. Clevedon: Channel View.

Graham, A. (2009) *Managing Airports*. Oxford: Elsevier Butterworth-Heinemann.

Lohmann, G. and Duval, D.T. (2015) 'Tourism and transport', in C. Cooper (ed.), *Contemporary Tourism Reviews, Volume 1*. Oxford: Goodfellow. pp. 129–82.

Lumsdon, L. and Page, S.J. (eds) (2004) *Tourism and Transport: Issues and Agendas of the New Millennium*. Amsterdam: Elsevier.

Mill, R.C. and Morrison, A. (1985) *The Tourism System: An Introductory Text*. Englewood Cliffs, NJ: Prentice Hall.

Peeters, P., Szimba, E. and Duijinisveld, D. (2007) 'Major environmental impacts of European tourism transport', *Journal of Transport Geography*, 15 (1): 83–93.

Prideaux, B. (2018) 'Tourism and surface transport', in C. Cooper, S. Volo, W.C. Gartner and N. Scott (eds), *The Sage Handbook of Tourism Management: Theories, Concepts and Disciplinary Approaches to Tourism*. London: Sage. pp. 297–313.

Wozniak, D. (2018) 'The economic, social, and environmental impacts of cruise tourism', *Tourism Management*, 66: 387–404.

MAJOR CASE STUDY 10.1

Low-cost Carriers and the Environment: The Dilemma

Both easyJet and Ryanair claim to be flying 'green'

Source: 'Ryanair-Turbine' by andreastrojak is licensed under CC BY 2.0

Introduction

Low-cost carriers (LCCs) are one of the most significant developments in air transport in recent years – with their innovative business model, they have reduced both the fares and levels of service on routes. Yet the jury is out as to whether LCCs are as environmentally responsible as they claim.

As air travel continues to expand across the world, there is no doubt that LCCs have fuelled this growth by creating a more competitive environment for air travel, but with this growth comes a greater impact on the environment. This case study examines the green credentials of LCCs and focuses particularly upon easyJet and Ryanair, two of Europe's most successful airlines.

The Low-cost Carrier Concept

Low-cost carriers are airlines that work to a business model of low fares and few extra services for the passenger. LCCs have a business model that delivers much lower operating costs and a different debt structure to network carriers (Table 10.1). This is because network carriers trade on their convenience and levels of service to passengers, both of which imply higher operating costs. A range of innovations characterise the LCC business model:

- Paperless ticketing;
- Internet-based bookings;
- Minimising staffing levels and encouraging the multi-skilling of staff, so they can take on a variety of roles in the organisation;
- Using only one type of aircraft to reduce training costs;
- One class for passengers;

TABLE 10.1 Comparison of strategies of LCCs and network carriers

	Network carriers	LCCs
Business model	Global strategy and high cost	Niche strategy and low cost
Network	Hub band spoke	Point to point
	Global alliance	Regional airports
Fleet	Different types of aircraft	One type of aircraft
	Moderate aircraft utilisation	High aircraft utilisation
Product	Full-service	Self-service
	Branding supports full-service concept	Branding emphasises price
	Complex fare structure	Simple fare structure
Sales policy/distribution	Sales departments	Direct sales
	Global distribution system	Internet-based
Operations	Traditional check-in procedures	eTicketing and self-service check-in
	Multiple classes	One class
	In-flight service	In-flight extras available for purchase

Source: based on Duval, 2007; Boniface and Cooper, 2009

- Unbundling fares so that extra charges apply for, say, checking in luggage;
- Earning income from services that are provided free on network carriers – such as catering, headphones and pillows;
- Flights to regional airports that charge lower landing fees and often have spare capacity. This reduces congestion at the busier airports;
- Flying point-to-point without the need to set up a feeder network for their airports; and
- Operating a yield management system by selling seats at different prices according to supply and demand. On any one flight there may be many different fares, allowing loss-leading (and headline-grabbing) fares to be charged.

This business model allows LCCs to charge significantly lower prices than the network carriers.

(Continued)

In turn, this increases load factors and allows LCCs to make a profit on smaller operating margins. From an environmental perspective, the low-cost business model means that they try to reduce use of fuel and try to have high load factors.

Both easyJet and Ryanair are large European airlines which claim to be flying 'green'. Ryanair is a major low-cost airline carrying over 130 million passengers in Europe (Ryanair, 2018), whilst easyJet carried 88.5 million passengers in 2018 (Easyjet PLC, 2018).

Their main environmental initiatives

Addressing CO2 Emissions

For both airlines, the major environmental concern is fuel consumption and the associated carbon emissions. Ryanair and easyJet are attempting to reduce emissions per passenger kilometre on their flights. For example, since 2000 easyJet has reduced its carbon emissions per passenger per kilometre by 32.5 per cent. Its current target is a 10 per cent reduction from its 2016 financial year performance by 2022, which would be a 38 per cent improvement from 2000. However, both easyJet and Ryanair's success has meant the number of flights and passengers carried has grown, thus increasing total CO2 emissions, even if the emissions per passenger are reducing. Ryanair also claims that the model of flying point to point with high load factors using fuel-efficient aircraft reduces CO2 emissions per passenger. Its policy includes single-engine taxiing, use of solar power, LED lighting and use of ground power units instead of the aircraft's power on the ground. There is also a move towards the use of alternative fuels.

Efficient Aircraft

Both airlines are introducing more energy-efficient aircraft. For example, easyJet introduced the Airbus A3230neo aircraft in 2017 (equipped with CFM LEAP-1A engines and wingtip 'Sharklets'), which are expected to be 15 per cent more fuel-efficient than current generation aircraft. These larger aircraft allow easyJet to maximise the use of airport capacity, particularly at airports across Europe that are slot constrained. Ryanair is working with designers to deliver a step change in fuel-efficient, next-generation aircraft design, including drag and noise reduction.

Operating Efficiently

easyJet continues to use operational measures to reduce fuel usage and carbon emissions. This includes installation of lightweight Recaro seats and use of electronic devices rather than paper documents in the flight deck.

Local Air Quality

Local air quality impact arises from nitrogen oxide (NOx) emissions during aircraft take-off and landing. easyJet's new engines feature a technical fix which reduces NOx emissions by around 25 per cent. These are in use in more than two-thirds of easyJet's aircraft.

Waste

Both airlines seek to recycle as much waste as possible. For example, on-board, easyJet has a two-bag waste collection system which separates recyclable material from general waste. EasyJet also has recycling in place in its offices and hangars around its network, whilst Ryanair is aiming to eliminate non-recyclable plastic in operations and in the supply chain.

Reporting

Ryanair has a comprehensive environmental reporting system. The airline's chief operating officer has direct responsibility for environmental risks and impacts, reporting directly to the Board.

The Dilemma

Despite their green claims, low taxes on air travel mean that the rapid growth of LCCs poses a threat to the environment. And LCCs are particularly in the frame because, on many of their routes, more enviornmentally friendly forms of transport such as the train are available. So, here is the dilemma – to fly or not to fly?

Discussion Questions

1. Given the threat of climate change, draw up a balance sheet of the positive and negative sides of the environmental debate surrounding LCCs.
2. How credible is the claim by Ryanair to be Europe's 'greenest airline'?
3. Given the environmental concerns surrounding flying, how sustainable is the LCC model into the future?

Sources: British Airports Authority (2006) *Issue Brief Low-Cost Airlines*. London: BAA; Civil Aviation Authority (2006) *No Frills Carriers: Revolution or Evolution*. London: CAA; EasyJet PLC (2018) *Annual Report And Accounts 2018*. Luton: EasyJet; Gross, S. and Schroeder, A. (2007) *Handbook of Low Cost Airlines: Strategies, Business Processes and Market Environment*. Berlin: Kluwer; Ryanair (2018) *Introducing Europe's Greenest Airline*. Dublin: Ryanair; de Wit, J.G. and Zuidberg, J. (2012) 'The growth limits of the low cost carrier model', *Journal of Air Transport Management*, 21: 17–23.

11

GOVERNMENT AND TOURISM

LEARNING OUTCOMES

This chapter focuses upon the role of government in tourism, outlining the key reasons for government involvement in tourism and the roles played by government. The chapter is designed to provide you with:

- an understanding of why government is involved in tourism;

- an awareness of the tourism policy-making process;

- a comprehensive view of public sector tourism organisations;

- an appreciation of contemporary tourism governance;

- an overview of why tourism planning is important; and

- an outline of the tourism planning process.

INTRODUCTION

This chapter is concerned with the role of government in tourism. Some argue that tourism is a private sector activity and that government has no legitimate reason for being involved. However, this chapter shows that exactly the opposite is true – government plays a central role in organising, managing, regulating and governing the tourism sector; indeed, following 9/11 government stepped in to keep many airlines afloat. In addition, government owns and manages many iconic tourism attractions, including national parks, coastlines and heritage attractions such as museums, art galleries and historic monuments.

Of course, government has its own reasons for intervening in tourism. Tourism plays a leading economic development role in many countries, and for the developed world in countries such as Greece and Spain tourism represents a significant proportion of the economy. As a result, government cannot afford to leave such an important economic sector to the whim of the market and the private sector. Remember, too, that tourism is produced where it is consumed, creating many consequences for the environment and host communities (as shown in Chapters 4 and 5). It is government's role to alleviate the negative consequences of tourism and to ensure that the sector is regulated and planned effectively. As a result, all levels of government play an active role in tourism although, as shown later in this chapter, the trend is to devolve government responsibility for tourism to the regional and local levels.

THE ROLE OF GOVERNMENT IN TOURISM

Considering the role of government in tourism raises three key issues. Firstly, why should government be involved? Secondly, there is an observable shift of the government role towards *governance* rather than *regulation and control*. Finally, the complex nature of tourism demands government coordination of activity and policies, as shown in the classic paper by Scott chosen for this chapter.

Government has to be involved in tourism for a range of reasons:

- **Authority.** Government is the only body that has the authority to legislate and determine policy for tourism and is therefore able to coordinate the sector at national, regional and local levels.

- **Economics.** As noted above, tourism plays an important role in many national economies, not only in terms of contributing foreign exchange, but also as an economic development tool and a generator of employment.

- **Education and training.** Government has overall control of national education and training systems, including for tourism. These systems have an important role in supplying trained manpower to the tourism sector. With the human resources crisis in tourism (which is considered in Chapter 14), government plays an important role in boosting the image of tourism as a rewarding sector to work in.

- **Statistics and information.** As the private sector is reluctant to pay for large-scale tourism surveys, such as international arrivals and departures or surveys of domestic travel, government has to step in to supply this service.

- **Planning and control to ensure that tourism delivers benefits and outweighs the costs.** The potential negative consequences of tourism for both natural and man-made resources and for host communities are clear. It is the role of government to ensure that the benefits of tourism are maximised and the negative consequences managed to a minimum. Some governments, for example, view tourism as a social benefit for their populations and subsidise holidays for the disadvantaged through 'social tourism schemes'.

- **Market regulation and promotion.** Government has the authority to regulate and intervene in markets, particularly in a fragmented sector such as tourism where quality control and management may need to be imposed. Increasingly this is done in cooperation with the sector through 'public private partnerships' (PPPs). Government also has the resources to promote destinations and ensure that a positive image is projected.

- **The nature of destinations.** Chapter 2 showed that destinations can be viewed as loosely articulated amalgams of organisations and communities, so it commonly falls to government to provide the coordination and leadership needed for destinations to function. This includes destination marketing, visitor information provision, research, and planning and management.

From government to governance: The changing role of government

Traditionally, the role of government in tourism has been policy setting, regulation and planning. However, as the importance of tourism has grown and government's role has matured, the public sector is expected to provide a wider range of functions, including marketing and promotion, destination management, strategy and sector coordination. Government agencies have struggled to deliver all of these roles alone and so they have sought out partnerships with 'non-state actors' such as the industry and communities to deliver these functions. This approach recognises the importance of market forces and reflects a fundamental trend in government to more collaborative ways of working. As a result, government agencies now act to coordinate the activities of tourism through 'integrated tourism governance' rather than 'regulation'. Here, tourism governance can be thought of as representing the whole system of rights, processes and controls established internally and externally over the management of a destination, with the objective of protecting the interests of all stakeholders.

Mini Case Study 11.1 shows how government is being reinvented for the benefit of tourism.

MINI CASE STUDY 11.1

Reinventing Government for Tourism: Banyuwangi, Indonesia

Introduction

Banyuwangi is located on the eastern coast of the Indonesian island of Java, close to Bali – a major tourism destination. Until 2012 the town was neglected as a tourism destination but decided to radically transform its local government with the aim of boosting and developing tourism. This flies in the face of its former stereotype as a sleepy regional town with an ineffective government.

Gandrung is a traditional Indonesian dance performed at a series of Banyuwangi festivals

Source: ©Jhon R. Tambunan/Shutterstock.com

The Transformation

The transformation of local government in Banyuwangi is based on the following set of actions:

- Facilitating a 'whole of government' approach to services across education, health, social work and tourism;
- Maintaining and enhancing infrastructure, with a particular emphasis on digital;
- Developing a goal-oriented and powerful group of local government officials to brand the town by changing mindsets, emphasising the need to be profit-oriented, budget efficient, goal-oriented, and to work in teams across government; and
- Speeding up the decision-making process and facilitating mutual interdependency among government officials. This is facilitated by use of communication technologies such as WhatsApp, reducing the normal three to four days of paperwork in order to make decisions swiftly, and certainly within a day.

This process of reinventing government developed four key strategies to embrace the tourism sector:

1. **Region as a product**. Here the core of the strategy is the transformation of government.
2. **Branding and promotion**. The strategic position of Banyuwangi is based upon the concept of an ecotourism destination, optimising and sustaining culture and nature. Promotion embraces digital culture and the town is promoted as a digital hub.
3. **Innovation**. This is based upon speeding up the decision-making process and green innovation through green architecture and energy saving. The strategy invested in Internet marketing training for 2000 people across Banyuwangi.
4. **Event management**. One of the core tenets of the tourism strategy is event management – all events are managed and delivered by civil servants. This includes the anchor Banyuwangi Festival and up to 40 other festivals.

Results

The results of the transformation have been spectacular:

- Poverty has been reduced from almost 25 per cent of the population to less than 10 per cent;
- Banyuwangi is now 35 minutes by air to Bali as opposed to over eight hours before the transformation;
- A neglected, sleepy, voodoo town has become an Internet and festival town;
- Tourism has boomed, attracting over 50,000 international and almost 1.8 million domestic tourists by 2015; and
- The tourism industry has grown, with over 350 hotels.

Discussion Questions

1. Banyuwangi has transformed its local government to work for tourism. How would you go about a similar transformation for your home town?
2. Draft a list of the possible barriers that might have been encountered in managing this transformational change. How would you overcome them?
3. Banyuwangi is a classic example of leveraging tourism from events. Do you think this is a sustainable strategy?

Sources: www.banyuwangitourism.com; Office of Culture and Tourism (2016) *Four Winning Strategies*: *Keys to Success of Developing Sustainable Tourism in Indonesia – The Case of Banyuwangi*. Banyuwangi Regency, East Java: Office of Culture and Tourism.

Coordination across government

Tourism is a complex sector and impacts upon other sectors such as transport, labour and the environment. Equally, tourism interests range from the international and national level to the regional and local. As a result, it is important for government agencies to coordinate their actions and policies with respect to tourism. This is done in two ways (Scott, 2015):

1. **Horizontal coordination of tourism policy and actions.** Effective tourism governance demands that activities and policies are coordinated horizontally across the relevant

government departments and ministries. For example, air transport policy has a fundamental impact upon the tourism sector yet is normally not part of the tourism portfolio. In many countries, such as Australia, a cross-departmental committee has been formed to ensure that the interests of tourism are heard in relevant government ministries and departments.

2. **Vertical coordination of tourism policy and actions.** Vertical coordination in tourism governance ensures that national, regional and local activities and policies are linked and reinforcing. In addition, with the trend to devolution of tourism powers to regional and local levels, new mechanisms are being designed to ensure that vertical coordination takes place and that the regional and local authorities do not act independently of national policies and plans.

TOURISM POLICY

A key role of government is the determination of tourism policy. Tourism policy is a macro-level instrument that looks to the long term and, by showing the intention of government, it provides a clear sense of direction for the tourism sector. The key aims of tourism policy are to create competitive destinations, to ensure that the tourism sector functions efficiently and to deliver benefits, including income and employment, to the government's stakeholders (Scott, 2015). Tourism policy therefore sets the priorities and administrative framework for tourism and allows for coordination with other policy areas such as transport or the environment, as noted above. Definitions of policy continue to evolve – the UNWTO (2019), for example, defines tourism policy as: 'All the actions carried out under the coordination of public administrations with the objectives of achieving previously defined aims in the processes of analysis, attraction, reception and evaluation of the impacts of tourism flows in a tourism system or destination.' The process of determining tourism policy is a continuous one, with constant revisions and iterations. Table 11.1 shows the policy cycle for tourism.

TABLE 11. 1   The tourism policy cycle

Stage of the cycle	Activity
Define the scope and philosophy of the policy	A period of reflection, consultation and debate to define the parameters of the policy and a framework for action, including roles and responsibilities
Analyse the existing policy framework, identify issues	An analytical and diagnostic stage scoping the internal and external factors that will influence the policy
Determine the policy objectives	Objectives are developed on the basis of the analysis above and set the framework for the policy action programmes
Develop the tourism policy plan	The tourism policy plan develops a set of coherent programmes and actions that have been agreed by consensus. These programmes and actions will relate to the competitive positioning of the destination or system
Policy implementation and outcome	Policy will be implemented by the public sector institutions, increasingly in partnership with other stakeholders. This stage will determine the relative roles, funding, timing and monitoring

Wanhill (2008) classifies the main policy instruments that governments use to manage tourism into two basic types:

1. **Managing tourism demand.** The policy instruments available here include:

    *   Marketing and promotion, where government funds and coordinates destination marketing activities, particularly international promotion;

    *   Information provision and network development for incoming tourists;

    *   Pricing intervention to control competition and regulate the tourism market;

    *   Controlling access through, say, visas and immigration policy. This is often not part of tourism policy but lies in the domain of immigration policy. China's tourism policy, for example, has used the control of entry and exit to the country strategically to develop its international tourism sector;

    *   Security and safety which form another area which impacts upon tourism but is often implemented by another public sector agency as in the USA.

2. **Managing tourism supply.** The policy instruments available here include:

    *   Land-use planning, building regulations and environmental control, which allow government to control the location and scale of tourism development;

    *   Market regulation which is used to govern how firms behave in the marketplace and to prevent, say, mergers which may act against the public interest – examples would include mergers of airlines which may create monopolies on certain routes;

    *   Market research and planning which form an important aspect of government policy for tourism as government is seen as the candidate to fund large-scale surveys;

    *   Taxation – here tourism taxes, as in, say, Bermuda, are levied as well as other taxes which can be levied on tourism, such as entry taxes that are used in Venice;

    *   Education and training which are a critical area for tourism manpower development, although they are often implemented by ministries other than tourism;

    *   Ownership of tourism plant which is more unusual, but in the past this has been part of government policy as in some African countries and New Zealand;

    *   Investment incentives which are used to influence the actions of investors in tourism.

From a public sector perspective, however, tourism is a relatively new focus for policy. Stevenson et al. (2008) state that this has a number of implications for the process of tourism policy making:

*   It takes place in a rapidly changing environment;
*   It is essentially about communication with other stakeholders;
*   It takes place on the margins of political activity; and
*   It is closely linked to other policy areas.

3. **Sustainability.** Tourism policy for sustainable tourism can be added to Wanhill's (2008) classification. This is because the market alone cannot facilitate sustainable development and government interventions are needed. However, Hall (2011) states that policy for sustainable tourism presents a paradox. It can be said to have been successful as it

has been increasingly adopted across all tourism sectors, yet it also represents a policy failure as negative environmental, social and cultural impacts still occur at the hand of tourism. The UNWTO's (2019) review of the integration of sustainability into tourism policies is also cautious, suggesting that the policies themselves are often vague on sustainability, falling back on voluntary initiatives and lacking data. Governments, therefore, need to take a leadership position with policy for sustainability so that decisions can be made in a more systematic manner, effectively championing a re-balancing from a dominance of economic thinking towards environmental and social considerations (Butler, 2018). Mini Case Study 11.2 shows how policy can be implemented for sustainable tourism.

MINI CASE STUDY 11.2

Policy for Sustainable Tourism Development in Guanajuato State, Mexico

Introduction

The State of Guanajuato in Mexico has devised specific public sector policies for sustainable development, including tourism. Tourism is important in the state, ranking second in the economy. Guanajuato has two world heritage cities and is one of Mexico's cultural heritage destinations as well as being an important location in Mexico's road to independence. The concept behind the policy development is to both transform tourism in the state and to work across government to promote 'transversality'.

Sustainability Policy

The strategic vision of the state is to 'create major economic and social welfare opportunities for the people of Guanajuato'. This has been achieved by adopting four principles of sustainability:

1. Create sustainable awareness;
2. Increase economic and cultural benefits;
3. Increase the protection of the environment; and
4. Get sustainable competitive advantage.

This has been embedded by seeking sustainability certification and awareness raising amongst residents, businesses and visitors.

The State Tourism Programme

The goals of the State Tourism Programme are to:

- Promote Guanajuato to be one of the six most visited destinations in Mexico by developing tourism circuits (including the Nopal, Tequila, Cajeta, Mezcal and wine circuits), encouraging inward private investment, developing an events and festivals programme (including gastronomy festivals, the International Hot-Air Balloon Festival and the World Rally Championship), and developing the state's infrastructure;

- Keep tourism as the second most important economic sector in the state, by increasing the number of tourists, capitalising on their spend, boosting air connectivity and increasing the number of jobs generated by tourism; and
- Internationalise the Guanajuato brand.

As part of the State Tourism Programme, specific policy actions were developed to boost the state's competitive position in tourism. These include:

1. Enhancing the statistical base of tourism by pioneering a UNWTO Tourism Observatory to ensure that public policy is based upon accurate and comprehensive data, particularly from the point of view of sustainability – measuring carbon footprint and impacts;
2. Developing a training excellence model, using national certification to train over 1000 tourism businesses; and
3. Developing sustainable infrastructure across 36 municipalities, representing 177 projects.

A key part of the transformation of tourism has been to develop and promote the region's gastronomy, rooted in Guanajuato's agricultural sector and national leadership in farming. The gastronomy programme is part of the re-branding of the state as 'Guanajuato sí sabe'. The programme involves certification of gastronomy across the state, training and celebrating traditional cooks and developing events and festivals such as the Gastronomic Summit and the Grape Harvest Festival. The overall aim of the programme is for Guanajuato to become the Iberoamerican capital of gastronomic culture, which in turn delivers internationalisation of the brand.

Discussion Questions

1. Is Guanajuato's state tourism programme more about increasing tourism generally than taking a sustainable approach?
2. Research the state's tourism attractions and resources. Do you think they are managed sustainably?
3. Do you think that tourism would have grown anyway without policy intervention?

Source: www.guanajuato.mx

CLASSIC PAPER

Scott, N. (2015) 'Tourism policy', in C. Cooper (ed.), *Contemporary Tourism Reviews*, Volume 1. Oxford: Goodfellow. pp. 57–90

Noel Scott has written a comprehensive, deep and wide-ranging review of tourism policy. The review delivers an extensive list of the policy literature, not just in tourism but also the core literature of political science. This paper is a classic simply because of the synoptic approach of the author, reviewing over

(Continued)

250 pieces of policy-related literature – a literature that Scott admits is diverse and fragmented – indeed the value of this review is in drawing together this disparate literature. The second distinguishing mark of the paper is the intellectual structure used – that of the policy cycle as a narrative for the paper.

The paper opens with an introduction outlining the purpose of the review as 'the study of government policy seek[ing] to understand how policy decisions are created, the information, interests and values involved in policy processes and what their impact are' (p. 58). The article goes on to explain that tourism policy is important because it has a practical impact on the sector; indeed the literature can be thought of as splitting into both practical and academic approaches. Here, the academic approaches examine definitions of policy and different types and levels of tourism policy.

Scott then spends some time on examining the policy-creation process itself and how policy is evaluated. The review begins with policy aims, objectives and ideologies before moving on to the different geographic levels of policy. The policy-making process is examined in detail and the role of stakeholders and interested parties clearly outlined through the 'relational approach'.

The review concludes, rightly, with the fact that the policy literature is a vibrant and active field – much aided by this excellent classic paper by Noel Scott.

GOVERNMENT TOURISM ORGANISATIONS

There is a large variety of government agencies that have responsibility for tourism. These range from intergovernmental organisations such as the UNWTO to local authority tourism offices. As these agencies mature, their roles, structure and funding are changing, as explored later in this chapter.

International organisations

At the international level, it is notoriously difficult for the public sector to design and implement tourism policy, simply because it requires agreement of all the nation states involved. The European Union, for example, has limited tourism powers; instead, tourism policy and decisions are taken at the national level. Whilst there are a number of intergovernmental agencies working in tourism, there are two that stand out for their contribution:

1. **The UN World Tourism Organization (UNWTO) (www.unwto.org).** The UNWTO is the peak public sector body for tourism, based in Madrid. It is a specialised agency of the United Nations and serves as a global forum for tourism policy issues and a repository of tourism expertise. The agency is committed to the development of responsible, sustainable and universally accessible tourism and to promoting the role of tourism in achieving the United Nations Sustainable Development Goals. Its major contribution, however, has been the development of statistical measurement systems for both tourism demand and supply.

2. **The Organisation for Economic Cooperation and Development (OECD) Tourism Committee (www.oecd.org).** Based in Paris, the OECD represents the governments of the world's leading economies. The OECD has an active tourism committee, formed shortly after the Second World War to advise countries on how tourism might be used to rebuild shattered economies. The committee is in a unique position to serve as an international forum for coordinating tourism policies and actions, and it acts as a global forum for discussions of tourism policies.

National organisations

In contrast to the international level, it is on a national scale that government has real powers in relation to tourism. Government intervention at the national level is achieved through ministries of tourism or national tourism organisations (NTOs). Wanhill (2008) states that the way that these agencies for tourism are organised differs significantly across the world, but that they can be summarised into five types:

1. A ministry of tourism is common where tourism represents a significant proportion of the economy. Mauritius is an example (www.mauritius.net).

2. An NTO located within the ministry is another variant, where the NTO delivers the marketing and planning functions of tourism and the ministry takes care of policy and international relations, as in Greece (www.visitgreece.gr).

3. An NTO located outside the ministry is increasingly common as the specialist technical functions demanded by today's tourism require specialist staff and terms of reference. In this model, the majority of funding still comes from government, although the agency may be called upon to meet some costs from entrepreneurial activities. Tourism Australia is an example here (www.australia.com).

4. A semi-governmental agency with its own board and constitution is a more unusual approach although, again, the majority of funding comes from government. An example here is the Canadian Tourism Commission (www.canada.travel).

5. A Convention and Visitor Bureau (CVB) may be established which is independent of government and often formed by the private sector. This type of organisation may be based upon membership, with members' fees forming a significant part of the CVB's funding.

For all NTOs, the source and scale of their funding is an important issue. In part, it is determined by the importance of tourism to the national economy – for example, the Spanish government is generous with its funding to support tourism, but of course politics also plays a part in the level of funding. Where government provides significant funding to tourism agencies, there is an increasing trend to attempt to assess the effectiveness of that funding through, for example, calculating the return on investment (ROI) of marketing campaigns or development funding. More controversially, governments may also choose to fund their agencies through a tourism tax. This can be on bed nights or, more commonly, on passenger movements into and out of the country, or on spending through a value added tax. Other sources of funding available to governments include:

- Levies upon tourism businesses, normally based upon turnover. Investment and foreign exchange levies are also used, as are levies on tourism businesses to fund tourism training, as in Kenya (https://tourismfund.go.ke); and

- The user pays approach where organisations pay the NTO for services rendered, such as promotion or booking services.

The role of NTOs

The effectiveness and scope of the roles that an NTO plays is obviously dependent upon the funding issue discussed above. Whilst the roles of NTOs do vary globally, there is a set of core competencies common to most NTOs. These focus around the complementary roles of 'planning and development' and 'marketing and promotion' that are particularly suited to the coordinating role that government can play, and to the fact that government has a mandate for planning.

Planning and development

In terms of planning and development, it falls to government to plan and manage tourism at all scales, from the national to the local, and including thematic planning such as for ecotourism or heritage-based tourism. The planning and development role is discussed in more detail later in this chapter. As part of the planning role, NTOs are often given responsibility for managing the quality of the tourism product through the issuing of licences for accommodation and food and beverage outlets to operate, as well as inspecting, registering and grading accommodation. In many countries, such as Saudi Arabia, this is a major activity of the NTO and a legal framework has been developed to support the organisation in this role. NTOs also use their development role to influence investors and the types of tourism facilities that are encouraged. This is done through tax and investment incentives and, along with re-investing tourism taxes, is a powerful tool to shape destinations. NTOs also tend to be responsible for the collection of tourism statistics and research, both internationally and domestically. Education and training for tourism is also an area of competence for NTOs, although this is often shared with education and manpower ministries and agencies. In particular, NTOs commonly are responsible that for specialist tourism training such as that for guides, as in Malaysia.

Marketing and promotion

Whilst it may be expected that marketing and promotion of destinations are the preserve of the private sector, in fact they are an important part of the work of NTOs. This is for three reasons:

1. NTOs act in a coordination role for destination marketing, providing an 'umbrella' marketing function for the destination, under which individual organisations then market their own products.

2. Destination marketing and promotion are expensive, particularly at the international level – it therefore falls to government to provide this role for destinations.

3. It should also be said that government is involved in the marketing of destinations because the spin-off in terms of attracting inward investment and features such as

mega events can be considerable. In the twenty-first century, for example, there have been a number of new entrants to staging the Formula One motor racing Grand Prix, which can be overtly linked to the ambitions of those countries in the tourism marketplace.

As a result, the public sector tends to provide leadership and coordination in destination branding, promotion and the provision of visitor information. Many NTOs, for example, have extensive networks of visitor information centres and other means of delivering information to visitors, particularly at gateways and popular tourism spots. They are also active in developing new markets, as in Singapore where the education market is seen as an important part of tourism, and they nurture high-yield markets such as the business market.

The public sector's marketing role is not an easy one, however. It could be argued that the public sector is ill equipped to perform a professional marketing role, although as agencies have matured this criticism is less valid. Public sector budgets are set on an annual basis and this hampers long-term market planning, and the very nature of destinations, with their many stakeholders and interest groups, makes even the coordination role of the public sector difficult at times. But perhaps the most challenging aspect of the role is the fact that they have no control over the product that they are promoting. In some countries, this can be partly overcome when the prices of products are regulated and, as mentioned above, development incentives can be used as a lever to influence a particular destination, but for the most part the public sector marketing role is dependent upon the good will and involvement of the private sector stakeholders at the destination. A further stumbling block to the effectiveness of NTOs is their lack of expertise in technology, as shown in the below Focus on Technology.

FOCUS ON TECHNOLOGY

Egypt's e-Tourism Strategy 2020

The Advisory Council of the Tourism Ministry, Egypt has developed an innovative e-tourism strategy to help the country recover from the impact of terrorism and political upheaval on tourism demand since the 2011 revolution.

The goal of the strategy is to encourage innovative and digital solutions for the tourism sector to enhance its competitiveness and change Egypt's image. The main actions of the strategy are for the Ministry to:

- Draw together key stakeholders in the tourism sector, including local communities, tourists, hotels, airports, enterprises, universities and the Ministry of Tourism to work together to develop the strategy;

- Collaborate with business innovation centres to enable an environment for technology innovation;

- Develop an advanced communication programme to link the public and private sectors to facilitate knowledge exchange on technology and e-tourism;

(Continued)

- **Use a 360-degree feedback process between travellers and the Ministry of Tourism to research and change visitors' image of Egypt;**
- **Provide online marketing training to all stakeholders. This includes training in website use, Google ads and other e-marketing tools; and**
- **Create a new marketing campaign using online forums and the hashtag: 'This is Egypt'.**

CONTEMPORARY APPROACHES TO INTEGRATED TOURISM GOVERNANCE

The pivotal role that government plays in tourism means that tourism cannot escape from the changes in how government operates, and from the pressures that are placed upon government. These include the impact of globalisation and changing global politics, which have combined to flatten administrative structures and to demand that governments are networked into a wider world. In addition, there are pressures associated with ageing societies, environmental challenges including climate change, and the changing skill base of tourism as technology changes. As a result, government is becoming more accountable, more participative and more responsive to community activism. In tourism this is compounded by changing industry structures, in part driven by technology and globalisation, but also by the impact of the knowledge economy. This demands that the tourism sector in general leverages from the knowledge, competencies and skills of its employees and wider stakeholders. In other words, contemporary governments are actively encouraging the involvement of 'non-state actors' in tourism decision-making.

In many respects, government tourism agencies have been leaders in responding to these challenges through the emergence of a new style of public sector involvement in tourism which can be thought of as 'contemporary integrated tourism governance'. Three key features characterise this new approach:

1. Devolution of government power and responsibility away from the national level to the regional and the local – in other words, closer to where the tourism product is actually delivered;

2. The development of policy and governance networks which manage the relationship between the public sector and destination stakeholders at the local and regional levels; and

3. Metagovernance, which attempts to draw all institutions together to influence outcomes. This recognises the fact that tourism is comprised of many 'self-governing actors' and that influence and coherence of actions are more effective than traditional top-down approaches to governing (Jenkins, 2018). The major case study at the end of this chapter illustrates this approach.

This new approach is designed to be more effective and efficient, to encourage partnerships and, above all, to deliver a more holistic approach to governing the destination of benefit to both residents and tourists alike.

The anatomy of integrated tourism governance

This integrated approach to tourism governance is a quantum leap from past approaches. Forging partnerships between the public sector and other destination stakeholders creates a more holistic approach to governing the destination, effectively leading to more 'joined up' tourism administration. Because decisions are being taken closer to the public sector's clients – the industry, other public sector organisations and the host community – the approach integrates public sector services closer to the point of delivery. For example, local and regional tourism stakeholders are encouraged to be involved in marketing and planning decisions in the spirit of true partnership.

The integrated approach to tourism governance is a trend that can be seen across the world with Canada, Scotland and New Zealand as leaders in the field. The approach is based upon the concept of destinations being made up of a relatively stable set of public and private sector actors who are linked to each other and defined by their relevant administrative boundaries. The linkages allow communication for information, communication, expertise, trust and other policy resources. Of course, in the past, stakeholders were in touch with others, but the difference here is the involvement of the public sector, which pumps resources into the network and makes it a more formal arrangement. Above all though, the involvement of the government makes the networks more democratic and all stakeholders are given the opportunity to engage and participate in decisions.

Integrated tourism governance structures

The detailed structures and operation of these new public sector arrangements for tourism vary across the world but some common features are emerging as the approach gains momentum:

- A disciplined approach to identifying the types, roles and functions of all destination stakeholders and their relationships;
- Strong public sector leadership backed by political commitment;
- Technology used to deliver a single point of access for all stakeholders – destination web portals and social media sites are increasingly being used;
- Flexible funding arrangements, essential to respond to differing local and regional tourism contexts; and
- Performance measures being factored in.

This approach to governance is a clear departure from past approaches but is proving to be highly effective in engaging the tourism sector at the local and regional levels in decision-making and policy formation. Of course, there are tensions and strains as systems change and power shifts from the national level to a more dispersed regional and local level, but the successful approaches are ones where resistance to change has been anticipated and planned for. The very fact that the public sector is being taken closer to the point of delivery of the tourism product means that every context is different and so there is no 'one size fits all' model of integrated tourism governance; rather it tends to be destination specific. The potential of the approach is clear and can lead to genuine 'learning destinations' as tourism slowly comes to terms with the knowledge economy. It is interesting though that the approach is also dependent upon intangible elements such as personalities, trust, leadership and a cohesive vision. Of course, this new approach demands new competencies from government tourism officers, as shown in the below Focus on Employability.

FOCUS ON EMPLOYABILITY

The Role and Competencies of Government Tourism Officers

Government tourism officers have an increasingly wide range of responsibilities. These focus around responsibility for the development of the tourism strategy, promotion of tourism and support for local tourism. An increasing responsibility is to raise funding and income as governments withdraw support for tourism. A government tourism officer's job description includes:

- Managing staff and budgets;
- Promotion (including digital media);
- Research;
- PR;
- Event management;
- Attracting business conventions/conferences;
- Local business support;
- Attracting inward investment;
- Assessing impacts of planned developments;
- Consulting across the sector; and
- Managing tourist information offices.

The competencies needed include:

- IT;
- Enthusiasm;
- Adaptability;
- Communication;
- Creativity and innovative strategic thinking;
- PR and marketing;
- Customer service;
- Budget management;
- Organisation;
- Energy;

- **Resourcefulness; and**
- **Confidence.**

Anyone can apply for a government tourism officer role but a degree or diploma is preferred, often in languages, travel, tourism, leisure, business studies, marketing, management or journalism. These jobs are extremely highly sought after, so the relevant work experience is usually essential for tourism officer roles. Once in the role, progression within government is often easier than in the private sector and managerial positions in, say, tourism development or economic development are possible.

TOURISM PLANNING

This chapter has shown that an important reason for public sector involvement in tourism is the mandate from the public to plan and manage. In the case of tourism, the public sector acts as the lead planning agency, ensuring that tourism is beneficial for the economy, environment and society (Morpeth and Yan, 2015). This is essential as tourism occurs in many diverse settings and is attracted to fragile resources, such as the natural heritage and cultural attractions that are both unique and special – but this also makes them vulnerable to the inseparable nature of tourism – the fact that the tourist has to be physically present to consume them. In other words, there is a pressure on the resource, often focused in both space and time, that has to be planned and managed to minimise the costs and maximise the benefits of tourism to that resource. However, there is criticism of the traditional tourism planning approach rooted in the industrial organisation of economic development (see Dredge, 2016). Critics argue that planning is too managerial and unsuited to the contemporary fluid world of social media and smartphone communications and that instead an approach based on stewardship and partnerships is more appropriate – something that this chapter has also argued.

The anatomy of tourism planning

Planning is about taking a disciplined and ordered approach to organising the future – and tourism is no exception here. Effectively, tourism planning is one part of the implementation of tourism policy. Tourism planning can be defined as: 'Anticipating and regulating change in a [tourism] system to promote orderly development so as to increase social, economic and environmental benefits of the development process' (Murphy, 1985: 156). Table 11.2 catalogues why this is important in tourism in particular.

As noted earlier in this chapter, government's approach to tourism is changing with the active involvement of 'civil society'. As a result, tourism planning now closely involves both the private sector and the host community at the destination (Sharpley and Telfer, 2014). In the section on contemporary approaches to integrated tourism governance, the chapter showed how tourism agencies are devising mechanisms and formalising networks to involve destination stakeholders in tourism decisions, including planning. Of course, this is just one further evolution of the 'public participation' debate, where there has long been concern that the loudest voices would be heard at a destination rather than a balanced representative view.

TABLE 11.2   The imperative for tourism planning

Tourism is not well understood	The lack of expertise in tourism means that planning is essential to put in place guidelines and codes of practice and to ensure a holistic view of the destination.
Complexity of tourism	The multifaceted nature of tourism demands that planners coordinate and organise all of the destination elements.
The destination is where tourism is delivered	The destination is the focus of tourism, and the inseparable nature of tourism means that benefits must be maximised and costs minimised.
Establish objectives	Planning allows the establishment of destination objectives which help to unite stakeholders.
Work together as a destination	Plans provide a rallying call for the destination with allocated roles and responsibilities to bring all stakeholders together behind one purpose.
Guidelines and standards	Plans put in place for guidelines and standards which raise the quality of the destination offering and ensure that new developments comply.
Sustainable development	Planning ensures the sustainable development of all the destination elements through integrated planning approaches.
Baseline and monitoring process	Plans allow for the disciplined monitoring of destination elements to observe the success, or otherwise, of the plan.
Place-making and differentiation	Competitive destinations are those that emphasise local features and design to deliver the tourist experience.

The contemporary approach to integrated tourism governance delivers a 'whole of destination approach' to tourism planning. This reflects the realities of tourism, which demand collaboration and partnerships reflecting the many stakeholders involved in delivering the product to the tourist. To reach this point, tourism planning has gone through a series of stages, beginning with plans that prioritised economic goals and moving towards contemporary plans where sustainability is the key. The evolution of tourism planning is shown in Table 11.3.

Five traditions can be seen to have characterised tourism planning (Getz, 1986; Hall, 2007):

1. **Boosterism** – where tourism is viewed uncritically as a means to 'boost' the profile of the destination;

2. **Economic planning** – based on economic and regional development where the state is involved in managing the economy, and economic analysis is used to make and evaluate planning decisions;

3. **Physical planning** – where land use zoning and the use of geographical information systems (GIS) is dominant and based upon concepts from regional and land use planning;

4. **Community-based planning** – where tourism plans take account of the views of the host community, often being developed from the community upwards – there are a variety of approaches here, ranging from 'token' participation to full control by the host community (Figure 11.1); and

5. **Sustainable planning** – where the plans are increasingly concerned with the long-term viability of the destination and encompass issues such as environmental sustainability, carbon footprints and climate change.

TABLE 11.3   The evolution of tourism planning

Physical-based plans	These were site-specific plans, emphasising economic development with no consideration of the wider impact of the development.
Strategic-based plans	Plans began to take into account the wider regional impacts of tourism developments and were more integrated, including environmental considerations – early tourism master plans took this form.
Master plans	Tourism master plans took all the destination elements, including transport, marketing, human resources and the impacts of development into one overarching plan. These tended to be 'one off' plans that were updated every few years.
Integrated and rolling plans	The next evolution of tourism plans was away from the 'one off' plan towards a more continuous planning process with monitoring and adjustments made over the plan period.
Whole of destination approach	Contemporary approaches to tourism planning take a 'whole of destination approach' including the host community and all legitimate stakeholders to deliver competitiveness and sustainability.

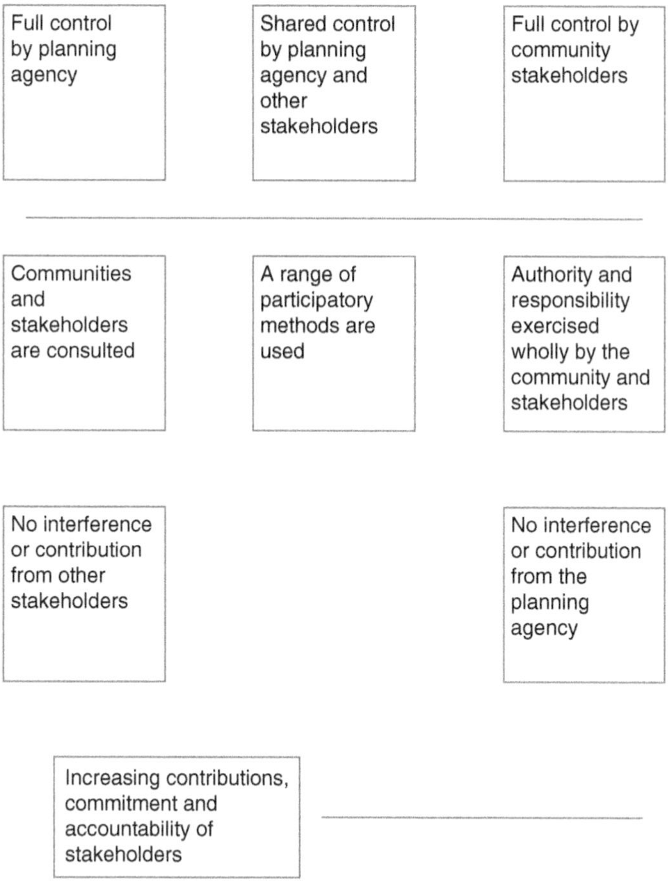

Full control by planning agency	Shared control by planning agency and other stakeholders	Full control by community stakeholders
Communities and stakeholders are consulted	A range of participatory methods are used	Authority and responsibility exercised wholly by the community and stakeholders
No interference or contribution from other stakeholders		No interference or contribution from the planning agency

Increasing contributions, commitment and accountability of stakeholders

FIGURE 11.1   A continuum of host community involvement in tourism planning

Source: based on Selman, 2004

Finally, tourism planning operates on a range of geographical scales:

- **International planning** is unusual, mainly for the reasons identified above, when considering international government operations in tourism. Simply, it is difficult to get agreement across borders, and national planning systems differ substantially. Nonetheless, an increasing number of international planning initiatives are being launched – particularly across borders, such as the tourism strategy for the Greater Mekong Delta Region or the Danube Regional Strategy. There is also no doubt that new destinations such as Antarctica will require an international approach to tourism planning.
- **National planning** in tourism is common and sets the framework for regional and local plans. In the past this has been the scale for master plans, as, for example, in former Eastern European states such as Romania and Bulgaria, although, as shown above, the trend is now to focus more on the regional and local levels.
- **Regional plans** allow for detailed tourism plans within the national framework. They will focus more closely on access, development, infrastructure and policy.
- **Development planning** is where specific areas have been zoned for tourism. These plans deal with site and facility layout, zoning and design issues as well as infrastructure and investment planning, and tend to be the most common type of tourism plan.
- **Special plans** cut across geographical scales; instead they focus on tourism themes such as the Australian State of Victoria's Aboriginal Tourism Development Plan (Tourism Victoria, 2006).

Of course, the pace of change in new thinking and approaches to planning and policy creates its own challenges, not least of which is technology and how to introduce knowledge into the tourism planning system (Costa and Brandao, 2018). This allows contemporary planning to deliver 'smart' destinations which invest in their human capital, use technologies to facilitate sustainable growth and ensure participatory governance balancing the delivery of experiences to tourists with the quality of life for residents (Trufino and Campana, 2019).

The tourism planning process

Tourism planning takes many forms and acts at a variety of scales. However, there are a number of common threads running through contemporary approaches to the planning process.

At the beginning of any tourism planning exercise, a number of key questions have to be asked, including:

- What type of tourist is wanted?
- What is the scale of tourism wanted?
- Where and how will tourism take place?
- Who will finance development?

- What is the government's view about tourism?
- Where will the manpower and infrastructure come from?

The answer to these questions will depend upon how important tourism is to the destination and the role that government plays in the planning process.

The stages of planning

There are many accounts of the various stages of tourism planning but the one presented by Mill and Morrison (1985) is both comprehensive and logical. Table 11.4 outlines the various stages and the tasks involved.

The stages of tourism planning outlined in Table 11.4 cover the key functions of a tourism plan, although the sequencing and the details will vary according to the goals and objectives, and the scale of the plan.

TABLE 11.4   Stages of the tourism planning process

Stage of planning	The tasks involved
Background analysis	Desk research to set the context for the plan and identify information gaps
Situation analysis	Review current and past plans and policies, including the needs of the plan sponsors
Resource analysis	Inventory of tourism resources
Demand analysis	Market demand for the destination – volume, value, trends and characteristics
Tourism sector analysis	SWOT analysis of the tourism sector
Research	This stage plugs the gaps identified in background analysis and will involve visiting the destination
Resource research	A detailed review of the tourism resources through field visits to determine locations, types and capacities of the resources
Activities research	Identification of potential products available at the destination, using the resource base
Market and competition analysis	Market research to expand on the background analysis and will include a competitor analysis
Synthesis	Here, the information from the first two stages is drawn together to inform the plan's development
Position statements	A series of reports for stakeholders to review the current situation and design the way forward. These reports will be focused on development, marketing and the sector
Goals and objectives	Based upon the research stages, plan goals and objectives are designed. They can be varied (for example, they may be economic or environmental), but they must be achievable, quantifiable and give the plan direction

(Continued)

TABLE 11.4   (Continued)

Stage of planning	The tasks involved
Plan development	The plan is then developed into a series of actions that will deliver the goals and objectives. This may take the form of a draft plan which is then approved or modified
Programmes and actions	This is the 'engine room' of the plan, with detailed approaches for each of the plan's goals – they identify roles and responsibilities, timing, funding and monitoring
Plan monitoring	This final stage is vital. The quantified goals and objectives will be monitored on a regular basis and adjustments made to the plan if any are not being achieved. An excellent example of contemporary tourism planning using a monitoring approach is the Tourism Optimisation Management Model for Kangaroo Island in Australia

Source: Mill and Morrison, 1985

Plan failure

A major issue for tourism planners is the fact that many plans are never implemented, or worse, they go wrong, or even fail. Consultants often tell of their expensive and detailed master plans that lie unopened on ministry shelves. This may be because the plan could not be resourced or because the political will to implement the plan was lacking. The response to this issue by funding agencies has been to place more emphasis on the implementation and monitoring of tourism plans. Nonetheless, despite the fact that this chapter has shown the importance of public sector involvement in tourism – and of tourism planning – there are those who oppose this approach on the grounds that planning exercises are expensive, that tourism is a complex sector where planning is inappropriate, and, in particular, view tourism as a private sector activity where public sector intervention is unwelcome.

Plans may also fail for a variety of reasons:

- Public policy towards tourism may change and make the plan redundant.
- Tourism demand may have been poorly estimated by the plan and the expected visitors do not materialise.
- Expected developments such as access and transportation fail to materialise.
- The competitor analysis may have underestimated particular competitors who surge ahead.
- The plan was badly conceived and out of scale with the destination and its own vision.
- The plan failed to convince key stakeholders to be involved.
- The plan was drawn up by planners without a clear understanding of how tourism operates or the needs of the market.

When plans do fail, or are not implemented, the destination will suffer. McKercher and Mak (2019) have developed a novel tool to identify destinations 'at risk', based on two dimensions:

1. **Market indifference** – there is little interest in the destination; and

2. **Market irrelevance** – over-reliance on markets that are not interested.

Destinations where planning has failed have three characteristics. Firstly, there will be no disciplined allocation of resources across the destination, not simply within the tourism sector, but tourism may also lose out to other economic sectors such as power generation at the coast. Secondly, failure will result in undisciplined competition between resources within tourism – for example, the clash between nature conservation and tourism access to national parks will not be resolved – and, thirdly, the very integrity of tourism resources at the destination will be threatened without a tourism planning framework.

SUMMARY

This chapter has demonstrated why government is so important for the tourism sector and outlined the agencies and mechanisms that deliver tourism policy, planning and marketing. Fundamentally, the contribution of tourism to economies and societies is too valuable to leave to the private sector and so governments legislate and provide a policy framework for tourism. This policy is delivered through a wide range of tourism public sector organisations and, whilst their roles vary, they can be summarised as policy, planning and marketing. With increased pressure on the public sector, a new type of tourism governance is emerging where the organisations closest to the delivery of tourism are being empowered and networks of tourism stakeholders have developed to assist these organisations to deliver their tasks. One of these tasks is tourism planning and the chapter details why it is so vital for tourism, an activity which is potentially very damaging to the destinations. The chapter outlines the tourism planning process and the fact that other destination stakeholders are increasingly involved in planning as the 'whole of destination approach' to planning becomes more widespread. Finally, the chapter identifies the reasons for plan failure and its consequences.

DISCUSSION QUESTIONS

1. Draft a briefing paper for a councillor explaining why their local authority should be involved in tourism.

2. Taking a public sector tourist organisation for a destination that you know, visit their website and map their key functions.

3. For a destination that you are familiar with, create a list of the stakeholders who you would like to be involved in a policy network to assist in government decision-making for tourism.

4. Justify why tourism planning is important.

5. Taking a destination that you are familiar with, design a strategy for the fair and balanced involvement of the host community in the tourism planning process.

ANNOTATED FURTHER READING

Costa, C. and Brandao, P. (2018) 'Tourism planning: evolution and trends for the future', in C. Cooper, S. Volo, W.C. Gartner and N. Scott (eds), *The Sage Handbook of Tourism Management: Theories, Concepts and Disciplinary Approaches to Tourism*. London: Sage. pp. 538–55.

Thorough and synoptic view of tourism planning.

Jenkins, J. (2018) 'Tourism policy', in C. Cooper, S. Volo, W.C. Gartner and N. Scott (eds), *The Sage Handbook of Tourism Management: Theories, Concepts and Disciplinary Approaches to Tourism*. London: Sage. pp. 297–313.

Contemporary review of tourism policy.

Morpeth, N.D. and Yan, H. (2015) *Planning for Tourism: Towards a Sustainable Future*. Wallingford: CABI.

Contemporary tourism planning text.

Murphy, P.E. and Murphy, A.E. (2004) *Strategic Management for Tourism Communities*. Clevedon: Channel View.

A thorough and expanded update on Peter Murphy's seminal work on community tourism and the role of the host community in the contemporary planning process.

Sharpley, R. and Telfer, D.J. (2014) *Tourism and Development: Concepts and Issues,* 2nd edn. Bristol: Channel View.

Excellent account of the different approaches to development that underpin tourism planning.

REFERENCES CITED

Butler, R. (2018) 'Sustainability and resilience: two sides of the same coin?' in C. Cooper, S. Volo, W.C. Gartner and N. Scott (eds), *The Sage Handbook of Tourism Management: Theories, Concepts and Disciplinary Approaches to Tourism*. London: Sage. pp. 407–21.

Costa, C. and Brandao, P. (2018) 'Tourism planning: evolution and trends for the future', in C. Cooper, S. Volo, W.C. Gartner and N. Scott (eds), *The Sage Handbook of Tourism Management: Theories, Concepts and Disciplinary Approaches to Tourism*. London: Sage. pp. 538–55.

Dredge, D. (2016) 'Are DMOs on a path to redundancy?' *Tourism Recreation Research*, 41 (3): 348–53.

Getz, D. (1986) 'Models in tourism planning towards integration of theory and practice', *Tourism Management*, 7 (1): 21–32.

Hall, C.M. (2007) 'Planning and managing the contemporary destination', in C. Cooper and C.M. Hall (eds), *Contemporary Tourism*. Oxford: Butterworth-Heinemann Elsevier. pp. 188–215.

Hall, C.M. (2011) 'Policy learning and policy failure in sustainable tourism governance: from first- and second-order to third-order change?' *Journal of Sustainable Tourism*, 19 (4–5): 649–71.

Jenkins, J. (2018) 'Tourism policy', in C. Cooper, S. Volo, W.C. Gartner and N. Scott (eds), *The Sage Handbook of Tourism Management: Theories, Concepts and Disciplinary Approaches to Tourism*. London: Sage. pp. 297–313.

McKercher, R. and Mak, B. (2019) 'Identifying destination health: developing the concepts of market indifference and destination dependence/market irrelevance', *Journal of Travel Research*, https://doi.org/10.1177/0047287519867139

Mill, R.C. and Morrison, A.M. (1985) *The Tourism System: An Introductory Text*. Englewood Cliffs, NJ: Prentice Hall.

Morpeth, N.D. and Yan, H. (2015) *Planning for Tourism: Towards a Sustainable Future*. Wallingford: CABI.

Murphy, P. (1985) *Tourism: A Community Approach*. London: Methuen.

Scott, N. (2015) 'Tourism policy', in C. Cooper (ed.), *Contemporary Tourism Reviews, Volume 1*. Oxford: Goodfellow. pp. 57–90.

Selman, P. (2004) 'Community participation in the planning of management of cultural landscapes', *Journal of Environmental Planning and Management*, 47 (3): 365–92.

Sharpley, R. and Telfer, D.J. (2014) *Tourism and Development: Concepts and Issues,* 2nd edn. Bristol: Channel View.

Stevenson, N., Airey, D. and Miller, G. (2008) 'Tourism policy making: the policymakers' perspectives', *Annals of Tourism Research*, 35 (3): 732–50.

Tourism Victoria (2006) *Aboriginal Tourism Development Plan*. Melbourne: Tourism Victoria.

Trufino, M. and Campana, S. (2019) 'Drivers and emerging innovations in knowledge-based destinations: towards a research agenda', *Journal of Destination Marketing and Management*, 4: 1–11.

UNWTO (2019) *Baseline Report on the Integration of Sustainable Consumption and Production Patterns into Tourism Policies*. Madrid: UNWTO.

Wanhill, S. (2008) 'Public sector and policy', in C. Cooper, J. Fletcher, A. Fyall, D. Gilbert and S. Wanhill (eds), *Tourism Principles and Practice*. Harlow: Prentice Hall. pp. 438–73.

MAJOR CASE STUDY 11.1

The Heart of St. Kitts Foundation

The 'St. Kitts Scenic Railway' tourist attraction

Source: ©Gem Russan/Shutterstock.com

Introduction

This chapter has been clear that the growing responsibilities of government in tourism mean that they have to seek the assistance of 'civil society' organisations to fulfil their commitments. Governments have taken different approaches to the issue and this case study unpacks an award-winning destination-based foundation established by a Caribbean ministry of tourism to expand its activities. The destination is St. Kitts and Nevis, part of the Leeward Islands – destinations that

have not pursued mass tourism. St. Kitts is the larger of the two islands and the focus of this case study.

Development of Sustainable Tourism on St. Kitts 2005–2016

St. Kitts has overtly shunned mass tourism, turning instead to a policy of sustainable tourism development. Tourism on the island has grown in response to the government's economic policy of diversification away from sugar cane exports and a focus on tourism as a major part of the economy. The last of the sugar plantations closed in 2005 and this triggered the development of the island's tourism strategy. The Ministry of Tourism decided upon a sustainable tourism strategy to create a 'Pro-Planet, Pro-People' tourism plan, and in order to implement the plan, the St. Kitts Sustainable Destination Council (SDC) was established. The SDC is a public–private organisation created to promote collaboration across island stakeholders both within and outside the tourism sector.

The plan has clearly worked, with a growth in annual visitor numbers from 360,000 in 2005 to over 1 million visitors in 2016 on both St. Kitts and Nevis. This growth prompted a series of initiatives from the Ministry and the SDC to ensure that growth was sustainable, reflected good practice in destination management and did not bring negative consequences for the island. These initiatives included:

- *Environmental and sustainability education* – a key action has been environmental and sustainability education from primary school upwards, aiming to create environmental awareness across the island. The education initiative was led by the SDC focusing on all dimensions of sustainability. The results of the education programme have been positive for the island, with 80 per cent of residents believing tourism is a positive rather than a negative development.

- *Partnerships* – as well as working with the SDC, the St. Kitts Ministry of Tourism opened up a partnership with Sustainable Travel International (STI) in 2012. This partnership was designed to enhance the island's sustainable destination management programme by agreeing a common agenda – to improve lives and protect places through travel and tourism, and to implement the Ministry's 'Pro-People, Pro-Planet' tourism strategy.

- *Standards* – St. Kitts was an early adopter of the Global Sustainable Tourism Council's (GSTC) Destination Criteria (see Chapter 6). By adopting the criteria, the island was prompted

to create the Inter-Agency Sustainable Destination Management Council (IASDMC) to streamline sustainability operations across government agencies to address the needs of the GSTC criteria and to train over 30 local leaders on the island to become better destination stewards.

The Heart of St. Kitts Foundation 2016 to date

The Ministry of Tourism established the Heart of St. Kitts Foundation in 2016. The main reason for its creation was to embed the Ministry's achievements to date within the local industry and community and to achieve buy-in for sustainable tourism across St. Kitts. The Foundation was also designed to work closely with the IASDMC and STI. A key to the success of the Foundation has been the collaboration between the Ministry of Tourism and tourism enterprises on the island. This collaboration acts to build awareness of sustainability priorities in St. Kitts and to provide funding for local projects. To quote the website, the vision of the Foundation is: 'Through support from local tourism businesses and visitors to the island, the Heart of St. Kitts Foundation aims to inspire better stewardship of the environment, culture and lasting legacy of St. Kitts' (www.heartofstkitts.org/about).

This vision is achieved through the projects that the Foundation is developing. These projects are pioneering a number of key tourism initiatives across the island related to conserving land and marine habitats, improving waste management, preserving local culture and heritage/historic sites and supporting community-driven tourism products. The following projects exemplify the work of the foundation:

Cotton Ginnery Restoration

Spooner's Cotton Ginnery was the first ginnery on St. Kitts, dating back to 1901. It is the only remaining ginnery on the island, abandoned since its closure in 1970.

(Continued)

The Heart of St. Kitts Foundation is restoring the ginnery to tell the story of the island's agro-industrial past through the creation of a new cultural attraction for both visitors and residents.

Rails to Trails Project

The Heart of St. Kitts Foundation is part of a strategic partnership involved in restoring the old sugar railway on the island as a hiking and biking trail. The railway stretches over 22 kilometres. The initiative began in 2015 and will provide a safe and educational new tourism product – 'Rails to Trails'.

Waste Management

This project is designed to improve the waste management infrastructure on the island where residents are not able to recycle waste.

Beach Clean-Ups

St. Kitts has over 78 kilometres of coastline with valuable ecosystems. The Heart of St. Kitts Foundation is supporting regular beach clean-up activities as well as awareness-building of the damage done to the coastline by human pressure, including littering.

Discussion Questions

1. Do you think the Ministry of Tourism could have achieved its sustainable tourism vision without the creation of the Foundation and other bodies?
2. Research the island of St. Kitts – do you agree that the Foundation has protected the island from negative tourism impacts?
3. Do the Foundation's projects reflect the organisation's vision?

Source: www.heartofstkitts.org/about

PART 4
TOURISM DEMAND AND MARKETING ESSENTIALS

This part focuses upon the tourist, analysing how they demand tourism and are the focus of tourism marketing. Here, the emphasis is upon the 'generating region' of Leiper's tourism system. By focusing upon the tourist, this part demonstrates the influences upon their decision-making process and how tourism demand can be conceptualised. Of course, consideration must be given to those who do not travel but wish to, perhaps due to particular constraints such as illness. In other words, it must be recognised that every tourist is an individual with particular motivations, wants and needs. This makes it possible to devise effective consumer decision-making models although, as shown, the current models for tourism do not take into account contemporary methods of information search using the Internet and social media, failing to factor in the 'wild card' events that are so influential on demand.

In Chapter 12, the personal influences upon tourist demand are analysed and the chapter shows how these can be drawn together into models of consumer decision-making for tourism, where technology is having an increasing influence. Personal determinants and influences of demand can be aggregated to provide a worldview of tourism demand, a picture that is influenced by factors such as economic development and demographics. In the twenty-first century, the global pattern of tourism demand has been impacted by 'wild card' events, of which 9/11 was the defining one. These events have had a significant impact upon demand patterns and decision-making.

A thorough understanding of the influences upon tourism demand is essential for effective tourism marketing. Current thinking in terms of the scope and definition of marketing has identified a shift in focus from goods to a 'service-dominant logic' of marketing. This new approach recognises that tourism marketing thinks of the product as a bundle of both tangible and intangible elements as well as focusing on consumer needs and their involvement in the co-creation of the tourism experience. The service-dominant logic is presented in the classic paper for Chapter 13. This paper by Vargo and Lush pervades the chapter's thinking on tourism marketing.

Chapter 13 shows how technology, and particularly the Internet, has transformed the business of tourism marketing, and introduces the dimensions of digital and e-marketing, announcing the new era of 'marketing 4.0' where digital and physical marketing are combined. It then goes on to discuss the nature of tourism market planning and strategy and the elements of the marketing mix, and especially the implications of the nature of tourism for the mix. The chapter closes with a review of the concept of tourism 'product markets', which draw together the market and the product in a neat framework that explains the various sub-products of tourism, such as heritage or special interest tourism.

12
DEMAND

LEARNING OUTCOMES

This chapter focuses upon the tourist and their demand for travel. It outlines the reasons for tourism travel and the various influences that shape travel behaviour. The chapter is designed to provide you with:

- an awareness of the concepts and definitions of tourism demand;
- an understanding of the tourist consumer decision-making process;
- an appreciation of the factors that determine tourism tourist demand;
- an ability to identify the constraints on travel; and
- an understanding of the issues surrounding the forecasting of tourist demand and the techniques used.

INTRODUCTION

In Chapter 1, Leiper's tourism system was identified as an effective organising concept for tourism; this chapter focuses upon the generating region of the system. In order to manage tourism demand, it is important to understand the nature of demand in terms of definitions, the various components of demand, the consumer decision-making process in tourism, the role of social media and how we forecast demand, as well as some of the more fundamental aspects of demand such as motivation, chosen as the focus of the classic paper for this chapter.

There is no doubt that managing tourism demand is one of the challenges for tourism in the twenty-first century as the volume of tourists grows and the remotest corners of the world are visited. In fact, perceptions of demand have changed over the years with early pronouncements such as the UN's Universal Declaration of Human Rights encouraging everyone to travel as a 'right' (www.un.org/en/universal-declaration-human-rights), to the present day when the tourist is urged to travel 'responsibly' and to offset the carbon emissions generated from flying, or even not fly at all.

There are three key reasons to have a thorough understanding of tourism demand:

1. It is an essential underpinning for policy and forecasting.

2. It provides critical information to allow the balancing of provision of supply and demand at destinations.

3. It allows the tourism industry to better understand consumer behaviour and the tourism marketplace.

DEFINITIONS AND CONCEPTS

Definitions

Of course, definitions of demand vary according to the perspective of the author. The differing perspectives of various disciplines help us to fully understand tourism demand. For example, economists consider demand to be the schedule of the amount of any product or service that people are willing and able to buy at each specific price in a set of possible prices during a specified period of time. This introduces the idea of elasticity – which describes the relationship between demand and price or other variables. In contrast, psychologists view demand from the perspective of motivation and behaviour, scratching beneath the skin of the tourist to examine the interaction of personality, environment and demand for tourism. Finally, the geographers' definition encompasses a wide range of influences, in addition to price, and includes not only those who actually participate in tourism, but also those who wish to but for some reason do not. This chapter adopts this approach and uses Mathieson and Wall's (1982: 182) definition of demand: 'The total number of persons who travel, or wish to travel, to use tourist facilities and services at places away from their places of work and residence'.

Concepts

The fact that some individuals may harbour a demand for tourism but are unable to realise that demand suggests that demand for tourism consists of a number of components. Three basic components make up the total demand for tourism:

1. **Effective or actual demand** is the actual number of participants in tourism or those who are travelling, that is, de facto tourists. This is the component of demand most commonly and easily measured, and the bulk of tourism statistics refer to effective demand.

2. **Suppressed demand** is made up of that section of the population who do not travel for some reason. Despite burgeoning demand for tourism across the world, only a very small percentage of the world's total population engages in international tourism, as shown in Chapter 1. Of course, a considerably greater number participate in domestic travel, but in many parts of the world tourism remains an unobtainable luxury.

    Two elements of suppressed demand can be distinguished. First, *potential demand* refers to those who will travel at some future date if they experience a change in their circumstances – such as an increase in their purchasing power. Second, *deferred demand* is a demand postponed because of a problem in the supply environment, such as a lack of capacity in accommodation, weather conditions or, perhaps, a natural disaster such as a hurricane. When the supply conditions are more favourable, those in the deferred demand category will convert to effective demand at some future date.

3. **No demand.** Finally, there will always be those who simply do not wish to travel or are unable to travel, constituting a category of *no demand*. Increasingly people are in this category because they choose to spend their discretionary income on goods rather than tourism.

Demand for tourism may also be viewed and influenced in other ways. For example, *substitution of demand* refers to the case when demand for one activity (say, a self-catering holiday) is substituted for another (staying in serviced accommodation, or taking surface transport rather than flying). A similar concept is *redirection of demand* where the geographical location of demand is changed – say, a trip to Spain is redirected to Italy because of over-booking of accommodation. Finally, the opening of a new tourism supply – say, a resort, an attraction or accommodation – will:

- Redirect demand from similar facilities in the area;
- Substitute demand from other facilities; and
- Generate new demand.

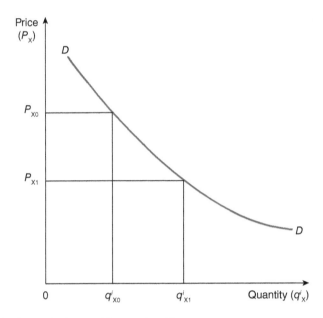

FIGURE 12.1   An individual's demand for product X

Source: Wanhill and Airey, 1980

Economists refer to the first two of these as the *displacement effect* – in other words, demand from other facilities is displaced to the new one and no extra demand is generated.

Leiper's model of tourism makes it clear that tourism demand results in *flows* between the generating region and the destination region. These flows are complex and determined by a wide variety of factors, including geographical proximity, historical trade and cultural ties, and, of course, the notion of contrasting environments, exemplified by the flow of tourists from northern Europe to the warmer countries of the Mediterranean.

In economic terms, a *demand schedule* refers to the quantities of a product that an individual wishes to purchase at different prices at a given point in time. Generally, the higher the price of the product, the lower is the demand; the lower the price, the greater is the demand. This is shown in Figure 12.1. It is normal to characterise the demand curve

DD in Figure 12.1 by an appropriate measure that expresses the responsiveness of quantity to changes in price. Such a measure is termed the *elasticity of demand.*

Finally, a key concept to consider is *seasonality.* Most patterns of tourism demand demonstrate regular fluctuations due solely to the time of year known as seasonality. Although this is often the result of changes in climate over the calendar year, there are other influencing factors, such as the timing of school and work holidays, or regular special events. The perishable nature of the tourism product means that seasonality can cause major problems and is a major influence upon both employment and capital investment. It can result in seasonal employment, and the under-use or even closing down of facilities at certain times of the year. It can also result in an over-stretching by some destinations and businesses at times of peak activity to compensate for low demand off-season. This leads to overcrowding, over-bookings, high prices and ultimately to customer dissatisfaction and a worsening reputation. Strategies to reduce seasonality vary. Typically, they involve attempts to create or shift demand to the shoulder or trough months, either through setting price differentials or through the introduction or enhancement of all-year facilities. Marketing may be targeted at groups that have the time and resources to travel at any time of the year, notably the elderly, or at the development of products that are less climate or weather sensitive. Mini Case Study 12.1 outlines an approach to overcoming seasonality in Uruguay.

MINI CASE STUDY 12.1

Punta del Este, Uruguay – Overcoming Seasonality

Introduction

Overcoming seasonality of demand is a perennial challenge for destinations. It is a particular issue for mass tourism resorts where the summer season dominates demand. Punta del Este is such a resort on the Atlantic Coast in the Maldonado Department of southeastern Uruguay. The UNWTO has developed an approach to defeat seasonality in the resort at the request of the municipality.

The Approach

The key to the approach has been collaboration across the tourism sector and beyond, including to other destinations both regionally and internationally, including Cape Town. A variety of agencies are involved in the initiative:

- The Uruguay Ministry of Tourism and Sports;
- The Maldonado regional government; and
- Destino Punta del Este.

On the supply side, private sector stakeholders have been closely involved in the process. Their approach is based on developing new tourism products and other innovations to create a year-round tourism offering.

(Continued)

These include working with the agri-food sector to develop culinary tourism, developing sports tourism, wellness tourism, language tourism and academic training, theme-based events and convention/MICE (meetings, incentives, conferences and events) tourism based upon a new convention centre.

The demand side of the project has focused on contemporary forms of tourism demand, including the conscious traveller, the trans-modern tourist, the transformative tourist, and also takes into account the demands of the baby boomer generation, all incorporating demand based upon simplicity and meaningful experiences.

The success of the approach is based upon three key pillars:

1. **Collaboration**. The Punta del Este approach has achieved collaboration across a variety of destination stakeholders, based upon a public–private partnership approach. This has allowed for common solutions to seasonality which embrace the destination's economic and social development.
2. **Creative strategy**. The approach is based upon a unifying and guiding theme of energy to allow innovation in experiences to underpin the tourism offer.
3. **Mainstreaming**. The approach has taken a disciplined approach to seasonality by utilising disciplines such as social analytics, positioning, continuous innovation, communication and quality.

Discussion Questions

1. Visit the website of Punta del Este. Does the site communicate the concept of year-round tourism?
2. Assess the demand-side approach – how effective is it?
3. Taking a destination that you know well, what can you learn from the Punta del Este approach to reduce seasonality there?

Sources: www.maldonado.gub.uy/?mi=PuntadelEste#municipio; UNWTO (2018) *Seasonality, Challenge and Opportunity: Punta del Este 365*. Madrid: UNWTO.

THE TOURIST CONSUMER DECISION-MAKING PROCESS

The tourist consumer decision-making process is complex. Not only is it influenced by the characteristics of the tourists themselves, but also their images of the many destinations available, their engagement with social media and the fact that tourism is a 'high involvement' purchase and increasingly 'technology enabled'. It is important to understand the psychology of the tourist consumer decision-making process, not only so that marketers know when, and how, to intervene in order to influence the process in terms of price and promotion, but also to understand how best to educate the tourist in their buying behaviour – for example, in their choice of travel mode vis-à-vis carbon emissions (Pearce, 2011).

Influences on the tourist consumer decision-making process

Kotler et al. (2020) view the consumer decision-making process as a response to a set of marketing stimuli. For tourism these marketing stimuli will include price, promotion and distribution as well as the 'product'. Here, an important part of the product is the destination itself and the image that the potential tourist holds of a destination. Destination image can be defined as: 'The attitude, perception, beliefs and ideas one holds about a particular geographic area formed by the cognitive image of a particular destination' (Gartner, 2000: 295).

Effectively, an image is a simplified version of reality, a way of making sense of the many stimuli received and processed by an individual. In tourism, the image of a destination is critical as it affects both an individual's perception of a destination and their decision whether to visit. The generation of the image is different for destinations when compared to other consumer goods. Two factors make the image particularly critical for tourist decision-making:

1. The intangible nature of tourism means the image is the only evidence that a visitor has of the destination before they visit.

2. The inseparable nature of the production and consumption process of tourism means that once they visit, the tourist's image of the destination is immediately changed by the experience.

The theories of image are divided into two camps. The first suggests that images can be disaggregated into many attributes and elements that can be measured. The second, 'gestalt approach' views the image as a whole, or holistic, concept that cannot be disaggregated.

The formation of a destination image is based upon information acquired by the tourist from three sources (Gartner, 2018):

1. **Induced agents** are controlled by sources external to the individual, such as advertisements and websites.

2. **Organic agents** are acquired through personal experience. These are normally the most trusted sources of information and include actual visits, social media and e-word of mouth.

3. **Autonomous agents** are media sources or popular culture. They are powerful because they can quickly alter a tourist's image of a destination.

A second set of influential variables relates to the characteristics of the tourists themselves. Kotler et al. (2020) have developed a fourfold classification of these characteristics:

1. Cultural characteristics are an important determinant of purchasing behaviour and include elements such as social class. An important aspect of marketing is to closely follow changes in culture in a society.

2. Social characteristics refer to how tourists make purchasing decisions as part of a group, whether it is within a family or amongst peers. Here, we are seeing substantial shifts in how we view our peers and reference groups – particularly with respect to membership of online communities and social media.

3. Personal characteristics are the lifestyle and life cycle factors that are dealt with later in this chapter.

4. Psychological factors relate to the personality of the tourist and how they view themselves and the world. This is influenced by four key psychological concepts – motivation, perception, learning and attitude.

For tourism decisions, 'perception' of the destination is critical, as noted above. A second key concept that has received much attention is 'motivation'. Of course, the most well-known theory of motivation is Maslow's (1970) hierarchy of needs, reproduced in Figure 12.2.

However, the tourism literature has developed its own approach to motivation as it applies to tourist decision-making. For example, in the classic paper for this chapter we present a contemporary view of tourist motivation. Other approaches include the traditional focus on:

- **Physical motivators** around 'recreation' and refreshment' of body and spirit through physical activity or soaking in the essence of a destination through sun or sea bathing;
- **Cultural motivators** around curiosity to see new places and to scratch under the skin of destinations to understand the people, their cultures and cuisine – this is how many tourists now justify their travel, and characterises the 'new tourist';
- **Interpersonal motivators** around people, whether it is meeting new people, visiting friends or relatives, or indeed escaping from the people we interact with on a daily basis; and
- **Status and prestige motivators** around the need for recognition through travel, whether it be a trip for culinary education or a culture tour of Europe.

Gray's (1970) classification of travel motivators shows how the market has evolved:

- **Wanderlust** is simply curiosity to experience the strange and unfamiliar. It refers to the basic trait in human nature to see, at first hand, different places, cultures and peoples. Status and prestige motivators would be included under this heading.
- **Sunlust** can be literally translated as the desire for sunshine and a better climate, but in fact it is broader than this and refers to the search for a better set of amenities for recreation than are available at home.

Here we can identify a change in tourist consumer behaviour with a shift away from 'sunlust' to 'wanderlust' motivators, partly driven by fears of the effects of the sun, but also by the desire to fully experience the culture as well as the physical attractions of the destination.

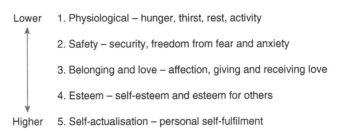

Lower   1. Physiological – hunger, thirst, rest, activity

2. Safety – security, freedom from fear and anxiety

3. Belonging and love – affection, giving and receiving love

4. Esteem – self-esteem and esteem for others

Higher   5. Self-actualisation – personal self-fulfilment

FIGURE 12.2 Maslow's hierarchy of needs

Source: Cooper et al., 2008, p. 45 © Chris Cooper, John Fletcher, Alan Fyall, David Gilbert and Stephen Wanhill, 2005

CLASSIC PAPER

Pearce, P.L. and Lee, U. (2005) 'Developing a travel career approach to tourist motivation', *Journal of Travel Research*, 43: 226–37

This classic paper provides a fresh way of viewing motivation in a tourism setting. Philip Pearce is well known for his work on tourist psychology and behaviour and here he writes with Lee to develop the idea of how tourist motivation can be linked to the idea of a 'travel career'.

Motivation is the driving force of tourism and the place to start when trying to understand tourist demand and behaviour but, as we have seen, there are many conflicting theories and ways of viewing motivation in tourism studies. This paper makes a major contribution by outlining the 'travel career ladder' (TCL) theory of motivation and then further developing the concept. The TCL is similar to Maslow's hierarchy of needs and is described by Pearce and Lee as having five levels of need:

1. Relaxation needs;
2. Safety/security needs;
3. Relationship needs;
4. Self-esteem and development needs; and
5. Fulfilment needs.

One or more of these needs motivates each trip, but one need will dominate. The TCL then links this idea to the fact that a traveller's needs would be expected to change with experience, equating to a 'travel career'. In other words, the mix of 'needs' will change over the course of a person's life and their travel experiences. Whilst it is difficult to generalise, the TCL theory suggests that people ascend the TCL over their life, often moving from 'level 1, relaxation needs' to 'level 5, fulfilment needs'. Alternatively, some people may remain at one particular level of the TCL.

The paper by Pearce and Lee takes the idea of the TCL theory of motivation one stage further. The authors test the theory on travellers and conclude that the original theory is perhaps too simplistic. They find that the idea of a simple 'one direction' movement up the 'ladder' over a person's travel career is misleading. Instead, the article's findings lead to the idea of travel career patterns (TCPs) of multiple motivations rather than a simple travel career ladder. These TCPs are influenced by previous travel experience and age. More recent research by Wu et al. (2019) investigates the links between the TCL and travel career, finding that income is an important additional variable to age.

Pearce and Lee's paper therefore makes a major contribution to our understanding of tourist behaviour, with a clear and intuitively appealing set of findings.

Source: Wu, J., Law, R., Fong, D.K.C. and Liu, J. (2019) 'Rethinking travel life cycle with travel career patterns', *Tourism Recreation Research*, 44 (2): 272–7.

MODELS OF CONSUMER BEHAVIOUR IN TOURISM

There are a number of traditions of modelling consumer behaviour dating back to the 1960s, with each best suited to particular situations (Woodside, 2018):

- **Cognitive approaches,** where the purchase is the outcome of problem-solving behaviour and the consumer is credited with rational behaviour;
- **The habitual approach,** where brand loyalty and inertia mean that few alternatives are considered; and
- **The reinforcement approach,** where the purchase is based upon learned past behaviour.

Each of these approaches views buying behaviour as sequential, triggered by recognition of a need from when the individual begins the decision-making process. The main advantage of these models is that they force marketers to understand the whole process, rather than simply the end point – the purchase decision. For a tourism purchase, Sirakaya and Woodside (2005) structure this behaviour into a series of eight well-defined stages. Whilst the assumption is that purchasers will pass through all stages, in reality some stages may be skipped. The stages are as follows (Figure 12.3):

1. Need arousal and recognition that there is a decision to be made. Here, there is a discrepancy between a consumer's 'actual' state and their 'ideal' state;

2. Formulation of goals and objectives for the purchase;

3. Identification of alternatives for the purchase;

4. Generation of an alternative set of products from which to choose;

5. Search for information about the properties of the alternatives under consideration, using information from a variety of sources, although research shows that information from personal networks and 'e-word of mouth' are the most influential. The end of chapter major case study examines TripAdvisor's role in information search;

6. Decision made – ultimate judgement or choice among the alternatives;

7. Acting upon the decision – purchasing travel and tourism; and

8. Post-purchase behaviour and feedback – the feelings experienced after the purchase, which may involve 'cognitive dissonance' – a feeling that an alternative may have been better – and sharing memories such as photographs and videos on social media.

Sirakaya and Woodside's (2005) approach is based upon generic models of consumer behaviour, but it also recognises that a tourism purchase is different from many others. For a tourism purchase:

- The consumer is highly involved;
- The purchase represents a major outlay of resources;
- The purchase is high risk as, firstly, the tourist may have little experience of the product and, secondly, the purchase is for a service and the product is intangible;

- It takes time and effort to choose so there is a considerable investment in information search; and

- Technology increasingly makes it possible to co-create the product with the supplier.

On this last point, there is no doubt that social media has become an important influence on tourists' search and buying behaviour. Social media facilitate information and content sharing amongst like-minded groups as well as social networking (see Garay, 2019). Here 'trust' is an important feature of social media and its users and is reflected in the term 'e-word of mouth', a relatively new source of information for tourists that does not depend purely upon their own social circle.

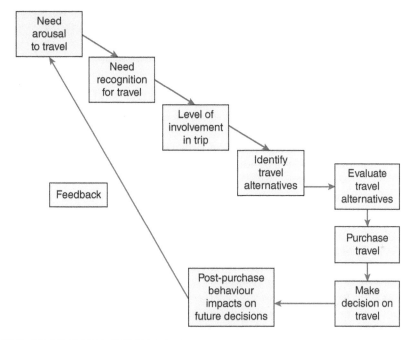

FIGURE 12.3   Model of consumer behaviour

FOCUS ON TECHNOLOGY

Travel Influencers

As shown above, social media has become a powerful source of information for tourists choosing their trip. Social media influencers are growing in number, including in tourism, and from a cottage industry a few years ago it is now a mature and sophisticated business model. Travel influencers have the ability to 'influence' potential travellers to take action and book a particular trip. They are vey different from traditional travel journalists. Leading travel influencers work to grow their

(Continued)

followers and develop content. When travel companies embark on influencer marketing, it is important to take a disciplined approach rather than adopt the approach because it is fashionable. This involves setting metrics to measure the success of the influencer, including measuring increases in website traffic, page views versus reads, growth in social media followers for the company and level of engagement. Indeed, when the relationship between an influencer and a travel company works well it can be very effective, often more so than conventional channels.

However, the presence of influencers has become controversial in the travel industry as they frequently request substantial discounts or free travel or accommodation in return for their endorsement on social media or their blog. Some companies feel that these demands have reached saturation point and requests are refused, raising the question as to whether influencers really do have the power that they claim.

AN EVALUATION OF CONSUMER BEHAVIOUR MODELS IN TOURISM

Despite a considerable literature, models of consumer decision-making in tourism have been criticised on a number of grounds (Decrop, 2000; Swarbrooke and Horner, 2007):

- They are too theoretical and not grounded in any empirical testing.
- They are beginning to date and no new models have been developed since the mid-1990s, yet the travel sector has changed considerably – what, for example, is the impact of Internet bookings, Internet information sources or social media on such models (see Mills and Law, 2015)? And how do they factor in new patterns of behaviour such as 'ethical decision-making', or the importance of experiences as opposed to destinations in the decision to travel?
- They do not help in understanding how the market would react to 'shocks' to the system such as 9/11.
- They fail to take into account the differing purchasing situations a tourist may experience – for example, a repeat versus a first-time trip.
- They view tourism from a Western developed-country perspective, yet we know that China and India will be major generators of international travel in the future.
- They fail to predict or identify the behaviour of tourists or markets and do not assist the manager in when to intervene in the buying process to secure a purchase.

It is this last point that is critical. If models of consumer behaviour in tourism cannot be used by marketers to fit products to particular market segments, then their use has to be questioned.

DETERMINANTS OF DEMAND FOR TOURISM

This section focuses upon the key determinants of demand for tourism and goes on to show how an understanding of these underlying influences allows us to forecast tourism demand.

Determinants at the individual scale

Although an individual may be motivated to travel, their ability to do so will depend on a number of factors related to both the individual and the supply environment. These factors can be termed *determinants of demand* and represent the 'parameters of possibility' for the individual – even within the developed world, many are unable to participate in tourism for some reason. For example, a certain level of discretionary income is required to allow participation in tourism, and this income, and indeed the type of participation, will be influenced by such factors as job type, life cycle stage, mobility, level of educational attainment and personality.

Once a decision to travel has been taken, the ability to undertake the trip, and the nature of that trip, will be determined by a wide range of interrelated factors. These can be broadly divided into two groups:

1. The first group of factors can be termed *lifestyle,* and includes income, employment, holiday entitlement, educational attainment and mobility.

2. The second group can be termed *life cycle* where the age and domestic circumstances of an individual affect both the amount and type of tourism demanded.

Naturally, these factors are interrelated and complementary. In a Western society, a high-status job is normally associated with an individual in middle age with a high-income, above-average holiday entitlement, education and mobility.

Lifestyle determinants of demand for tourism

Income and employment

Income and employment are closely linked and exert important influences upon both the level and the nature of tourist demand. Tourism is an expensive activity that demands a certain threshold of income before participation is possible. Gross income gives little indication of the money available to spend on tourism – rather, it is discretionary income that provides the best indicator – that is, the income left over when tax, housing and the basics of life have been accounted for.

The relationship between income and tourism is a complex one. For example, certain tourism activities are highly sensitive to income – additional holidays and expensive pursuits such as skiing holidays are a particular case in point. The relationship is also characterised by the fact that, at the extremes of the income spectrum, tourism demand is strongly affected, whereas in the middle of the spectrum it is much more difficult to discern a clear relationship.

A fundamental distinction is between those in employment and those unemployed. The impact of unemployment on the volume of tourism demand is obvious, but the nature of demand is also changed by employment uncertainty, particularly in times of economic recession. This encourages later booking of trips, more domestic holidays and shorter lengths of stay, and switches demand away from commercial accommodation to VFR, therefore leading to lower spending levels.

Paid holiday entitlement

The increase in leisure time experienced by most individuals in the developed world since 1950 is well documented. However, the relationship between an individual's total time budget, leisure time and paid holiday entitlement is complex. A number of surveys suggest that in a developed Western economy individuals have anything from 35 to 50 hours free time a week at their disposal. This free time is greater for males, the young and single adults. However, to enable tourism, leisure time has to be blocked into two or more days to allow a stay away from home. While this obviously is the case with paid holiday entitlement, patterns of leisure time have changed to allow three-day weekends, flexitime and longer periods of absence for those in employment.

Individual levels of paid holiday entitlement would seem to be an obvious determinant of travel demand, but again the relationship is not straightforward and, rather like the income variable, it is clearer at the extremes. Paid holiday entitlement tends to be more generous in developed economies and less so in the developing world. The pattern of entitlement is also responsible in part for the seasonality of tourism in some destinations simply because some of the entitlement has to be taken in the summer months. To an extent, this is historical and is rooted in the holiday patterns of manufacturing industries. It does, however, have an impact upon the nature of demand for tourism. In some countries, notably France, the staggering of holiday entitlement has been attempted to alleviate seasonality.

Education and mobility

Level of educational attainment is an important determinant of travel demand as education broadens horizons and stimulates the desire to travel. Also, the better educated the individual, the higher the awareness of travel opportunities and exposure to technology, information, media and promotion.

Personal mobility also has an important influence on travel demand. The car is the dominant recreational tool for both international and domestic tourism (as shown in Chapter 10). It provides door-to-door freedom, can carry tourism equipment (such as tents or boats) and has all-round vision for viewing. Ownership of a car stimulates travel for pleasure in all but recessionary times.

Race and gender

Race and gender are two critical determinants of tourist demand, but the relationships are not clearly understood. Most surveys of participation in tourism in the developed world suggest that whites and males have the highest levels of effective demand for tourism. However, changes in society are acting to complicate this rather simplistic view.

Clearly, for the purposes of analysing each variable, we have to separate them but it must be remembered that they are all complementary and interrelated. Indeed, this is such that some writers have attempted to analyse tourism or leisure lifestyles by performing multivariate analysis on the determinants of tourism demand and then trying to group individuals into particular categories. To date these analyses have met with limited success. Even where they have been commercially adopted as market segments, it is difficult to correlate them with other variables such as media habits.

Life cycle determinants of demand for tourism

The demand to travel, and indeed the type of tourism experience demanded, is closely related to an individual's age. Although the conventional measurement is chronological age, *domestic age* better discriminates between types of tourist demand and levels of travel demand. Considering an individual's domestic age – or position on the *family life cycle* (FLC) (childhood, young adult, married, etc.) – is an effective explanatory variable of travel behaviour with a distinctive pattern of demand found at each stage in the cycle. Table 12.1 outlines the stages of the FLC and the type of tourism demanded.

The explanatory framework provided by the FLC approach is a powerful one. It has implications for the supply of facilities, for the analysis of market needs of particular groups and is used as a basis for market segmentation by the tourism sector. However, the FLC as outlined is only appropriate for developed Western economies and even here it is a generalisation as it does not take into account, for example, one-parent families, divorcees or other ethnic groups living within Western economies.

TABLE 12.1   Family life cycle stage and tourism characteristics

Family life cycle stage	Tourism characteristics
Childhood	At this stage, decisions are taken for the individual in terms of holiday taking. However, children do have a significant influence upon both their parents' decisions. By the age of 10 or 11 years, some children take organised holidays with school or youth groups and day trips are common. These are usually domestic with self-catering arrangements.
Adolescence/ young adult	At this stage, young single people not living at home are preoccupied with independence, socialising and a search for identity. Typically, holidays independent of parents begin at around 15 years, constrained by finances but compensated for by having few other commitments, no shortage of free time and a curiosity for new places and experiences. This group has a high demand to travel, mainly on budget holidays using surface transport and self-catering accommodation. Here the preoccupation is simply to 'get away' – the destination is unimportant and is often associated with rites of passage such as the American 'Spring Break'.
Married	In married adulthood, the preoccupations are more with establishment, lifetime investments and social institutions. This FLC stage can have a number of options. For example, newly married couples who are young and have no children may have few constraints on travel, a high income and few other ties, giving them a high travel demand, frequently overseas. The arrival of children totally changes the influences upon tourism demand as holidays become more organisational and less geographical and constraints of time and finance may depress travel demand. Holiday preferences switch to domestic destinations, self-catering accommodation and VFR. This is known as the full nest stage and constraints on travel will depend on the age of the children.
Empty nest	As children grow up, reach the adolescence stage and begin to travel independently, constraints of time and finance are lifted from parents and their travel demand increases. This is often a time for long haul travel – the cruise market typically comprises this group.
Old age	The emergence of early retirement at 50 or 55 years is creating an active and mobile group in the population of many countries who will demand both domestic and international travel. However, it is too simplistic to view senior travellers as homogeneous, and there are many different categories – partly defined by the tension between physical health and financial resources In later retirement, lack of finance, infirmity and often the loss of a partner act to offset the increase in free time experienced by this group. Holidays become more hotel based and travel demand decreases. Recent changes in pension and social security arrangements in leading generating countries may depress senior travel in the future (see Pak, 2019).

FOCUS ON EMPLOYABILITY

Travel Writing

This book has focused on career positions in tourism, but self-employed travel writers play a significant role in the industry. Travel writers play a key role in influencing demand for destinations and in shaping destination image. Travel writing comes in many forms, including hotel reviews, destination guides, guidebooks themselves, travel blogs and pieces in travel magazines. Above all though, travel writers have to be able to write to gain attention and write accurately. Professional and budding travel writers recognise that they may need to supplement their income with a 'day job' and successful writers religiously keep a diary or journal. They treat writing as a business and try to find a particular niche for which they become known.

The world of travel writing is changing as traditional print media publications are declining and being replaced by online outlets. This means that travel writers have to understand these new media and be able to promote themselves effectively online. This may be through their own named portfolio domain websites where writing can be posted, blogs and Instagram feeds. However, it is also important to recognise the need to be well networked and to understand the industry and new trends in the sector. In terms of skills, journalism or creative writing courses are useful, as are photographic skills.

SUPPRESSED DEMAND FOR TOURISM

Despite a seminal paper by Haukeland in 1990, non-travellers receive short shrift in the study of tourism demand. There are two main reasons why people do not travel: firstly, they exert a preference not to travel and, secondly, they are unable to participate in travel for some reason. Nyaupane and Andereck (2008) have taken the well-known model of leisure constraints and adapted it for tourism. They structure constraints on travel into three types:

1. **Interpersonal constraints.** Lack of interest, peer group pressure and/or fear are real constraints on travel for some individuals. Physical limitations (such as ill health) are a significant reason for many people not travelling. In particular, heart disease and mental/physical handicap act as a major constraint on travel.

2. **Intrapersonal constraints.** Lack of companions to travel with acts as a constraint for some, as do the family circumstances of, say, single parents or those who have to care for elderly relatives.

3. **Structural constraints.** These tend to be the most significant constraints. Travel is expensive and demands a certain threshold of income before people can enter the market. It also competes with other products for available funds. A second structural constraint is lack of time, which may be for business or family reasons. Government restrictions such as currency controls and visas may also act as a real barrier to travel (both inbound and outbound) for some countries. Finally, peer pressure can be added as a constraint on travel, particularly the demand to reduce carbon emissions through, say, offsetting, or not flying at all.

MINI CASE STUDY 12.2

Climate Change and Tourism Demand: The Climate Index for Tourism

Introduction

It is clear that climate change will impact upon absolute levels of tourism demand in some parts of the world where, for example, there will be greater incidences of extreme weather events, extreme heat and water shortages. More subtly, it is also expected that climate change will shift the seasonality patterns of tourism in some destinations away from the summer peak and into the shoulder months. Climate is therefore a key part of the resource base of destinations, demonstrating a complex relationship with tourism demand.

Many alpine destinations are now experiencing a receding snow line with unreliable snowfall which, in the past, supported skiing and winter sports activities

Source: 'Ski Track' by timo_w2s is licensed under CC BY-SA 2.0

The Climate Index for Tourism

As a key resource of destinations, climate impacts upon the type of tourism activities that are demanded. For example, many alpine destinations are now experiencing a receding snow line with unreliable snowfall, which in the past supported skiing and winter sports activities. These destinations are having to change their product offering to more of a walking and lakes and mountains product. In other words, different tourist activities have different weather requirements, particularly in relation to human comfort levels. This has led to the development of climate indices specific to tourism activities, which were discussed in Chapter 4. These indices allow the assessment of climate attractiveness for different types of tourism activity (Cavlek et al., 2018). De Freitas et al. (2008) have conceptualized a climate index for tourism (CIT) that integrates the thermal, aesthetic and physical facets of the atmospheric environment important for tourism. This allows for estimates of a set of weather thresholds for different activities from surveying of groups of tourists spending time on the beach (sun, sea and sand, and picnicking). This was taken further by Bafaluy et al. (2014), using consultations with experts and practitioners. They established a set of thermal, aesthetic and physical thresholds for a number of other tourist activities including cycling, hiking, golf, motor boating, sailing and cultural tourism.

There are three components of the CIT:

1. The thermal component is a measure of the body-atmosphere energy balance expressed by a biometeorological index that integrates physiological, thermal and environmental variables comprising temperature, relative humidity, wind speed and radiation.
2. The aesthetic component includes the condition of the sky.
3. The physical components include wind and rain, which can have an overriding effect on demand when certain values are exceeded.

(Continued)

These components are then combined to determine the level of demand for different activities at a destination, as affected by the prevailing weather conditions. This is done by creating a weather typology matrix which rates each activity, ranging from unacceptable conditions, through acceptable to ideal conditions. This allows planners to predict levels of demand for these activities at destinations, and by season, and so scientifically defines the relationship between tourism demand and climate.

Discussion Questions

1. In class, debate the ideal weather conditions for beach tourism and for sightseeing.
2. Using a map of the world, identify climate hotspots which will no longer be able to support tourism.
3. Taking a destination that you know well, how do you expect climate change to influence seasonality in the next 50 years?

Sources: Bafaluy, D., Amengual, A., Romeo, R. and Homar, V. (2014) 'Present and future climate resources for various types of tourism in the Bay of Palma, Spain', *Regional Environmental Change*, 14: 1995–2006; Cavlek, N., Cooper, C., Krajinovoc, V., Srnec, L. and Zaninovic, K. (2018) 'Destination climate adaptation', *Journal of Hospitality and Tourism Research*, 43 (2): 314–22; de Freitas, C.R., Scott, D. and McBoyle, G. (2008) 'A second generation climate index for tourism (CIT): specification and verification', *International Journal of Biometeorology*, 52: 399–407.

It is common for people to experience a combination of two or more of these constraints. For example, a one-parent family may find lack of income and time will combine with family circumstances to prevent tourism travel. Obviously, it is just these groups who would most benefit from a holiday, and research has shown the significant impact upon families when they cannot afford a holiday (Sedgley et al., 2012). As a result, tourism planners are increasingly concerned to identify these barriers and devise programmes to encourage nonparticipants to travel. Perhaps the best-known examples of this are the 'social tourism movement', which is concerned with facilitating participation in travel by disadvantaged or disabled people, and the measures used to encourage this participation, and increasing numbers of destinations and facilities that provide specifically for disabled people.

MACRO DETERMINANTS OF TOURISM DEMAND

In order to demonstrate how these individual influences upon demand can be aggregated to explain patterns and rhythms of tourist demand globally, different geographical scales have to be considered. For example, from what is already known, countries with a high level of economic development and a stable, urbanised population would be expected to be major generators of tourism demand.

At the aggregate level, the relationship between tourist demand and the characteristics of a population is not straightforward. In particular, it must be remembered that the variables which determine tourist demand are all related. A high travel demand would be expected for a developed Western economy with a high degree of urbanisation, high incomes, small household sizes and high levels of mobility. Conversely, low travel demand would be expected for rural societies with large family sizes and low incomes.

When individual purchasing patterns and the influences upon them are aggregated to the national level, it is possible to gain a clearer view as to the influences upon global patterns of demand for tourism (Song, 2018). This is known as performing a STEP analysis (sometimes known as PEST if the acronym is changed). It analyses the impact of:

S   social factors;

T   technological factors;

E   economic factors; and

P   political factors.

Social factors

Levels of population growth, its development, distribution and density affect travel demand. Population growth and development can be closely linked to the stages of economic growth of a society by considering the demographic transition where population growth and development are seen in terms of four connected phases (Table 12.2). However, some criticise the demographic transition on the basis that it does not include migration and is less applicable to very advanced economies.

Population density has a less important influence on tourist demand than has the distribution of population between urban and rural areas. Densely populated rural nations may have low travel demand owing to the level of economic development and the simple fact that the population is mainly dependent upon subsistence agriculture and has neither the time nor the income to devote to tourism. In contrast, densely populated urban areas normally indicate a developed economy with consumer purchasing power, giving rise to high travel demand and the urge to escape from the urban environment.

TABLE 12.2   The demographic transition and tourism

Stage of the demographic transition	Tourism characteristics
High stationary phase	This corresponds to many undeveloped countries with high birth and death rates, keeping the population at a fluctuating, but low, level. Here, many forms of tourism are impossible.
Early expanding phase	High birth rates continue, but death rates fell due to improved health, sanitation and social stability. The population expands, characterised by young, large families. Tourism is a luxury that cannot be afforded by many.
Late expanding phase	Here, birth rates fall with the growth of an industrial society and birth control technology and both outbound and domestic tourism begin to develop.
Low stationary phase	Here, birth and death rates have stabilised at a low level and some countries are not replacing their population, leading to an ageing market.

The distribution of population within a nation also affects patterns, rather than strict levels, of tourist demand. Where a population is concentrated into one part of the country, tourism demand is distorted. This asymmetrical distribution of population is well illustrated by the USA where two-thirds of the population live in the eastern third of the country. The consequent east to west pattern of tourist flows (and permanent migrants) has placed pressure on the recreation and tourist resources of the western states.

Technological factors

There is no doubt that technology has been a major enabling factor in terms of converting suppressed demand into effective demand. This is particularly the case in terms of transport technology where the development of the jet engine in the late 1950s gave aircraft both speed and range, and stimulated the variety of tourism products available in the international market to meet pent-up demand for international travel. Developments in aircraft technology have continued but so has the level of refinement and access to the motor car. Similarly, the development of information technology, and, in particular, the Internet and mobile technology, is a critical enabling factor in terms of tourism demand. Generally, technology acts to increase access to tourism by lowering the cost or by making the product more accessible. Examples here include access to travel information and booking on the Internet, and developments in 'recreational technology' such as off-road recreational vehicles.

Economic factors

A society's level of economic development is a major determinant of tourist demand because the economy influences so many critical, and interrelated, factors (Song, 2018). One approach is to consider a simple division of world economies used by the International Monetary Fund (IMF, 2012). The IMF classifies countries into 'advanced economies' and 'developing economies'. This classification has evolved over time and is based on many variables including gross domestic product, source of exports, net debt or credit and population. Advanced economies are further divided into major advanced economies (the USA, Japan, Germany, France, Italy, the UK and Canada), members of the euro area and newly industrialised Asian economies.

As a society moves towards the advanced economy classification, a number of important processes occur. The balance of employment changes from work in the primary sector (agriculture, fishing, forestry) to work in the secondary sector (manufacturing goods) and the tertiary sector (services such as tourism). As this process unfolds, an affluent society usually emerges and the percentage of the population who are economically active increases from less than a third in the developing economies to half or more in the advanced economies. Similarly, discretionary incomes increase and create demand for consumer goods and leisure pursuits such as tourism.

Other developments are closely linked to the changing nature of employment. The population is healthier and has time for recreation and tourism (and mostly has paid holiday entitlement). Improving educational standards and media channels boosts awareness of tourism opportunities, and transportation and mobility rise in line with these changes. Institutions respond to this increased demand by developing a range of leisure products and services. These developments occur in conjunction with each other until, as a country reaches the advanced economy classification, all the economic indicators encourage high levels of travel demand. Clearly, tourism is a result of industrialisation and, quite simply, the more highly developed an economy, the greater the levels of tourist demand.

As more countries enter the advanced economy classification, so the volume of trade and foreign investment increases and business travel develops. Business travel is sensitive to economic activity, and although it could be argued that increasingly sophisticated communication systems may render business travel unnecessary, there is no evidence of this to date. Indeed, the very development of global markets and the constant need for face-to-face contact should ensure a continuing demand for business travel.

Political factors

Politics affects tourist demand in a variety of ways. For example, the degree of government involvement in promoting and providing facilities for tourism depends upon the political complexion of the government. Governments that support the free market try to create an environment in which the tourism industries can flourish, rather than the administration being directly involved in tourism itself. Socialist administrations, on the other hand, encourage the involvement of the government in tourism and, through 'social tourism', often provide opportunities for the 'disadvantaged' to participate in tourism. Governments in times of economic problems may control levels of demand for travel overseas by limiting the amount of foreign currency that can be taken out of a country. Government restrictions on travel also include visa and passport controls as well as taxes on travel. Generally, however, these controls are not totally effective and, of course, they can be evaded.

We can also identify inadvertent political influences – for example, a government with an economy suffering high inflation may find that inbound travel is discouraged. In a more general sense, unstable political regimes or regions (where civil disorder or war is prevalent) may forbid non-essential travel, and inbound tourism will be adversely affected. In more extreme cases, inbound travel becomes impossible, such as with the ISIS (Islamic State of Iraq and Syria) controlled areas.

Other factors

Finally, there are a number of further factors that will determine the demand of a population to travel to particular destinations. Destination image, for example, will strongly influence demand and would be expected to be related to promotional spend, but this relationship is notoriously difficult to measure. Other factors include:

- **Economic distance** – the time and cost of reaching a destination; and
- **Cultural distance** – the difference in culture between the origin area and the destination – for more adventurous travellers, this may attract rather than deter a visit.

Costs at a destination are not an absolute quantity but have to be considered relative to the value of the traveller's own currency. This is graphically demonstrated by the ebb and flow of traffic across the Atlantic depending upon the relative strengths of the dollar, euro and pound sterling.

FORECASTING TOURISM DEMAND

An understanding of demand determinants is fundamental to forecasting future demand (Liu et al., 2018). For example, as discussed above, effective demand for tourism will be expected to be highly concentrated among the affluent, industrialised nations. This information is important for managers, and accurate forecasts in tourism are essential to inform decision-making in both governments and the industry. Frechtling (2001) identifies why tourism demand forecasting is important:

- The tourism product is perishable and assets such as beds cannot be stored.

- In an industry as volatile as tourism and in times of rapid and unexpected change, it is important for both governments and the tourism industry to have reliable and accurate forecasts to allow them to plan and make decisions.

- The inseparability of the production and consumption of tourism means that enterprises have to be aware in advance of the level of demand for their product.

- The tourism product comprises a range of complementary providers – forecasts ensure that these are available when they are needed.

- The tourism product needs large investment in fixed costs, meaning that accurate forecasts of demand are essential.

As a result, failure to forecast tourism demand accurately can have devastating consequences, as supply and demand will be unbalanced. Indeed, forecasting is difficult in tourism due to the lack of good statistical information from the past, the complex and volatile nature of tourism demand, seasonality and the occurrence of one-off 'wild card' events that have a major influence on demand (Liu et al., 2018).

Forecasting methods

There is a wide variety of methods available for forecasting tourism demand (UNWTO, 2008). There are five key factors that determine the choice of method to use:

1. **Purpose of the forecast** – this relates to the level of detail required and the scope of the forecast;

2. Time period required;

3. Level of accuracy required;

4. **Availability of information** – there is no point in recommending a complex quantitative approach if the information is not available to support it; and

5. **Cost of the forecast** and the available budget.

Choice of forecasting method basically comes down to two options: quantitative approaches and qualitative approaches. However, in practice, the most successful forecasts are those that use a combination of these two methods, utilising the relative strengths of each.

Quantitative forecasting approaches

There are numerous quantitative approaches to forecasting demand, ranging from the simplistic to the highly technical.

- **Causative models.** At the complex end of the spectrum are causative models. These models attempt to predict changes in the variables that cause tourist demand and to analyse the relationship between those variables and the demand for tourism. The most well-known of these approaches is econometric modelling, commonly using multiple regression. A mathematical relationship is sought that establishes demand as a function of influencing variables (such as income levels and price). The advantage of this approach is that it allows for an understanding of the underlying causes of tourist demand and a forecasting of how these will change in the future. It also allows for questions such as 'What if…?' to see how demand will change under a certain set of circumstances.

- **Non-causative models.** These models are often known as time series models. Essentially they rely on extrapolating future trends from the past and use techniques such as moving average, exponential smoothing and trend curve analysis. While these models can be criticised for being inappropriate for a volatile industry such as tourism, where past situations may not carry forward into the future, they do deliver surprisingly accurate forecasts.

- **Artificial intelligence models (AI).** There are two approaches to forecast demand using AI. The first uses artificial neural networks (see Law et al., 2019) whilst the second uses fuzzy logic. However, these are relatively new approaches and Lui et al. (2018) are critical of them as they do not provide explanations for the forecasts.

Qualitative forecasting approaches

Qualitative approaches to forecasting demand are mainly used to predict long-term trends, or to examine specific scenarios in the future such as climate change or technological influences. The most common techniques are the Delphi technique and scenario writing:

- **The Delphi technique.** The Delphi technique relies upon a panel of experts to deliver a consensus view of the future. The panel is selected according to their expertise and a questionnaire is compiled relating to the particular future trend or forecast required. Once the panel members have completed the questionnaire, results are combined and circulated to the panel to give them a chance to change their views once they have seen the forecasts of other panel members. This process goes through a number of iterations, often three or four, before a consensus forecast is reached.

  There are significant advantages to this approach as it does not rely on one individual view and can be tailored to particular needs. However, the Delphi technique can be expensive to implement and may be subject to the influence of a strong panel member, and its effectiveness depends on both the choice of questions and the selection of panel members.

- **Scenario writing.** Scenario writing is not only a technique to forecast future tourism demand but also an approach that clarifies the issues involved. It relies upon creating alternative hypothetical futures relating to particular 'states' or sets of circumstances that will impact upon demand in the future. It involves assessing the variables that we examined in the section on STEP analysis and then creating long-term scenarios of how they may change, based upon the current situation as a baseline.

In a world of rapid and unexpected change, it could be argued that forecasts are irrelevant. However, the changing nature of the environment within which tourism occurs makes it all the more important to forecast future patterns of tourist demand in order to anticipate and manage them.

SUMMARY

This chapter has focused upon demand for tourism. It began by clearly identifying definitions and concepts of demand, including the notion that many people cannot travel due to particular constraints such as illness. The chapter then focused on the personal influences upon tourist demand and showed how these can be drawn together into models of consumer decision-making for tourism with a classic paper re-examining the concept of motivation. The chapter went on to show how these personal determinants and influences of demand can be aggregated to provide a worldview of tourism demand, a picture that is influenced by factors such as economic development and demographics.

DISCUSSION QUESTIONS

1. Compare the advantages and disadvantages of the main techniques of forecasting tourist demand.

2. Review the relevance of the life cycle and lifestyle determinants of tourist demand for the developing world.

3. Taking a country of your choice, identify the main determinants of tourist demand and evaluate their importance.

4. How does social media influence tourism consumer behaviour?

5. When planning its marketing campaigns, does the tourism industry take full advantage of what is known about the buying decision in tourism?

ANNOTATED FURTHER READING

Liu, A., Ling, S.V. and Song, H. (2018) 'Analysing and forecasting tourism demand', in C. Cooper, S. Volo, W.C. Gartner and N. Scott (eds), *The Sage Handbook of Tourism Management: Theories, Concepts and Disciplinary Approaches to Tourism*. London: Sage. pp. 202–21.

A thorough and contemporary review of tourism demand forecasting.

Pearce, P.L. (2011) *Tourist Behaviour and the Contemporary World*. Bristol: Channel View.

An excellent research-based text reviewing the major theories and concepts of tourist behaviour.

Song, R. (2018) 'Emerging markets in tourism', in C. Cooper, S. Volo, W.C. Gartner and N. Scott (eds), *The Sage Handbook of Tourism Management: Applications of Theories and Concepts to Tourism*. London: Sage. pp. 111–28.

A rare analysis of demand patterns in the developing world.

Swarbrooke, J. and Horner, S. (2007) *Consumer Behaviour in Tourism,* 2nd edn. Oxford: Routledge.

A thorough textbook reviewing all aspects of consumer behaviour and broader elements of tourism demand.

World Tourism Organization (WTO) (2011) *Tourism Towards 2030: Global Overview*. Madrid: WTO.

An excellent and comprehensive review of future patterns of tourism demand and the key changes in determinants across the world.

REFERENCES CITED

Decrop, A. (2000) 'Tourists' decision-making and behaviour processes', in A. Pizam and Y. Mansfield (eds), *Consumer Behaviour in Travel and Tourism*. New York: Haworth. pp. 103–33.

Frechtling, D. (2001) *Forecasting Tourism Demand: Methods and Strategies*. Oxford: Butterworth-Heinemann.

Garay, L. (2019) '#Visitspain: breaking down affective and cognitive attributes in the social media construction of the tourist destination image', *Tourism Management Perspectives*, 32: 100560.

Gartner, W.C. (2000) 'Image', in J. Jafari (ed.), *Encyclopedia of Tourism*. London: Routledge. pp. 295–6.

Gartner, W.C. (2018) 'Tourism destination image', in C. Cooper, S. Volo, W.C. Gartner and N. Scott (eds), *The Sage Handbook of Tourism Management: Applications of Theories and Concepts to Tourism*. London: Sage. pp. 207–18.

Gray, H.P. (1970) *International Travel – International Trade*. Lanham, MD: Lexington Books.

Haukeland, V.J. (1990) 'Non-travellers: the flip side of motivation', *Annals of Tourism Research*, 17 (2): 172–84.

International Monetary Fund (IMF) (2012) *World Economic Outlook 2012*. Washington, DC: IMF.

Kotler, P., Bowen, J., Makens, J. and Baloglu, S. (2020) *Marketing for Hospitality and Tourism,* 7th edn. Harlow: Pearson.

Law, R., Li, G., Ka, D., Fong, C. and Han, X. (2019) 'Tourism demand forecasting: a deep learning approach', *Annals of Tourism Research*, 75: 410–23.

Liu, A., Ling, S.V. and Song, H. (2018) 'Analysing and forecasting tourism demand', in C. Cooper, S. Volo, W.C. Gartner and N. Scott (eds), *The Sage Handbook of Tourism Management: Theories, Concepts and Disciplinary Approaches to Tourism*. London: Sage. pp. 202–21.

Maslow, A.H. (1970) *Motivation and Personality,* 2nd edn. New York: Harper and Row.

Mathieson, A. and Wall, G. (1982) *Tourism: Economic Physical and Social Impacts*. London: Longman.

Mills, J. and Law, R. (2015) *Handbook of Consumer Behavior, Tourism, and the Internet*. London: Routledge.

Nyaupane, G.P. and Andereck, K.L. (2008) 'Understanding travel constraints: application and extension of a leisure constraints model', *Journal of Travel Research*, 46: 433–9.

Pak, T.Y. (2019) 'Old-age income security and tourism demand: a quasi-experimental study', *Tourism Management*, https://doi.org/10.1177/0047287519878512

Pearce, P.L. (2011) *Tourist Behaviour and the Contemporary World*. Bristol: Channel View.

Sedgley, D., Pritchard, A. and Morgan, N. (2012) '"Tourism poverty" in affluent societies: voices from inner-city London', *Tourism Management*, 33: 951–60.

Sirakaya, E. and Woodside, A.G. (2005) 'Building and testing theories of decision-making by travellers', *Tourism Management*, 26: 815–32.

Song, R. (2018) 'Emerging markets in tourism', in C. Cooper, S. Volo, W.C. Gartner and N. Scott (eds), *The Sage Handbook of Tourism Management: Applications of Theories and Concepts to Tourism*. London: Sage. pp. 111–28.

Swarbrooke, J. and Horner, S. (2007) *Consumer Behaviour in Tourism,* 2nd edn. Oxford: Routledge.

UNWTO (2008) *Handbook on Tourism Forecasting Methodologies*. Madrid: UNWTO.

Wanhill, S.R.C. and Airey, D. (1980) 'Demand for accommodation', in R. Kotas (ed.), *Managerial Economics for Hotel Operation*. Guildford: Surrey University Press. pp. 23–44.

Woodside, A. (2018) 'Consumer behaviour in tourism', in C. Cooper, S. Volo, W.C. Gartner and N. Scott (eds), *The Sage Handbook of Tourism Management: Applications of Theories and Concepts to Tourism*. London: Sage. pp. 238–56.

MAJOR CASE STUDY 12.1

User-generated Reviews – TripAdvisor.com

Introduction

Star ratings and recommendations in guidebooks were once the information cues used by tourists to make purchasing decisions. With the advent of the Internet, however, it is *user-generated reviews* that have revolutionised the way tourists make the decision to travel. The Internet has drastically altered people's information search patterns and decision processes when it comes to travel, allowing everyone's opinions and thoughts to be instantly accessible to others. In travel this has led to a number of *user-generated content sites* which review travel products (Gretzel, 2018). These user-generated opinions and reviews are hugely influential in travel information search and decision-making and carry considerable credibility, with users saying that they are more up to date, enjoyable and reliable than, say, a company or tourist board website (see Fang et al., 2016).

The official TripAdvisor website

Source: ©PhotoStock10/Shutterstock.com

TripAdvisor.com

One of the first and most successful of these websites is TripAdvisor.com, representing the largest online network of travel consumers. The mission of TripAdvisor is to 'help people around the world plan and have the perfect trip'. The website was founded in 2000, originally as a means of linking to official guides or other media but it soon evolved into a social media site and is now owned by the major online travel provider Expedia (www.expedia.com). In 2009 a Chinese version of the site was launched and, in 2011, TripAdvisor was floated on the stock exchange. The statistics are impressive and testament to the power of this new medium:

- Annual revenue exceeded $1.6 billion in 2018, including substantial revenues from its subsidiaries and from advertising.

- It employs over 3000 people.
- Estimates suggest that 10 per cent of all trips worldwide are planned using TripAdvisor.
- TripAdvisor-branded sites attract more than 300 million monthly visitors.
- More than 760 million travel reviews and opinions are posted on the site.
- TripAdvisor reviews cover more than 4.9 million accommodation units/attractions and 1.2 million restaurants in 136,000 destinations.
- TripAdvisor manages and operates 25 travel websites.

The website has been significantly revamped to link more closely with social media to become the 'Facebook' of travel. It features:

(Continued)

- Online reviews for accommodation, restaurants and attractions;
- Traveller articles where users can add information on destinations;
- Third-party social networking applications through applications on sites, including Facebook, which is seen by TripAdvisor as a way to personalise the site;
- Photograph uploading – over 6 million to support reviews;
- A range of apps and planning features for booking;
- Just for You – tailored recommendations;
- Holiday ideas; and
- 'Best of' reviews.

Clearly, TripAdvisor has evolved from a small website serving the needs of a group of travellers to a major commercial empire with 'white branding' and syndicating of review sites, meaning that existing reviews occur on other, seemingly independent sites. The success and development of TripAdvisor raises some important issues for tourist consumer decision-making and marketing:

1. Its users are affluent, well educated and frequent travellers, making them an ideal target demographic for travel companies. As a result, TripAdvisor has become an important advertising medium as more and more reviews are posted and they become more timely and accurate – the more so as mobile technology allows for 'instant posting'.
2. A second commercial application of TripAdvisor is to extend recommendations and reviews to bookings and referrals. TripAdvisor provides easy access to online travel agencies, including its own sites. Such is the power of the site that tour operators and tourist boards are adding TripAdvisor's reviews to their websites as this transparency fosters trust in their brands. However, this power does mean that its own websites are favoured in listings and page position and businesses can pay for preferential treatment.
3. Of course, this approach may be compromised by false reviews posted to enhance a company's reputation or tarnish that of competitors. This has arisen because TripAdvisor allows reviews to be posted by anyone. However, the site clearly states that its staff moderate all reviews, that they have algorithms and filters to detect and block abuse and that suppliers have the opportunity to respond to every review. However, there is no doubt that this is the Achilles heel of TripAdvisor. In 2013 it was forced to remove the word 'trusted' from its slogan due to the number of fake reviews. A reputation management industry has developed that generates these reviews for a price.
4. Other issues include the fact that sites such as TripAdvisor are vulnerable to being copied and their content used by other providers such as Google. There is also suspicion amongst potential partners that Expedia could use their intelligence to compete with them. Finally, it has been suggested that sites such as TripAdvisor have made travellers less adventurous and more risk averse.

Discussion Questions

1. Taking a destination with which you are familiar, visit TripAdvisor.com and look up hotel reviews for the destination. Do they match your own local knowledge of the hotels?
2. Why do you think user-generated content sites have become so powerful in influencing travel decision-making?
3. Draft an advertisement for an attraction or a hotel to be placed on TripAdvisor.com. What distinct features would you use given the mission and nature of the site?

Sources: Fang, B., Ye, Q., Kucukusta, D. and Law, R. (2016) 'Analysis of the perceived value of online tourism reviews: influence of readability and reviewer characteristics', *Tourism Management*, 52: 498–506; Gretzel, U. (2018) 'Tourism and social media', in C. Cooper, S. Volo, W.C. Gartner and N. Scott (eds), *The Sage Handbook of Tourism Management: Applications of Theories and Concepts to Tourism*. London: Sage. pp. 413–32; www.tripadvisor.com; www.expedia.com

13

TOURISM MARKETING

LEARNING OUTCOMES

This chapter considers tourism marketing as a key component of any tourism organisation. It outlines the meaning of a marketing approach, how marketing is undertaken in tourism and, finally, discusses market planning and the marketing mix. The chapter is designed to provide you with:

- an understanding of what marketing means in tourism;

- an awareness of the service-dominant logic approach;

- an appreciation of the role of technology in tourism marketing;

- an understanding of market strategy and planning and the elements of the marketing mix; and

- an awareness of the concept of tourism product markets and how they give rise to different types of tourism.

INTRODUCTION

This chapter introduces the dimensions of tourism marketing. It outlines current thinking in terms of the scope and definition of marketing and, in particular, charts the shift in focus from goods to a service-dominant logic of marketing. This new approach recognises that tourism marketing thinks of the product as a bundle of both tangible and intangible elements as well as focusing on consumer needs and their involvement in the co-creation of the tourism experience. The chapter shows how technology, and particularly the Internet and social media, has transformed the business of tourism marketing as organisations embrace a digital approach. It goes on to discuss the nature of tourism market planning and strategy and the elements of the marketing mix, and especially the implications of the nature of tourism for the mix. The chapter closes with a review of the concept of tourism product markets.

THE CONCEPT OF MARKETING

Marketing takes a particular approach and is a distinctive way of thinking about the world. Effectively, it is a management philosophy that prioritises a focus on the consumer. Marketing as a concept is evolving quickly and, interestingly for tourism, there is a growing trend to conceptualise marketing based upon services rather than physical goods. Whilst there are many definitions of marketing, they all focus around the need to identify and supply customer needs, and the contemporary approach is to go beyond satisfying those needs to delighting the customer. Contemporary definitions of marketing reflect this thinking with a focus upon the many actors in the marketplace. Kotler et al.'s (2003) definitions are the most commonly used:

- A market is: 'A set of actual and potential buyers who might transact with a seller. This market can be a physical or virtual space' (Kotler et al., 2003: 20).
- Marketing is: 'A social and managerial process by which individuals and groups obtain what they need and want through creating and exchanging products and value with others' (Kotler et al., 2003: 12).

These definitions work well for tourism as they include the non-profit sector (such as destination marketing organisations – DMOs), but do not lose sight of the two central concepts of marketing – the concept of exchange and relationships, and the imperative to supply consumer needs:

1. The concept of exchange states that exchange takes place when parties agree about a transaction and will be worse off without the exchange – it therefore creates 'value'. Relationships in the tourism marketplace lead to exchanges and naturally have led to the concept of relationship marketing where the nurturing of the relationship is more important than single exchanges. Given the nature of tourism as a high-involvement product, relationship marketing plays an important role. However, social media has changed the balance of this relationship, as shown later in the chapter.

2. The process of identifying and supplying consumer needs lies at the heart of tourism marketing. The marketing concept is tightly focused on delivering value to the consumer, where value is viewed as the difference in the benefits that the consumer receives from the product and the costs of obtaining the product. There is an important difference here between tourism marketing and that of physical goods.

EVOLUTION OF MARKETING APPROACHES

There are four key stages that mark the evolution of marketing. These stages are:

1. **Production orientation**. Here the dominant preoccupation is to produce as many goods as possible to meet strong demand. In tourism, this can be likened to the industrialisation of tourism in the 1960s and 1970s when many products were made available (beds and airline seats).

2. **Sales orientation**. Once more product was available, the emphasis switched to securing sales. Major tour operators in the 1970s and 1980s had huge sales teams and developed computer reservation systems (CRS) to boost sales. Here the focus was on exchange rather than building a longer-term relationship, simply persuading consumers to buy rather than understanding their decision-making process.

3. **Marketing orientation**. The next logical stage of evolution is to focus on consumer needs and to reorientate thinking to ensure that products are formulated, and marketing processes designed, to meet the needs of the tourist. This has not happened quickly in tourism. Initially, the trend to marketing simply meant taking down the 'sales department' sign and replacing it with a 'marketing department'

sign, but gradually a shift in thinking took place such that the whole company was encouraged to think about meeting customer needs and delivering high-quality service. For tourism, a marketing orientation implies that an organisation displays four characteristics:

a. A dominant marketing philosophy which demonstrates an unwavering focus on the consumer and which is underpinned by research;

b. It encourages exchange and strengthens both its networks and loyalty through recognising the importance of developing long-term relationships with customers;

c. A thought process accepting that strategic planning and tactical planning go hand in hand and include constant evaluation and review of activities; and

d. It demonstrates an integrated organisational structure geared to the organisation's goals of delivering value to the consumer.

The road to achieving these characteristics is shown in Table 13.1.

TABLE 13.1 Translating marketing orientation into action

Task	Marketing function
Identifying consumer needs	Marketing research
Analysing marketing opportunities	Market segmentation and understanding relationships
Translating needs into products	Product planning and formulation
Determining product value in different seasons	Pricing policy and creation of value delivery
Making the product available	Distribution policy
Informing and motivating the customer	Promotion strategy and tactics, engagement with social media

Source: Cooper et al., 2005: 593

4. **Societal and social marketing**. More recently, as the negative impacts of tourism have come to the fore, and issues such as climate change have emerged, marketing has evolved further to embrace concepts of corporate social responsibility (CSR) and ethical behaviour (Hudson and Hudson, 2017). This is known as *societal marketing* – in other words, marketing takes into account the broader needs of society rather than just the consumer. Of course, a CSR or an ethical approach to the tourism marketplace may be cynically used to pre-empt the development of legislation applying to, say, the greening of hotels, as noted by Font et al. (2012). However, there is no doubt that the ethical tourism marketplace also attracts particular groups of consumers. Goodwin (2003), for example, notes the growth of the ethical purchasing of tourism with an ethical purchasing index which calibrates the ethical marketplace. Nonetheless, with societal marketing, the organisation is still focused on profits, in contrast to *social marketing* where the organisation uses marketing to promote a social or an environmental message that benefits individuals and society as a whole. The case study of the Faroe Islands is a good example here.

MINI CASE STUDY 13.1

De-marketing the Faroe Islands

Introduction

The challenges of balancing visitor use and conservation in heavily used, but sensitive, spaces such as Denmark's Faroe Islands has prompted some public management agencies to consider de-marketing. For marketers, de-marketing may seem counterintuitive as it is premised on the idea of discouraging customers.

The Faroe Islands are characterised by dramatic volcanic scenery, an abundance of birdlife, friendly people and clean air

Source: 'Gásadalur' by aevarg is licensed under CC BY 2.0

The Faroe Islands

The Faroe Islands belong to Denmark. The archipelago lies between Iceland and Norway and is characterised by dramatic volcanic scenery, an abundance of birdlife, friendly Faroese people and clean air. It is one of the most unspoiled and unpolluted places on earth. Tourism numbers are increasing by around 10 per cent each year and currently stand at around 110,000 visitors each year.

Closing the Faroes to Visitors

Whilst overtourism is not yet an issue for the Faroes, the islanders want to maintain their fragile natural beauty and character, particularly at some popular tourist sites. As a result, they turned to de-marketing in 2019 and closed the islands to visitors for a short period. This pilot project saw the temporary closure of popular tourist sites and key maintenance projects were identified by local municipalities, tourism centres and villagers. In a clever marketing move, the Islands then invited volunteer visitors to come during the closure period and engage in 'clean up' tourism to assist with these maintenance projects. The pilot project attracted 100 volunteers from 25 countries to help lay the groundwork for a sustainable future for the Islands.

The volunteers were provided with accommodation and food for three nights by the Faroese nation but had to pay for their own flights to the islands. The volunteers stayed in villages where they met and dined with locals, and at the end of the project there was a celebratory meal for all helpers. The volunteers could then extend their trip to the Faroe Islands.

The approach was successful and will continue with another closure in Spring 2020 when the maintenance projects will include:

- VÁGAR – signpost erection and cairn restoration;
- TJØRNUVÍK – path and stonewall restoration;
- EIÐI (SLÆTTARATINDUR) – the path to the Islands' highest mountain is worn and dangerous so an alternative route will be signposted, and some stretches will be maintained;

(Continued)

- FUNNINGUR – erection of signposts and ladders, and provision of information at a well-known viewpoint;
- HELLURNAR – mending footpaths;
- SELATRAÐ – path maintenance;
- NORÐAGØTA – the path and steps will be restored to a telescope mounted on the mountain ridge;
- KLAKSVÍK (KLAKKUR) – Klakkur is one of the tallest mountains surrounding Klaksvík, the second-largest town in the Faroe Islands. Because of its easy accessibility, the hike to the mountaintop is very popular but there is no path so this will be built;
- KIRKJUBØUR – the popular hiking route between Tórshavn, the capital, and Kirkjubøur, an important historical site, has old cairns that need to be maintained and new cairns that need to be built. Moreover, the path needs to be mended and drained, and way-finding posts set up;
- SANDOY & SKÚVOY – path restoration, way marking and signage to help protect birds.

Discussion Questions

1. Is this really a de-marketing exercise or a cynical publicity stunt?
2. How effective are volunteers in doing professional jobs such as way marking paths?
3. Does the Faroe Islands' approach have lessons to be learned for other destinations?

Source: www.visitfaroeislands.com/closed

An alternative view: From goods-dominant logic to service-dominant logic

The classic paper in this chapter is by Vargo and Lusch (2004), two authors who have had a major impact on recent marketing thought and who see marketing as having a 'service-dominant logic' (S-D logic) rather than the traditional 'goods-dominant logic' (G-D logic). In their paper, they chart the evolution of marketing thought and show how it has swung from one extreme to the other:

1. Nineteenth-century thinking viewed marketing as based upon the exchange principle inherited from economics. This focuses on the unit of output and places the 'good' at the centre of the stage. When marketing is based upon goods, it focuses on tangibility, embedded value and transactions.

2. A new paradigm emerged in the 1970s and 1980s that viewed services as being different from goods. This contemporary thinking shifted marketing thought to a service-oriented view where the key drivers are intangibility, co-creation of value and relationship marketing.

Vargo and Lusch (Vargo and Lusch, 2004; Lusch and Vargo, 2014) have articulated this second approach as the contemporary logic of marketing, and it is now informing the way that tourism marketers approach their craft (Shaw and Agarwal, 2018). Vargo and Lusch state that whilst the 4 Ps are a handy framework, they are in fact meaningless in an age where marketing is seen as an innovating and adaptive force and where the focus is on the continuous nature of relationships between all market actors. Their view is shared by Lovelock and Gummesson (2004), who agree that the dominant logic of marketing is reflected in an emphasis on provision of service. For tourism marketing, the implications are fundamental as it means that organisations must reposition themselves to get closer to their consumers (Li and Petrick, 2008). For example, intermediaries must recognise that (i) consumers can easily access information on products; (ii) consumers have transparent price comparisons such that the traditional 'one-to-one' distribution channels are now many-to-many; and (iii) intermediaries themselves have the choice of going electronic, being replaced or repositioning themselves (as shown in Chapter 9).

Of course, the true situation often lies between the two extremes and there is an increasing view that goods and services are both part of the marketing offering, and in fact what has occurred is more of a shift away from manufacturing to a customer-centred approach. This approach to the product as a mix of both services and goods has been termed 'the molecular approach' by Shostack (1977). He views products as being made up of many parts, some tangible, some intangible – in other words, an amalgam that is exemplified by the fragmented nature of the tourism product. This 'molecular' approach allows managers to manage the total product and to realise the synergies between parts of the amalgam.

CLASSIC PAPER

Vargo, S.L. and Lusch, R.F. (2004) 'Evolving to a new dominant logic for marketing', *Journal of Marketing*, 68 (January): 1–17

This paper by Vargo and Lusch represents a significant milestone in marketing thought and it has been hugely influential in setting research agendas and the way that marketers view the world. Basically, Vargo and Lusch argue that marketing has viewed the world from an economics perspective where the currency is one of 'exchange' and products are manufactured. The thrust of the Vargo and Lusch paper is that since the closing decades of the twentieth century 'new perspectives have emerged that have a revised logic focused on intangible resources, the co-creation of value and relationships' (p. 1). For tourism, this is a significant development as it heralds a new era of marketing thought where service provision and their characteristics, rather than goods, have become the 'dominant logic' of marketing.

The paper begins with a thorough and insightful review of how marketing thinking has evolved and, in particular, details the new approaches, often based on services, that allowed thinking to break away from the 4 Ps concept. Vargo and Lusch conceptualise a timeline of marketing thought as follows:

1800–1920	Classical and neo-classical economics
1900–1950	Early/formative marketing
1950–1980	Marketing management
1980–2000 and beyond	Marketing as a social and economic process

(Continued)

However, as stressed in this chapter, the paper is not a plea for a separate field of services marketing, but instead an appeal for 'service-dominant logic' to be applied across the whole field of marketing, including goods. Indeed, it is rare to think of a marketing offering that is not a bundle of both goods and services, as we saw above. Yet it is the services aspect that has long been neglected. The paper then goes on to outline the key features of the new 'service-dominant logic' (p. 5):

1. The core competencies of an organisation are the fundamental knowledge and skills, and this represents potential competitive advantage. This recognises the importance of knowledge management, the importance of the 'learning organisation' and how the skills and competitions of the workforce provide a competitive edge.

2. Organisations identify other entities (potential customers) that could benefit from these competencies. This recognises the imperative to develop relationships with customers to allow co-creation – an increasingly important aspect of marketing facilitated by the Internet and networked online communities, as we have seen elsewhere in this book.

3. Organisations cultivate relationships that involve the customers developing customised, competitively compelling value propositions to meet specific needs. This means developing networked organisations that allow enterprises to leverage from others in the network.

4. Organisations gauge marketplace feedback to learn how to improve the firm's offering to customers and improve firm performance. In other words, the enterprise continually improves.

Throughout the paper, Vargo and Lusch weave contemporary approaches of relationship building, networked organisations and knowledge management into the writing and show how these approaches support the 'service-dominant logic'. This tripartite approach is supported by a further paper by Li and Petrick (2008) and a later book by Lusch and Vargo (2014). To conclude with the words of Vargo and Lusch (2004: 15): 'the focus is shifting away from tangibles toward intangibles, such as skills, information and knowledge, and toward interactivity and connectivity and ongoing relationships. The orientation has shifted from the producer to the consumer.'

A TOURISM MARKETING GAP?

So far, this chapter has dealt with generic concepts of marketing. When considering tourism marketing, however, there is a question as to whether many of these ideas have been accepted. In tourism, the very strong traditions of custom and practice, reflected in the conservative nature of the industry, mean that organisations are often a number of years behind other economic sectors in terms of the adoption of new ideas such as the service-dominant logic. In part, this is due to the tradition of promoting managers up through the ranks rather than educating them, the view that tourism products somehow need a different approach, and the later adoption of technology in the sector. However, as the tourism market matures, there will be less of a place for the amateur entrepreneur and professional marketing managers will be more in demand. The question is then whether the tourism sector has the professional and technical capacity to cope with the contemporary marketing environment.

Marketing approaches for tourism organisations

There are two considerations to take into account in order to understand how best to approach tourism marketing:

- Firstly, technology and, in particular, the Internet and social media, have transformed the way that tourism marketing is done; and
- Secondly, it is vital to understand the nature of the tourism product itself, and the nature of the purchasing process (Table 13.2).

TABLE 13.2 Distinguishing features of tourism purchasing

Distinguishing features of a tourism purchase	Distinguishing features of tourism products
A tourism purchase is highly involving of the customer.	Tourism products comprise a bundle of tangible and intangible (experiential) goods.
A tourism purchase offers great ability to develop relationships with the customer.	Tourism products are characterised by unstable demand which is not only highly elastic but also tends not to be loyal.
A tourism purchase offers the ability for co-creation of the tourism product with the customer.	Tourism products are distributed by intermediaries (traditional or electronic) who can influence the purchase decision.
A tourism purchase is high risk as it is difficult to predetermine value and the intangible elements of the product.	There is considerable regulation and consumer legislation of tourism products. On purchase, the consumer does not own the tourism product. The tourism product is fragmented and delivered by many different suppliers.

The role of technology

The Internet influences every aspect of tourism and has changed the culture and behaviour of how people purchase, search and communicate (Benckendorff et al., 2014). It connects companies, customers and governments at low cost and without constraints of time or space and as such is a transformative marketing tool. This is because it has significant advantages over traditional communication media, such as reach, low cost, richness, speed of communication and interactivity. Indeed, technology facilitates many of the processes that are needed in the new marketing paradigm of relationship building and co-creation (UNWTO, 2014). These include two-way communication with customers, interactivity, tools for research, massive data storage and the ability to build, track and maintain relationships.

Technology has created a whole new marketing industry – e-marketing – which can be defined as the promotion of a tourism product, company service or website online and can include a variety of activities from online advertising, through communication on social media, to search engine optimisation. It also provides a medium and delivery mechanism for consumers to gather information and to make purchasing decisions.

E-marketing is ideally suited to tourism. It allows the development of online brochures that can deliver rich multimedia content, blending text, images, sound and video into multimedia documents to overcome the intangible nature of the product. Through video and interactivity, it delivers the ability to 'test drive' the product. It also gives tourism organisations the ability to instantly change dates, prices and availability online, saving expensive brochure reprints. Technology also allows organisations to individually target customers through 'narrow casting' to customise messages, utilise social media and web links to engage in 'viral marketing' and, of course, the Internet gives small businesses and destinations a degree of global market reach previously unheard of.

E-marketing in tourism aims to generate traffic to an organisation's website, to engage the customer and to convert that traffic into sales. There is a range of mechanisms for closely engaging with the consumer through e-marketing, social media and tracking use of the website. This includes how often they visit, for how long and which pages are browsed.

Despite the obvious advantages of its use, technology does bring with it certain constraints when used in marketing. For example, there are concerns over the security of financial information and personal identity (Mills and Law, 2015). Most websites are in English so creating a barrier to access, and in some countries access to the Internet comes at a high cost. In the future, the limits to this technology will be economic, in terms of investment; human, in terms of attitude and habits; and technological, in terms of computing power, storage and bandwidth.

Digital marketing approaches now enable overlapping and ubiquitous use of computer systems with devices such as entertainment systems, smartphones, tablets and other devices. For tourism, an increasingly pervasive marketing application is the use of mobile devices to deliver marketing messages and information, as shown in the major case study at the end of the chapter. Technology has also empowered the consumer. Social media and the Internet have revolutionised the information search for products, online reviews and search engines (Xiang and Gretzel, 2010). However, evaluation of the effectiveness of social media as a tourism marketing medium is at an early stage (see Wozniak et al., 2017).

FOCUS ON TECHNOLOGY

Phillip Kotler's new conceptualisation of the development of marketing since the adoption of the Internet has much to offer tourism. In this Focus on Technology, his approach is summarised in Table 13.3. A useful exercise is to examine the table and then add an extra column and populate it with tourism applications and insights for each stage.

TABLE 13.3 Kotler's Marketing Stages from Marketing 1.0 to 4.0

Kotler's four stages of the relationship between marketing and the Web	Characteristics of each stage
Marketing 1.0 Product-centric	This represents the early stage of the relationship between marketing and the Web. It is characterised by one-way communication between organisations and customers and is focused on providing products and services from offline companies. The customer is passive and their activity is confined to browsing the Web.
Marketing 2.0 Customer-centric	The relationship evolves to true interaction between organisations and their customers where the social and technological aspects of the Web are combined. This allows for knowledge sharing across organisations and customers through the creation of virtual communities, use of blogs, wikis and content sharing through social media. The customer becomes integral to the development of the product and its marketing and is now an active rather than passive participant.

Kotler's four stages of the relationship between marketing and the Web	Characteristics of each stage
Marketing 3.0 **Human-centric**	By this stage, the relationship between the customer and the Web is one characterised by deep changes in behaviour. Technology allows for vast amounts of data to be synthesised and personalised for the user. Networking allows marketing to be collaborative across all players – investors, customers, employees and partners. Transparency and consistency are facilitated by the openness of the technology, leading to a values-oriented 'social marketing' approach.
Marketing 4.0 **Human Spirit**	At this stage, the relationship moves almost full circle as online marketing meets offline (traditional) marketing in an attempt to gain from the best of each in a blended approach. This has become known as 'phygital', as noted in Chapter 9 on intermediaries where it is most clearly seen. Machine-to-machine interactions are complemented by human-to-human interactions. By now, the substance, values and essence of a brand have become more important than style. Marketing functions change such that customers are treated as 'equals', not 'kings'; the marketing mix expands to peer-to-peer channels, and promotion becomes more of an interactive conversation. The focus changes to how marketing can touch the human spirit.

Source: Kotler et al., 2016

The nature of tourism

This chapter argues that tourism is simply a particular type of offering to the marketplace that demands a differentiated approach from other products. This view includes the following approaches:

- Wherever possible, the product should be made tangible – for example, through the use of staff uniforms and careful design of the environment – or service-scape – where the product is delivered.

- Employees become an additional part of the marketing mix and therefore need to be well trained. The tourism product is produced where it is consumed and this means that employees can influence not only the successful delivery of the product, but also the tourist's evaluation of the service during the short time that they are exposed to it.

- Perceived risk should be managed through strong quality assurance, to ensure consistent and standardised service delivery. This consistency should be communicated to the customer through strong branding of the product, which itself acts to reassure the customer about the service.

- Other elements of the mix should be carefully aligned with tourism, with promotion stressing emotive aspects and relationship building with intermediaries.

- The nature of services as perishable means that it is essential to manage both capacity and demand through yield management, which adjusts pricing to demand and so smooths out the demand curve.

These points can be summarised into two key approaches that characterise tourism marketing and are designed to help retain and build relationships with customers, avoid price competition, retain employees and reduce costs:

1. Relationship marketing has evolved to embrace the use of social media where the power has shifted to the customer as they engage with products and services in real time. Organisations therefore link with the customer base through social media to secure loyalty and commitment, allowing for co-creation of the product, so creating, maintaining and enhancing strong relationships with consumers.

2. Service quality management is designed to 'industrialise' service delivery by guaranteeing standardised and consistent services.

MARKET PLANNING IN TOURISM AND HOSPITALITY

It is essential for tourism organisations to plan their marketing strategically as well as tactically. Tourism market planning provides a common point of reference for the organisation, acting as a coordination mechanism – particularly important for destination marketing. It also encourages a disciplined approach to marketing by ensuring that objectives are set for markets and products, that each market has activities and resources allocated and, of course, the planning process itself sets key performance indicators (KPIs) against which the success – or otherwise – of the plan can be monitored. Market planning takes both strategic long-term and tactical short-term approaches. Increasingly these plans are flexible and subject to constant revision. The process is summarised in Figure 13.1.

Strategic approaches

There are a number of approaches to determining market strategy in tourism. These include:

*   Product market portfolios;
*   Growth and development strategies; and
*   Branding.

Product market portfolios

The product market portfolio approach lends itself well to tourism and the most well-known is the Boston Consulting Group Growth Share Matrix (BCG matrix). The BCG matrix is a management tool that allows an organisation to classify its products and then apply particular strategies to them. The matrix has two dimensions and four cells (Figure 13.2). The two dimensions are relative market share and market growth:

1. **The market share dimension** is a measure of the health of the product relative to its competitors; and

2. **The market growth dimension** is a measure of the product life cycle and can be used to estimate the level of resources needed.

This creates four cells in the matrix:

1. Cash cows are highly profitable and do not need significant investment.

2. Stars are product leaders in high-growth markets.

3. Question marks have not achieved a dominant market position, and hence do not generate much cash.

4. Dogs are a drain on the organisation's resources, with low market share in a low-growth market.

According to where a product lies within the matrix, a particular marketing strategy is appropriate. The BCG matrix is not perfect as it is subjective and requires substantial amounts of data; however, it is widely used due to its intuitive appeal.

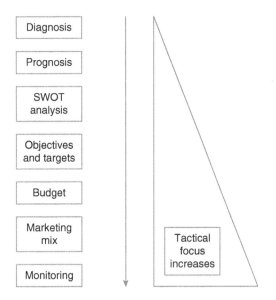

FIGURE 13.1   The marketing planning process

Source: Kotler et al., 2003

Growth and development strategies

Also using a matrix approach, the best-known tool for growth and development strategies is the Ansoff product market growth matrix. Ansoff's matrix is a simple tool that combines markets and products to allow organisations to consider how to grow and develop their business according to the market that they are in (Figure 13.3). There are two dimensions which create a four-cell matrix. The dimensions are:

1. Existing and/or new products; and

2. Existing and/or new markets.

The cells then provide strategy options:

•   **Market penetration**, which involves increasing market share at the expense of competitors.

- **Product development**, which involves developing new products to serve existing markets.
- **Market development**, which involves seeking new markets for existing products.
- **Diversification**, which involves entering new markets with new products.

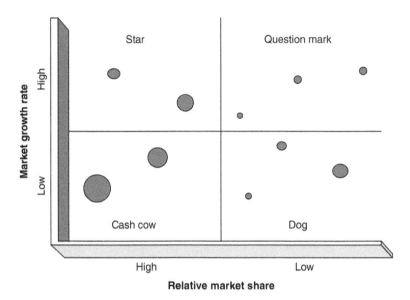

FIGURE 13.2   Market growth – market share portfolio analysis matrix

Source: Kotler et al., 2003

	Existing Product	**New Product**
Existing Market	Ski tours in Europe	Lakes and mountains walking tours
New Market	Ski tours in southern hemisphere to give 12 month sales	Ski clothing and accessories

FIGURE 13.3   Ansoff product market growth matrix for a British ski tour operator

Source: based on Ansoff, 1957

Branding

Branding is an important strategic tool in the tourism marketing process. To quote Kotler et al. (2003: 418): 'branding is the art and cornerstone of marketing'. A brand can be defined as: 'A name, term, sign, symbol or design or combination of them, intended to identify the goods or services of one seller or group of sellers and to differentiate them from those of competitors' (Kotler, 2000: 404).

Brands can be approached from two viewpoints:

1. **The product plus approach** views the brand as an addition to the product (along with, say, price) and is concerned with communication and differentiation.

2. **The holistic approach** views the brand as greater than the sum of its parts such that brands reside in the minds of consumers. This approach is common in destination marketing.

Brands signify identity and originated as a means of ownership and identification by farmers or craftsmen. Brands became important as mass markets developed for products in the twentieth century. This was for two reasons: firstly, consumers became more sophisticated and were faced with greater product choice; and, secondly, branding was developed for 'fast moving consumer goods' (FMCG) as they are characterised by low-involvement products with the need for branding to build loyalty and communicate benefits over competitors. Nonetheless, whilst it may appear that brands are fabricated, they are real entities, based upon products, resistant to change and dependent upon occupying defensible niches within product categories. Developing and managing tourism brands is therefore as much a strategic operation as it is tactical.

MINI CASE STUDY 13.2

Should Destinations Be Marketed?

This case study debates whether marketers should treat destinations as products to be marketed and branded. Indeed, there is a view that destinations do not readily lend themselves to traditional marketing approaches.

Destination Marketing

The *process* of destination marketing involves dealing with the complexities of destinations and their many stakeholders, whilst the *outcome* is a brand or the image of the destination. In other words, a good destination marketer will focus upon two key operations:

1. Managing the destination's many stakeholders and networks; and
2. Formulating and managing the destination brand.

The idea of destination marketing continues to evolve, and a view is emerging that it is 'branding' that is the glue that holds the marketing of the destination together. The two key components of destination marketing are image and brand.

Should Destinations be Marketed?

There are three key areas of controversy regarding destination marketing:

1 The Role of the Public Sector

The public sector tends to take the lead in destination marketing, coordinating other inputs and stakeholders. However, we have to question whether government is the most appropriate agency to deliver

(Continued)

destination marketing. Government does not control destination product quality or private sector suppliers and so cannot address deficiencies in the product mix. It also has to be even-handed in its dealings with stakeholders and cannot be seen to 'back winners'. Traditionally, government tends not to be entrepreneurial, lacking in both marketing and technological expertise, and commonly can only facilitate bookings and often cannot close a sale. Finally, the nature of the public sector means that budgets may be inadequate for significant promotion and market research. Government does, however, have the ability to act in a leadership and coordination role when it comes to destination marketing.

2 The Role of Destination Stakeholders

A second key issue for destination marketing is to ensure involvement and commitment by all stakeholders in the destination marketing process. Here, destination politics are notoriously destructive, and it is therefore vital to be inclusive from the outset. The key here is to manage the relationship between collaboration and power and to recognise that the views of the local community must be included in destination marketing as destinations are also places where people live, work and play.

3 The Nature of the Tourist Destination

Should the places where people live, work and play be transformed into brands and products? The development of destination brands may conflict with a community's perception and feelings for the place where they live, work and play. This can be exacerbated by the delivery of the brand on the ground through the use of signage, street furniture and landscaping. Destinations are contested spaces and the various users of this space each hold their own images, identities and interests.

Does the very nature of the tourist destination run counter to the ability to transform it into a brand? The theory on branding is built largely upon the experience of manufactured products. It could be argued that this theory cannot be simply transferred to the marketing of destinations. The nature of the destination as a fragmented and complex amalgam of attractions and support facilities, delivered by many different providers, means that the definition and formulation of the destination product is problematic. If it is to succeed, destination marketing must recognise that it is a more collective activity than is normally found in marketing.

Discussion Questions

1. What are the benefits of destination marketing?
2. Debate whether the public sector is the appropriate agency for destination marketing and, if not, who should assume this role?
3. Is marketing theory overstretched when applied to destinations?

Tactical level

For most organisations, the tactical level of tourism marketing is focused upon marketing campaigns. Here, the starting point is to identify the target market and then to use elements of the marketing mix to approach that market. The marketing mix can be thought of as the set of marketing tools that the organisation uses to pursue its marketing objectives in the target market, where each element of the mix supports the others and none stand alone.

Also, as noted above, with the move to a service-dominant logic, the marketing mix can be expanded from the traditional 4 Ps to include other influencing variables, such as (i) the people involved in delivering the service, (ii) the physical setting – or service-scape – where the service is delivered, (iii) the actual process of delivering the service, and (iv) productivity or performance, which examine how well an organisation's services compete in the marketplace. This may include how consistent the service is and how well its features translate into benefits as it is being delivered. Performance also considers how to measure financial goals and whether they are being achieved.

Target market

Defining the target market is an essential first step in the market planning process. It represents a concentrated or differentiated approach in contrast to a mass market approach where every consumer is targeted. Dolnicar (2018: 258) is clear on the approaches used:

> Market segmentation is not an isolated marketing strategy. It goes hand in hand with targeting and positioning … *Segmentation* means splitting a market into groups of similar consumers. *Targeting* refers to the selection of one or a small number of market segments to target. *Positioning* centres around building an image of the tourism destination, business or organisation that signals that the needs of the targeted segments are met.

Market segmentation therefore allows marketers to tightly define subsets of the market and those groups to be targeted in terms of formulating products and devising marketing campaigns. Despite the obvious importance of market segmentation, tourism has been slow to adopt a sophisticated approach, with some arguing that it is a rather arid and academic approach to marketing with little real-life relevance. Nonetheless, market segmentation has much to offer the tourism marketer (see Dolnicar et al., 2018). To be successful, market segments must have a number of key features. They must be:

- **Measurable**. There is no point in creating a sophisticated approach to segmentation if the group cannot be measured on variables that allow them to be identified and reached by the marketer.
- **Substantial**. Segments must be substantial enough to be worth devising campaigns or products to meet their needs.
- **Durable**. The segments must be durable in terms of time. If a company is targeting a particular segment, it needs to be confident that the segment will remain stable for a number of years.
- **Competitive**. The company must be confident that it has a competitive offering to attract purchasers from the particular segment.

Segmentation in tourism has taken a traditional 'common sense' approach in the past – for example, segmenting by demographics or by geography. In part, this is because tourism statistics are organised in this way, making it relatively easy to identify these segments. However, in the twenty-first century, and with the support of sophisticated market research and technology, it is possible to be much more creative in segmentation. This involves adopting a 'data-driven' approach, including variables such as use of technology, preference for adventure and overall leisure lifestyles. It is also possible to apply social technographics, which segment consumers according to their behaviour on social networking sites. These contemporary approaches to market segmentation demand sophisticated research techniques, including qualitative market research and multivariate analysis. Deep and meaningful research underpins new approaches to segmentation that can deliver detailed customer profiles and identify elements of consumer behaviour. The following are common segmentation approaches used in tourism:

- **Demographic**, using standard census-based data to segment the market by gender or age;
- **Socio-demographic**, which combines demographic data with social variables such as family size;
- **Geographic**, using standard geographic data such as address or country of residence;
- **Geo-demographic**, which is a more sophisticated approach combining demographics with data such as post- or zip codes to map where particular segments live;
- **Buyer behaviour**, where particular purchasing groups, such as business or leisure tourists, are grouped together. This can be more sophisticated, however, using segments of late bookers or adventure travellers; and
- **Psychographics**, which is a more sophisticated approach, reliant on qualitative market research and multivariate analysis to segment the market by psychological profiles.

Increasingly, segmentation based upon experience and use of technology is being developed.

A key component of market planning is the positioning of the destination or product against the competition. This ensures that the destination or product delivers a unique position in relation to its competitors and occupies a particular place in the minds of potential tourists. Positioning is based upon differentiation, cost and developing a unique focus. Positioning must be consistent with cost and value for money, market trends and consumer preferences, convenience of purchase, technology and demographic trends. Finally, positioning must take into account the capability and resources of the destination or product to deliver the promise.

THE TOURISM PRODUCT

The tourism product represents the utilities and benefits offered to the marketplace. Kotler et al. (2020) view the product as comprising three parts:

1. **The core product** is the essence of the offering. In tourism this may be the core idea of a holiday on a tropical island.

2. **The tangible product** is the offering itself and, for the holiday to the tropical island, will be made up of the actual elements (tickets, accommodation) of the holiday. These elements of the product must all be present for the tourist to use the services.

3. **The augmented product** is where the supplier of the product adds extra features to be competitive. These may include additional free nights, transfers at no extra cost, or a free champagne breakfast on arrival.

Tourism products are complex and multifaceted and, as a result, there are a number of ways of viewing the product:

- **The product as a bundle of tangible and intangible elements**. It is a myth that the tourism product is entirely intangible, although of course elements of it are. Instead, the tourism product can be thought of as a bundle of tangible elements (such as hotel rooms and the destination environment) and intangibles (the experience of travelling). This reflects the service-dominant logic view, incorporating notions of relationships, the co-creation of value, the recognition of intangible products and the consideration of all market actors.

- **The product as a destination amalgam**. A second approach is to view the product as being synonymous with the destination, such that the tourism product is an amalgam of destination elements, including attractions, supporting services such as accommodation and food and beverage, and transportation. There are significant implications of this amalgam for tourism marketing, particularly the challenge of managing quality across the various elements, each of which is often supplied by a different organisation. Because each of these elements is normally supplied by a different organisation, this creates real challenges for the tourism marketer – especially, say, a destination manager who attempts to coordinate the delivery of the tourism product. The challenge is simple – any element of the product that is of poor quality compromises the rest of the product bundle and means that the tourist will leave with a negative impression of the destination and may not return.

- **The product as a series of stages**. The tourism product can be disaggregated into stages of the vacation from anticipation and planning, to booking, travel and evaluation. This stresses the importance of the consumer focus and of service delivery. Indeed, some companies have successfully integrated these stages into their products by, for example, keeping in touch with the customer during the run-up to the trip and providing free transfers from home to the transport terminal, as well as providing welcome home packs and reunion parties. Finally, tourists increasingly share memories and photographs of their trip through social media sites. Product life cycles are a further important consideration for tourism. Here the analogy is that products are developed, launched, grow and develop, eventually move into decline and, finally, are taken off the market. (This aspect of tourism destination is covered in detail in Chapter 2.)

- **The product as experience**. Gilbert (1990) takes the idea further, arguing that the tourism product is in fact the total experience. He defines the tourism product as 'an amalgam of different goods and services offered as an activity experience to the tourist' (p. 20).

Gilbert's idea can be extended to consider the tourism product as being developed and engineered as an experience; indeed, many tourism products are staged experiences, recognising that meaningful experiences cannot be guaranteed but that they can be managed. Here, the trend to combine tourism with the creative industries will see exciting new experience-based products develop. As tourism markets mature, they seek authentic tourism products. Suppliers and destinations are responding to this challenge by delivering experience-based products (Frochot and Batat, 2013). Pine and Gilmore (1999) have termed this trend the 'experience economy'. In the experience economy, changing values from older to younger generations mean that consumers are seeking new meaning and self-actualisation in their tourism consumption patterns as they move beyond material possessions and services to experiences. Tourism products are increasingly being formulated to serve this demand by engineering experiences to match the expectations of the marketplace, not only in tourism but also across the services sector (Scott and Gao, 2018). Here, Pine and Gilmore (1999) see experiences along two dimensions: passive to active and absorption to immersion, with the ability of a good experience to 'transform' the visitor. Experiences are therefore personal, memorable, evoking an emotional response as the tourist enters into a multifaceted relationship with both the actors and destination setting of the experience. They cannot be guaranteed, but they can be managed (Kuiper and Smith, 2014).

Finally, an imperative for tourism marketing is innovation through new product development (NPD). Changing tastes, technology and heightened competition mean that new product development in tourism is vital. As products and destinations progress through the life cycle, they need to be continuously refreshed and revitalised. Moutinho (1994) states that new products are the lifeblood of tourism organisations, delivering increased revenue, competitiveness and facilitating market positioning, diversification and growth. Failure to innovate risks failing to meet consumer demands, engage with new technology and keep up with the competition. New service development is also important for tourism but here the process is less well understood, and it is important to recognise the pre-conditions for delivering the service are unlikely to change.

Price

Tourism is both perishable and highly price elastic, which means that consumers will switch products on the basis of price. As a result, pricing is a critical element of the marketing mix, yet it is also one that is subject to government regulation (for example, air fares), reducing the options of the marketing manager. There are both strategic and tactical approaches to pricing. Tactical approaches can be clearly seen in the windows of travel agents and on airline websites where prices are reduced to offload excess capacity close to the date of departure. Strategic approaches to pricing include:

- **Cost-oriented pricing** – where the price is determined by the cost of providing the product. Not always easy to do in tourism;
- **Rate of return pricing** – where the price is determined to deliver a set rate of return for the company;
- **Demand-oriented pricing** – where the price is set according to what the market is prepared to pay;
- **Discrimination pricing** – where prices differ according to different market sectors (students, for example) or time of the year (high and low season);
- **Backward pricing** – where the price is decided upon and then the product is 'reverse engineered' to deliver that price – for example, using hotels a few blocks from the beach or flying at night to achieve a low price;
- **Penetration pricing** – where a low price is set in the early stages of the life cycle in order to build market share; and
- **Skimming pricing** – with this strategy the company often has a monopoly on a shortage product and can charge a premium price.

Promotion

The nature of tourism as an experience product, albeit with many tangible elements, means that it particularly lends itself to promotion. Remember, too, that the tourism market tends not to be loyal and so demand for tourism products is unstable, as well as seasonal and price sensitive. This means that promotion can play a powerful role in influencing demand, reducing seasonality and creating loyalty. Promotion is about persuading, informing, reminding and communicating benefits to the potential consumer. Promotion in tourism marketing does not stand alone and is used to support other elements of the mix; for example, it can communicate pricing strategy. Smart tourism promotion intervenes in the tourism purchasing process to influence behaviour. (The purchasing process was examined in detail in Chapter 12.) Here the key decisions for the marketer are what type of message to promote and when to send the message to ensure maximum impact. Of course, the media used are also critical and increasingly promotion is done using electronic media, social media and viral campaigns on websites such as YouTube (www.YouTube.com). These decisions are part of the promotion planning process which is outlined in Figure 13.4.

Distribution

In tourism marketing, a distribution channel is (Goeldner and Ritchie, 2009: 182): 'an operating structure, system or linkages of various combinations of travel organisations through which a producer of travel products describes and confirms travel arrangements to the buyer'. Sometimes known as intermediation, distribution is an important element

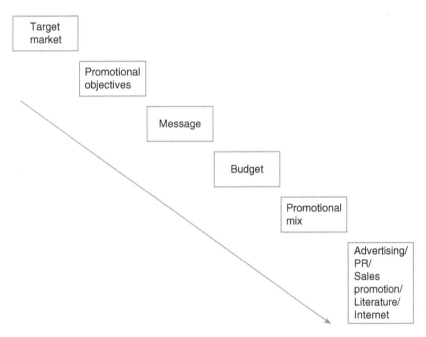

FIGURE 13.4　Promotion planning

of the tourism industry (as shown in Chapter 9). Distribution of the product is carried out by intermediaries – travel agents and tour operators/wholesalers – who have increasingly been impacted upon by newcomers in the market in the form of e-distribution companies such as Expedia (www.expedia.com). Indeed, the nature of tourism distribution has been transformed by the Internet and its use by both new-style e-intermediaries and tourists themselves, seeking to bypass intermediaries.

In tourism, distribution channels link suppliers with the customer. Distribution in tourism has particular characteristics that are not shared by other products:

- The nature of intermediaries means that they can influence the purchasing decision through advice and selective offerings. This is because intermediaries provide access to a range of products and can facilitate their purchase.

- The distribution process transfers risk from the supplier to the intermediary as a travel agent or tour operator holds stock until it is sold.

- It reduces the marketing costs of suppliers, as they do not have to reach the consumer directly – this is done by the intermediary.

- The fact that the tourism product cannot be stored means that the distribution process in tourism has become very sophisticated, utilising real-time reservation systems that can be accessed globally.

- The intermediary becomes a repository of advice and knowledge, acting as a one-stop shop for consumers.

Distribution channels in tourism can be thought of as having a number of steps (Figure 13.5). They can be classified by the nature of the power, relationships and arrangements within the channel:

- **Consensus channels** are found when all members of the channel are in agreement with the objectives and business models of the others – for example, tour operators who are supporting their destinations and often investing in them.

- **Integrated channels** demonstrate contractual arrangements, and often ownership arrangements, within the channel – for example, airlines may own their own tour operator and travel agent or e-intermediary.

- **Adversarial channels** were common in the 1990s where each member of the channel was jockeying for position and intent on a competitive battle with the rest of the channel.

As with other elements of the marketing mix, it is important for organisations to take a disciplined and planned approach to distribution. This will ensure that the type of channel used will conform to the product's promotion and design, as well as supporting the pricing strategy. It also ensures that management can control distribution costs and the strategy adopted. Here distribution strategy options include:

- **Intensive distribution**, where the product is sold through every available channel;

- **Exclusive distribution**, where the product is sold through a small number of highly appropriate channels which meet the product's image; and

- **Selective distribution**, which is a combination of the above two approaches – the product is sold through a wide number of channels, but these channels closely meet the product's image and campaign objectives.

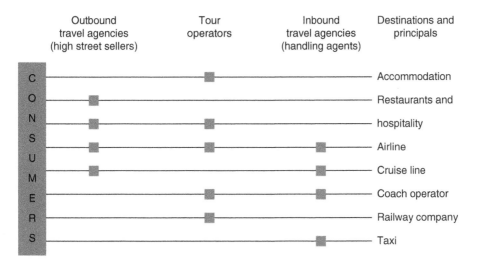

FIGURE 13.5   Tourism distribution mechanisms

Source: Buhalis and Laws, 2001; Page and Connell, 2009

Distribution is one of the elements of the marketing mix that has been transformed by technology. Liu (2000) notes that electronic distribution has a number of advantages:

- Drastic cost reduction, achieved through the electronic processing of bookings (such as e-tickets and electronic confirmations) and other transactions;
- Automation, reducing labour costs and office space;
- Direct and personal links to the customer; and
- Encouraging customer-driven distribution through social media and websites (such as www.tripadvisor.com).

Of course, electronic distribution has decimated traditional intermediaries such as 'bricks and mortar' travel agents. Tour operators, on the other hand, are reinventing themselves with the ability to flexibly package the product (dynamic packaging) and deal directly with their customers (as shown in Chapter 9). This shows that electronic distribution works well for tourism where the product is fragmented and web portals allow companies to provide and deliver a dynamic assembly of all of the elements of the product (Expedia is a good example here). Buhalis (2003) suggests that in the future tour operators will fall into two distinct groups:

1. Multinational, large and vertically integrated operators with economies of scale, wide distribution and a global network, taking a high-volume, low-profit approach; and

2. Small, niche differentiated operators focusing on particular destinations or products, taking a low-volume, high-profit approach.

FOCUS ON EMPLOYABILITY

Hotel Marketing Professionals

The role of a hotel marketer is to maximise revenues and increase profits for their property or chain. A key part of the role is understanding how to boost occupancy and manage the yield from the guests through rooms, meeting and leisure facilities. Hotel marketers help to determine the hotel's mission and goals and will increasingly use digital marketing to achieve their goals. Hotel marketers work closely with other staff and departments in the hotel.

Their job encompasses:

- Conducting marketing research, including monitoring customer reviews and tracking and analysing the performance of advertising campaigns;
- Promoting the hotel and its facilities, including events and functions;
- Building relationships with customers, partners and suppliers;
- Designing and implementing marketing strategy;
- Designing and implementing tactical marketing campaigns;
- Designing and policing the creative side of the hotel's brand; and
- Managing the marketing budget and allocating funds.

Job Requirements

Hotel marketing roles are highly sought after. To stand a chance of being employed, it is often a good idea to have been an intern in a property as prior experience is valuable. It is also important to have contemporary marketing tools such as web analytics and understand digital marketing. Increasingly, a degree in marketing or hospitality is required.

PUTTING IT ALL TOGETHER: TOURISM PRODUCT MARKETS

The 'product market' concept recognises that products and markets are inextricably linked, and treats 'product markets' within a framework of the interaction of buyers and sellers in a marketplace (Figure 13.6). The concept of product markets is intuitively appealing and fundamental to marketing theory. This is because they help explain how markets function and evolve, how new products are accepted and whether market boundaries are distinct or shifting. In other words, because product markets are formed by the interaction of tourists and suppliers, their boundaries are flexible as they represent the aggregate of many exchanges. This is outlined in Rosa et al.'s pioneering paper on the subject (Rosa et al., 1999). They see product markets as 'meeting grounds for buyers and sellers' (Rosa et al., 1999: 64).

Product markets are very helpful in understanding different types of tourism and how they can be classified. In tourism, each exchange between a tourist and a supplier is unique, simply because of the nature of tourism supply as highly heterogeneous and the many different levels of involvement by the tourist. There are two processes at work here:

1. Exchanges can be grouped and aggregated into a product market; and

2. The product market concept shows that both the supplier and the tourist can influence these exchanges.

In other words, different tourism product markets are defined by the interaction between suppliers and tourists and include ecotourism, dark tourism, adventure tourism, heritage tourism and cultural tourism. In each product market, tourists can be classified by their behaviour and involvement, as their 'wants' will tend to cluster, whilst suppliers will tend to specialise in particular product markets. It must be remembered, however, that product markets are not destinations. Destinations are bounded geographical entities which act as the 'setting' for product markets and therefore different 'types of tourism' (as shown in Chapter 2). Destinations can therefore be the stage for many product markets – each with its own group of customers and suppliers. An example here is volunteer tourism – or 'voluntourism' – a contemporary and growing 'type' of tourism which is beginning to attract its own set of suppliers, which include charitable bodies. Volunteer tourism is characterised by:

- A market that is somewhat altruistic, often seeking self-development and offering their time for free; and

- A product that is based upon environmental or social improvement at the destination – for example, cleaning up Everest, or helping rural villages to develop their education.

Putting these together into a product market for the type of tourism known as volunteer tourism results in a 'conscious, seamlessly integrated combination of voluntary service to a destination' (www.voluntourism.org).

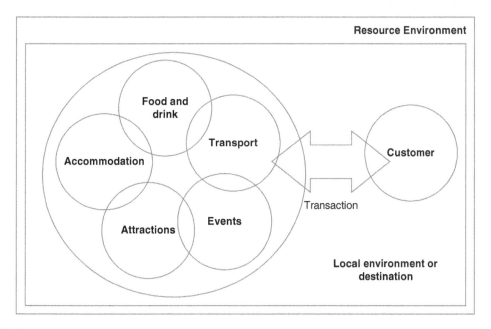

FIGURE 13.6 The tourism product market

Source: Cooper et al., 2006

SUMMARY

This chapter has introduced the nature and scope of tourism marketing. In particular, it has charted the evolution of the marketing concept and shown how the service-dominant logic is now replacing the previous goods-dominant logic of marketing. It presented the ground-breaking paper by Vargo and Lusch on the service-dominant logic as the classic paper for the chapter and introduced Kotler's new marketing concepts. The particular nature of tourism as a fragmented product has a number of implications for tourism marketers and may have led to a 'marketing gap'. The chapter also showed how the creative use of technology has transformed the business of tourism marketing and then presented the process of tourism market planning and strategy and showed its uses in tourism. The chapter went on to consider the marketing mix, focused as it is upon a target market. Each element of the mix was discussed, along with the implications for the nature of tourism and how these elements of the mix can be applied. Finally, the chapter outlined the very useful concept of the tourism product market as a way of thinking about tourism marketing and types of tourism.

DISCUSSION QUESTIONS

1. Taking a tourism company of your choice, discuss to what extent it displays the characteristics of a societal marketing approach, or whether it is in an earlier stage of evolution (marketing, production or sales).

2. Discuss the advantages and disadvantages that digital marketing brings to tourism marketers.

3. Taking a tourism product of your choice, dissect the dimensions of the product and chart the various companies and organisations responsible for their delivery.

4. Construct a table of the eight elements of the marketing mix in one column. In the second column, list the considerations the mix should take into account when focusing on tourism markets.

5. How does distribution for tourism differ from distribution for physical goods?

ANNOTATED FURTHER READING

Fyall, A. and Garrod, B. (2005) *Tourism Marketing: A Collaborative Approach*. Clevedon: Channel View.

Edited volume thoroughly reviewing the use and role of collaboration and partnership in tourism marketing.

Hudson, S. and Hudson, L. (2017) *Marketing for Tourism, Hospitality and Events: A Global and Digital Approach*. London: Sage.

Contemporary, all-embracing text with a strong digital flavour.

Kotler, P., Bowen, J., Makens, J. and Baloglu, S. (2020) *Marketing for Hospitality and Tourism*, 8th edn. Harlow: Pearson.

Classic marketing text reoriented with a tourism flavour.

Lovelock, C. and Gummesson, E. (2004) 'Whither services marketing? In search of a new paradigm and fresh perspectives', *Journal of Service Research*, 7 (1): 20–41.

Classic paper on services marketing.

Lusch, R.F. and Vargo, S.L. (2014) *The Service-Dominant Logic of Marketing: Dialog, Debate, and Directions*. London: Routledge.

Contemporary debate on their approach.

McCabe, S. (2013) *The Routledge Handbook of Tourism Marketing*. London: Routledge.

Comprehensive overview of current tourism marketing themes.

REFERENCES CITED

Ansoff, I. (1957) 'Strategies of diversification', *Harvard Business Review*, 25 (5): 113–25.

Benckendorff, P.J., Sheldon, P. and Fessenmaier, D. (2014) *Tourism Information Technology*, 2nd edn. Wallingford: CABI.

Buhalis, D. (2003) *eTourism: Information Technology for Strategic Tourism Management*. Harlow: Pearson Education.

Buhalis, D. and Laws, E. (eds) (2001) *Tourism Distribution Channels: Practices, Issues and Transformations*. London: Continuum.

Cooper, C. Fletcher, J. Fyall, A. Gilbert, D. and Wanhill, S. (2005) *Tourism Principles and Practice*. Harlow: Pearson.

Cooper, C., Scott, N. and Kester, J. (2006) 'New and emerging markets', in D. Buhalis and C. Costa (eds), *Tourism Business Frontiers: Consumers, Products and Industry*. London: Elsevier Butterworth-Heinemann. pp. 19–29.

Dolnicar, S. (2018) 'Understanding and satisfying customer needs: segmenting, targeting and positioning', in C. Cooper, S. Volo, W.C. Gartner and N. Scott (eds), *The Sage Handbook of Tourism Management: Applications of Theories and Concepts to Tourism*. London: Sage. pp. 257–68.

Dolnicar, S., Grün, B. and Leisch, F. (2018) *Market Segmentation Analysis: Understanding It, Doing It, and Making It Useful*. New York: Springer.

Font, X., Walmsley, A., Cogotti, S., McCombes, L. and Häusler, N. (2012) 'Corporate social responsibility: the disclosure performance gap', *Tourism Management*, 33: 1544–53.

Frochot, I. and Batat, W. (2013) *Marketing and Designing the Tourist Experience*. Oxford: Goodfellow.

Gilbert, D. (1990) 'Conceptual issues in the meaning of tourism', in C. Cooper (ed.), *Progress in Tourism, Recreation and Hospitality Management*. London: Belhaven Press. pp. 4–27.

Goeldner, C.R. and Ritchie, J.R.B. (2009) *Tourism Principles, Practices, Philosophies*. Hoboken, NJ: Wiley.

Goodwin, H. (2003) 'Ethical and responsible tourism: consumer trends in the UK', *Journal of Vacation Marketing*, 9 (3): 271–83.

Hudson, S. and Hudson, L. (2017) *Marketing for Tourism, Hospitality and Events: A Global and Digital Approach*. London: Sage.

Kotler, P. (2000) *Marketing Management: The Millennium Edition*. Englewood Cliffs, NJ: Prentice Hall.

Kotler, P., Bowen, J. and Makens, J. (2003) *Marketing for Hospitality and Tourism*, 3rd edn. Englewood Cliffs, NJ: Prentice Hall.

Kotler, P., Bowen, J., Makens, J. and Baloglu, S. (2020) *Marketing for Hospitality and Tourism*, 8th edn. Harlow: Pearson.

Kotler, P., Kartajaya, H. and Setiawan, I. (2016) *Marketing 4.0: Moving from Traditional to Digital*. Hoboken, NJ: John Wiley & Sons.

Kuiper, G. and Smith, B. (2014) *Imagineering Innovation in the Experience Economy*. Wallingford: CABI.

Li, X. and Petrick, J.F. (2008) 'Tourism marketing in an era of paradigm shift', *Journal of Travel Research*, 46: 235–44.

Liu, Z. (2000) 'Internet tourism marketing: potential and constraints', paper presented at the Fourth International Conference, Tourism in South East Asia and Indo China: Development, Marketing and Sustainability.

Lovelock, C. and Gummesson, E. (2004) 'Whither services marketing? In search of a new paradigm and fresh perspectives', *Journal of Service Research*, 7 (1): 20–41.

Lusch, R.F. and Vargo, S.L. (2014) *The Service-Dominant Logic of Marketing: Dialog, Debate, and Directions*. London: Routledge.

Mills, J. and Law, R. (2015) *Handbook of Consumer Behavior, Tourism, and the Internet*. London: Routledge.

Moutinho, L. (1994) 'New product development', in S.F. Witt and L. Moutinho (eds), *Tourism Marketing and Management Handbook*. Hemel Hempstead: Prentice Hall. pp. 350–3.

Page, S.J. and Connell, J. (2009) *Tourism: A Modern Synthesis*. Andover: Cengage Learning.

Pine, J. and Gilmore, J. (1999) *The Experience Economy*. Cambridge, MA: University of Harvard Press.

Rosa, J.A., Porac, J.F., Spanjol, J.R. and Saxon, M.S. (1999) 'Sociocognitive dynamics in a product market', *Journal of Marketing*, 63 (4): 64–77.

Scott, N. and Gao, L. (2018) 'Tourism products and experiences', in C. Cooper, S. Volo, W.C. Gartner and N. Scott (eds), *The Sage Handbook of Tourism Management: Applications of Theories and Concepts to Tourism*. London: Sage. pp. 191–206.

Shaw, G. and Agarwal, A. (2018) 'The development of service dominant logic within tourism management', in C. Cooper, S. Volo, W.C. Gartner and N. Scott (eds), *The Sage Handbook of Tourism Management: Applications of Theories and Concepts to Tourism*. London: Sage. pp. 173–90.

Shostack, G.L. (1977) 'Breaking free from product marketing', *Journal of Marketing*, 41: 73–80.

UNWTO (2014) *Handbook on E-marketing for Tourism Destinations*. Madrid: UNWTO.

Vargo, S.L. and Lusch, R.F. (2004) 'Evolving to a new dominant logic for marketing', *Journal of Marketing*, 68 (January): 1–17.

Wozniak, T., Stangl, B., Schegg, R. and Liebrich, A. (2017) 'The return on tourism organizations' social media investments: preliminary evidence from Belgium, France, and Switzerland', *Information Technology and Tourism*, 17: 75–100.

Xiang, Z. and Gretzel, U. (2010) 'Role of social media in online travel information search', *Tourism Management*, 31 (2): 179–88.

MAJOR CASE STUDY 13.1

Digital Marketing Strategy: Etihad Airways

The Etihad Airways smartphone mobile app

Source: ©BaniHasyim/Shutterstock.com

(Continued)

Introduction

Etihad Airways was launched in 2003 and is the national airline of the United Arab Emirates (UAE). It is a global airline and the second largest airline in the UAE. It carries almost 15 million passengers each year on over 1000 flights per week to more than 120 destinations.

Etihad Digital Guest Innovation Strategy

Etihad is one of three major airlines operating out of the Gulf States. Clearly these three airlines have hubs that are well positioned geographically and they all emphasise their luxury product. As the youngest of the three airlines, Etihad therefore needed a differentiation strategy to mark itself out from competitors. As part of the differentiation approach, Etihad established a Digital Guest Innovation strategy. This uses multiple digital channels to deliver customised packages tailored to customers' preferences. Here, there are ten different social media channels, including Chinese channels. This approach to placing digital at the core of its marketing marks Etihad out as an innovator in the field. In part, this is to be expected from one of the world's youngest airlines. Each channel is used in a different way to play to its strengths and the peculiarities of the audience. This has been particularly challenging for two reasons:

1. The airline's core market is in the Middle East and communicates in Arabic. However, the airline also has to provide support for its followers in their own native language such as English whilst they are booking and flying; and
2. The airline's various markets use social media in very different ways. For example, the Arabic language market views news on traditional visual channels such as Instagram, whilst they tend to follow influencers on channels such as Snapchat, which allows for more anonymity.

Etihad's digital strategy is firmly based on building a community of followers by fostering meaningful relationships with the audience. Messaging is designed to amplify positive messages and to turn negative messages into positive ones using empathy and tone of voice techniques. The strategy uses a communication style to deliver a highly personalised and empowering message to each follower.

Elements of the Strategy

Instagram

Etihad has been an extensive user of Instagram. Once it reached one million followers on Instagram, Etihad decided to launch a photo contest. This was designed to further drive engagement with Instagram. Over the ten-day period of the contest, a winner was announced each day on the airline's 'Instagramstory'. The prizes went to the most impressive travel photos and followers were encouraged to view a gallery of the best entries.

Snapchat

Etihad Airways worked with Snapchat to produce a campaign entitled 'The AR Fly-By'. This campaign featured an Etihad jumbo jet flying over the Etihad Stadium at the same time as Manchester City football club's iconic blue moon was rising on the horizon. The campaign was activated via a Snapcode promoted at the Etihad Stadium. Further similar campaigns are planned at key football matches.

WhatsApp

As a further part of the airline's customer engagement strategy, Etihad uses WhatsApp to allow its premium passengers to communicate directly with the airline when they are at Abu Dhabi International Airport. This allows customers to chat with agents about their flights in a fast, personal and efficient manner. For the future, Etihad will work with WhatsApp to deliver information messages such as flight reminders to customers.

YouTube and Virtual Reality

In a highly innovative approach, Etihad created a virtual reality film, *Flying Reimagined* starring Nicole Kidman using Google Cardboard, and delivered it via a YouTube blast. This had an immediate and tangible impact with an 8 per cent growth in revenue and a 25 per cent increase in referral traffic. Viewers of the film were 22 per cent more likely to consider Etihad, 7% were more likely to pay extra for the Etihad flying experience and Etihad's app was downloaded 26,000 times in the weeks following the campaign.

Discussion Questions

1. Discuss the effectiveness of these digital marketing approaches compared to more traditional campaigns.
2. How important are the tone of voice and messaging protocols in a digital marketing campaign?
3. What other marketing techniques can be used to differentiate an offering aside from digital?

Source: www.etihad.com

PART 5
TOURISM FUTURES: THE ESSENTIALS

The final part of this book turns to the futures of tourism. This is uncharted territory where few authors dare to tread – though there are notable exceptions such as the *Journal of Tourism Futures*. Because the future is unknown, everything is possible. Because there is an infinite number of futures to consider, this chapter talks of *tourism futures* rather than a single *tourism future*. Predicting tourism futures is not an easy task. Since publication of the second edition of this book, for example, climate change has climbed high on the global agenda, social media, smartphones and texting have grown exponentially, the fourth industrial revolution has brought artificial intelligence and robotics to the fore of human resources and everyone is connected – leading us towards a world of driverless cars, smart cities and digital wallets. The United Nations World Tourism Organization (UNWTO) has termed the uncertainty caused by the radical change experienced in the twenty-first century as the 'new normal', suggesting that tourism will never return to the relatively stable conditions of the twentieth century. Indeed, tourism is inextricably integrated with society and other economic sectors and so is exposed to their changes and influences.

Whilst it is easy to hype up a sensationalist future for tourism, the future is indeed an exciting one, of biofuels and carbon sinks, transformational travel to move people rapidly between continents, flying cars, nanorobotics, biochips and teleportation, and China, South Asia and Latin America becoming global superpowers. Nonetheless, it is important to take a disciplined and structured approach to the issue. Indeed, despite pessimistic accounts of the human race being wiped out by disease, meteorites or aliens, it is likely that humans will be around for some time to come. It is also possible that with gloomy scenarios of energy shortages and carbon emissions, the early years of this century may be viewed as one of privileged travel. This chapter provides two frameworks within which to consider and analyse tourism futures:

1. Firstly, the drivers of the future are analysed along with how tourism might respond in the future. These drivers, such as demographics and technology, will have a fundamental influence upon tourism futures, but it is misleading to treat each one in isolation. For example, social and economic drivers will

encourage the growth of tourism, but they will also determine social attitudes to processes such as climate change and, as a consequence, the very nature of tourism operations will begin to change. Underpinning these drivers will be cross-cutting variables such as technology that will increasingly pervade every aspect of tourism in the future.

2. Secondly, the response of tourism to these drivers is analysed using Leiper's tourism system (introduced in Chapter 1), which provides an all-encompassing approach to studying tourism. Tourism futurists commonly focus only on the tourism destination part of the system. But this fails to recognise the complexity of the tourism sector and the need to match trends on both demand and supply sides. To consider any one of these in isolation would provide an unbalanced assessment of the futures of tourism. A good example here is the concept of product markets (introduced in Chapter 13). Here, drivers of future market trends will combine with technology and destination management to create the products of the future, whether they are in space or deep under the sea.

All of this means that tourism futures are an exciting and stimulating area of study. What is clear is that the tourism of the future will have to embrace the principles of the low-carbon economy to deliver 'smart tourism': a clean, green, ethical and quality tourism underpinned by a concern for the environment, for the destination, for local communities and particularly the poor. Above all, it will use technology and networked enterprises to deliver a high-quality experience to the discerning tourists of the future.

And so, let's take a shot at a prediction …

Imagine it is the year 2040 and you are booking a holiday. You want to recreate your honeymoon but the news last night confirmed that this is now impossible: the last inch of the Maldives has just disappeared under the Indian Ocean. You have saved hard for this trip – not financially, as all flights are incredibly cheap, but in terms of your rationed air miles. For two solid years, you have saved your carbon allowances so that you will be able to fly almost anywhere in the world without paying hefty premiums on what is not covered by your ration cards. Going onto the Web, you enter a virtual travel office and walk around the badly deteriorated ruins of Angkor Wat for a while before clicking through to a virtual reality beach on the east coast of Australia. Here, other visitors have left virtual versions of themselves, which tell you about the facilities, what to do, where to stay and what to avoid. Australia is attractive now that the flight goes into space and only takes six hours, but the carbon rations needed make you feel that it may be a waste, now that all the coral of the Great Barrier Reef has been bleached …

14

TOURISM FUTURES

LEARNING OUTCOMES

This chapter focuses upon the futures of tourism, outlining the key drivers of the future and possible scenarios for both the tourist and the tourism sector itself. The chapter is designed to provide you with:

- a disciplined approach to analysing and anticipating the futures of the tourism system;

- an understanding of the key drivers of tourism futures;

- an awareness of the way that tourism markets will evolve in the future;

- an approach to understanding how both destinations and the tourism sector, including transport, will be shaped in the future; and

- an awareness of the cross-cutting issues that will impact upon tourism futures.

INTRODUCTION

The future is as yet unknown and there are therefore many possibilities, hence the term *tourism futures*. This chapter adopts a disciplined approach to studying tourism futures, beginning by examining the leading reports on tourism future scenarios and going on to examine the key drivers of tourism futures. It will then move its focus to the response of markets, destinations and the sector itself to these drivers before closing with an examination of cross-cutting issues.

FUTURE TOURISM SCENARIOS

Futurists say that the future cannot be predicted, but alternative futures can, and that to be useful, futures studies should be linked to strategic planning and policy (Yeoman and McMahon-Beattie, 2018). Scenario planning is an approach that is being used increasingly in tourism to predict alternative futures and to assist agencies in planning, and it is a useful tool to analyse sustainable tourism futures. The approach was developed by the oil company Shell in the 1960s and has grown out of futures studies and strategic analysis. It is a tool that develops a range of pictures and stories of multiple, plausible futures, constructed using future-shaping drivers and trends. In tourism the approach has been pioneered by the 2025 Scenario Planning Group based at VisitScotland (VisitScotland and Future Foundation, 2005). There are a number of influential reports that have attempted to develop scenarios for tourism futures:

- On the demand side, the UNWTO's forecasts of international tourism are essential reading for anyone interested in global trends to 2030 (UNWTO, 2001, 2007, 2011a).

These forecasts show that, despite the setbacks of the early twenty-first century, international arrivals will approach two billion by 2030, although climate action may reduce this figure. Nonetheless, this continuous growth is unusual for any economic sector. Demand for domestic tourism will expand at a slower rate and some countries will reach demand-side ceilings of capacity and available leisure time which will constrain further growth. International arrivals will continue to be concentrated in Europe, East Asia and the Pacific, and the Americas, and the major growth areas will be long haul travel and newer destinations such as those in East Asia and the Pacific.

- On the supply side, there are a number of influential sources, including:

  o *World, Transformed*, a report by the world's peak tourism industry body, the World Travel and Tourism Council (WTTC), is concerned about the implications of entwined megatrends and their impact upon tourism. It makes a set of recommendations for how the sector can respond to these trends (WTTC and Bloomberg Media Group, 2019).

  o The European Tourism Futures Institute (ETFI) (2014) has developed a set of four scenarios for tourism in 2040. They are based upon future states where the commercial interests of the tourism sector are balanced and moderated by concerns for sustainability to create competitive advantage (Postma, 2014).

  o The European Tourism Future's Institute's (2014) *The Future of European Tourism* and Sara Nordin's (2005) *Tourism of Tomorrow* utilise techniques from futures research to analyse the driving forces of change for tourism. Nordin's report is noteworthy for the adaptation of the STEEP methodology to understand the environment within which tourism operates. STEEP can be characterised as comprising social, technological, environmental, economic and political forces, all of which work together. The report then draws in the idea of 'wild cards' – events that have a low probability of occurring, but which are devastating when they do. Of course, 9/11 is the defining 'wild card' for contemporary tourism but events such as the financial crisis of 2008/09 were also not foreseen and impacted severely upon tourism.

  o The European Travel Commission (2006) has written a tight and comprehensive analysis of European tourism futures, scanning both demand- and supply-side trends.

  o In Australia, the Sustainable Tourism Cooperative Research Centre (STCRC) (Dwyer et al., 2007) has published an influential report on tourism megatrends, with the aim of alerting the tourism sector to upcoming trends and mapping their implications for tourism.

  o The Forum for the Future (2009) has developed four scenarios for tourism to 2023 using expert opinion across the sector. They strongly feature sustainable tourism and resource use. The scenarios are: (i) 'boom and burst' where growth in the economy creates growth in tourism globally with travellers going further, more often and faster than before; (ii) 'divided disquiet' where extreme climate change, clashes over resources and social unrest create an uncertain and fearful world; (iii) 'price and privilege' where oil prices have soared and the travel and aviation sector have been hit hard; and (iv) 'carbon clampdown' where governments have developed tradable carbon allowances to help combat climate change.

  o The Northern Ireland Tourist Board (NITB) (no date) has predicted what tourism will look like in 2030. From a number of drivers and results, two scenarios focus particularly on sustainable tourism futures: (i) zero impact tourism, a utopian vision of a zero-carbon destination; and (ii) changing trends, preferences and policies in sustainability, focusing on a growing demographic known as 'lifestyles of health and sustainability' (LOHAS). This group is driven by eco-conscious, well-educated consumers.

This chapter adopts a similar approach to these reports by analysing the drivers of tourism futures and then outlining possible scenarios for both the tourist and the sector itself. The classic paper for this chapter is, however, cautious about predictions and observes that few have the courage to write about tourism futures.

CLASSIC PAPER

Special Issue of the journal *Futures* (2009): Cole, S. and Razak, V. (2009) 'Tourism as future', *Futures*, 41 (6): 335–45

This issue of *Futures* focuses exclusively on the futures of tourism and features papers by leading tourism scholars, overall evidencing the case that: 'futurists should address the topic of tourism, and that tourism specialists and policy-makers should use futures thinking to better address their concerns and explore wider perspectives' (p. 335).

The introduction by Cole and Razak is particularly useful, synoptically mapping the scope of tourism and its futures. But it also, perhaps surprisingly, speaks of the 'missing futures' of tourism, pointing out that papers on tourism futures are hard to find. It is interesting to speculate as to why this is; certainly it may be explained by the fact that tourism is comprised of so many component parts and has a fickle market.

As the exception to the rule, this volume provides a range of excellent papers on tourism futures. To quote the editors:

> Papers in this special issue elaborate the issues involved both through historic review and theoretical analysis, and by providing case studies that demonstrate possible directions for international tourism analysis and policy. Collectively, the papers explore the relationships between destination countries and their markets, and the extent to which tourism might fulfil its promise to promote economic development and stability, peace, poverty reduction, and sustainable development. (p. 3)

THE FUTURE DRIVERS OF TOURISM

This section examines the major drivers of tourism futures. In reality, most of these trends and variables are interlinked and mutually reinforcing. For example, the very economic development that has fuelled tourism growth is contributing to climate change, which threatens to alter the nature of many destinations and travellers' transport choices. There is no doubt that these trends, when combined, will have a fundamental impact upon future tourism scenarios and, as a consequence, cannot be ignored. Yet, no single trend will dominate and each will impact upon tourism futures in a different way, but at key times some trends will tip and become significant – and irreversible; the adoption of the Internet in the 1990s is an obvious example – as a result, the possible futures of tourism are many and varied (Buckley et al., 2015).

Social drivers of change

Demographic drivers

Despite the fact that the world will be home to 9.6 billion people in 2050, for most of the traditional generators of domestic and international tourism, population growth is either static or even negative, with populations ageing as people live longer in North America, Europe and Japan (UNWTO, 2010). Ageing populations tend to be associated with urbanisation and conservative politics, and markets for their goods and services have clear implications for the tourism sector – the influence of the ageing baby boomer generations of the developed world is waning, to be replaced by younger generations who will shape tourism futures. Generations X, Y and Z will remain in the youth market longer as they marry later and continue with their youth lifestyle, so changing the nature of the traditional nuclear family household. Generation Y, roughly speaking those born between 1978 and 2000, is the largest population bulge since the baby boomers and they are influencing consumer behaviour: they are technologically adept and more savvy consumers, sceptical about marketing messages, and seek networked, virtual communities. Emerging generators of international tourism such as China and India are experiencing rapid population growth: in the future, the majority of population growth will take place in the developing world, with Africa set to grow the most, creating a new middle class and young workforce that will benefit tourism.

Social drivers

Throughout much of society, there is a move to more flexible working practices and a fluid balance between work and leisure. The knowledge economy places a premium on education, creating a 'creative class' of educated, networked and self-motivated individuals where English is the dominant language. With education comes an increasing concern for ethical consumption, environmental concerns which will change attitudes to mobility in general, and a conflicting emphasis on pleasure-seeking, conspicuous consumption. Family structures in the developed world are changing, with a trend to later marriage, more one-parent families and having children at a later age. Here, there are three key social trends that have specific implications for tourism:

1. Worldwide, more people are choosing to live in cities such that in 2020 more than 60 per cent of the world's population already live in urban areas. Urbanisation has important policy implications in terms of the growth of city-states, which have their own tourism markets, the use of tourism to market cities and the fact that tourist resources will be increasingly located adjacent to the urban market, favouring artificial types of development such as theme parks, as has occurred in Japan. Here the UNWTO's (2019) Lisbon declaration on 'Cities for All: Building Cities for Citizens and Visitors' is an important initiative.

2. In many countries, both the status and influence of women are on the increase. Women will have an increasing say not only in purchasing decisions, but also in the types of products offered by the tourism sector and in the senior management decisions of

major travel corporations. This is leading to provision of women-only hotels and excursions, such as the 'women only' luxury spa retreat in Marrakech, Morocco, offered by Responsible Travel (responsibletravel.com).

3. Populations are becoming more culturally diverse as improved communications, increasing wealth and mobility stimulate people to try to understand other cultures. Tourism products and their marketing will increasingly have to embrace cultural diversity, and niche products – such as gay tourism – are emerging as a consequence.

Political and economic drivers of change

Tourism futures are intricately linked to politics and economies at all levels. Politics demonstrates the rapidity of change experienced in the world and the vulnerability of tourism to this change – witness, for example, the BREXIT decision in the UK which will profoundly change European tourism, and the election of Donald Trump as US president introducing a 'climate sceptic' to power. Elsewhere, the world order is changing with the rising economic power of newly emerging economies such as Brazil, Russia, India and China (the BRIC economies) and the newer group of strong economies of Mexico, Indonesia, Nigeria and Turkey (MINT). Indeed, some commentators now characterise future global economic power as a struggle between the 'Anglosphere' and the 'Sinosphere' as the USA strives to maintain its influence on the world stage. At the international level, tourism futures will be influenced by four key trends – the forging of international trading blocs, globalisation, religion and economic growth.

Trade blocs and regionalism

Opportunities for tourism will be enhanced by the formation of a number of trading blocs across the globe as country groupings come together in deregulated economic alliances. Notable here are the North American Free Trade Agreement (NAFTA) and the creation and expansion of the European Union (EU). In the EU, adoption of the euro has demonstrated the power of these blocs, as the currency has encouraged tourism across Europe, while the expansion of the EU itself will begin to change the balance of tourism flows within Europe.

A contradictory trend at the regional level is the rise of regionalism and a search for cultural identity. Here, 'city-states' are emerging as major visitor destinations where tourism plays a key role in 'boosting' their reputations, lifestyle and economies. Cities can significantly leverage their image by staging a major event; for example, Sydney benefited from hosting the Olympic Games, as did Singapore from the first night-time Formula One Grand Prix. Similarly, regionalism is growing, with pressure for independence from regions such as Scotland and Catalonia creating tensions within the large mega trading blocs. However, there is a darker side to regionalism, exemplified by the growth of extremist groups such as ISIS (Islamic State of Iraq and Syria) creating no-go areas for travel.

Globalisation

Underlying the changing world order is the globalisation of tourism businesses – a powerful force shaping national and regional economies, which are linked and interdependent as never before. Globalisation can be defined as: 'the interaction, and sometimes integration, of industries, peoples, governments and economies through international arrangements, trade, travel, information technology' (Timothy, 2018: 570).

Globalisation is therefore the combination of the revolution in information technology, telecommunications and transport, a consensus among governments for free trade and the democratisation of financial markets. Globalisation results in the increasing interdependence of markets and production in different countries, creating a 'borderless world' (Dwyer, 2014). Key drivers of globalisation in tourism are:

- Decreasing costs of international travel, allowing access to most markets in the world;
- Increasing income and wealth in the generating countries;
- Newly emerging destinations and the increased demand for international travel;
- Adoption of free trade agreements, removing barriers to international transactions;
- Digital and communications technology encouraging networked businesses; and
- Worldwide acting suppliers.

Some of the consequences of globalisation for the tourism sector will include:

- Increasingly standardised products, procedures and global brands, such as Disney;
- Pressure for alliances and mergers;
- Increased concentration in the marketplace; and
- Pressure on vulnerable businesses such as local SMEs.

Indeed, it is the larger, international companies that can take advantage of these consequences as globalisation encourages increased concentration in the tourism industry as major companies gain market share and market influence. At the same time, we are seeing the concentration of capital in a few tourism companies, a trend that also drives tourism towards the key performance indicators (KPIs), return on investment measures (ROI) and business practices demanded by the finance industry.

A particular problem associated with this trend is that most of the larger corporations do not have a relationship with a specific destination. They may therefore be less sensitive to the impact of their operations on that destination. In addition, SMEs and local destinations fear the 'neo-colonial' relationship which can emerge from dealing with large companies. This is an important consideration for tourism where, at the end of the day, the product is delivered locally – hence the conundrum of balancing against the global forces upon an essentially 'local' product.

Economic drivers

In the long term, the economies of most generating countries will grow, leading to higher per capita incomes. This enhances the ability to consume tourism products as discretionary income rises proportionately, which will be particularly the case in the emergent economies of China and India. However, environmental concerns may check growing levels of consumption. The STCRC's report (Dwyer et al., 2007) identifies seven drivers of economic growth:

1. Political pressures for higher living standards;
2. Improved macroeconomic policies;

3. Deregulation/liberalisation;

4. Rising trade and investment;

5. Diffusion of information technology;

6. An increasingly dynamic private sector; and

7. Evolving global financial markets.

Science and the environmental drivers of change

Science helps to understand environmental change and its potential impact upon tourism futures as the sector continues its imperative for sustainable development. One of the major factors that will impact upon tourism futures is concern for the environment. And as the STCRC's (Dwyer et al., 2007) report so clearly states, environmental change will be with us for the remainder of the century, whereas most of the other drivers of the futures identified here have a much shorter time horizon.

The United Nations Environment Program (UNEP, 2002) has identified three environmental concerns for the future:

1. Climate change;

2. Depletion of natural resources (energy, water and land use); and

3. Loss of biodiversity.

Of these, climate change has become the major issue for tourism (as shown in Chapter 4). This is because not only is the scientific evidence compelling, but also tourism is a climate-sensitive sector. Climate determines tourism seasons and destination choice, and impacts upon tourism product development. Concern for the impact of human activity upon the climate is altering consumer behaviour and has increasingly become a focus for tourism policy and management initiatives. There is also no doubt that tourism is both a vector and a victim of climate change, with estimates suggesting that the tourism sector contributes 5 per cent of global greenhouse gas emissions.

Fortunately, understanding the science of climate change is increasing, as is the world's awareness of the seriousness of the issue, evidenced by global activism in 2019. Global climate change includes long-term factors such as global warming and the erosion of the ozone layer. Analysis of the impact of climate change on tourism needs to consider the total tourism system, including transport. On the supply side, there is no doubt that the increasing temperature of the earth and the consequent rise in sea level will affect tourism destinations such as wetlands, deserts, islands, mountains and coastal areas. Much of tourism investment is found in locations that fringe the coast, and global warming will irrevocably alter vital tourism resources. These include the disappearance of iconic destinations such as the Maldives, deterioration of coral reefs through coral bleaching and the loss of snow in winter resorts. On the demand side, fear of skin cancer and eye cataracts may reduce demand for products such as beach tourism which, in turn, will impact upon destination and product development. Finally, it has to be recognised that some transport modes used for tourism, particularly air transport, are high emitters of carbon, leaving the tourism sector with a poor image – this will need to change.

Other concerns raised by UNEP will also impact upon tourism futures. Water will become a precious asset in some regions of the world: indeed, estimates suggest that by 2025, 1.8 billion people will live in areas of absolute water shortage (see Gössling et al., 2015). Consumption of water across the globe is growing at double the rate of population growth and water is essential for tourism. The real concern for the future is that climate change will impact severely on the water cycle, impacting tourism as follows (Day and Chin, 2018):

- Water supports the tourist's basic needs such as sanitation and drinking water; and
- Water supports tourism products such as golf, lakes and river tourism.

Tourism is a voracious consumer of energy. In the future, this will have to be carefully managed as the days of abundant energy dwindle. As the years of 'peak oil' approach, when the maximum amount of oil is being extracted from the earth, there is a growing dialogue supporting the transition to a low-carbon economy. This will depend upon the development of renewable energy technologies for tourism operations and fossil-free, fuel-efficient, smart transport systems (Becken, 2015). Biodiversity, too, is being impacted upon by development in many regions of the world, and by climate change. For an industry that depends upon natural resources to attract tourists, this remains a serious issue.

MINI CASE STUDY 14.1
Food Futures

Introduction

There is no doubt that food is an important part of tourism, with gastronomy becoming a key part of local culture at the destination, and often the focus of visitors' conversations. In the future, demand for food globally will increase by 50 per cent by 2030 and 70 per cent by 2050 (https://population.un.org). Yet, combined with this burgeoning demand, linked to population growth (up to 9 billion by 2050), is the fact that food production is threatened by both climate

Livestock accounts for almost 20 per cent of the world's carbon emissions

Source: ©Syda Productions/Shutterstock.com

change and shifting patterns of trade. In other words, how secure are the world's food supplies going forward, and what will future food look like?

(Continued)

Drivers of Food Futures

There are a number of reinforcing factors which will influence not only the future supply of food, but also the nature of food itself:

- Firstly, there is a range of environmental stressors on future food supplies. These include higher temperatures, resulting in drought and damage to habitat diversity. There is also a decline in pollinating insects and a degradation of soil. However, it must also be remembered that in some regions of the world, crops will benefit from a changing climate.
- Secondly, food is political and will be impacted upon by shifting patterns of trade and political events such as Brexit.
- Thirdly, the current food production regime is designed for a high-carbon world, built on non-renewables. For example, meat has a high-carbon footprint, with livestock accounting for almost 20 per cent of the world's carbon emissions, and they consume up to a third of the world's food production.

Post Cow? Beyond Beef?

So, what are the alternatives for future foods at the destination? It is clear that with the cost of livestock rising and the negative impact of meat production on the climate, alternatives will need to be found. At the time of writing, non-meat and vegan alternatives are becoming fashionable, stocked in mainstream supermarkets and offered in fast food restaurants such as Burger King (www.bk.com) and Kentucky Fried Chicken (www.kfc.com). Many of these alternatives are based upon meat protein derived from plants. Here one of the pioneers is the American 'Impossible Burger' (https://impossiblefoods.com). In the future, this will be taken further as food technology delivers new types of food and food production. These might include:

- Insects and bugs as forms of protein – a much more efficient source of protein than meat;
- Algae- and seaweed-based foods;
- Genetic engineering of foods to match individual nutritional needs;
- Vertical farming to combat land shortages;
- Powdered food protein and nutrients such as Queal (a complete food with all necessary nutrients); and
- Lab-grown meat which drastically reduces the carbon footprint.

Discussion Questions

1. Over a weekend, sample fast-food alternatives to meat – debate the experience in class the following week.
2. How acceptable is food based upon crickets, cockroaches and grubs? Would you eat it?
3. Draft a list of the way that climate change may impact upon future food production to 2050 in your country.

TECHNOLOGICAL DRIVERS OF CHANGE

FOCUS ON TECHNOLOGY

Technology in 2050

Admittedly, 2050 seems a long way in the future but it is only 30 years from the publication of this book. It is therefore possible to make educated predictions about the technology of the future and its impact upon tourism, hospitality and events. This is expanded upon in the end-of-chapter major case study. Applications will include the following:

- For medical tourism, nanobots will diagnose and cure disease, delivering drugs direct to the body. More extreme is the idea that they will be able to permanently capture travel memories and even reincarnate human beings or extinct species with DNA sampling.

- At the destination, implant device technology in the form of a chip will allow for enhanced communication without external devices such as smartphones.

- AI will develop algorithms for weather forecasts, itinerary design and product search engines.

- The Internet of Things will develop its own ecosystem, seamlessly linking the home and travellers with the external environment.

- Space tourism will be a reality by 2050 and a stimulus for new jobs and product development (see Spector and Higham, 2019, for a review of space tourism products).

- Connected self-driving cars will be ubiquitous at all destinations and will reduce traffic-related deaths and injuries and boost ride sharing. This will allow smart destinations to develop transport ecosystems.

- Alternative energy technology will include ocean thermal energy – one of the world's largest potential energy resources – geothermal energy and more efficient solar power generation.

- Drone and robotic technology will make inaccessible destinations accessible and develop logistics delivery ecosystems.

- Exoskeletons will allow travellers to reach inaccessible mountain peaks and other resources.

- AI-enabled robots will impact upon tourism jobs.

- Sophisticated new realities will be in the home in the form of holograms on glass walls. Virtual and augmented realities will pervade much of tourism, hospitality and events, delivering totally immersive virtual destinations using nanobots to interface our brains with computers.

The UNWTO has stated that the world in the future will be characterised by the penetration of technology into all aspects of life. Tourism futures will be determined and facilitated by technology, where – to paraphrase the well-known commentator on technology trends, Donald Norman (2007) – the most successful technology will be invisible to the user. Where it does interface with the user, the experience will be organic. It is technology that demonstrates how unpredictable the future can be; for example, in the 1970s the Internet as we know it was not even predicted.

The following quote from Lewis (2002: 117) brings home the impact of the Internet on tourism futures: 'Wide-eyed amateurs, 15 year old teenagers and outsiders can nonchalantly take on the professionals, insiders and establishments and drub them into submission'. This quote underlines the fact that the Internet has levelled the playing field for tourism marketing. A good website means that small, remote destinations can compete equally with the giants of tourism such as Spain (see, for example, https://visitandorra.com/en), whilst SMEs can take on large corporations.

The fusion of information and communication technologies (ICTs) allows tourism enterprises to become more efficient and competitive, not simply by lowering costs and facilitating market access, but also by allowing them to network and integrate with other enterprises – and their consumers. Indeed, everything and everyone will be connected in the future. ICTs and Big Data will increasingly allow customisation of products and real-time access to demand, allowing flexible pricing and segmentation down to the individual; indeed, innovations such as facial recognition technology, allied to Big Data, will allow each and every indivdual visit to an event, museum or theme park to be personally curated. In the market we are also seeing the growth of online tourism communities; here, the evolution of the Internet is transforming the way that business is done, and for tourism the fusion of Internet technologies with social activities such as blogging facilitates content-rich sites and enables networked online tourism communities. By enhancing user-generated content, this will displace more traditional ways of seeking information about tourism. New generations of the Internet will advance booking systems and consumer access by introducing intelligent systems and enabling personal travel advisors and intelligent recommendation systems to deliver tailored information. TripAdvisor, for example, is evolving into a professional information hub, employing content moderators and peer reviewers, wrapped into a contemporary social media site – as shown in Major Case Study 12.1 (see also Future Foundation, 2015). Effectively, technology has increased the connections between the actors in the tourism system. However, as authorities become concerned at the openness of the Internet, there is a danger that, in the future, 'Balkanisation' of the Internet will create regional closed versions – in, say, Russia or China – curtailing the international nature of the medium.

FOCUS ON EMPLOYABILITY

Skills for 2050

The UNWTO is partnering with Google to identify the digital skills needed by tourism in the future. This has prompted this Focus on Employability to predict the skills and jobs that will be in demand in tourism, hospitality and events in 2050. These skills can be divided into three types:

1. **Higher cognitive skills** including critical thinking, complex information processing and problem-solving, mental elasticity and creativity.

2. **Soft, or people, skills** including communication, empathy, continual learning and management skills.

3. **Hard technological skills** including those required for software development, programming, robotics, nanotechnology and implantables, bio-facturing, gene-editing and AI.

So how will these skills be applied in a world dominated by technology, longer life spans and a merging of the virtual and the real? Future jobs might include: machine learning engineer, personal data broker, chief productivity officer, quantum data analyst, personal medical counsellor, virtual experience designer, drone manager, care-giving specialist, sustainable building regulator, waste engineer, commercial space pilot, extinct species revivalist, alternative energy consultant, climate scientist, organ/body part creator, mind transfer specialist/memory surgeon, and baby designer.

Two observations stand out here. Firstly, it is interesting that technology cannot replicate humanity, so successful individuals will be those who can major on these 'human' skills; and secondly, the majority of the jobs above will be of relevance to tourism and hospitality and events, but very few are directly related – a sobering thought for how the subject should be taught in the future.

Source: Daheim, C. and Winterman, O. (2016) *2050: The Future of Work. Findings of an International Delphi Study of The Millennium Project*. Gutersloh: Bertelsmann Stiftung.

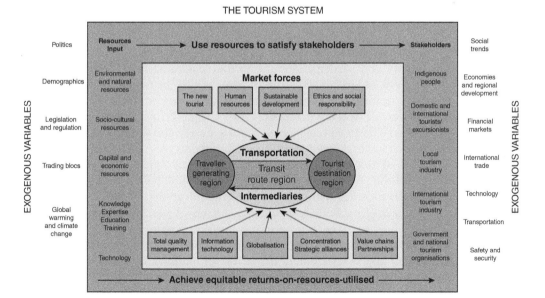

FIGURE 14.1   A framework for tourism trends analysis

THE RESPONSE – TOURISM FUTURES

Given the drivers of change identified above, the chapter now turns to examine how they will shape tourism futures. This section returns to the elements of Leiper's tourism system introduced in Chapter 1. Leiper's system recognises the complexity of tourism and the need to match up trends on the demand side in terms of markets and consumer behaviour, with trends on the supply side in terms of product developments and the destination. To consider any one of these elements in isolation would provide an unbalanced assessment of tourism futures. And, of course, the tourism system itself does not operate in isolation and is subject to a number of cross-cutting influences such as climate change and technology (Figure 14.1).

TOURISM MARKET FUTURES

In Leiper's 'traveller generating region', the demographic and social trends identified above have combined to change both the scale and nature of tourism markets, facilitated by technology and the economy, but tempered by crises and environmental and ethical concerns. Future tourism markets will be dominated by technology, characterised by fragmentation and they will be borderless. Many tourism futurists have suggested that the maturing of the tourism market is creating a 'new tourist', or a 'post-tourist', characterised as experienced, sophisticated and demanding. This means that the traditional annual family holiday, mostly spent in a beach resort, may be gradually superseded by multi-interest travel and a range of creative and innovative travel experiences – and, of course, holidays will be seen as a time to detox from the digital world. These trends will see the relative importance of conventional packaged tours decline in favour of independently organised tourism, often using 'dynamic packaging' or a more bespoke form of tourism.

The new tourist

The new consumer of tourism will demand more. They will be knowledgeable, networked, discerning, seek quality and participation and, in the developed world, be increasingly drawn from an older age group (Yeoman, 2008). Motivations for travel are moving away from passive sunlust towards educational and curiosity motives. At the same time, travel will be facilitated by flexible working practices. Tourists from the major generating regions of the world have become frequent travellers, are linguistically and technologically skilled, and can function in multicultural and demanding environments overseas. Add to this media and Internet exposure of tourism destinations and the reduction of perceived distance to reach such places and the stage is set for a reappraisal of holiday formulae. Education, too, has played a part, together with enhanced communications, and has led to more sophisticated requirements from holidaymakers who are now looking for new experiences combined with rewarding activities, but never too far from a wireless hotspot. Here, the emergence of the knowledge-based society is significant for tourism as travel products are merged with education and entertainment to create 'info-tainment' or 'edu-tainment' at many destinations. As technology has constantly improved the quality of entertainment, visual images and sound in our own homes, so we have come to expect a similar level of quality of our tourism experience. Pine and Gilmore (1999) have taken this one step further by suggesting that, in the future, consumption will be driven by 'experiences' and that suppliers will 'engineer' these experiences. Tourism is perfect for this approach as, for the new tourist, travel is less about being at the destination and more about the experiences associated with being there (either in reality or virtually) as travel becomes the medium for personal fulfilment and identity. Indeed, many commentators suggest that the 'experience' will increasingly drive the decision to purchase a holiday, rather than the 'destination' itself. Here, the Future Foundation (2015) has created six future traveller tribes for 2030 based on personality and the psychology of travel, influenced by 'social media, ethical concerns and a desire for well being' (p. 3). The tribes are fluid and consumers may identify with more than one. They are:

1. Simplicity searchers based on ease and transparency in travel;

2. Cultural purists immersing themselves in the destination;

3. Social capital seekers seeking social reward from travel;

4. Reward hunters seeking a return on their travel investment;

5. Obligation meeters such as business travellers; and

6. Ethical travellers shaped by their conscience.

The new tourist though will differ from earlier travellers in their embrace of ethical travel and their concern for the destinations and communities who live there. We will see an increase in philanthropic, conscientious travel and the growth of fair-trade tourism as the tourist recognises their responsibilities to the destination (Hall and Brown, 2008). Here, however, the consumer psychology of tourism will be critical in determining whether tourists really care about climate change enough *not* to fly. In recognition of this trend, the World Committee on Tourism Ethics was inaugurated in 2008 to track implementation of the UNWTO's Global Code of Ethics for Tourism (www.unwto.org/global-code-of-ethics-for-tourism), whilst in 2009 Tourism Concern issued a hard-hitting report on tourism and human rights (Tourism Concern, 2009) (www.tourismconcern.org.uk). In response to this trend, new forms of tourism such as volunteering (volun-tourism) are growing whilst suppliers are embracing the idea of corporate social responsibility (CSR), particularly with respect to local communities. This is in part facilitated by the Internet through online communities of new tourists.

Through social media, online communities are having an increased impact upon the tourism product itself and tourists trust each other in preference to advertisements or company endorsements as 'e-word of mouth' grows in importance. Of course, there will be an increased requirement for high standards of product design, efficiency and safety, but, more importantly, through user-generated websites such as TripAdvisor, the tourist is more critical and aware of the product and can compare offerings. At the same time, as the new tourist is conscious of value for money rather than simply price, other elements of the marketing mix will become important. In particular, this will mean that 'quality' will remain a key attribute in tourism product development, and customer convenience in all its forms will be demanded by the new travellers. Technology facilitates the involvement of travellers in the true co-creation of products and brands through social media interaction with suppliers. The issue of quality is increasingly important because the consumer is time poor and will increasingly demand that the products they purchase will be quality controlled and reliable.

Approaching future markets

Every new tourist is different, bringing a unique blend of experiences, motivations and desires, and the use of Big Data will allow the creation of a 'market of one'. Tourism will therefore increasingly follow the trend of other industries towards customising. Here, technology enables products to be tailored to meet individual tastes. This means that the way that these markets are approached will be different in the future:

- 'Co-creation' of tourism products will increase as customers help to formulate products along with the supplier, as noted above.
- Technology, through the use of social media, has seen power shifting to the customer; they are knowledgeable and engage with products and services in real time. Increasingly, businesses are engaging with the customer to engineer their brands.
- Approaches to tourism market segmentation are being reappraised and moving towards deep and meaningful research to understand tourism behaviour (as shown in Chapter 13).

DESTINATION FUTURES

For Leiper's 'tourist destination region', there is no doubt that destinations of the future will need to be better planned and managed and show more concern and respect for their environment and host community, as well as adapting to climate change. Indeed, everyone involved in tourism will have to take increased responsibility for social and environmental issues. In the future, the focus of tourism will be on the destination as new intelligent management systems and techniques are adopted, based on the Internet of Things, and the attention to volume will give way to concepts of visitor experience and value. These concerns will be addressed by enhanced tourism planning and visitor management techniques and a clear agenda to involve local communities in the futures of their destinations. In this way, the imperative will be for the sustainable management of tourism destinations, adaptation to climate change and the conservation of their unique characteristics. Examples here include the management of UNESCO world heritage sites such as Machu Picchu in Peru or Mount Everest (https://whc.unesco.org/en/list).

The central issue is the gradual shift from short-term to longer-term thinking and planning in tourism. It is no longer acceptable for the industry to exploit and use up destinations and then move on; indeed we are already seeing the results of this in the demise of some of the mass-tourism resorts built in the 1960s and 1970s – Acapulco in Mexico (www.acapulco.com/en) and Benidorm in Spain (www.benidorm. com) are examples here. The concepts of the tourism area life cycle and strategic planning provide a much-needed long-term perspective in this respect. This means that destinations can decide to remain at a particular point on the life cycle by using strategic marketing and planning approaches rather than being inexorably driven to grow – or decline. On the demand side, there are also drivers of sustainability as consumers place pressure upon the industry and destination managers to behave in a responsible manner; if they do not, then their destination may be shunned as being environmentally unacceptable to visit.

Managing the destinations of the future

Destinations are responding to these demands in a variety of ways. Resource-based destinations are adopting sophisticated planning, management and interpretive techniques to provide both a welcoming and a rich experience for the tourist, while at the same time ensuring protection of the resource itself. The innovative use of technology, through both virtual and augmented realities, is assisting here (see http://itoursaustralia.com.au) and as shown in Mini Case Study 14.1.

Enterprises at the destination are also responding to the drive for sustainable destinations in three ways:

1. The tourism industry is anxious to demonstrate that it is both responsible and acting to curb some of the excesses of past development. Increasingly, sustainable tourism practices are being adopted as guidelines and manuals; certification and eco-labelling are examples here. They encourage tourism enterprises to 'raise their game' in terms of sustainability and allow the consumer to discern those enterprises that are attempting to be sustainable in their practices (Fennell and Cooper, 2020). Indeed, it could be argued that sustainability has become a driver of innovation in the tourism sector, with the larger companies adopting three guiding principles for their actions:

    a. Sustainability is driven by business imperatives such as competitiveness;

    b. All the organisation's stakeholders are involved – including customers and suppliers; and

    c. Sustainability is underpinned by detailed research to guide decisions.

       An example of this trend is Green Tourism, which offers independent guidance on sustainability to tourism businesses (www.green-tourism.com).

2. Destinations will benefit from future trends in the tourism supply chain. In the past, this was a combat zone with each member feeling they had to compete. For destinations, this resulted in exploitation by tour operators who failed to recognise that the resort was, in fact, their product. In the future, tourism businesses will begin to recognise the importance of working with other members of the chain and this will include tour operators investing in the destination.

3. Networks or alliances of businesses and consumers along value chains will increase business efficiencies and improve communication. This trend is critical for the tourism sector and is leading to a shift in thinking away from the management of individual sectors of the industry to the concept of integrated management.

So, what of the future for tourism destinations? There are two clearly different and divergent trends:

1. The first is the trend towards the use of artificially, technologically enhanced destinations such as theme parks, cruises and resorts. Examples here include Las Vegas (www.visitlasvegas.com), the Disney theme parks and Carnival Cruise Line (www.carnival.com). The product is unashamedly artificial, creating a fantasy world that will be increasingly part of the 'experience' economy. Technology plays a major role here, with theme parks adopting the 'Internet of Things' and re-engineering their

parks to be computer interfaces to communicate with visitors' devices, such as wrist bands.

2. The second trend is for authentic, well-managed contact with nature and indigenous communities. Here, ecotourism and heritage tourism are the obvious examples, with sympathetic encounters with wildlife (gorilla encounters in Rwanda) or native peoples (meeting with Maori in New Zealand). This type of destination demands a different type of management to the artificial fantasy destination, as here it is the resource that is paramount in delivering the experience.

MINI CASE STUDY 14.2

New Realities

In the future, tourism will embrace new realities facilitated by technology:

-   Virtual reality (VR) is a completely immersive digital world that is neurologically indistinguishable from the outside world;
-   Augmented reality (AR) is a real environment with technological overlays; whilst
-   Mixed reality (MR) is perhaps the most visionary, a mix of virtual and real worlds where physical and digital objects interact.

Such is the power of the technology that there are concerns that these realities may one day merge and replace the authentic travel experience altogether. After all, the very nature of tourism as an 'experience' lends itself perfectly to VR – virtual reality is simply a further step along the road of engineering tourist experiences and one that reinforces the trend of leisure activity based upon the home with, say, gaming. In the future, the tourist will be able to engineer their visit such that they can eliminate, for example, pollution in the sea, or the homeless from their city tour. Already dedicated destinations are being developed for VR with advanced stagecraft and high-end components to deliver a much better experience than in the living room and visitors can roam imaginary worlds untethered.

Of course, truly immersive VR is some years away (though perhaps not too far in the future), but there are already many tourism applications (see Guttentag, 2010; Guttentag and Griffin, 2018). These include:

-   Virtual eating where VR tricks diners into thinking they are eating steak, but in fact it is a blob of amorphous protein. Similarly, it can be used for dieting, or for creating experiences in restaurants where the diners are transported to, say, Tuscany.
-   Creating simulated training environments where mistakes can be made and breakages happen, but in a virtual world, these are not a problem.
-   Replacing the real visit to a fragile destination, such as one based on heritage or wildlife viewing, with a virtual experience, or enhancing the visit through augmented reality delivering education and interpretation with strong storylines. It is, for example, already possible to take a virtual tour of Tutankhamen's tomb or Stonehenge, or to view hotel properties before visiting (www.shangri-la.com). This takes away pressure from the resource and, as with VR, the impacts are minimal: no environmental degradation, carbon emission, cultural demonstration effect or risk of disease.

- Allowing the elderly, the sick or the disabled to visit destinations that they can never visit in real life because of their physical limitations – or allowing travellers to visit destinations in 'no-go areas' such as war zones.
- Simulating future climates to bring the realities of climate change alive.

However, opponents contend that VR can never replace the real travel experience. Rather it will simply whet the appetite for more travel through enhanced exposure to, and awareness of, the product. Disputing this, however, Tussyadiah et al. (2017 and 2018) have found that VR creates positive attitudes towards destinations. So, the key question is just how easily will the market accept VR substitutes for the real thing, and if it does, then is VR the death of tourism as we know it?

Discussion Questions

1. Do you think that the various kinds of realities will replace the authentic travel experience in 20 years' time?
2. What other applications of VR might there be in tourism?
3. Try the Google cardboard VR application – how good is the experience?

Sources: Guttentag, D.A. (2010) 'Virtual reality: applications and implications for tourism', *Tourism Management*, 31 (5): 637–51; Guttentag, D.A. and Griffin, T. (2018) 'Virtual tourism/augmented reality', in C. Cooper, W. Gartner, N. Scott and S. Volo (eds), *The Sage Handbook of Tourism Management*. London: Sage. pp. 443–62; Tussyadiah, I.P., Wang, D. and Jia, C. (2017) 'Virtual reality and attitudes toward tourism destinations', in R. Schegg, and B. Stangl (eds), *Information and Communication Technologies in Tourism*. Cham: Springer. pp. 229–39; Tussyadiah, I.P., Wang, D., Jung, T.H. and Dieck, M.C. (2018) 'Virtual reality, presence, and attitude change: empirical evidence from tourism', *Tourism Management*, 66: 140–54.

TRANSPORT FUTURES

By its very definition, tourism is a transport-intensive activity and is therefore exposed to changes in energy and fluctuating oil prices. Historically, change in tourism has been closely linked to transport innovations in Leiper's 'transit route region', but in the future, the influence of transport will be diluted by the emergence of other new drivers of change. At the same time, transportation itself will benefit from technological change that will improve the speed, reduce the cost, improve fuel consumption and, most importantly, improve the environmental efficiency of travel. Nonetheless, the influence of transport as a driver of tourism futures should not be underestimated. Tourism remains dependent upon transport technologies which are largely carbon dependent and this therefore poses a problem. Tourism may therefore be constrained by transportation in the future as old systems fail to accommodate increased levels of demand, or travellers perceive the security risks of travel as being too great, or the environmental cost too onerous. Similarly, the inadequate capacity of transport infrastructure will act as a real constraint upon tourism growth in the future, particularly in Europe and the USA where the development of new airports or their extensions is furiously controversial.

The future will also see a change in the management of and approach to transport enterprises, with an emphasis on both marketing and building strategic alliances to gain market share. The airline sector, for example, was very heavily affected by the downturn in travel following 9/11 and has seriously re-thought its response to future markets and patterns of travel. Here there are two schools of thought. Boeing sees the future in medium-sized aircraft that can operate flexibly between hubs and also secondary regional airports (www. boeing.com). Airbus, on the other hand, sees the future in larger aircraft, with a longer range that will dominantly ply long haul routes (www.airbus.com). The key here will be to adjust the capacity and range of aircraft to 'match' market demand.

Environmental factors, however, are the overriding concern for all transport modes in the future, particularly in the case of air transport, as emissions are unlikely to be reduced in the medium term. Indeed, the Intergovernmental Panel on Climate Change estimates that air transport accounted for 2 per cent of total carbon emissions in the early years of the century and will rise to 3 per cent in 2050 (www.ipcc.ch). Environmental factors may bite in two ways:

1. The consumer has an increasing concern for energy consumption and carbon emissions, and this may lead to a gradual modal shift in transport away from air and towards surface modes, and in extreme cases the decision not to fly at all (see Major Case Study 1.1).

2. This trend may be reinforced by the imposition of environmental taxes on both air and car travel, which will prompt further changes in choice of transport mode as tourism is asked to pay its way (see Becken and Carmigani, 2020, for a review of passenger forecasts in the light of the climate crisis).

In response, the industry is developing more environmentally efficient, high-capacity, high-speed passenger vehicles. As a result, competition between transport modes will increase in the future, characterised by improved rail services and products, the realisation of the environmental advantages of rail and continued technological developments in the area of high-speed train networks. A magnetically levitated (maglev) fast train service is already operating in Shanghai (www.smtdc.com/en) and commentators suggest that by 2030 maglev technology may be replacing more traditional forms of traction. Road transport has not escaped this revolution, with cars and traffic prediction enabled by Wi-Fi and sensors and, of course, hybrid and electric cars increasing in popularity as battery technology improves (see Cohen and Hopkins, 2019 for a review of the impact of connected driverless cars on tourism). Forecasts of international transport predict that technological developments, use of aviation biofuels, increased airline efficiency and labour productivity savings will offset any rises in aviation fuel prices. This is supported by the fact that on short haul routes the low-cost carriers are gaining market share from the traditional 'scheduled' carriers.

FUTURE TOURISM PRODUCTS

The key to understanding Leiper's framework of tourism, and indeed the study of tourism, is that all elements of tourism are interlinked. This is clear when considering the question: What will tourism products look like in the future? To answer this question, we could, of course, revert to the hype of commentators with their flying cars, but in fact it is more helpful to understand the underlying process of how these products will merge. This involves the concept of 'product markets' (introduced in Chapter 13).

In the future, tourism products and markets will remain inextricably linked. As shown in Chapter 13, the 'product market' concept helps explain how markets function and will evolve in the future, and therefore helps to understand different types of future tourism products and how they can be classified (Cooper and Hall, 2019). The concept is based upon the 'exchange' between tourists and suppliers and how the two partners in this exchange will change in the future. For example, we have already seen that:

- The consumer will be more demanding but also more concerned about issues such as CSR, fair trade and ethical consumption; whilst
- Suppliers will use technology to engineer experiences for the tourist and provide 'immersive previews' of their products so that you can 'try before you buy' (Future Foundation, 2015).

This evolving exchange will lead to the creation of new types of tourism into the future. These will range from the emerging products of today such as dark and adventure tourism, through to products that will characterise tourism futures – such as space tourism and virtual reality theme parks. For professional futurists, it is not so much the list and type of these new product markets that is important but, rather, the underlying approach of analysing how they will emerge. Here, in each product market, tourists can be classified by their behaviour and involvement, as their 'wants' will tend to cluster, whilst suppliers will tend to specialise in particular product markets. Taking space tourism, for example:

- In terms of the characteristics of the market, demand will depend upon price, the length of stay in space, motivations and the associated facilities (Cater, 2010). Also, medical advances, such as drugs to combat motion sickness, would make space tourism more appealing. On earth, demand will be stimulated by the development of spaceports and space-tourism centres – such as Florida's Space Coast – where prospective tourists can experience simulated space flights.
- In terms of the product, accommodation may be on orbiting hotels which offer views of the earth, astronomy, space walks and activities designed to make use of micro-gravity, such as swimming, diving or gymnastics.

CROSS-CUTTING ISSUES FOR TOURISM FUTURES

The final section of this chapter examines the response of the tourism sector to four cross-cutting issues that will have considerable impact upon tourism futures.

Risk and security

Perception of safety will always be a paramount consideration for the traveller, influencing the reputation of destinations and enterprises as security becomes part of a destination's value proposition. Despite the economic growth scenarios outlined above, tourism is vulnerable to natural and man-made crises, unexpected events that affect traveller confidence in a destination, whether the risk is real or perceived (see Ritchie and Jiang, 2019, for a comprehensive review of the field). Quite simply, this is because destinations are where people gather, and they are often fixed locations with the potential for a large number of casualties. And, of course, absolute security is impossible as it has to be weighed against the tension of being open and welcoming to visitors.

A crisis can be defined as: 'An event or set of circumstances which severely compromises the marketability and reputation of a tourist destination or tourism business' (Beirman, 2018: 155). The events of the twenty-first century have already tended to focus attention on the security risks to travel associated with terrorism (or by the future threat of cyber-terrorism and acts of war), and political groups such as ISIS creating effective 'no-go' areas for tourism (Piekarz et al., 2015). However, Beirman (2018) is clear that tourism is affected by many other threats, including:

- Poor governance of food and water standards;
- Threats to property or valuables through, say, crime;
- Threats to psychological wellbeing;
- Threats to physical security through natural disasters including climate change;
- Threats to physical safety through product failures such as air disasters;
- Threats to physical security through negligence; and
- Threats to physical safety and wellbeing through pandemics or epidemics.

The impact of an unexpected 'wild card event' will vary according to its duration and the degree of preparedness of the destination. And, of course, these events are more significant because society is more connected through social media so bad news travels fast, and people are more mobile and therefore more exposed to events, whilst destinations are often in locations vulnerable to earthquakes, hurricanes and avalanches (Ritchie, 2009).

These 'wild card' events have changed the way that travel occurs. Within a few weeks of the attacks on 9/11, the tourism sector had adopted a new vocabulary, including phrases such as 'risk management', 'destination recovery' and 'crisis management'. As the sector has become more resilient to and experienced in dealing with such events, it is clear that 'time is of the essence' and this has shaped the evolving approach (UNWTO, 2011b; see Figure 14.2). Beirman (2002) has coined a new scale for tourism to describe the magnitude of a crisis that can have an impact upon a destination. He calls this the DESTCON scale, with DESTCON 1 the most severe crisis that tourism can experience, down to DESTCON 5 when normality resumes.

International travel can also be a bio-security threat as it facilitates the spread of infectious diseases, such as the coronavirus, as well as the introduction of alien species into countries. As a result, quarantine, customs and bio-security procedures have been increased at many borders – a contradictory trend to the 'borderless' world of globalisation. Threats such as bird flu or the African Ebola outbreak prompt the UNWTO to establish a bio-security procedure. This procedure is advantaged by the fact that epidemics are crises that can be predicted, unlike terrorist attacks, which are not predicable.

Elsewhere, disease and decreasing levels of safety will constrain the uninhibited expansion of tourism. The spread of AIDS, for example, may render some otherwise attractive destinations no-go areas, while increasingly vociferous campaigns against sex tourism may also alter tourism flows and motivations. For the developing world, there is a fine balance between reporting such occurrences and protecting the income from tourism.

Climate change and the low-carbon economy

Growing recognition of the seriousness of climate change has prompted tourism policy and management intervention as well as a call for the tourism sector to embrace the 'low-carbon economy'. At the international level, various agencies have been active in promoting concerns through meetings, reports and calls to action. This has led to a series of meetings and declarations by the major intergovernmental and private sector organisations, and all the international agencies now have reports on tourism and climate change which can be accessed on their websites.

For the future, the solutions are challenging. One of the ways that tourism contributes to climate change is through carbon emissions from tourism-related activity such as transportation. Whilst approaches such as green taxes on carbon emitters, or carbon trading schemes, will undoubtedly target tourism in the future, carbon offsetting has emerged as a popular but controversial way to neutralise the greenhouse gases emitted by travel. For the future, solutions will coalesce around four areas:

1. Consumer education with a view to adapting behaviour, hastened by climate activists such as Extinction Rebellion (https://rebellion.earth);

2. Destination adaptation to climate change;

3. Reduction of carbon emissions and adoption of carbon trading schemes; and

4. Scientific advances in the use of alternative energy forms and the sequestering of carbon through natural 'sinks' such as forests.

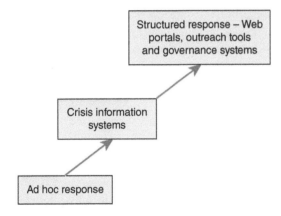

FIGURE 14.2   The evolving response to crises in the tourism sector

All of these solutions combine to demand that tourism embraces the principles of the 'low-carbon economy'. This can be achieved by the sector mainstreaming policies and technologies that change the way tourists and the industry operate, adopting a quadruple bottom line where climate is added as the fourth element, and accounting for the carbon footprint of tourism using contemporary approaches such as the tourism satellite account.

Technology

The creative use of technology has allowed the tourism sector to add value, reduce costs and build a close relationship with their customers. Yet, it is interesting that the major innovations in the use of technology have come from outside tourism. It was the computer industry that devised the concept of e-intermediaries, for example, a concept that has revolutionised how tourism is sold, as shown in the previous chapter. Technology, too, is allowing the creative use of databases and Big Data to individualise tourist experiences, understand patterns from social media posts and develop sophisticated customer relationship management. Of course, technology also gives the tourist much greater control over how they interact with enterprises and purchase their travel. Shirky (2010), for example, says that the Internet creates engaged, connected consumers who share experiences as time online through social media increases and passive activities such as watching TV decrease. Tourism enterprises will increasingly use technology to reduce operating costs and, as a result, their structures will change, becoming flatter and more networked organisations.

Technology will also impact upon tourism futures in two further ways:

1. There will be a mushrooming of embedded technology in cities and destinations, allowing, for example, hand-held devices for guides and navigation (such as https://nodeexplorer.com). When combined with mobile computing, Big Data and the participatory social media culture, this means that managers will be able to track a tourist's digital and contextual footprint to communicate market opportunities, facilitating dynamic destination management. At the same time, tourists will be able to communicate with each other through geo-social networking sites such as www.Foursquare.com and www.yelp.co.uk. These sites allow tourists to find out who is nearby, make recommendations and play interactive games.

2. Technology is empowering the consumer in the marketplace to reverse the traditional supply chain from company-to-customer to customer-to-company. Here, the customer drives the relationship with the tourism enterprise, turning marketing on its head with the customer in control, co-creating products with the sector and forming 'customer managed' relationships with companies. So powerful is this trend that companies can now evolve their brands in tune with shifting consumer opinion, monitored by posts on social media.

Human resources

Many of you reading this book will be looking towards the tourism sector for a career. Indeed, the challenges facing the tourism sector will only be met successfully by a well-educated, well-trained, bright, energetic, multilingual and entrepreneurial workforce who understand the nature of tourism and have a professional training. A high quality of professional human resources in tourism will allow enterprises to gain a competitive edge and deliver added value with their service. This book has outlined a professional and analytical approach to tourism, an approach that demands high standards of professionalism and education. Achievement of many of the best practices outlined will only be possible with a well-trained tourism workforce.

Tourism is a high-touch, high-tech, high-involvement industry where it is the people that make the difference. Yet, in a number of countries, an acute shortage of trained manpower and skills are impacting upon the growth of tourism; hence the move to using robots in many hospitality enterprises. The ability to succeed and the future performance of tourism and related activities will depend largely upon the skills, qualities and knowledge that managers will be able to bring to their business (Ladkin, 2018).

In the past, tourism has been characterised by a lack of sophistication in human resource policies and practices, imposed by outmoded styles of human resource management and approaches to operational circumstances. This leaves tourism vulnerable to ideas, takeovers and domination by management practices found in other economic sectors. Indeed, practices that are commonplace in other service industries – comprehensive induction, regular appraisal, effective employee communications – are underdeveloped in many tourism and leisure businesses.

A high-quality tourism workforce can only be achieved through high standards of contemporary tourism education and training. Tourism education and training involve the communication of knowledge, concepts and techniques that are specific to the field of tourism, but which draw upon the core disciplines and themes of areas such as geography, finance and marketing. The future of tourism education will lie in changing the modes of delivery of courses by using blended approaches through technology, making material available through 'massive online open access courses' (MOOCs), greater customisation of education to meet the needs of particular student groups, and a rethink of the content of tourism courses, which currently have become mired in twentieth-century thinking. This brings us back to the influential Tourism Education Futures Initiative (http://tourismedu cationfutures.org), which was showcased in Chapter 1. TEFI is attempting to draft tourism education approaches for a changing world, stressing skills such as managing change and environmental stewardship.

SUMMARY

The futures of tourism are exciting but this chapter guards against being too confident in predicting the future. The chapter has examined the key reports on tourism futures, which confirm the fact that tourism is a difficult sector to predict. Each of the drivers of the future identified in the chapter is influential in its own right, but when combined they deliver a powerful force shaping the futures of tourism. Futurists counsel against predictions of a single 'future of tourism', but it is possible to see some of the likely scenarios. The chapter discussed the type of tourist that might be expected in the future and how they will differ from the tourists of today. Future markets, too, will be more fragmented and dominated by technology and new products, including trips to space. At the same time, the destination will come under increasing pressure and will need careful and appropriate management, whilst transportation will be greener and more efficient. The chapter closed by examining cross-cutting issues that will be of key concern in the future.

Of course, tourism cannot control all the forces that impact upon it. However, the message of this book has been that, whatever tourism futures bring, tourism will only be successful by taking a scientific and disciplined approach. This book offers you the challenges of tourism management and an exciting future as you, the readers, become 'future makers'.

DISCUSSION QUESTIONS

1. Why is the future of tourism so difficult to predict?

2. Critically review the key drivers of tourism futures and show how they are related.

3. How can destination marketing organisations leverage from the content available on mobile devices?

4. Write a report on how you see the tourism labour market developing in the future. How can companies prepare for this new market?

5. In the future, the ethical consumption of tourism and CSR concerns will be increasingly important. Discuss this statement in the light of the need for companies to make a profit and return on investment.

ANNOTATED FURTHER READING

Fayos Sola, E. and Cooper, C.P. (eds) (2019) *The Future of Tourism: Innovation and Sustainability.* Cham: Springer.

Innovative, cutting-edge volume on tourism futures.

The Journal of Tourism Futures, Bingley: Emerald.

The first tourism journal to focus on the future.

Pine, J.B. and Gilmore, J.H. (1999) *The Experience Economy.* Boston, MA: Harvard Business School Press.

A visionary book, casting glimpses into the way that tourism products will be engineered and themed as 'experiences' in the future.

www.spacetourismsociety.org

A comprehensive website covering all aspects of space tourism.

UNWTO (2011) *Tourism Towards 2030 – Global Overview.* Madrid: UNWTO.

A report delivering a thorough analysis of future markets and products.

REFERENCES CITED

Becken, S. (2015) *Tourism and Oil.* Clevedon: Channel View.

Becken, S. and Carmigani, F. (2020) 'Are the current expectations for growing air travel demand realistic?' *Annals of Tourism Research*, 80: doi.org/10.1016/j.annals.2019.102840

Beirman, D. (2002) *Restoring Tourism Destinations in Crisis: A Strategic Marketing Approach.* Wallingford: CABI.

Beirman, D. (2018) 'Tourism crisis and safety management', in C. Cooper, S. Volo, W.C. Gartner and N. Scott (eds), *The Sage Handbook of Tourism Management: Applications of Theories and Concepts to Tourism*. London: Sage. pp 154–70.

Buckley, R., Gretzel, U., Scott, D., Weaver, D. and Becken, S. (2015) 'Tourism megatrends', *Tourism Recreation Research*, 40 (1): 59–70.

Cater, C.I. (2010) 'Steps to space: opportunities for astrotourism', *Tourism Management*, 31: 838–45.

Cohen, S. and Hopkins, D. (2019) 'Autonomous vehicles and the future of urban tourism', *Annals of Tourism Research*, 74: 33–42.

Cooper, C. and Hall, M. (2019) *Contemporary Tourism*. Oxford: Goodfellow Publishing.

Day, J. and Chin, N. (2018) 'Tourism, energy, oil and water', in C. Cooper, S. Volo, W.C. Gartner and N. Scott (eds), *The Sage Handbook of Tourism Management: Theories, Concepts and Disciplinary Approaches to Tourism*. London: Sage. pp. 466–81.

Dwyer, L. (2014) 'Transnational corporations and the globalization of tourism', in A.L. Lew, C.M. Hall and A.M. Williams (eds), *The Wiley Blackwell Companion to Tourism*. Chichester: Wiley. pp. 197–209.

Dwyer, L., Edwards, D., Mistilis, N., Scott, N., Cooper, C. and Roman, C. (2007) *Trends Underpinning Tourism to 2020: An Analysis of Key Drivers for Change*. Gold Coast, Australia: STCRC.

European Tourism Futures Institute (2014) *The Future of European Tourism*. Leeuwarden: ETFI.

European Travel Commission (2006) *Tourism Trends for Europe*. Brussels: ETC.

Fennell, D.A. and Cooper, C. (2020) *Sustainable Tourism: Principles, Contexts and Practices*. Bristol: Channel View.

Forum for the Future (2009) *Tourism 2023*. London: Forum for the Future.

Future Foundation (2015) *Future Traveller Tribes, 2030*. London: Future Foundation.

Gössling, S., Hall, C.M. and Scott, D. (2015) *Tourism and Water*. Bristol Channel View.

Hall, D. and Brown, F. (2008) 'The tourism industry's welfare responsibilities: adequate response?' *Tourism Recreation Research*, 33 (2): 213–18.

Ladkin, A. (2018) 'Tourism human resources', in C. Cooper, S. Volo, W.C. Gartner and N. Scott (eds), *The Sage Handbook of Tourism Management: Theories, Concepts and Disciplinary Approaches to Tourism*. London: Sage. pp. 254–68.

Lewis, M. (2002) *Next: The Future Just Happened*. Philadelphia, PA: Coronet Books.

Nordin, S. (2005) *Tourism of Tomorrow – Travel Trends and Forces of Change*. Östersund: European Tourism Research Institute.

Norman, D.A. (2007) *The Design of Future Things*. New York: Basic Books.

Northern Ireland Tourist Board (NITB) (no date) *The Future of Sustainable Tourism*. Belfast: NITB.

Piekarz, M., Jenkins, I. and Mills, P. (2015) *Risk and Safety Management in the Leisure, Sport, Tourism and Events Industries*. Wallingford: CABI.

Pine, J.B. and Gilmore, J.H. (1999) *The Experience Economy*. Boston, MA: Harvard Business School Press.

Postma, A. (2014) 'Anticipating the future of European tourism', in I. Yeoman, A. Postma and J. Oskam (eds), *The Future of European Tourism*. Leeuwarden: European Tourism Futures Institute, Stenden University of Applied Sciences. pp. 290–305.

Ritchie, B.W. (2009) *Crisis and Disaster Management for Tourism*. Bristol: Channel View.

Ritchie, B W. and Jiang. Y. (2019) 'A review of research on tourism risk, crisis and disaster management: launching the annals of tourism research curated collection on tourism risk, crisis and disaster management', *Annals of Tourism Research*, 79: doi.org/10.1016/j.annals.2019.102812

Shirky, C. (2010) *Cognitive Surplus*. Harmondsworth: Allen Lane.

Spector, S. and Higham, J. (2019) 'Space tourism in the Anthropocene', *Annals of Tour Research*, 79, doi.org/10.1016/j.annals.2019.102772

Timothy, D. (2018) 'Globalisation, supranationalism and tourism', in C. Cooper, S. Volo, W.C. Gartner and N. Scott (eds), *The Sage Handbook of Tourism Management: Theories, Concepts and Disciplinary Approaches to Tourism*. London: Sage. pp. 569–81.

Tourism Concern (2009) *Putting Tourism to Rights*. London: Tourism Concern.

UNEP (2002) *Global Environment Outlook 3 – Past, Present, and Future Perspectives*. New York: United Nations Environment Program.

UNWTO (2001) *Tourism 2020 Vision*. Madrid: UNWTO.

UNWTO (2007) *Tourism Market Trends*. Madrid: UNWTO.

UNWTO (2010) *Demographic Change and Tourism*. Madrid: UNWTO.

UNWTO (2011a) *Tourism Towards 2030 – Global Overview*. Madrid: UNWTO.

UNWTO (2011b) *Toolbox for Crisis Communications in Tourism – Checklists and Best Practices*. Madrid: UNWTO.

UNWTO (2019) *Lisbon Declaration on 'Cities for All: Building Cities for Citizens and Visitors'*. Madrid: UNWTO.

VisitScotland and Future Foundation (2005) *Our Ambition for Scottish Tourism: A Journey to 2025*. Edinburgh: VisitScotland.

WTTC and Bloomberg Media Group (2019) *World, Transformed: Megatrends and Their Implications for Travel & Tourism*. London: WTTC.

Yeoman, I. (2008) *Tomorrow's Tourist*. Oxford: Butterworth Elsevier Heinemann.

Yeoman, I. and McMahon-Beattie, U. (2018) 'Framing tourism futures research: an ontolological perspective', in C. Cooper, S. Volo, W.C. Gartner and N. Scott (eds), *The Sage Handbook of Tourism Management: Applications of Theories and Concepts to Tourism*. London: Sage. pp. 461–75.

MAJOR CASE STUDY 14.1

Artificial Intelligence, Robotics and Automation Technologies

Pepper Robot Assistant at a Tokyo tourist information center

Source: ©VTT Studio/Shutterstock.com

Introduction

As noted already in this book, there is a view that tourism jobs are not the 'decent jobs' demanded by the International Labour Organization. Rather, they are low-skill, part-time and seasonal jobs. In response, with the fourth industrial revolution, or industry 4.0, breaking over the sector, the development of artificial intelligence

(AI) and robotics is taking over jobs in tourism to bridge this gap in the future. Lower-level tourism jobs demand predictable routines and highly structured environments which can be replicated easily by robots. The McKinsey Global Institute (2017) suggests that up to 30 per cent of current jobs will be obsolete by the early 2030s and that robots, particularly in the hospitality sector, will be the norm as soon as 2025. As the future unfolds, there

(Continued)

is no doubt that these trends will be facilitated by AI. Artificial Intelligence has a long pedigree, dating back to John McCullach's work in 1955 when he described AI as science and engineering making smart machines. There is now a convergence of robotics, artificial intelligence and automation technologies (RAIA) driving the future of employment.

Robots

As a result, and as shown in Chapter 8, the hospitality sector has begun adopting robots in their properties as technology costs have fallen and guests have become less fearful of robots. Indeed, guests see them as both entertaining and a novelty with families (Murphy et al., 2017). In the future, robots will play two key roles in the hospitality system – of course, they are ideal for routine and dirty jobs but they are also increasingly being used to interact with guests (Kervenoaela et al., 2020). Additionally, they can free up human staff for other roles and they can constantly collect data as they operate. However, as Cooper and Hall (2019: 334) note:

> whilst robots are intended to replace more fallible humans – who are expensive, get sick, make mistakes and leave, robots are not perfect. They still cannot make beds and have to be monitored 24/7, meaning that the hotel environment has many security cameras, and needs real people to monitor both the safety of guests and the security of the expensive robots.

Robots are not infallible and 2019 saw the first example of Japanese robots being 'sacked' from their role for being irritating and incompetent. Nonetheless, there are quite a few examples of robots working in hospitality environments. Of these, one of the most well known is the 'Weird' Hotel in Tokyo. The hotel is 'manned' almost totally by robots to save labour costs (www.h-n-h.jp/en). AI-powered robots can be used as butlers, to deliver information to guests, to deliver room service and also to act as chatbots at reception, or in restaurants, coffee shops or at events.

What the Future May Hold

As more and more jobs in tourism, hospitality and events are done by machines, there will be a 'technological transformation' driven by digitisation as robotics and artificial intelligence (AI) converge to underpin innovations and developments. Daheim and Winterman (2016) see this development as split into stages:

- Firstly, up to 2040 there will be a 'transformational phase' where more and more jobs and even professions are replaced by automation.
- Secondly, this will be followed by a 'completely new system' of working and of economic development as AI and robotics begin to dominate. By this stage, economic and social systems will have to adapt and innovate, and governments will need to consider a replacement for salaries and wages as fewer people will have actual jobs. Already, in Scandinavia, there is consideration of a basic wage for everyone.

Discussion Questions

1. Tourism jobs are often said to need human skills as well as technological ones. What might these skills be?
2. How realistic is the scenario of 80 per cent of jobs being mechanised by 2060?
3. How should tourism education begin to respond to RAIA?

Sources: Daheim, C. and Winterman, O. (2016) *2050: The Future of Work. Findings of an International Delphi Study of The Millennium Project*. Gutersloh: Bertelsmann Stiftung; Gretzel, U., Sigala, M., Xiang, Z. and Koo, C. (2015) 'Smart tourism: foundations and developments', *Electron Mark*, 25 (3): 179–88; Stanislav, I. and Webster, C. (eds) (2019) *Robots, Artificial Intelligence and Service Automation in Travel, Tourism and Hospitality*. Bingley: Emerald; Kervenoaela, R., Hasana, R., Schwob, A. and Goh, E. (2020) 'Leveraging human–robot interaction in hospitality services: incorporating the role of perceived value, empathy, and information sharing into visitors' intentions to use social robots', *Tourism Management*, 78, doi.org/10.1016/j.tourman.2019.104042; McKinsey Global Institute (2017) 'Jobs lost, jobs gained: What the future of work will mean for jobs, skills, and wages'. New York: McKinsey Global Institute; Murphy, J., Hofacker, C., & Gretzel, U. (2017) 'Dawning of the age of robots in hospitality and tourism: Challenges for teaching and research', *European Journal of Tourism Research*, 15, 104–111.

INDEX